THE EPISTLES OF ST. PAUL

WITH INTRODUCTIONS AND COMMENTARY FOR PRIESTS AND STUDENTS

VOLUME II

EPHESIANS, PHILIPPIANS, COLOSSIANS, PHILEMON, FIRST AND SECOND
THESSALONIANS, PASTORALS, AND HEBREWS

THE
EPISTLES OF ST. PAUL

*With Introductions and Commentary
for
Priests and Students*

BY THE

Rev. CHARLES J. CALLAN, O.P., S.Th.M., Litt.D.

PROFESSOR OF SACRED SCRIPTURE IN THE CATHOLIC FOREIGN MISSION SEMINARY
MARYKNOLL, N. Y.

06353

VOLUME II

EPHESIANS, PHILIPPIANS, COLOSSIANS, PHILEMON, FIRST AND SECOND
THESSALONIANS, PASTORALS, AND HEBREWS

NEW YORK
JOSEPH F. WAGNER, Inc.
LONDON: B. HERDER

COLLEGIO PONTIFICIO INTERNAZIONALE "ANGELICO"

Via San Vitale, Roma

Attente perlegimus commentarium Adm. R. P. Callan, O.P., in S. Pauli Epistolas, scilicet ad Ephesios, Philippenses, Colossenses, Philemonem, Thessalonicenses, Timotheum, Titum, Hebræos; atque nihil obstare credimus quin typis mandari possit.

Romæ die nona Maii, 1931

Fr. Vincentius Rowan, O.P., S.Th.L., S.Scrip.Lic.

Fr. Seraphinus M. Zarb, O.P., S.Th.L., S.Script.Lic.

Imprimi Permittimus:

FR. M. S. GILLET, Mag. Gen. O.P.

Imprimi Potest:

FR. T. S. McDERMOTT, O.P., S.Th.L.,
Provincialis

Nihil Obstat

ARTHUR J. SCANLAN, S.T.D.
Censor Librorum

Imprimatur

✠PATRICK CARDINAL HAYES
Archbishop of New York

New York, July 23, 1931

PREFACE

IT is hardly customary to write a Preface to the second volume of a work, and yet in the present instance a few introductory words may not be out of place. First of all, several years have intervened since the publication of our first volume on the Epistles of St. Paul. This we have much regretted, but we can only say that the delay has been unavoidable. A work like this requires prolonged study and concentration, which many other duties and pressing occupations have made generally impossible for years, to say nothing of the interruptions often caused by physical infirmities. But since we have been teaching these Epistles in the Seminary all along, we trust that the lapse of years has enriched our knowledge and thus made more serviceable the volume we now offer to the public. The delay in its appearance has enabled us to take account of the latest and best works that have come out on the different Epistles.

In the second place, we would say that the method followed in this second volume is precisely the same as that adopted in the first volume of this work, with the exception that here we have made use of the valuable suggestion offered by *The Irish Ecclesiastical Record* in its review of Volume I, and so have revised the Douay-Challoner text of the Epistles wherever it was notably obscure or out of harmony with the best Greek reading. Corresponding corrections have likewise been indicated for the Latin Vulgate. Such revision has helped to save space in the comments, though many times we have still had to deal in the notes with different readings and difficulties of text.

If all priests only knew St. Paul thoroughly, they would find little trouble in preaching, for he is an inexhaustible ocean of doctrine, most elevated and sublime as well as most practical and useful for every phase of the Christian life. May this work contribute to a better and more ready understanding of the great Apostle and of the vast riches of his heavenly teaching!

CHARLES J. CALLAN, O.P.

v

CONTENTS

THE EPISTLES OF SAINT PAUL

THE
EPISTLE TO THE EPHESIANS

INTRODUCTION

I. Captivity Epistles. Four letters of St. Paul—those to the Ephesians, to the Philippians, to the Colossians, and to Philemon—are known as the *Captivity Epistles,* because the Apostle was a prisoner when he wrote them, most probably at Rome (61-63 A.D.), as mentioned in Acts xxviii. 30. This opinion is according to a very ancient tradition which the contents of those Epistles support. First of all, there is a similarity of vocabulary and style in these four letters, and Philippians seems to point directly to Rome when St. Paul speaks of himself as a prisoner, of the number of local preachers, and of Cæsar's household (Phil. i. 7-17, iv. 22). Moreover, that these four letters emanated from the Eternal City and were written about the same time is further made very likely from the following: (a) Timothy is associated with St. Paul in writing to the Philippians, to the Colossians, and to Philemon; (b) Rome, the capital of the Empire, was the natural resort of the runaway slave from Colossæ, Onesimus, whose meeting with St. Paul occasioned the letter to Philemon (Phlm. 10-12, 18); (c) in Ephesians vi. 20, the Apostle calls himself an ambassador in chains, that is, a representative of Christ the King in the imperial city, but without honor; (d) he is free to preach and to receive all who come to him (Phlm. 7 ff., 24; Eph. iii. 12, vi. 19, 20; Phil. i. 12, 20 ff.;

Acts xxviii. 30, 31); (e) he expects an early release, and asks Philemon to make ready a lodging for him (Phil. ii. 24; Phlm. 22); (f) Tychicus and Onesimus are together in bearing these three letters to Asia (Eph. vi. 21; Col. iv. 7-9; Phlm. 12, 22).

In view of these considerations there is nothing of moment to be said in favor of the opinion that the three letters last named were written during the Cæsarean captivity (58-60 A.D.). The arguments just given favoring Rome would not fit Cæsarea. Still less can be said in support of the opinion which makes Ephesus the place whence St. Paul wrote the Captivity Epistles (see Pope, *Aids to the Study of the Bible,* vol. III., p. 160).

As to the order of these four Epistles, it is evident from what has been said above that those to the Ephesians, the Colossians, and Philemon are not to be separated; but whether the Colossian Epistle preceded or followed the composition of that to the Ephesians cannot be determined with any degree of certainty, though it is clear that both were carried from Rome at the same time by Tychicus (Eph. vi. 21; Col. iv. 7). Nor can it be decided whether the letter to the Philippians was the first or the last of these four Captivity Epistles.

With regard to their general contents Dr. Vosté, O.P., very appropriately remarks that "there is nothing in the whole New Testament which so nearly approaches the doctrinal and mystical sublimity of the Fourth Gospel as do these Epistles. There is the same loftiness of dogmatic and ethical teaching, the same marvelous boldness of expressions, the same divine revelation of the union of the faithful with Christ or of the branches with the vine, and finally the same glorification of the love and person of Christ. John, the beloved disciple, has revealed to us the glory of the Word made flesh; Paul, rapt to the third heaven, has made known to us the glory of Christ exalted on high. And then, also, it was that the Apostle described this sublimity when, like the exile of Patmos, he was an ambassador in chains for Christ; when, like Stephen the First Martyr when being stoned to death, he saw the heavens opened and the Son of man standing on the right hand of God" (*Ep. ad Eph.,* Introd., pp. 6, 7).

The style and manner of treatment in these Captivity Epistles is very different from that in St. Paul's previous letters—Romans,

Corinthians, and Galatians. In those great Epistles the Apostle was at the height of his career; he was founding Churches; he was unfolding his great revelations; he was defending his authority and his teachings; he was in the thick of the battle. In these letters his work is mostly done; he is quietly surveying the fruits of his many labors, and is only anxious that they may be preserved. He is now reflective, meditative, and on the whole at peace in his mind.

His surroundings are also very different here. Formerly he was writing from Greek cities, with their individualistic outlook and cultured environment; but now he is writing from Rome, the centre of the great empire, with its worldwide outlook and its emphasis upon the family, the community, the state, and the race. Hence, Paul's vision assumes a wider range here—especially in Ephesians, Colossians and Philippians—taking in the whole world and uniting all men of all time under the universal sovereignty of Christ. Christ, the King, and His universal Church are uppermost in the Apostle's mind in these letters.

II. Ephesus. Situated on the great highway of trade between the East and the West, and under Roman rule the capital of Proconsular Asia, Ephesus was one of the most important cities of ancient times. It was to the province of Asia what Corinth was to Greece, what Antioch was to Syria, and what Alexandria was to Egypt. It was built on the Cayster River only about three miles inland from the Ægean Sea, and was the sea terminal of the great trade route which extended eastward, up the valley of the Mæander to that of the Lycus, and thence to central Asiatic and far eastern points. Miletus was indeed the natural terminus and seaport of the road which, from central Asia Minor and eastern lands, led down the valleys of the Lycus and the Mæander to the West, but the journey was shortened some thirty miles by a pass only six hundred feet high over the mountains from the Mæander to Ephesus. Moreover, during later centuries, and especially under the Romans, the silt carried down by the Mæander seems to have been permitted to spoil the harbor of Miletus, thus giving Ephesus undisputed supremacy as the seaport of Proconsular Asia until, in course of time, a similar fate befell the port of Ephesus through the alluvium which the Cayster deposited at its mouth. Even in St. Paul's age the channel between Ephesus and the sea had to be cleaned out repeatedly, but later, after the sway of Rome had passed away, it was allowed to fill up and become a mere marsh, and the glory of Ephesus as a port and the great coastal terminal of trade from Central Asia and eastern countries ceased to exist and became a mere matter of the past.

In the days of its prosperity the trade and wealth of Ephesus were augmented also by the coast-line ships from north and south, and by the vast numbers of visitors who were passing from Rome to the East or from the Orient to the West, as well as those who came to the city to worship at the shrine of Diana, to enjoy the Roman festivals, and to assist at the public games and shows. For, as already said, Ephesus was the principal seaport of the Roman province of Asia and the roads from the interior all converged there, thus making it most easily accessible for land travelers. Just outside the city stood the marvelous Temple of Diana (Artemis), one of the seven wonders of the world, and on the western side of Mt. Coressus was the largest theatre of the Hellenic world, open to the sky, and capable of accommodating 50,000 spectators; while a little to the north was situated the Stadium or Race Course where the public games and fights were exhibited.

The road from Ephesus to the east up the valley of the Cayster was too steep and precipitous for commercial purposes, but, as it was considerably shorter than the lower and more level route down the valleys of the Lycus and the Mæander, foot-passengers, like St. Paul, naturally preferred it. Hence, the Apostle going on foot from Pisidian Antioch to Ephesus would follow the higher, though steeper, Cayster route; and this is why he seems never to have visited Colossæ and Laodicea, which were on the main highway of trade down the valleys of the Lycus and the Mæander.

III. **The Church of Ephesus.** Being so situated, the terminal of trade and travel from Asia and the East westward, and as the Asiatic port for commerce and travelers from the West to the East, Ephesus was naturally sought by St. Paul as a centre from which his preaching and missionary activities should radiate. Already at the outset of his second great journey (51 A.D.) he seems to have had Ephesus in mind as his goal, but being "forbidden by the Holy Ghost to preach the word in Asia" (Acts xvi. 6), he passed through Mysia over to Troas, and from there to Neapolis and Philippi, and then down through Macedonia and Greece (Acts xvi. 11–xviii. 18). But at the close of that missionary journey, on his way from Greece to Syria, he paid a brief visit to Ephesus, leaving there, as he proceeded back to the East, Aquila and Priscilla whom he had brought thither, and promising to return later himself (Acts xviii. 18-21).

Accordingly, on his third missionary journey (55-58 A.D.), St. Paul, after visiting the Churches previously founded in Galatia, came directly to Ephesus by way of the "upper coasts," that is, following the Cayster valley route (Acts xix. 1). The seed planted there on his first brief visit and nourished to some extent by the efforts of Aquila and Priscilla, aided for a time by Apollo, had already produced a little fruit in the establishment of a small group of catechumens who had received only the baptism of John (Acts xix. 1-3). These St. Paul at once instructed and baptised, imposing hands upon them and thus endowing them with the gifts of the Spirit (Acts xix. 4-7). Then entering the synagogue where he had preached on his first visit to Ephesus, "he spoke boldly for the space of three months, disputing and exhorting concerning the Kingdom of God," until, forced by the opposition of some of his Jewish hearers, he made "the school of one Tyrannus" his place of worship and instruction (Acts xix. 8, 9). In this new abode he continued his spiritual labors for two whole years, discoursing every day and proving by miracles the divinity of his doctrine and claims, with the grand result that great numbers embraced the faith in Ephesus, the magical practices in honor of Diana were exposed as frauds, and the Gospel was heard by both Jews and Greeks throughout the whole province of Asia (Acts xix. 10-26). It seems that St. Paul himself remained in Ephesus all the time (Acts xx. 18), but his influence and efforts were extended by co-workers, like Epaphras and Tychicus of Colossæ, and by the multitudes who came to Ephesus for various purposes, and, having heard the glad tidings of the new religion, carried them back to their homes. Although his personal work in Ephesus was nearly finished and he was contemplating an early visit to Macedonia and Corinth (1 Cor. xvi. 5 ff.), the Apostle's stay was somewhat shortened by the tumult raised by the silversmith Demetrius and his craftsmen; whereas he had intended to prolong his labors in that fruitful field until Pentecost, and then go to Macedonia and Achaia (Acts xix. 21 ff.; 1 Cor. xvi. 8, 9).

On his way from Corinth back to Syria at the close of his third missionary journey (58 A.D.), St. Paul, unable to spare the time for a visit to Ephesus itself, halted at Miletus on the coast of Caria (Acts xx. 15), some thirty miles southwest of Ephesus, and called thither the ancients of the Church of Ephesus, and addressed to them the solemn discourse of which St. Luke has given us the substance in Acts xx. 18-35—which discourse is at once an indication of the strong and flourishing condition of the Ephesian Christian community and of St. Paul's abiding interest in and affection for the Church there.

The next mention of Ephesus in connection with St. Paul is in the *Pastoral Epistles*, written towards the end of the Apostle's life. In 1 Tim. i. 3 ff., we read that Paul exhorted Timothy to remain at Ephesus as head of that Church to teach and to correct, while he himself went to Macedonia; and in the Second Epistle to Timothy, written during the Apostle's last imprisonment in Rome and shortly before his death, he recalls the kindness of the Ephesian Onesiphorus (2 Tim. i. 18), and says he has sent Tychicus to Ephesus (2 Tim. iv. 12).

Ephesus is mentioned twice in later Apostolic history, namely, in Apoc. i. 11 and ii. 1. There it was, after Timothy had passed, that St. John the Evangelist, as Bishop of that see, spent his declining years and wrote his Gospel and Epistles; there he was heard by Polycarp, Ignatius Martyr, and Papias; and there he died and was buried about the close of the first century of our era.

The Church of Ephesus continued to exercise a great influence for many centuries. It was the scene of the Ecumenical Council of 431 and of the "Robber Synod" of 449, and at the end of the fourth century its Bishop bore the title of Exarch or Grand Metropolitan of Asia. Ultimately, however, the primacy of Asia was taken over by the Patriarch of Constantinople, and the Christian community of Ephesus gradually declined with the rest of the city to its present desolate state of a small Turkish village.

IV. **To Whom Ephesians Was Addressed.** It is extremely difficult to decide for whom this letter was destined. A great variety of opinions have been advanced, the merits of all of which it is neither possible nor useful to discuss here. Hence we shall confine ourselves to those which seem most likely, and which are or have been most generally held.

According to tradition this Epistle was intended for the faithful of the city of Ephesus, which St. Paul visited at the close of his second missionary journey and where he spent over two years on his third journey. In favor of this opinion we have: (a) the testimony of all extant Manuscripts containing St. Paul's Epistles, which —with the exception of the Vatican (B), the Sinaitic (א), the cursive 67, and that of Mt. Athos recently found—read ἐν Ἐφέσῳ (at Ephesus) in i. 1; (b) the title given this Epistle by every known MS., which has "To the Ephesians"; (c) the most ancient versions, going back to the middle of the second century, which follow the MSS. in reading "at Ephesus" in i. 1, and which therefore seem to indicate that this reading was already old when they were made; (d) the Muratorian Fragment in Rome, St. Irenæus in Gaul, Tertullian in Africa, and Clement in Alexandria. These Fathers appear to have held the Ephesian destination of this letter on the authority of tradition, and not on the evidence of the MSS. before them. Thus it seems that, at the end of the second century, tradition was wellnigh unanimous in affirming that this letter was written for the faithful of Ephesus. Internal evidence, however, in support of this ancient opinion is, practically speaking, entirely lacking.

Against the Ephesian destination we have: (a) the indirect and negative testimony of the four MSS. referred to above, two of which are the oldest and best in existence, going back to about the middle of the fourth century; (b) Marcion, about the middle of the second century, who said this letter was addressed to the Laodiceans, and who, since he could have had no dogmatic reason for saying so, may have been guided by some ancient codex which read this way; (c) Tertullian, who, arguing against Marcion for the Ephesian destination, was influenced only by tradition, making no reference to the words "at Ephesus" in i. 1, which must therefore have been absent from the MSS. known to him; (d) Origen, St. Basil, and St. Jerome, from whose writings we see that the phrase "at Ephesus" in i. 1 was lacking in the MSS. they made use of. With regard to the argument from Marcion, just given above, we are not obliged to believe that he had before him a codex which read "to the Laodiceans," for his opinion may have been based only on the reference in Colossians to a letter at Laodicea (Col. iv. 16). However, all this external evidence seems to show, at least, that the words ἐν Ἐφέσῳ of verse 1 of this Epistle are not authentic, and consequently do not prove anything for the Ephesian destination of the letter.

Internal evidence is strongly opposed to an Ephesian destination. For example, (a) this Epistle has no personal greetings of any kind, which is nearly impossible to understand if Paul was writing to Ephesus where he had lived and labored so long and so successfully; (b) the tone of the letter is formal and distant, terms of familiarity and endearment (like "beloved" and "brethren"), being entirely absent; (c) there is no allusion to the Apostle's previous relations with his readers (as in Thess., Gal., Corinth., etc.), but, on the contrary, he seems to be unknown to the recipients of this Epistle, he has only heard of their faith (i. 15), they have perhaps heard of the ministry committed to him (iii. 2 ff.), and he hopes they have been taught aright regarding Christ (iv. 20, 21). We cannot imagine St. Paul addressing the Ephesians, either exclusively or inclusively, in this manner; and hence it seems to us that not only was this letter not addressed solely to the faithful of Ephesus, but it also could not have been written to any group of Churches which would include Ephesus.

If, therefore, we are to follow the theory commonly accepted nowadays (namely, that this was a Circular Epistle addressed to a number of Christian communities in Asia Minor), we ought to exclude the Church at Ephesus, and perhaps confine ourselves to the faithful of Laodicea and Hierapolis. But here again we encounter difficulties. Since these cities were only a few miles from Colossæ, and must therefore have been affected by the same errors as endangered the faithful to whom Colossians was sent, it is hard to see why two letters so different in tone and object should have been directed to readers so near together and so similarly circumstanced. We admit, of course, that this objection has weight only in the supposition that Ephesians was addressed exclusively to the Churches at Laodicea and Hierapolis, and not to a group of Churches of which those two were only a part. If then we hold that we have here a Circular Epistle, and yet exclude the Church at Ephesus for the reasons given at the end of the preceding paragraph, and also the Churches at Laodicea and Hierapolis because of their nearness to Colossæ, what group of Churches unknown to St. Paul shall we designate as readers of this letter? In reply it must be observed, first of all, that it seems next to certain that the readers addressed by this Epistle were living in Asia Minor somewhere and not too far from Colossæ, since Tychicus was the bearer of this Epistle and of that to the Colossians at one and the same time. Arguing thus, some scholars have concluded that this letter was written for that rather isolated group of Churches in northeastern Asia Minor, near the Black Sea, to which St. Peter addressed his first letter (1 Pet. i. 1). The Ephesian designation given the letter, we are told, was due to the fact that, when the official collection of St. Paul's Epistles was prepared some time in the second century, the copy which had been made at Ephesus when Tychicus first arrived there with the original from Rome, and which naturally bore the inserted reference to that central Church of Asia, was the one that was chosen for the Canon and that was copied generally in subsequent codices (cf. Ladeuze, *Cath. Encycl.*, vol. V, pp. 487, 488; *Revue Biblique*, 1902, pp. 573-580.) This conjecture is worth some reflection, but one may well ask why St. Paul sent the crown of all his Epistles only to such a comparatively insignificant body of the faithful.

In view of the unsatisfactory character of the conclusions so far arrived at touching the destination of this letter, perhaps it is best after all to hold with the majority of modern scholars that we have in Ephesians a circular letter written to the various Churches of Asia Minor, including Ephesus, Laodicea and Hierapolis, and that the impersonal tone and distant, formal character of the Epistle are to be explained by the very fact that so many of the faithful were addressed, not a few of whom were strange and unknown to the Apostle. Along with this opinion the words ἐν Ἐφέσῳ which are found in so many MSS., can be explained quite reasonably as in the preceding paragraph.

The opinion of Harnack, however, which Fr. Knabenbauer regarded as not improbable and which Dr. J. M. Vosté, O.P., adopts in his learned work on Ephesians, deserves our serious consideration. The opinion goes back to Marcion's view that our Epistle was addressed to the Laodiceans. We give here a summary of Dr. Vosté's reasoning on this theory.

In the first place, the best text of verse 1 of this Epistle seems to be defective, as if the name of a city which ought to be in it had dropped out or had been purposely omitted. After the words τοῖς οὖσιν we should expect a noun, as in Rom. i. 7 τοῖς οὖσιν ἐν Ῥώμῃ, and in Phil. i. 1 τοῖς οὖσιν ἐν Φιλίπποις; (cf. also 1 Cor. i. 2; 2 Cor. i. 1; Gal. i. 2; Col. i. 2). Therefore, it is concluded that verse 1 of Ephesians ought to read: τοῖς οὖσιν ἐν Λαοδικίᾳ, κ.τ.λ. (to those that are at Laodicea, etc.). The phrase ἐν Λαοδικίᾳ, we are told, was in time suppressed because of the unworthiness which later crept into the Church of Laodicea, and to which St. John refers in Apoc. iii. 14-19; but that it belongs there and that this Epistle was consequently directed to the Laodiceans is further made probable by the following references to the Church at Laodicea in the Epistle to the Colossians:

1. "For I would have you know what manner of care I have for you and for them that are at Laodicea, and whosoever have not seen my face in the flesh" (Col. ii. 1). Here we observe that, while speaking to the Colossians, only the Laodiceans are expressly named.

2. St. Paul says of Epaphras: "For I bear him testimony that he hath much labor for you, and for them that are at Laodicea, and them at Hierapolis" (Col. iv. 13). These three cities—Colossæ, Laodicea and Hierapolis—were not far apart in the valley of the Lycus River.

3. The Apostle says to the Colossians: "Salute the brethren who are at Laodicea, and Nymphas, and the church that is in his house" (Col. iv. 15). Here Hierapolis is not included.

4. Finally, the Apostle says: "And when this Epistle shall have been read with you, cause that it be read also in the church of the Laodiceans: and that you read that which is of the Laodiceans" (Col. iv. 16). Here again there is question only of the Churches at Colossæ and Laodicea, and both have received a letter from St. Paul.

As Dr. Vosté goes on to observe here, it is manifest from the foregoing texts that the Churches at Colossæ and Laodicea were

intimately connected one with the other and in the heart of the
Apostle. And hence it would *a priori* be very strange if, while
the Epistle to the Colossians has been preserved, that to the Laodiceans should have been lost—all the more so, since, having been
read at Colossæ, most likely a copy of it would have been made by
the Colossians. That no copy of a letter so important as this one
seems to have been should have come down to us, while that to the
Church of Colossæ and even the little personal letter to Philemon
written at the same time have been preserved, borders on the in-
credible. But, on the other hand, if among the Epistles of St. Paul
that we have there is one which, as regards time of composition and
contents, is like our Epistle to the Colossians, though its traditional
inscription gives rise to various hypotheses, there results great probability that this is the Epistle to the Laodiceans.

Now, we have an Epistle to the Ephesians, written at the same
time as the Epistle to the Colossians and in many ways very much
like it, which seems certainly not to have been written to the Ephesians but to some other Church. The suspicion, therefore, naturally
arises that this letter which now bears the title "to the Ephesians,"
but which in the best MSS. and in ancient tradition appeared without any special inscription, is that lost Epistle of St. Paul's which
was sent to the Laodiceans. With this admission, we shall find no
difficulty in the absence of salutations and of particular characteristics, because, as a matter of fact, the Laodiceans had never seen St.
Paul, and, moreover, certain things in the Epistle to the Colossians,
which was also to be sent to the Laodiceans, would pertain to the
latter.

Hence, it seems very probable that our Epistle to the Ephesians
in the beginning carried in its salutation the phrase ἐν Λαοδικίᾳ, and
that Marcion in the middle of the second century still read these
authentic words in his text. We can account for the early suppres-
sion of the Laodicean designation, as said above, by the great corruption which invaded the Church of Laodicea towards the end of
the first century (Apoc. iii. 14-19), and which rendered it no longer
worthy of so great a privilege and special distinction. This sup-
pression would naturally be soon forgotten at large, and in course
of time, when the collection of St. Paul's Epistles was made, the
illustrious name of Ephesus, the capital city of Roman Asia where

St. Paul had lived so long, was substituted for the omission, in order to satisfy the grammatical construction of the first verse of the letter, as well as to give to this glorious Epistle a complete and specific inscription, like those of St. Paul's other letters. The fact that not all MSS. adopted the Ephesian inscription only proves that the Epistle had for long been known to lack the name of any special city or place.

The foregoing explanation is in substance the theory of Harnack as given by Dr. Vosté in his work on Ephesians (Introduction, pp. 18 ff.). As said above, this opinion was also accepted by Fr. Knabenbauer, S.J., as not improbable, and it has been followed by a number of non-Catholic exegetes. To us it seems very plausible, though not entirely free from difficulties. Perhaps it is open to fewer objections than any of the other explanations.

V. **Authorship of Ephesians.** This letter was circulated in the Church to some extent by the end of the first century, at the close of the second century it was in common use and widely known, and it was always ascribed to St. Paul as its author. In fact, the authenticity of this Epistle was admitted without question by every ancient authority that can now be cited. Thus, the Muratorian Canon includes Ephesus among the Churches to which St. Paul wrote letters. St. Irenæus quotes v. 30 as the words of "the blessed Paul in his Epistle to the Ephesians." Tertullian argues against Marcion for the Ephesian destination of this letter. Clement of Alexandria, Origen and St. Basil are equally explicit; and Eusebius includes this Epistle among the sacred writings which were admitted by the whole Church without hesitation.

It is even probable that we have an allusion to this Epistle in Col. iv. 16, and a number of references to it in the First Epistle of St. Peter. For the latter compare Eph. i. 3-14 with 1 Pet. i. 2; Eph. i. 20 with 1 Pet. iii. 22; Eph. ii. 18-22 with 1 Pet. ii. 4-6; Eph. iii. 10 with 1 Pet. i. 12; Eph. iv. 9 with 1 Pet. iii. 19; Eph. v. 22-vi. 9 with 1 Pet. ii. 18-iii. 7. There are also quotations from and allusions to this Epistle, or echoes of it, in the writings of St. Ignatius Martyr, Clement of Rome, Polycarp, Tatian, The Teaching of the Twelve Apostles, and the Epistle of Barnabas.

Moreover, the heretics of the second century not only admitted that St. Paul was the author of this letter, but they even cited it as Sacred Scripture. Marcion, for example, included it in his Canon (cf. St. Epiphanius, *Hær.*, xlii. 9), Valentine made use of it to justify his own doctrine (cf. St. Iren., *Adv. Hær.*, i. 3, 8), Basilides did likewise (*Philosoph.*, vii. 26), and other heretics likewise had recourse to it when they thought it served their purpose.

Among modern Rationalists and non-Catholic writers there are some who have doubted or denied the authenticity of our letter, but there is an equal if not a greater number who admit its genuineness, or incline towards it. In the former group are Schleiermacher, De Wette, Weizacher, Ewald, Baur, Holtzmann, Renan, Schwegler, Davidson, Cone, Moffatt, Dobschutz, Pfleiderer, Clemen, Scott, von Soden, etc.; whereas in the latter group we find such names as Weiss, Zahn, Shaw, Knowling, Lunemann, Lock, Robertson, Bacon, Schenkel, Salmon, Godet, Harnack, McGiffert, Howson, etc. Dr. Hort says he is sure that Ephesians bears "the impress of Paul's wonderful mind." Jülicher appears to be uncertain.

One of the main reasons for suspecting the authenticity of this Epistle is based upon its similarity to Colossians, from which it is concluded that one or the other or both are the work of some falsifier, living perhaps early in the second century.

We may reply, in the first place, by freely conceding that the resemblances between these two letters are many and striking. For example, (a) the salutations are practically the same; (b) both have the same general structure; (c) in both the principal subjects and leading thoughts are much the same, the relations of Christ to His Church and to the Universe being the dominant thoughts in Ephesians and Colossians respectively; (d) there are many parallel passages, the same words, phrases and similitudes, and, in the practical part, the same counsels and exhortations. But are not these similarities just what we should expect in two letters written by the same author at about the same time to two Churches in practically the same spiritual condition and general environment? They are both Captivity Epistles (Eph. vi. 20; Col. iv. 10), and Tychicus is the bearer of them both (Eph. vi. 21, 22; Col. iv. 7-9), very probably to neighboring Churches known to him. Is it surprising, then, that both letters should discuss similar themes in a similar style?

In the second place, let it be observed that, while there are notable resemblances between Ephesians and Colossians, there are also marked differences. Thus, (a) Colossians is personal and concrete, Ephesians impersonal and general in application. (b) The former inclines to the controversial and polemical; the latter is poetical and mystical, and more Johannine than any other of the Pauline writings. "In Colossians Paul is the soldier, in Ephesians the builder" (Farrar). "Colossians is a letter of discussion, Ephesians of reflection. In the former we behold Paul in spiritual conflict, in the latter his soul is at rest" (Findlay). (c) The former is Christological, dealing with Christ's relation to the universe; the latter is the ecclesiastical Epistle, treating of the relation between Christ and the Church. Under this last heading there are five passages in Ephesians which have no parallel in Colossians, namely, i. 3-14, iv. 4-16, v. 8-14, v. 22-33, vi. 10-17. (d) There are twelve references to the Holy Ghost in Ephesians, and only one in Colossians; there are nine quotations from the Old Testament in the former Epistle, and none in the latter.

In view of the foregoing, it seems to us that no valid argument against the Pauline authorship of Ephesians can be drawn from the resemblances between that Epistle and Colossians. But our objectors find another difficulty in the style and diction of this letter, where, we are told, there are some forty strange words or expressions (ἅπαξ λεγόμενα) that do not occur elsewhere, either in the writings of St. Paul or in the whole New Testament; and some forty more which, while they are found elsewhere in the New Testament, are not to be found in St. Paul. Moreover, it is objected that the style here is dull and sluggish; that it is overtaxed with phrases, clauses, synonyms and qualifying epithets; and that it is lacking in the sharpness, vigor, and overpowering eloquence so characteristic of St. Paul.

In reply to the first difficulty it need only be said that peculiarities of expression may be found more or less in all the letters of St. Paul, and as frequently in those whose authenticity the Rationalists admit as in the others. Thus, for example, we find ninety-six ἅπαξ λεγόμενα in the Epistle to the Romans; ninety-one in 1 Cor.; ninety-two in 2 Cor.; thirty-three in Gal.; thirty-six in Philippians, etc. On the other hand, it should be noted that this letter contains many words not found in the New Testament except in the writings of St. Paul, which is an additional, positive proof of its authenticity.

As regards peculiarities of style and composition, we can say that these are easily and satisfactorily explained by a consideration of the time, place, and conditions in which Paul wrote this letter, as well as the circumstances of the faithful to whom he addressed it. The Apostle was nearing the end of his eventful life; he was a prisoner in Rome, the central city of a vast empire, and he had leisure for meditation on the great mysteries that had been revealed to him. He was writing to Churches unknown to him, at least for the most part, with which he had no reason for discussion or controversy, but which he wished to remind of the spiritual treasures that were theirs. In language, therefore, which often takes on the qualities and proportions of a hymn of adoration he unfolds to his readers in this letter the wealth of sublime thoughts and reasonings that flooded his soul. It is not wonderful, then, that his language here becomes rich and overflowing, soaring up like a cloud of incense to the very throne of God. Paul was writing from his prison cell in Rome, but his heart and soul were with Christ in heaven; he was enchained to a Roman soldier, but his mind swept over the vast Roman domains and took in the conditions of all the Churches scattered throughout the Christian world; he was still bound to his earthly tabernacle, but his thoughts penetrated to the "heavenly places" and pondered the mystery, the plenitude, the light, the love, the peace and glory of the Godhead as revealed in Christ and made known to the Church.

There are few advocates today of the argument against the authenticity of this letter which Baur, Schwegler and other Rationalists based on the Epistle's relation to the Gnosticism of the second century. First of all, it is well known now that the Gnosticism which was a developed system in the second century had its beginning and early growth in the time of St. Paul. On this point we need only consult Irenæus (*Adv. Hær.*, i. 23), Clement of Alexandria (*Strom.*, vii. 18), and Eusebius (*Hist. Eccl.*, ii. 13; iv. 7).

In the second place, it is altogether doubtful whether there is any allusion in the Epistle to the Ephesians to Gnosticism, as it appeared in the second century. It is far more likely, on the contrary, that the propagators of this heresy made deliberate use of some of the expressions of St. Paul in this letter to help the spread and acceptance of their own doctrines.

VI. **Date and Place of Composition.** At the close of Paul's third missionary journey, while he was fulfilling a vow in the Temple at Jerusalem, he was arrested by the Jewish authorities on a false charge (Acts xxi. 26 ff.) and carried away as a captive to Cæsarea, where he was kept in prison for two years (Acts xxiii. 23–xxiv. 27). At the end of this period, when the Roman Governor Festus was about to bring him to trial, the Apostle asserted his Roman citizenship and appealed to the tribunal of Cæsar; and Festus, having heard Paul's story and found him guilty of no crime, decided to send him to Rome (Acts xxv. 1-27). After making the long and perilous journey Paul with Luke finally arrived in the Eternal City and was there kept in prison two more years (Acts xxvii. 1–xxviii. 31).

Now we shall assume that the Cæsarean imprisonment occurred 58-60 A.D., that St. Paul set out from Cæsarea for Rome in the autumn of 60 A.D., arriving in the latter city in the spring of 61 A.D., and that consequently the Apostle's ensuing Roman captivity was from 61 to 63 A.D. We accept these years, not because they are certain or the only ones, but because they are just as probable as (if not a little more so than) any others that may be given. With these data premised, we ought not to find it difficult to fix the date and place of composition, not only of Ephesians, but also of the three other Captivity Epistles—Philippians, Colossians, and Philemon—on account of the very close relationship between these four letters.

As in the case of the three last-named Epistles, the Apostle was a prisoner on behalf of the Gentiles when he wrote our letter (Eph. iii. 1; iv. 1; vi. 20), and his imprisonment had lasted a considerable time (Eph. iii. 1; vi. 22). Our letter was carried to its destination by a certain Tychicus (Eph. vi. 21), who was at the same time entrusted with a similar letter to be delivered to the faithful at Colossæ (Col. iv. 6), and who therefore was recommended to both these Churches in almost the same words. On this mission Tychicus was accompanied by Onesimus, a fugitive slave from Colossæ, whom the Apostle was sending back with a letter of commendation to his master, Philemon, a well-to-do Christian of that city (Col. iv. 7-9). From these clear indications it seems evident that Ephesians, Colossians, and Philemon were all written from the same place, during the same imprisonment, and therefore about the same time. But whether Rome or Cæsarea was the place of Paul's captivity at this time is still a disputed question, with the great weight of evidence pointing to Rome. For, if we examine the letter to the Philippians, we shall find that that Epistle was written either shortly before or shortly after these other three, while the Apostle was in the same imprisonment (Phil. i. 12 ff.), and that the indications are all Rome-ward. Thus the reference to the prætorium in Phil. i. 13, the relations between Jewish and Gentile Christians as reflected in Phil. i. 15-20, the mention of Cæsar's household in Phil. iv. 22, the freedom to preach and teach which St. Paul enjoyed (Phil. i. 12; Eph. vi. 23; cf. Acts xxiv. 32 ff., and xxviii. 31 ff.), are all much more applicable to Rome than to Cæsarea. Again, it must have been when St. Paul was in Rome that he was expecting a speedy release (Phlm. 22), for surely he was not expecting a release from Cæsarea that would soon enable him to visit Philemon in Colossæ. Finally, the points of contact between these four Epistles and the Pastoral Epistles in phraseology, in Christology, in the stress laid on an organized Church and family life, etc., all indicate the later date, and so favor Rome, during the Apostle's first captivity there between 61 and 64 A.D. (cf. Hastings, *Dict. of The Bible,* vol. I, p. 718).

In conclusion, then, we hold with the traditional opinion that not only Ephesians, but also Philippians, Colossians, and Philemon, were written by St. Paul in the Eternal City, during his first Roman captivity (61-63 A.D.).

VII. **Occasion and Purpose.** We have just seen that the Apostle was a prisoner in Rome when he wrote this letter. Epaphras had brought him news of the dogmatic and moral errors that were springing up in the Church at Colossæ and the neighboring cities. Perhaps the Apostle had been accused of a lack of interest in those Churches which he had not personally evangelized, and which had not seen his face (Col. ii. 1-5). He had heard of the faith and charity of the "Ephesians," and he was greatly pleased at this (Eph. i. 15, 16); they also had heard of him and of his work among the Gentiles (Eph. iii. 2 ff.).

While, therefore, dispatching Tychicus with a letter to the Colossians, St. Paul seized the opportunity to send this letter to those other Churches which he addressed in this Epistle, to remind them of their dignity as Christians and of the glorious life in Christ; to assure them that, though not evangelized by him, they were nevertheless members of the one vast Catholic Church which had been predestined before the ages to unite all mankind, Jews and Gentiles, in one common brotherhood living the life of God; to exhort them, consequently, to a higher activity and a greater unity in accordance with God's eternal decrees and purposes for His Church; to warn them against the dangers of sin and possible errors which would imperil their divine life here on earth and their sublime prospects in the eternal life hereafter; and to stimulate them to ever greater efforts in the pursuit of virtue and in the fulfillment of their various duties. That such were the occasion and purpose of the letter to the "Ephesians" an analysis of its contents seems to show, as well as the hints that we can gather from the Epistle to the Colossians.

VIII. **Argument and Division.** In general, this Epistle consists of a brief introduction, in which St. Paul greets his readers in his usual manner (i. 1, 2); a dogmatic part, in which he discusses God's eternal purpose, realized in Christ, of uniting all mankind, Jews and Gentiles, in the one Church of Christ (i. 3—iii. 21); a moral part, in which are outlined the duties incumbent upon the members of the Church in the Christian life (iv. 1—vi. 20); and a conclusion, containing some personal matters and a benediction (vi. 21-24). A more detailed analysis of the dogmatic and moral parts will help to a better understanding of the Epistle.

A. DOGMATIC PART (i. 3—iii. 21).—(a) A solemn act of thanksgiving to God for our union with Christ (i. 3-14). In lyric fashion, the Apostle begins by recalling the divine benefits for which Almighty God from eternity has chosen and predestined us, that, namely, through the grace of Christ we should be His holy and adopted children (i. 3-6). It was Christ, he says, who in time carried out the divine decree, redeeming us from our sins by His blood, and revealing to us the supreme mystery of God, which was to reconcile to Himself all things in Christ (i. 7-10); for in Christ we have become God's portion, both we Jews, who had the Messianic promises, and you Gentiles, who by faith have also received the Holy Ghost, the pledge of our eternal inheritance (i. 11-14).

(b) A prayer that the Ephesians may understand the glories of being united to Christ in His Church (i. 13-23). In a special manner the Apostle first thanks God for the faith and love which are already characteristic of the "Ephesians" (i. 15, 16). He then prays for a still greater outpouring of the Spirit upon them that they may realize their Christian dignity and their future glory, as well as the greatness of the divine power exerted in our behalf (i. 17-19), and pre-eminently manifested in raising Jesus from the dead, and in making Him Lord of the universe and head of the Church, which is His mystical body (i. 20-23).

(c) The Gentiles' former heathen life and condition are contrasted with their present privileges in the Church of Christ (ii. 1-22). Formerly the "Ephesians" were dead in their sins, walking according to the course of this world and obeying the lusts of the flesh; but God out of pure mercy raised them from their miserable state to a participation in the resurrection and glorification of Christ, by whose grace we are saved (ii. 1-10). In order that the "Ephesians" may understand the greatness of the grace they have received, St. Paul bids them recall the state in which they were living before their conversion, and to contrast that with the exalted benefits they now enjoy through their union with Christ (ii. 11-13), who has broken down the wall that separated Jews and Gentiles and has reconciled both the one and the other with the Father (ii. 14-18). Henceforth the "Ephesians" are admitted to full membership in the household of God and are made parts of His spiritual edifice (ii. 19-22).

(d) A renewed prayer that the "Ephesians" may know and appreciate the greatness of their Christian vocation (iii. 1-19). At the thought of the call of the Gentiles into the Church of Christ, St. Paul breaks forth in an act of thanksgiving (iii. 1); but the very mention of the Gentiles causes him to interrupt his prayer and to digress upon the part his preaching and ministry have had in their admission into the Church (iii. 2-13). Resuming his prayer (iii. 14), the Apostle asks God out of the riches of His glory to give the "Ephesians" spiritual strength and the grace necessary to become perfect Christians (iii. 14-19).

(e) Doxology, which concludes the Dogmatic Part of the Epistle: Glory to God in the Church, and in Christ Jesus, the head of the Church, throughout all coming generations, to all eternity (iii. 20, 21).

B. MORAL PART (iv. 1—vi. 20).—(a) The general character of the Christian life, as manifested in the diversity of gifts and functions of the members of the Church within the one Church (iv. 1-16). The Apostle, bound a prisoner in the Lord, exhorts his readers to live a life worthy of their vocation in all charity, being careful to preserve the unity of the Spirit in the bond of peace (iv. 1-6). The diversity of the gifts of the Holy Ghost should not be an obstacle to unity, but rather a means of greater solidarity, because all the faithful are members of the one mystical body of Christ (iv. 7-16).

(b) The contrast between the old life of paganism and the new life of Christianity (iv. 17-24). The "Ephesians" must live no longer as they did as pagans, in ignorance and impurity (iv. 17-19); but, putting away the old man according to the flesh, they must put on the new man according to God (iv. 20-24).

(c) Virtues required of all Christians (iv. 25–v. 21). Our life and unity in Christ require that we refrain from the vices of lying, anger, etc., and practice the contrary virtues (iv. 25-32), that we be followers of God and imitators of Christ in our lives, avoiding the works of darkness and walking as children of light (v. 1-14). Let us be truly wise, using well our time, fulfilling the will of God, filled with the Holy Spirit, etc. (v. 15-21).

(d) Admonitions for special classes in the Church (v. 22—vi. 9). After a general exhortation to obedience (v. 21), the Apostle now takes up the duties of special classes in the Church, namely, those of wives and husbands (v. 22-33), of children and parents (vi. 1-4), and of slaves and masters (vi. 5-9)—all of which duties are to be faithfully discharged for the sake of Christ and in Christ.

(e) The warfare of the Church (vi. 10-20). From a consideration of things pertaining to the internal welfare of the Church, St. Paul now turns to external needs and reminds his readers of the battles that must be fought against spiritual forces without. Each member of the Church must be prepared to do his part in this warfare, and his weapons must be those of God Himself.

So much for the Dogmatic and Moral Parts. The Conclusion, like the Introduction, has been noticed at the beginning of this section.

BIBLIOGRAPHY

Of all the ancient commentators on Ephesians who lived before the Council of Trent, St. Chrysostom stands far in the lead among the Greeks and St. Thomas Aquinas is easily first among the Latins. St. Chrysostom, indeed, is at all times the prince of commentators on St. Paul, the supreme master who understood both the Apostle's mind and language as perhaps no one else has ever understood them. And the Angelic Doctor, following in the footsteps of the Patristic masters and commenting on all the Pauline Epistles, has embodied in his works not alone the results of his own marvelous erudition and critical acumen, but also the best conclusions of the principal ancient Fathers whose commentaries have come down to us. It is not too much to say that St. Thomas is invariably correct in his analysis and explanation of the text except when misled by a wrong reading of the Latin version which he used. Had he possessed the fine critical editions of the Greek New Testament which are now at our disposal, along with the other discoveries of modern research, he would without a doubt as far surpass all our present expositors as he did surpass those of his own day.

Next after St. Thomas, but over two hundred years later, we should place Cardinal Cajetan, who was not only the greatest theological commentator on the *Summa Theologica,* but was also a Scriptural exegete of a very high order. He was objective, concise, and thoroughly independent in his examination of the sacred text. His commentaries cover all the Pauline letters.

After the Tridentine Council, until we reach modern times, the following are in the first rank: Estius (1613), *In Omnes Pauli Apostoli Epistolas Commentarii;* Justinianus (1622), *Explorationes;* Calmet (1757), *Commentaire,* and the others mentioned by Cornely in his *Introduction to the New Testament* and by Vigouroux in *Dict. de la Bible.*

In recent times there have been many Catholic commentaries on this Epistle, of which the following are among the best: Bisping, *Erklärung der Briefe an die Epheser, Philipper, und Kolosser* (Munich, 1866); Padovani, *Comm. in Epist. ad Eph., Philip., Coloss.* (Paris, 1892); Van Steenkiste, *Comm. in omnes S. Pauli Epist.* (Bruges, 1899); Rohr, *Les Epîtres de l'Apôtre Paul aux Col. et aux Eph.* (Paris, 1905); Rickaby, *The Epistles of the Captivity,* in *Further Notes on St. Paul* (London, 1911); Knabenbauer, *Comm. in S. Pauli Epist. ad Eph., Phil., Coloss.* (Paris, 1912); Hitchcock, *The Epistle to the Ephesians* (London, 1913); Sales in *La Sacra Bibbia,* vol. II (Turin, 1914); Vosté, *Comm. in Epist. ad Eph.* (Rome, 1921); MacEvilly, *Exposition of the Epistles of St. Paul,* vol. II (7th ed., London, 1922); Rickaby in *Westminster Version of Sacred Scripture,* New Testament, vol. III (2nd ed., London, 1927).

Non-Catholic commentators on Ephesians are very numerous, and many of them are very excellent. We recommend with some reservations the following: Macpherson, *Comm. on St. Paul's Epistle to the Eph.* (London, 1892); von Soden, *Die Briefe an die Kolosser, Epheser* (Freiburg, 1893); Abbott, *The Epist. to the Eph. and Coloss.,* in *The International Critical Comm.* (London, 1897); Gore, *The Epist. to the Eph.* (London, 1898); Robinson, *St. Paul's Epist. to the Eph.* (London, 1904); Shaw, *The Pauline Epistles* (2nd. ed., Edinburgh, 1904); Westcott, *St. Paul's Epist. to the Eph.* (London, 1906); Murray, *The Epist. to the Eph.,* in *The Cambridge Greek Test.* (London, 1914); Graham, *The Epist. to the Eph.,* in *New Comm. on Holy Scripture* (New York, 1928); Dodd, *Ephesians,* in *The Abingdon Bible Commentary* (New York, 1929).

The Epistle to the Ephesians

CHAPTER I

1. Paul, an apostle of Jesus Christ, by the will of God, to the saints who are at Ephesus, and to the faithful in Christ Jesus.

1, 2. St. Paul addresses his readers in the usual manner, asserting his divine election and commission to preach the Gospel of Christ, and wishing them grace and peace, which divine favors are respectively the source and the fruit of their supernatural union with God through Christ.

1. **Paul.** It is to be noted that, whereas in the other Captivity Epistles Timothy's name is associated with Paul's, here, as in Rom., Gal., and the Pastoral letters, only the name of Paul is mentioned. As Timothy had been with Paul at Ephesus and was therefore well known to the Ephesians, the omission of his name in the greeting of this Epistle is taken as an argument that the letter was not directed to the Church of Ephesus (see *Introduction*, No. IV).

Apostle, that is, a legate to whom is committed a mission with power and authority. Hence, the term implies more than *messenger* and it is applied in the New Testament to those who have been designated to preach the Gospel. By this title, therefore, Paul claims to be Christ's legate, sent and commissioned by Christ to preach the Gospel. Thus, our Lord said: "As thou hast sent Me into the world, I also have sent them into the world" (John xvii. 18).

By the will of God, that is, Paul's mission is both gratuitous and divine, and not the result of his own merits or choice. He has not taken the honor to himself, but has been called by God, as Aaron was (cf. Heb. v. 4).

To all the Saints. The *omnibus* of the Vulgate is not represented in the Greek. "Saints," that is, those who by Baptism have been consecrated to God and live in union with Jesus Christ.

2. Grace be to you, and peace from God the Father, and from the Lord Jesus Christ.

At Ephesus. These words are wanting in some of the best MSS., and are omitted by Origen, Basil, and other Fathers; they are probably not authentic. Tertullian tells us that Marcion in the second century knew this letter as the Epistle "To the Laodiceans," which may have been the correct inscription (see *Introduction,* No. IV).

Faithful. This is a term frequently used by St. Paul. It designates those who with mind and heart have freely embraced the faith of Christ, subjecting themselves to His will and service.

2. **Grace . . . peace.** This is Paul's usual salutation. Grace, God's special help and favor, is the root and source of our supernatural union with Him and with Christ, and peace is the blessed fruit of that same union.

From God the Father, etc. In these words we have indicated the author and the fountain-head of the blessing which the Apostle imparts. Since the same divine favor is asked from God the Father and from the Lord Jesus Christ, we have here a proof of the divinity of our Lord: He and the Father are one (John x. 30).

THE DOGMATIC PART OF THE EPISTLE, i. 3—iii. 21

These three chapters constitute a sublime hymn of praise to God for the special divine blessings that have been vouchsafed to the whole world through Christ, our Redeemer and the Head of the Church. The Apostle begins with an act of thanksgiving, which recalls God's eternal decree of love in our behalf (i. 3-14) ; then he considers this decree as fulfilled in the Church, where the distinction between Jews and Gentiles has been blotted out (i. 15—ii. 22) ; next he reflects on the special part that has fallen to him in revealing this mystery to the Gentiles (iii. 2-13) ; finally, he utters the prayer for the "Ephesians," begun in iii. 1 and continued in iii. 14-19 after being interrupted by the digression of iii. 2-13, and closes with a doxology (iii. 20, 21). See *Introduction,* No. VIII, A.

A HYMN OF PRAISE TO GOD FOR THE BLESSINGS WE HAVE RECEIVED THROUGH CHRIST, 3-14

3-14. In St. Paul's time it was the custom to begin an ordinary letter with thanksgiving and prayer. The Apostle conformed to this

3. Blessed be the God and Father of our Lord Jesus Christ, who blessed us with all spiritual blessings in heavenly *places,* in Christ:

convention in opening his Epistles, varying as a rule the wording of the formula.

This whole section in the original forms but one sentence, consisting of a long chain of clauses and constituting a sort of hymn in three parts, of which each ends with the refrain, "to the praise of his glory" (verses 3-6, 7-12, 13-14)! Verse 3 is an outburst of praise to God for all the blessings conferred on us in Christ, and the following verses are an amplification of this central thought as it unfolds in meditation. As his conceptions evolve, the Apostle ascribes to each of the three divine Persons of the most holy Trinity the action which by appropriation belongs to Him in the work of our redemption. Thus, in verses 3-6 he speaks of the eternal Father who from eternity chose us as His adopted children; in verses 7-13a he considers the execution of this eternal decree in time towards Jews and Gentiles through the meritorious blood of Christ; and in verses 13b-14 he turns to the Holy Ghost who through grace applies redemption to all, and whom believing we have received as the pledge of our eternal inheritance.

3. **Blessed,** i.e., worthy of praise.

The God and Father, etc. More probably both **"God"** and "Father"—and not the word "Father" only—govern the genitive case that follows, because in Greek there is just one article, modifying "God," and none before "Father"; so that the sense is: "Blessed be our God and Father, who is the God and Father of our Lord Jesus Christ." Cf. John xx. 17: "I ascend to my Father and to your Father, to my God and to your God."

Who blessed us, i.e., you Gentiles and us Jews, all of whom are made partakers of the blessings of the Gospel. The reference is to God's eternal purpose towards the elect, and hence we should read, "Who blessed us," the definitely past tense.

With all spiritual blessings. The blessings now conferred on the faithful in Christianity are spiritual, as opposed to carnal and terrestrial goods, and as coming from the Holy Ghost and pertaining to man's higher nature, such as redemption, remission of sins, filiation, and the like. In the Old Testament the rewards promised were temporal (cf. Gen. xxii. 17; Deut. xxviii. 1-13, etc.).

In heavenly places (literally, *In the heavenlies*). This unusual

4. As he chose us in him before the foundation of the world, that we should be holy and unspotted in his sight in charity.

phrase occurs four more times in this Epistle (i. 20, ii. 6, iii. 10, vi. 12), but nowhere else; and each time there is question of locality, save the last, perhaps. These blessings therefore come from heaven and lead to heaven, they are both present and future; and they are given "in Christ"—that is, through Christ, by virtue of our union with Christ, who is the way, the truth and the life that lead to the Father. Christ is the head, and we are the members of His mystical body, the Church; we share in His life. This doctrine of the union of the faithful with Christ, their mystical head, is uppermost in this section and throughout the whole Epistle. The phrase "in Christ" is found twenty-nine times in the Pauline Epistles, and only three times elsewhere, and that in 1 Peter. In forty-three other passages of St. Paul we find the enlarged phrase, "in Christ Jesus," and four times "in the Christ." Everywhere these phrases denote our close union with Christ as members of His mystical body.

4. The Apostle now begins to explain God's eternal decree in behalf of Christians. The Eternal Father chose us from eternity, that we might be holy and immaculate in His eyes, and out of love for us He freely predestined us to be His adopted children through His beloved Son, our Lord Jesus Christ (ver. 4-6).

As. This word connects the preceding verse with the present one, and the meaning is that the spiritual blessings which Christians now enjoy are the logical consequence of God's eternal decree in their regard.

He chose us, i.e., He selected Christians, apart from the rest of mankind, to be His special people, "the Israel of God" (Gal. vi. 16).

In Him, i.e., in Christ, as members of His mystical body. Christians are not conceived apart from Christ, their mystical head, either in God's eternal decree or in time.

Before the foundation, etc., i.e., prior to all creation, from everlasting.

That we should be holy, that is, graced with virtues and free from vice. The reference is to an actual state of moral rectitude, and not to a future condition, nor to a merely external and imputed justice.

In his sight, i.e., in the eyes of God, who reads the secrets of

5. Who predestinated us unto the adoption of children through Jesus
Christ unto himself: according to the purpose of his will:

the heart, to whom nothing is hid (Ps. vii. 9; Matt. v. 48, vi. 4, 6, 18;
Heb. iv. 13).

In charity, i.e., in love. Whether this love is divine or human,
depends on the connection of this phrase with what precedes in the
verse or with what follows. Some authorities connect it with
"chose," and so there would be question of God's love which chose
us; but this explanation is not likely, as the verb "chose" is too
far separated from the phrase "in charity." Many others, ancient
and modern, connect the phrase with "holy and unspotted," and thus
the meaning would be that charity is the formal cause of our sanctification, and that charity is at once the bond and the crown of Christian virtues. St. Jerome and St. John Chrysostom, however, make
the connection with what follows in the next verse, "predestinated,"
and hence make the love of God for us the supreme cause of our
predestination to be His adopted children. In this whole section the
Apostle seems to be saying that love for us has been at the bottom
of God's free choice of us, and the motive of our predestination.
Thus also St. John says: "God so loved the world, as to give His
only-begotten Son, etc." (John iii. 16). Our adoption as children
through Christ, therefore, is due only to God's paternal love for us.

5. **Who predestinated us.** Those who connect "in charity" of
the preceding verse with this verse read as follows: "Who predestinated us in charity." According to our way of thinking, predestination presupposes election, and election presupposes love. Thus, God
first loved us, then chose us, and then predestined us. It is to be
noted that there is question here, directly, only of predestination to
faith and grace in this life; but of course, since faith and grace are
themselves ordained to eternal salvation and given for that purpose,
there would be also question here, indirectly, of predestination to
final salvation. In either sense the predestination is gratuitous, in
no way dependent on our merits.

Unto the adoption, etc. The proximate purpose of divine predestination was that we might become adopted children of God.
The Son of God became man that men might become the sons of
God, as St. Augustine says (cf. Gal. iv. 4-6). Perfect adoption
consists in our transformation into the likeness of the glorious

6. Unto the praise of the glory of his grace, by which he graced us in the beloved.

risen Saviour in the life to come, and presupposes as a means to this great end our present transformation by virtue into the likeness of Jesus. The use of the term "adoption" as applied to Christians is peculiarly Pauline. It is found five times in his Epistles (Gal. iv. 5; Rom. viii. 15, 23, ix. 4; Eph. i. 5), and nowhere else in the Bible.

Through Jesus Christ. Our adoption as sons of God is conferred through our Lord, as our Redeemer and Mediator: "You are all the children of God by faith, in Christ Jesus" (Gal. iii. 26).

Unto himself, i.e., unto the Father. Our redemption originated with the Father and goes back to Him as its end. The eternal purpose of the Father was "that we should be called, and should be the sons of God" (1 John iii. 1). A less probable interpretation refers "unto himself" to the Son, our Lord Jesus Christ.

According to the purpose, etc. Better, "according to the good pleasure, etc." Here we have indicated the radical reason and the true efficient cause of our redemption, election, etc., namely, the gratuitous will of God. Hence St. Thomas says: "Prædestinationis divinæ nulla alia causa est, nec esse potest, quam simplex Dei voluntas. Unde patet etiam, quod divinæ voluntatis prædestinantis non est alia ratio, quam divina bonitas filiis communicanda."

The will of God is "the ultimate account of all divine procedure, from the creature's point of view. Nothing in that Will is capricious; all is supremely wise and good. But it enfolds an 'unseen universe' of reasons and causes wholly beyond our discovery; and here precisely is one main field for the legitimate exercise of faith; personal confidence as to the unknown reasons for the revealed action of a Known God" (Bishop Moule, *Epistle to the Ephesians, hoc loco*).

6. **Unto the praise,** etc. Now the Apostle points out the final cause of God's love, choice, predestination and adoption of us Christians. The divine will actuated by love was the prime moving cause on God's part, and His glory is the final cause of the whole divine process in our regard. "Grace" here means not so much the supernatural gift of grace as the fountain of God's gifts, or His liberality and benevolence; and this benevolence of God towards us is described as shining, or gloriously manifesting itself. Hence, the

7. In whom we have redemption through his blood, the remission of sins, according to the riches of his grace,

final cause of our adoption as sons of God through Christ—that to which our adoption was ordained as regards God—is *praise,* or the public and jubilant exaltation in the sight of men and angels of the divine munificence gloriously manifesting itself towards us (Vosté, *Epist. ad Eph.*).

By which, etc. The preposition *in* of the Vulgate should be omitted here, as it is not represented in the best Greek MSS., where we read ἧς (a genitive by attraction of the preceding noun χάριτος, for the accusative or the dative). We should therefore translate: "By which, etc."

He graced us. The verb here is aorist, referring to a definitely past action. It is a rare verb which is found elsewhere in the New Testament only in Luke i. 28, and its meaning here goes back to the corresponding word in the verse, χάρις, which we said meant *benevolence.* Therefore the sense of the verb χαριτοῦν in this passage is *to pursue with benevolence.* Hence the meaning is that God, pursuing us with His benevolence, has rendered us lovable or gracious. Explaining this verb St. Chrysostom says: "He not only delivered us from sin, but He made us lovable"; and Theodoret has: "The death of the Lord made us worthy of love."

In the beloved (ἐν τῷ ἠγαπημένῳ). In the Vulgate the words *filio suo* are added as an explanation of *dilecto.* The meaning is given by Monod: "The Son, lovable in Himself, is essentially The Beloved; we, unlovable in ourselves, are accepted because of, and in, the Beloved; and if we are called *beloved* in our turn, it is because God sees us in His Son" (*Aux Ephés.*, quoted by Moule, *op. cit., hoc loco*). Thus, the grace of adoption has come to us, not on account of any merit of ours, but only through the merits of our Lord Jesus Christ, the beloved Son of God. It is to be noted that St. Paul is everywhere insistent on the mediatorial merits of Christ.

7. Having considered the eternal decree by which God chose and predestined us to be His adopted children, the Apostle now proceeds (ver. 7-14) to speak of the execution of this decree in time. "Loving us from eternity, He has rendered us lovable in time" (Corluy). Jesus, the Incarnate Word, has redeemed us from sin by His blood (ver. 7); in consequence we have received in the

8. Which he caused to abound in us in all wisdom and prudence;

supernatural order all wisdom and prudence (ver. 8), the supreme
mystery of the will of God to unite all things in Christ being made
known (ver. 9-10). All these things have happened to Jews and
Gentiles, called together into the New Israel (ver. 11-13a), the Holy
Spirit, the pledge of our eternal inheritance, being poured out on all
(ver. 13b-14). Cf. Vosté, *op. cit., hoc loco.*

In whom, i.e., in the beloved, our Lord Jesus Christ. In virtue
of our union with Him "we have redemption, etc.," that is, liberation from the devil and sin, and from the anger of God, which
redemption our Saviour has purchased for us by the shedding of
His blood for us on the cross (Matt. xx. 28; Col. i. 14, 20; 1 Pet.
i. 18 ff.; 1 Cor. vi. 20, etc.). Our redemption has been effected
by the voluntary offering on the part of Christ of His life as a
ransom-price for our souls; Christ died that we might live.

The remission of sins. This explains in what our redemption
consisted, namely, in the forgiveness of our sins (or, literally, *tres-
passes* of all kinds).

According to the riches, etc. This is a favorite phrase with St.
Paul, by which he wishes to show the immensity of God's goodness
and love towards us. It would have been a great favor merely to
have received God's forgiveness, and a still greater favor to have
received it through the giving of His divine Son for us; but to be
forgiven at the price of the pouring out of the very blood of God's
only Son, this manifests a love for us on the part of the Eternal
Father which surpasses all bounds, and which is, therefore, "according to the riches of His grace." The shedding of blood was an
acknowledgment of God's supreme dominion over life and death
which sin had challenged, suffering made atonement for transgression, and merit won back the graces lost (cf. Hitchcock, *op. cit.,
hoc loco*).

8. Which he caused to abound in us. The Greek here reads:
ἧς ἐπερίσσευσε, the genitive of attraction ἧς being used for the accusative ἥν. The subject of the verb is God, understood. Hence
we should read: "Which (grace) he (God) caused to abound in us."

In all wisdom, etc. The grace of God which has abounded in
our favor has not only procured for us remission of sins, but it
has also given us insight into the mysteries of the divine will.

9. Having made known unto us the mystery of his will, according to his good pleasure, which he purposed in him,

10. In the dispensation of the fullness of times, to re-establish all things in Christ, that are in heaven and on earth, in him.

"Wisdom" (σοφία) means a knowledge of principles, and here it has reference to a speculative knowledge of the great mysteries of faith. "Prudence," or "intelligence" (φρόνησις), pertains to actions, and is a practical knowledge of good to be done or evil to be avoided; prudence or intelligence is the wisdom of the just (Luke i. 17). Some expositors think there is question here of the wisdom and prudence which God has exercised, rather than of the wisdom and prudence which He has communicated to the faithful; but the common opinion and the context of verse 9 favor the latter view.

9. The Apostle now proceeds to show how God has made His grace to abound in all wisdom and prudence in the saints, namely, by making known to them and helping them to understand the divine purpose, long concealed but now revealed through the Incarnation, of uniting all things in Christ.

Having made known, etc. (γνωρίσας). The Greek word (γνωρίζειν) implies the revelation of hidden truths, and it occurs frequently in St. Paul. The time referred to is the actual revelation of the Gospel.

The mystery, etc., i.e., the hidden secret of His will or purpose to unite all, Jews and Gentiles, in Christ—to make Christ the term and, as it were, the synthesis of the whole re-established supernatural order (Vosté). The word μυστηρίον occurs twenty-one times in St. Paul, and six times in this Epistle. In the Vulgate it is rendered eight times by *sacramentum* (including the present passage), and at other times by *mysterium*. It would be better to translate it everywhere by *mysterium,* and thus avoid the confusion arising from the technical meaning now given to the word *sacrament.*

According to his good pleasure, i.e., according to the good pleasure of the Father who has made known to the saints the hidden purpose of His will.

Which he purposed in him, i.e., in the Son (ἐν αὐτῷ), the Messiah. The Father's purpose was in Christ, the Son, inasmuch as it was to be realized through the Son (omnia per Ipsum facta sunt, et iterum omnia per Ipsum reconcilianda et restituenda sunt).

10. **In the dispensation,** etc. The Greek word οἰκονομία, here

11. In whom we also were called by lot, being predestinated according to the purpose of him who worketh all things according to the counsel of his will;

rendered "dispensation," really means *stewardship, house-management;* and the sense of this passage, in connection with the preceding verse, is that, when sin had disrupted the primitive harmony of creation, the Eternal Father purposed or decreed to send His Son into the world when the time determined by Himself had arrived, and to make Him the supreme head and administrator of all things in His spiritual household, the Church, for the purpose of reuniting and reconciling all things to Himself through this same divine Son. This work of recapitulating and reconciling all things in Christ began with the Incarnation, but it will not be completed till the end of the world, at the general resurrection.

All things, etc., i.e., men and angels, the material universe and the spiritual, are all made subject to Christ, the supreme head of the supernatural order, and all are to be reunited and reconciled to the Father through Christ, since all are in need of this reunion and reconciliation, all having been thrown into disharmony by sin. The Greek verb here translated "to re-establish" means "to restore," "to reunite." In the beginning all creatures—angels, men and the physical world—formed one grand, harmonious family all subject to God. But sin disrupted this primeval unity and subordination of part to part and of the whole to the Creator; and so the Eternal Father sent His Son to reunite the dissevered parts of His Creation and to restore the original harmony between the rational and the irrational, earth and heaven, men and angels (cf. Rom. viii. 19 ff.). Thus, the redemption equals creation in its extension. All things were created through the Word, and all things must be summed up and reconciled to the Father through the Word.

In him, i.e., in Christ, a repetition for the sake of emphasis; but the phrase ought to be connected with the following verse.

11. **In whom we also,** etc. The *et nos* of the Vulgate is not represented in the Greek, and hence the *we* here is not emphatic; the Apostle is stressing not the persons that were called, but the *fact* of their call to the Gospel, both Jews and Gentiles.

By lot. The meaning of the Greek here is *to obtain an inheritance, a portion,* that is, to be made a part of God's inheritance, por-

12. That we may be unto the praise of his glory, we who before hoped in Christ:

13. In whom you also, after you had heard the word of truth (the gospel of your salvation); in whom also believing, you were signed with the holy Spirit of promise,

tion, lot. The Greek verb used here to express this allotment is found nowhere else in the Greek Bible, but its meaning is clear from the noun κλῆρος, *lot* (cf. also Deut. xxxii. 9). The Church is the New Israel of God (Gal. vi. 16). The call to Christianity is gratuitous, altogether independent of our merits, and infallible; it is in no way fortuitous or due to chance. For we were "predestinated" to this admission into the New Israel of God "according to the purpose, etc.," that is, according to the free and independent choice of the will of God. The Greek verb here used, ἐνεργεῖν, signifies the infallible efficacy of the divine action in moving all things to their respective operations and ends.

The counsel, etc. In Greek βουλή includes the deliberation of the reason, whereas θέλημα means native, active inclination. God's will is eminently free, but by no means arbitrary; it acts according to "counsel."

12. That we might be, etc. The final reason why God chose, predestined, and called us is His own glory. The final reason for every action of God must be Himself, because, as being all-perfect, He can act only for the highest and most perfect end, and this obviously is Himself.

We who before, etc., i.e., we Jews. It is more probable that the Apostle is speaking in this verse, not of Christians in general who are living in the hope of Christ to come at the end of the world, but of the Jews to whom the Messianic promises were given. To the Jews, living in hope of the Messiah to come, was given the prerogative of being first admitted into the New Israel of God, the Church. We hold, then, that the reference in this verse is to Jewish believers as against Gentile believers. The former, as having inherited and cherished the hope of the Messiah to come before the Gentiles were aware of this blessing, have a sort of prior claim with respect to the Gospel.

13. In whom you also, etc. Having spoken in the previous verse of the Jewish Christians, the Apostle now turns to the Gen-

14. Who is the pledge of our inheritance, unto the redemption of acquisition, unto the praise of his glory.

tile converts, who also have been called to share in the blessings
of the Gospel. Most probably the verb "were called" (as in ver. 11)
should be supplied to complete the first line of this present verse,
thus: "In whom you also were called, etc." Also the Gentiles have
been called through Christ, they have had preached to them "the
word of truth" (i.e., the Gospel), the purpose of which is their salvation; they have also believed in Christ and in the Gospel, and in
consequence they have received the Holy Spirit, the Spirit promised by the Prophets and by Jesus as the seal and pledge of their
divine filiation. This sign or seal is impressed on the soul in the
Sacraments of Baptism and Confirmation. These two Sacraments,
of Baptism and Confirmation, were usually conferred together in
the early Church (cf. Luke xxiv. 49; Acts i. 4 ff., ii. 16 ff.; John i.
32, vi. 27, etc.). Some authors take the second *in quo* of this verse
to refer to the Gospel rather than to Christ, but this does not change
the meaning.

14. **Who is the pledge, etc.** The Holy Ghost now given to
Christians is the earnest, or first installment, or part-payment of
the final and complete blessedness which will be theirs hereafter.
The Greek word ἀρραβών, here translated *pledge,* is Semitic in origin
and first meant something given as a guarantee of an agreement
between two parties, but which was to be surrendered upon the
fulfillment of the agreement. But by usage the word took on the
meaning of an *earnest,* or a certain part of the whole that is to be
paid in due time. This is the meaning of the word here.

Unto the redemption, etc., i.e., the Holy Ghost is now given
the Christians as the first installment of their full and final emancipation as God's people and possession, acquired by the blood of
Christ. The saints are the property or possession of God, and they
have already received a part or foretaste of their future inheritance;
the Holy Ghost has been given them as part-payment until the
redemption is complete, that is, until our "acquisition," or future
possession, has been fully redeemed. "Charitas viæ, quam hic
habemus per infusum Spiritum Sanctum, eadem numero est ac
charitas patriæ, qua beati (misericordia Dei) possidebimus Deum in
cœlo" (St. Thomas, *Ia IIæ,* Q. 67, art. 6).

15. Wherefore I also, hearing of your faith which is in the Lord Jesus, and of your love towards all the saints,

Unto the praise, etc. The last end of all God's benefits and gifts to us in His glory, that is, the praise of His glory in heaven. God will be the supreme object of the praise of the saved hereafter, and all else will be an object of that universal chorus of exultant song, inasmuch as it reflects God and His attributes. Thus did the Psalmist describe the future, spiritual joys of the citizens of Jerusalem, which was a type of the heavenly city: "And singing as well as dancing they shall chant: All my fountains are in thee" (Ps. lxxxvi. 7).

AN ACT OF THANKSGIVING AND A PRAYER THAT THE SAINTS MAY UNDERSTAND THE BLESSINGS THEY ENJOY IN CHRIST, 15-19

15-19. Having considered the benefits which God from eternity has bestowed on the "Ephesians," and also the privilege of their call to the Gospel in time, the Apostle now thanks God for the faith they have already received, and then goes on to pray for a further outpouring of the Spirit upon them, to the end that they may fully realize the divine prospects which are theirs, which God has in store for them, and which will be given them according to the measure of His omnipotent power displayed in the exaltation of Christ.

15. **Wherefore,** i.e., because of the many divine benefits which have been described above, namely, our election, predestination, adoption, redemption, etc.

I also, hearing, etc., i.e., Paul, a prisoner in Rome, had heard of the faith among the "Ephesians." This is taken as an argument that this letter was not addressed to the Christians of Ephesus, among whom Paul had lived so long and whose faith was known to him personally. But others say that the Apostle is here alluding to the increase and progress of their faith since he was with them.

Which is in the Lord Jesus, i.e., which reposes in Him and on Him as a basis and foundation; or, less likely, which is maintained in union with Him.

And your love, etc. The word "love" here is wanting in some good MSS., but it is found in other important ones and in all ancient versions, and is therefore to be retained as a parallel to "faith."

16. Cease not to give thanks for you, making commemoration of you in my prayers;

17. That the God of our Lord Jesus Christ, the Father of glory, may give unto you the spirit of wisdom and of revelation, in the knowledge of him:

18. The eyes of your heart enlightened, that you may know what the hope is of his calling, and what are the riches of the glory of his inheritance in the saints,

19. And what is the exceeding greatness of his power towards us who believe, according to the operation of the might of his power,

The faith of the saints issues in love toward the brethren who share that faith, that is, in a love of preference, one which favors the Christians, but does not exclude love towards all men (2 Peter i. 7).

16. **Cease not, etc.** This is a frequent phrase with St. Paul, especially at the beginning of his Epistles, and Egyptian papyri show that similar phrases were used in epistolary greetings in pre-Christian times; with St. Paul, however, such words have a spiritual meaning. The Apostle continually thanks God for the spiritual benefits conferred on the saints, and he prays that these blessings may be continued and extended.

17. In verses 17-19 we have the substance of St. Paul's prayer. This is the Apostle's first prayer in this letter; a second prayer occurs below in iii. 14-19, and a third in vi. 18-20.

That the God, etc. There should be no comma after *Deus* in the Vulgate here. The meaning of the passage is: The God whom our Lord Jesus Christ knew and manifested to the world (John xx. 17; Matt. xxvii. 46; cf. above, ver. 3). The Arians abused this text to prove that our Lord was not divine; and hence some of the Fathers interpreted the words "of our Lord Jesus Christ" as referring to the humanity of Christ.

The Father of glory, i.e., the author and source of all glory, who possesses in Himself the fullness of glory and diffuses it in the world outside the Godhead.

May give unto you the spirit, etc., not the Holy Spirit, but His gifts, especially that of heavenly wisdom which penetrates into the deep mysteries of God and ever reveals a fuller knowledge of the Father, the Divine Being, whom to know, together with the Son whom He has sent, is to know the secrets and the fullness of eternal life (John xvii. 3; Matt. xi. 27).

18-19. **The eyes of your heart,** etc., i.e., that the Father of glory may give you (v. 17) enlightened eyes, or enlightenment of eyes, so that you may thoroughly understand the following: (a) "what is the hope of his calling," i.e., what are the rewards to be hoped for by those whom God has called to Christianity; (b) "what are the riches of the glory, etc.," i.e., what are the treasures of glory in heaven which God has prepared for Christians who, as children of God, have become heirs of celestial riches; (c) "what is the exceeding greatness of his power, etc.," i.e., what is the infinite power of God which is able to confer on the saints all that God has promised them as a result of their Christian faith. Thus, the Apostle prays that his readers may grasp the hope of their calling, the object of their calling, and the infinite power by which God is able to fulfill His promises to the saints.

Heart, among the Semites and Hebrews, meant not only the seat of the affections, but of intelligence also.

What, i.e., the essence or *quiddity*. There is good MSS. evidence for rejecting the "and" after "calling," thus making "the hope of his calling" one question with "what are the riches of his glory," instead of there being two questions involved in those two clauses.

The glory of his inheritance, i.e., the state of glory which Christ, the King of glory, has inherited and prepared in heaven for the saints (John xiv. 2 ff.).

In the saints, i.e., in the Christians who are saved: "The sufferings of this time are not worthy to be compared with the glory to come, that shall be revealed in us" (Rom. viii. 18).

Of his power, etc., exercised in our sanctification and glorification.

Who believe is in apposition with "us"; the phrase is not to be connected with the words that follow.

According to the operation, etc. These words go back to "the exceeding greatness of his power," and the meaning is: "according to the working of the strength of his power."

Might of his power. This is an intensive phrase used to bring out the power of God working within us; nothing is impossible to that divine power which was able to raise Christ from the dead. God who calls us to the joys of the Infinite has infinite power to make effective that call. See parallel passages in Col. i. 27, and Rom. ix. 23.

20. Which he wrought in Christ, raising him up from the dead, and setting him on his right hand in the heavenly *places*,

21. Above all principality, and power, and virtue, and dominion, and every
name that is named, not only in this world, but also in that which is to come.

THE EXALTATION OF CHRIST, 20-23

20-23. Speaking of the infinite power of God manifested in the
raising of Christ from the dead, the Apostle is, as it were, carried
out of himself, and bursts forth into a sublime act of praise of
the risen and glorified Saviour, sitting at the right hand of God in
heaven, elevated above all angelic powers or dignities, with all things
beneath His feet, being made the head of the Church, which is His
mystical body. In these verses our Lord's exaltation and supremacy
are proclaimed, first over the universe (ver. 21-22a) and then over
the Church (ver. 22b-23).

20. **Which he wrought.** The reference is to the action of the
Eternal Father in raising our Lord from the dead.

In Christ, i.e., in the person and instance of Christ.

And setting him. Better: "making him to sit."

On his right hand, i.e., in the place of honor, sharing as the
Incarnate Son the throne of the eternal Father, which as God He
had never relinquished.

In the heavenly places, i.e., in a spiritual locality outside and
above our world of sense. Our Lord's glorified body is a real body,
and therefore it requires a real place in which to dwell. See above
on verse 3.

21. **Above all principality,** etc. The Apostle here mentions four
orders or classes or choirs of celestial beings above which Christ
in heaven is said to be exalted (cf. 1 Peter iii. 22, and below, iii. 10).
In Col. i. 16, we have a parallel passage where St. Paul adds the
order of "thrones," but omits the order of "virtue" here mentioned.
In that passage the thought is that Christ in His pre-existent glory
and divinity is the Creator of those angelic beings; whereas here
His Headship over them is the dominant thought. The division of
angels into nine orders and three hierarchies is due to the Pseudo-
Dionysius in his book *On the Celestial Hierarchy*, a notable work
which first appeared about 500 A.D., but which from then on exercised a great influence till the close of the Middle Ages.

22. And he hath subjected all things under his feet, and hath made him head over all the church,

23. Which is his body, and the fullness of him who is filled all in all.

Every name, etc., is a Hebraism which signifies every creature whatsoever, which can exist "not only in this world" (i.e., in the time that precedes the Second Coming of Christ), "but also in that which is to come" (i.e., the eternal and heavenly duration that will follow the Second Advent) : over all creatures, present or to come, Christ rules supreme (cf. Phil. ii. 9-11 ; Col. i. 13).

22. **And he hath subjected,** etc. An allusion to Ps. viii. 8, where man is described as the crown of the visible world (cf. 1 Cor. xv. 26 ff.; Heb. ii. 8 ff).

And hath made him head, etc. The Greek reads: "And gave him to the Church head over all." The words "over all" show the dignity and excellence of Christ whom the eternal Father has given to the Church as its head. Our Lord made St. Peter the visible head of the Apostolic College and of the Church, but He Himself ever remains the supreme head, not only of the Church Militant, but likewise of the Church Suffering and the Church Triumphant.

23. But Jesus is the head of the Church, not merely because He governs it and has subjected all things to Himself, but also because it is His mystical body. The Church exists by virtue of Christ its head, and we its members live by His life. Hence, to injure unjustly the Church and its members is to injure Christ, as Jesus affirmed to Saul the persecutor: "Saul, Saul, why persecutest thou me, etc." (Acts ix. 4 ff.). St. Paul frequently speaks of the Church as the mystical body of Christ (cf. Rom. xii. 5; 1 Cor. xii. 12 ff.; Eph. iv. 12-16, v. 23, 30; Col. i. 18-19, ii. 19).

The fullness of him, i.e., the totality or completion of Christ, or that which renders Christ complete. The Greek word πλήρωμα here is obscure and has received various explanations, the most probable of which we have just given in the preceding sentence. The Church is the body of Christ, and Christ is the head of the Church. From this union of head and body there results one whole, which is the mystical Christ. The Church, therefore, the body of Christ, completes Christ; or, to put it in another way, Christ, the head of the Church, is completed by the Church. In other words, as in the human body the members are the completion or complement of the head, since without them the head could not exercise the different actions, so the Church, which is the body of Christ, is the complement of Christ the head, because without it Christ would not be able to exercise His office of Redeemer and Sanctifier of souls.

Who is filled. Here again the meaning is very obscure. The verb *to fill* in the Greek of the present passage may be taken in the middle or in the passive voice. If we take it as a middle, the meaning would be that Christ for His own sake fills with all graces and blessings the members of the Church, His mystical body. If the verb be understood as a passive participle, the sense is that Christ, God Incarnate, is incomplete without the Church, as a head is necessarily incomplete without its body; and that, consequently, as the Church grows in holiness and progresses in the fulfillment of its divine mission, Christ, God Incarnate, is progressively completed.

All in all, i.e., all things in all ways. Cf. St. Thomas, *hoc loco;* Vosté, *op. cit., hoc loco;* Prat, *La Théol. de St. Paul,* I, pp. 410 ff.

CHAPTER II

THE POWER OF GOD IS MANIFESTED IN THE NEW LIFE GIVEN TO CHRISTIANS, 1-10

1. And you, when you were dead in your offences, and sins,

1-10. The Gentiles were formerly dead in their sins, and the Jews, following after the lusts of the flesh, were no better; but God in His mercy through Christ has raised up both the one and the other, and made them heirs to heavenly thrones, in order that He might manifest to the coming ages His infinite goodness. All this has been gratuitous on His part, for we are saved by grace, and not by our own natural works. Thus, we are new creatures in Christ, that henceforth we may live lives worthy of our high calling.

1. **And you.** The connection with what precedes is clear; the thought goes back to verse 20 of the preceding chapter, and is as follows: As God gave new life to Christ Jesus, raising Him from the dead, so has He also given new life to you, raising you from the death of sin to a life of grace. The phrases are suspended

2. Wherein in time past you walked according to the course of this world, according to the prince of the power of the air, of the spirit that now worketh on the children of unbelief:

3. In which also we all conversed in time past, in the desires of our flesh, fulfilling the will of the flesh and of *our* thoughts, and were by nature children of wrath, even as the rest:

here, having their subject ("God") in verse 4 and their verb ("quickened") in verse 5. This suspended construction is characteristic of St. Paul's nervous and vehement style.

When you were dead, etc., i.e., spiritually dead, bereft of the principle of supernatural life, which is the Holy Ghost dwelling by grace in the soul.

2. Wherein, etc., i.e., in which state of moral death you lived and wrought in your pagan past.

According to the course of this world, i.e., according to the evil principles and customs of this present order of things, which is under the sway and influence of Satan, who is "the prince of the power of the air" (i.e., who is the ruler of the authority of the air, or the evil ruler whose sphere of authority is the air, and who exercises his nefarious influence "on the children, etc.," on those who refuse to believe, or who reject the Gospel). Among the Jews the air was popularly regarded as the abode of evil spirits, as heaven was God's abode and the earth the place of man's sojourn. Moreover, Satan's legitimate sphere of activity is no longer in heaven (Apoc. xii. 9; Luke x. 18); nor is it on the earth, which has been reclaimed by the Death and Resurrection of Christ. Hence, the Apostle speaks of it figuratively as being between heaven and earth —in the air.

Power is more probably to be taken in an abstract sense for *domination,* and "spirit," a genitive in Greek, is governed by "prince," and means the mind or tendency by which the evil spirit, Satan, is actuated.

Children of unbelief, or better, "sons of disobedience," is a Hebraism to signify all those who do not accept the Gospel.

3. In which. This can refer to the "sins" and "offences" of verse 1, or to the "children of unbelief" of verse 2. If taken in the latter connection, we should render "among whom."

Also we all, i.e., the Jews, as well as the Gentiles.

Conversed, etc., i.e., lived and acted before they embraced

4. But God (who is rich in mercy), for his exceeding charity wherewith
he loved us,

Christianity. St. Paul is referring to the general unfaithfulness of
the Jews, in spite of their many privileges and graces (Rom. iii. 9) ;
he is not, of course, including faithful individual souls like the
Blessed Virgin, St. Joseph, the Prophets, etc. But the Jews as
a class, he says, like the Gentiles, lived according to the evil in-
clinations of their lower nature and the perverse counsels of the
mind of the natural man, disregarding the will of God and the dictates of an enlightened conscience. As a result, they were "by nature children of wrath," i.e., by reason of the corrupt nature they
had inherited from Adam, which inclined them to the actual sins
of which they were personally guilty, they had become objects of
God's great displeasure, "even as the rest" (i.e., like the pagans).
We are said to incur God's wrath when by willful transgression
we put ourselves in opposition to His will; the change is not in the
unchangeable God, but in us.

It is disputed whether "by nature" here is to be understood of
original sin, or of actual sins of which the Apostle has just been
speaking, or of both taken into the one account. St. Augustine took
the phrase to mean original sin, and this is the common opinion.
But Dr. Vosté thinks there is question here only of actual sins, since
the Apostle is speaking of sins in which the Gentiles "walked," and
in which the Jews "conversed" in times past—therefore, of sins
which both the Gentiles and the Jews had themselves committed.
The Jews and the Gentiles are both put in the same class here as
regards their sins, but that could not be with regard to original sin,
since the former, unlike the latter, were purified from it by circumcision before their conversion to Christianity. Of course, the innate
proneness to evil in both classes and in all men is best explained by
the doctrine of original sin.

4-6. The Apostle now goes on to say that, when both Jews and
Gentiles were spiritually dead because of their sins, God, moved
by His great love for them, "quickened" them (i.e., brought them
back to life), and "raised" them up from the grave of death, and
"made" them "sit together in the heavenly places" with the glorified Christ (i. 3). All this has been done by grace, without any
merit on their part; and of course what is here said of Jews and

5. Even when we were dead in sins, hath quickened us together in Christ (by whose grace you are saved),

6. And hath raised us up together, and hath made us sit together in the heavenly *places,* through Christ Jesus:

7. That he might shew in the ages to come the abundant riches of his grace, in his bounty towards us in Christ Jesus.

Gentiles is also true of all men of all time who are regenerated in Christ.

The compound verbs which appear here in the Latin and Greek of verses 5 and 6, and which can be respectively rendered in English by *co-vivified, co-raised,* and *co-seated,* show the intimate union that exists between Christ and the members of His Church, who constitute His mystical body. We are *with* Christ as His companions, and *in* Him as members of His mystical body, the Church. St. Paul is speaking of our spiritual restoration and our sanctification by which we are already admitted to a participation in the divine nature and to a foretaste of life eternal; hence the use of the aorist, or definitely past tense. Our glorification is already a fact in germ.

7. Here we have indicated the purpose of our present transformation by grace into the likeness of Christ, which is that in the life to come beyond the grave the Eternal Father might show to the angels and to the elect in heaven, where only so great a benefit can be perfectly understood, the infinite treasures of grace which of His own goodness He has bestowed on the saved through Jesus Christ, and by reason of their union with Christ. The Apostle never tires of repeating that all the graces and benefits we receive are given and shall be given us "in Christ Jesus," and this is why the Church always prays *through Christ.*

The phrase "in the ages to come" is understood by some interpreters to refer to the period during which the preaching of the Gospel will go on in the present world, by others to all future periods of development in God's kingdom; but it is better to take it as alluding to heaven, where the goodness of God towards us will be perfectly manifested and perfectly understood. We must not think of "the world to come as a monotonous stretch of time. As the life of God is pure activity without any element of inertia or passivity, the life of those who will share in the Divine Nature will be active. To us, wearied with labour, and burdened with care, heaven naturally becomes a symbol of rest. But labour implies a strength unequal

8. For by grace you are saved through faith, and that not of yourselves, for it is the gift of God;

to perfect mastery of the work; and the good, opposed to it, is not rest or inactivity, but the play of an artist or a child. So we may picture the life of God as one of play. And the life of the Church in heaven may be imaged as that of God's kindergarten, the knowledge of Him ever growing deeper, the vision of Him ever growing fuller, and His glory ever growing brighter. We cannot describe that life; but such an expression as 'the ages' implies a history of period after period, in which God will more and more exhibit the overflowing wealth of His grace by kindness to those in union with His Incarnate Son" (Hitchcock, *The Epistle to the Ephesians, hoc loco*).

8. In verse 5 St. Paul said we are saved *by grace*, and now he goes back to that thought and proves his assertion. Our justification and our salvation are the result of grace, with faith as a necessary condition (cf. Rom. iii. 22 ff.) ; and neither the faith that precedes nor the justification or salvation that follows can be said to be due in any way to our natural works, for the simple reason that there is no proportion between these supernatural gifts and our natural works; they belong to different orders.

For. This word shows the connection with the preceding verse, where it is said that God's favors to us are the consequence of His bounty towards us.

You are saved. The Apostle now addresses his Gentile readers, and hence changes to the second person.

Through faith, i.e., by means of faith, as a necessary condition of their salvation.

And that. The pronoun "that" here is neuter in Greek, and it is uncertain to what it may refer. St. Chrysostom, St. Jerome and others referred it to "faith"; but faith is a feminine noun. It seems better, therefore, to make the reference be to the whole preceding sentence, which declares in a positive manner that our salvation is entirely the work of God's grace. To this general positive teaching the Apostle then adds in a negative way that this salvation is not of ourselves, "for it is the gift of God." That faith alone is a pure gift of God is also certain (cf. 2 Cor. iv. 13; Phil. i. 29), though that is not the main point here. St. Paul is accustomed to use

9. Not of works, that no man may glory.

10. For we are his workmanship, created in Christ Jesus unto good works, which God hath prepared that we should walk in them.

11. For which cause be mindful that you, being heretofore Gentiles in the flesh, who are called uncircumcision by that which is called circumcision in the flesh, made by hands:

the pronoun "that" (τοῦτο) in reference to the preceding sentence, and not to the preceding word (as in 1 Cor. vi. 8; Phil. i. 28) ; hence we understand it here as referring to our deliverance by grace through faith.

9. The conclusion of the preceding verse is further reinforced in a negative way by saying here that our salvation is not the result of "works" (i.e., of any natural works), whether of the Law (Rom. iii. 28) or otherwise ; so that all the glory of our salvation may be referred to God, and not to any man, "that no man may glory" (i.e., boast that his salvation is due to himself). If anyone will glory in this matter, let him glory in the Lord (1 Cor. i. 31 ; 2 Cor. x. 17; Gal. vi. 14). And the reason for this is immediately given.

10. **For we are his workmanship,** etc., i.e., we as Christians are His making, for He has "created" us, as it were, anew "in Christ Jesus" (i.e., as members of Christ's mystical body in the super- natural order) "unto good works" (i.e., with a view to good works, as an inseparable condition of our new creation in grace) ; which good works God from eternity has decreed and prepared for us, not to the exclusion of our free will, but presupposing the right use of free will, for he adds "that we should walk in them" (i.e., God has so prepared those good works for us that we should freely do them in time).

THE GENTILES, TOGETHER WITH THE JEWS, ARE CALLED TO SHARE IN THE BLESSINGS OF CHRIST IN THE ONE CHURCH, 11-22

11-22. St. Paul's pagan converts will better understand the exalted life to which they have been elevated in the Church of Christ, if they first recall their former miserable condition as Gentiles, then reflect on the benefits they now enjoy, and finally compare their present with their former state.

11. **For which cause** (i.e., since you have been redeemed without any merit on your part) **be mindful,** etc. (i.e., remember your

12. That you were at that time without Christ, being aliens from the conversation of Israel, and strangers to the covenants, having no hope in the promise, and without God in this world.

13. But now in Christ Jesus, you, who some time were afar off, are made nigh by the blood of Christ.

former deplorable condition when you were "Gentiles in the flesh," that is, without even any external sign, like circumcision, of belonging to God), when you were contemptuously called the "uncircumcision" by those who were "called circumcision in the flesh"—that is, by the Jews, who bore on their bodies the external mark of belonging to the commonwealth of God, but in many of whom this physical mark was merely hand-made, and so without spiritual value, since it is the circumcision of the heart alone that counts in the sight of God (Rom. ii. 29; Col. ii. 11).

12. The Apostle continues the thought broken off after the phrase, "be mindful that you" (verse 11). The Gentiles before their conversion to Christianity were "without Christ" (i.e., apart from Christ), inasmuch as they had not the Scriptures and prophecies which contained the Messianic promises of a coming Redeemer; they were "aliens, etc.," as being excluded from the theocratic kingdom and from the family of God's chosen people; they were "strangers to the covenants" (i.e., to the promises of a Messiah made by God to Abraham and renewed to Isaac, Jacob, David, etc.); they were without "hope in the promise" of a Redeemer to come, and hence their best writers and philosophers all expressed the prevalent thoughts and sentiments of sadness and despair, the deep unhappiness at their existing state and the hopeless darkness of the future outlook, holding that the best thing that could happen to man was never to be born, and the next best thing was to die (cf. Mommsen, *Hist. of Rome,* Eng. trans., vol. IV, p. 586); they were "without God in this world" (i.e., without a correct knowledge of the true God in a dark and sinful world), having obscured by their sins the natural light of reason, and being devoid of the positive divine revelation which the Jews possessed.

13. The Apostle has just briefly reviewed the sad state of the Gentiles before their conversion to Christianity (ver. 11-12). Now he will speak of their new and glorious condition as Christians, and of the peace they enjoy in the Messianic Kingdom (ver. 13-18).

14. For he is our peace, who hath made both one, and breaking down the middle wall of partition, the enmity in his flesh:

Formerly they were without Christ, but now they are "in Christ" (i.e., living intimately united to the promised Messiah and in union with "Jesus," the Saviour of mankind). In their previous condition as pagans, they "were afar off" from the kingdom of God, being outside the citizenship of Israel and the covenants of promise; but now they "are made nigh, etc." (i.e., they have been incorporated in Christ by membership in His Church, through the merits of the passion and death of Jesus). It was Christ's blood offered in sacrifice for them, as for the whole world, that merited for these Gentile converts their redemption and the consequent peace they now enjoy in the Church of Christ: "This is my blood of the new covenant, which shall be shed for many unto the remission of sins" (Matt. xxvi. 28; Heb. ix. 12 ff.). The Apostle will now show how this has been done by the pacifying work of Christ.

14. **For he is our peace.** Isaias (ix. 6) foretold that the Messiah should be the Prince of peace. And Christ is said to be our peace, first because, through the abrogation of the Mosaic Law with its statutes and precepts, He has destroyed the barrier that made enmity between Jew and Gentile (ver. 14-15); and secondly because He has reconciled men with God by forgiving their sins (ver. 16). Thus, He "hath made both one" (i.e., He has made the Jewish and the Gentile sections of the human race one community), not by making Gentiles Jews, but by elevating both to the supernatural order and producing, as it were, a new race called Christians. The "middle wall of partition" refers to the Mosaic Law which kept the Jews separated from the Gentiles and was the cause of the enmity that existed between them. The figure here was likely suggested by the stone wall which separated the Court of the Gentiles from the Temple Court of the Israelites. Any Gentile who dared to trespass beyond this wall incurred the penalty of death.

Enmity. This word is more probably to be taken in apposition to "middle wall of partition," and it signifies the reality of which that wall was a figure. This enmity and its cause Christ has been broken down and removed "in his flesh" (i.e., by means of His passion and death).

15. Making void the law of commandments *contained* in decrees; that he might make the two in himself into one new man, making peace;

16. And might reconcile both to God in one body by the cross, killing the enmity in himself.

15. Some expositors connect "in his flesh" of the preceding verse with what follows here; but this does not affect the sense, since it was by His passion and death that Christ both removed the barrier between Jews and Gentiles and abrogated the Law with its statutes and precepts.

Making void, etc., by abrogating the Mosaic Law which contained numerous commands and ceremonies regarding foods, feasts, etc., all of which were calculated to isolate Israel from the rest of the world, and were figures or types of realities to come. With the advent, therefore, of Christ and the Gospel these ancient precepts and ceremonies were abrogated, as the shadow vanishes with the appearance of the light (cf. Col. ii. 14-20). It must be understood, of course, that the moral precepts of the Mosaic Law did not cease; they were rather perfected and confirmed (Matt. v. 17; cf. Rom. iii. 31; 1 Cor. iii. 14).

That he might make, etc. (better, "in order to create, etc."). The purpose was not merely to unite Jew and Gentile, but from the two to create a new human type that should be neither Jew nor Gentile, but Christian. The Apostle uses the masculine plural here (τοὺς δύο), because there is now question of two men, Jew and Gentile, and not of two systems, Judaism and heathendom, as in ver. 14 where the Greek neuter is used. The justification or sanctification of a soul is as much a generation in the supernatural order as the production of the soul and the human organism is in the natural order (cf. 2 Cor. v. 17).

In himself. Christ has united Jew and Gentile into one mystical body of which He is the head and life-giving source, thus "making peace" between them.

16. A further purpose of the propitiatory death of Christ was to reconcile both Jew and Gentile to God by means of the sacrifice of the cross, having destroyed by His own suffering the enmity that existed between them, and having united them both into one new man "in one body," which is His Church.

In one body. By this phrase some understand the physical

17. And coming, he preached peace to you that were afar off, and peace to them that were nigh.

18. For by him we have access both in one Spirit to the Father.

body of Christ affixed to the cross; but others with greater probability take the phrase to refer to the mystical body of Christ, the Church.

In himself should more likely be "in it," the reference being to the cross (ἐν αὐτῷ), rather than to Christ. The Greek, however, can refer to either Christ or the cross (cf. Col. i. 19-22).

17. And when the Saviour came into this world, He preached first in person to the Jews, and then through His Apostles to the Gentiles, the Gospel of peace among all men and reconciliation to God. The Gentiles were said to be "afar off," because they were without the Law and the special revelation which the Jews possessed, and in consequence of which the latter were said to be "nigh." The perfect peace which Christ brought to the world, and of which He spoke at the Last Supper (John xiv. 27, xvi. 33), rests on perfect justice; and hence, as St. Thomas says, it is impossible to have peace without justice. This peace of Christ which we enjoy is the fruit of our reconciliation with God, and the cause of it the Apostle will now explain in the following verse.

18. Christ is our peace, and He has given us peace because through Him we, Jews and Gentiles, have been freed from our sins, animated by the Holy Ghost, reconciled to God, and thus introduced to the Father. Note the mention here of the three Persons of the Blessed Trinity. It is more probable that the word "access" here should be given an active transitive sense, and so should be translated "introduction," because we have not ourselves come into the presence of the Father, but Christ has *introduced* us; "we do not come in our own strength, but need an introduction—Christ" (Sanday, on Romans v. 1-2).

Robinson and some others understand "one Spirit" here to refer to oneness of mind and heart among the Christians; but as the unity of the body results from the unity of the head, so the unity and concord of the faithful come from the unity of the Spirit by which they are animated. Thus, this second explanation is included in the first, and presupposes it.

19. Now therefore you are no more strangers and foreigners; but you are fellow citizens with the saints; and the domestics of God,

20. Built upon the foundation of the apostles and prophets, Jesus Christ himself being the chief cornerstone:

19. In verses 19-22 St. Paul will show the difference between the present and the former state of the Gentiles and their existing perfect equality with the Jews. He will illustrate this equality of Gentiles with Jews in the Christian commonwealth by several different metaphors—by a city or state, in which they enjoy the rights of naturalized citizens; by a household, in which they are members of God's family; by a building, of which they and the Jews are the living stones and Christ the chief cornerstone.

Now therefore. The Apostle is going to draw a conclusion from what he has just been saying in the preceding verses.

You are no more strangers, to the covenants of the promise (ver. 12), **and foreigners,** i.e., aliens, without the rights of citizenship in the spiritual commonwealth of God; **but you are fellow-citizens,** etc., i.e., full members of the mystical body of Christ and of the household of God, together with those of Jewish origin; you are all now inmates of the Father's house in Christ.

20. **Built,** etc., or better, "having been built upon the apostles and prophets" of the New Testament as a moral foundation, with "Jesus Christ himself" as the chief cornerstone of that foundation, who thus gives coherence and fixity to it and to the whole superstructure erected upon it. Having spoken at the end of ver. 19 of the inmates of the household of God, the Apostle in this verse passes to the building itself. The past tense of the verb here shows that the Gentiles became fellow-citizens in the New Jerusalem and members of God's family at the time of their conversion (Hitchcock, *op. cit., h. l.*). It is more probable that the "foundation" here refers to the apostles and prophets themselves, than to the doctrine they preached (1 Cor. iii. 10), since they are paralleled by "Jesus Christ" which follows. Nor is it likely that we should take Christ as the foundation here, as in 1 Cor. iii. 11, since just below He is said to be the "chief cornerstone." We are likewise to understand "apostles and prophets" to refer to the New Testament teachers and ministers of the Word (Acts xi. 28, xv. 32; 1 Cor. xiv), rather than to the Prophets of the Old Testament, as we judge from the

21. In whom the whole building, being fitly framed together, groweth up into a holy sanctuary in the Lord.

22. In whom you also are built together into a habitation of God in the Spirit.

order of the words here, from the fact that both nouns are preceded by only one article in Greek, from the parallel passages in Eph. iii. 5 and iv. 11, where the reference is certainly to New Testament prophets, etc. On the other hand, it is true that the Old Testament Prophets are frequently regarded in the New Testament as Evangelists before the time (Luke xxiv. 25; Acts iii. 18, 21, 24, x. 43; Rom. xvi. 26).

21. **In whom** (i.e., in which cornerstone, namely, Christ) **the whole building** (i.e., every part of the Church, becoming more intensely and solidly united, part with part and all the parts with the foundation and head) **groweth**—i.e., becomes ever more and more extended, as living stones are prepared and laid on living stones (1 Pet. ii. 5), rising to completion and perfection—**into a holy sanctuary,** worthy of the divine presence that dwells therein (cf. Apoc. xxi. 22), **in the Lord** (i.e., in Christ, who is the living bond of unity, coherence, growth, and sanctity of the entire Church). We have given what we consider the best and most probable rendering of the passage, "the whole building, being fitly framed together," the Greek of which is difficult and is variously translated.

"Sanctuary" (Gr., ναός), the more sacred part of the Temple, where the divine presence is especially manifested, as distinguished from the courts and outer area (ἱερόν).

22. **In whom.** The reference is again to Christ, the cornerstone.

You also, i.e., you Gentile readers of this Epistle.

Are built. Better, "are being builded" together with the rest of the Christians. The present tense is used in Greek, showing that the process is going on but is not yet complete; the Church is becoming more extended without and more united within as it gradually approaches its perfection and its goal as a permanent habitation for the Divine Presence in its glorified state hereafter.

Into a habitation is parallel to "into a holy sanctuary" above, and the thought is that of a building that is being perfected as an abiding dwelling place for God in the world to come, where "God shall be all in all" (1 Cor. xv. 28).

In the Spirit, i.e., in the Holy Ghost, "who sanctifieth the elect of God." "In the Spirit" is parallel to "in the Lord" of the preceding verse, and hence it is to be interpreted of the Spirit of God. The Church is built on the Son, by the Holy Ghost, for the Father; and the description here given of it by St. Paul, from the revelation he had received, began with a reference to the Messianic Kingdom of the Old Dispensation (ver. 11-12), then proceeded to a reflection on the peace now enjoyed in the Messianic Kingdom of the New Dispensation (ver. 13-18), and finally terminates (ver. 19-22) with a vision of the Messianic Kingdom of the New Jerusalem, where a manifestation of the glory to come (Rom. viii. 18), supreme and unimaginable, awaits all those who by perseverance in faith and good works are destined to be heirs of the riches of God in heaven.

CHAPTER III

THE REVELATION OF THE MYSTERY THROUGH THE PREACHING OF ST. PAUL, 1-13

1-13. Having spoken in the first Chapter of this Epistle of God's eternal purpose to unite Jewish and non-Jewish peoples in the one Church of Christ, and having shown in the second Chapter how this purpose has been realized in the present period of grace with its prospect of glorious consummation in the Church Triumphant hereafter, the Apostle, according to his custom after such meditations on the wondrous ways of God, begins a prayer of thanksgiving on behalf of the "Ephesians"; but he has only begun (ver. 1a) when he is somehow reminded of his chains and what has made him a prisoner for Christ, and this causes him to digress (ver. 1b-13) to consider the part he has played in the realization of God's eternal purpose to unite all the nations of the world in the one spiritual fold of Christ, and to unfold again the unsearchable wisdom of God hidden in the purpose of that divine mystery and age-old secret. For a parallel parenthesis see Rom. v. 13-18.

1. For this cause, I Paul the prisoner of Jesus Christ, for you Gentiles;
2. If at least you have heard of the dispensation of the grace of God which is given me towards you:

1. **For this cause,** a phrase repeated again in ver. 14, where Paul resumes his prayer; it refers back to what he has been saying in ii. 11-22.

I Paul is a characteristic way of introducing himself when he is about to treat matters of grave importance or defend his authority (cf. 2 Cor. x. 1; Gal. v. 2; Col. i. 23; 1 Thess. ii. 18; Phlm. 9, 19). St. Chrysostom would insert "am" here after Paul, so as to read: "I Paul am the prisoner, etc." But if this were the meaning, the article before "prisoner" in Greek should be omitted. Hence, it is better with Theodoret, Theodore of Mopsuestia, and all modern interpreters to recognize the break in the sentence here and its resumption at ver. 14.

The prisoner, etc., i.e., a prisoner according to the will of his Master, and for the cause of his Master (Phlm. 1, 9; 2 Tim. i. 8).

For you Gentiles, i.e., on behalf of you Gentiles, for preaching to you the Messianic salvation and admitting you on a level with the Jews in the Church of Christ (cf. Acts xxi. 21 ff.).

2. **If at least you have heard.** Abbott and many others hold that these words prove that St. Paul was addressing readers personally unknown to him. Westcott thinks there is nothing in the words to sustain such a conclusion. Moule believes we have here "a phrase of almost irony, an illusion to well-known fact under the disguise of hypothesis." Alexander says the words are expressive of gentle assurance. As a compromise, Robinson holds they mean that some, at least, of the readers were personally unknown to the Apostle. Hitchcock explains that St. Paul first had the intention of writing to the Ephesians, as he had written to the Colossians, but that his outlook changed as he wrote, embracing the Churches of the Lycus Valley and other Gentiles. Vosté would translate: "Since indeed you have heard, etc." If we explain the words as conditional, as in Eph. iv. 21, we still may hold that they are rhetorical, not implying any real doubt.

The dispensation of the grace, etc., better, "the stewardship of the grace, etc." The Messianic Kingdom is a reign of grace, and St. Paul was designated by Christ to be His steward in dis-

3. How that, according to revelation, the mystery has been made known to me, as I have written above in a few words;

4. Whereby, as you read, you may understand my knowledge in the mystery of Christ,

5. Which in other generations was not known to the sons of men, as it is now revealed to his holy apostles and prophets in the Spirit;

pensing the Messianic grace to the Gentiles. Cf. 1 Cor. ix. 17; Col. i. 24, 25.

3. The Apostle now begins to explain how the mystery of grace was made known to him, that is, his apostleship among the Gentiles, as he has explained above in ii. 11 ff.

How. The Vulg. *quoniam* should be *quomodo,* used to indicate the object of St. Paul's ministry, namely, that the Gentiles were to be fellow-heirs, etc. (ver. 6).

According to revelation, made to Paul directly on the road to Damascus at the time of his conversion, and elsewhere later on (Acts ix. 4 ff.; Gal. i. 12, ii. 2; 2 Cor. xii. 1, 7, etc).

The mystery, i.e., the purpose of God to save Gentiles as well as Jews through Christ (ver. 5, 6).

As I have written, etc., in this letter (i. 4-14, ii. 4-9, 11-22).

4. **Whereby, as you read,** etc. The meaning is that, as they read what he has already written in the first two Chapters of this letter, they will perceive his deep insight into God's world-purpose as revealed in the Incarnation of His Son, namely, the salvation of the world by means of the cross and the incorporation of the Gentiles with the Chosen People.

5. **Which** eternal purpose and deep mystery was never before known to mankind as it is now revealed in the Gospel by means of a special revelation communicated to chosen Apostles and prophets whom the Holy Ghost has inspired and set apart in order that they may make it known to the world.

Was not known, at all to the pagan world, and was only dimly shadowed forth among the Chosen People, the most of whom did not understand it.

Sons of men is a Hebraism meaning all men.

Holy apostles, etc., i.e., men especially selected and consecrated for their supernatural work, but not necessarily sanctified personally. That there is question here only of New Testament prophets is clear from the phrase "now revealed."

6. That the Gentiles should be fellow-heirs, and of the same body, and co-partners of the promise in Christ Jesus, by the gospel:

7. Of which I am made a minister, according to the gift of the grace of God, which is given to me, according to the operation of his power.

8. To me, the least of all the saints, is given this grace, to preach among the Gentiles the unsearchable riches of Christ,

In the Spirit, i.e., in the Holy Ghost, by whom the human mediums were inspired.

6. St. Paul now gives a brief definition of the content of the long-hidden mystery in so far as it pertained to the Gentiles, namely, that God has made the Gentiles equal to the Jews as regards salvation; they are now "fellow-heirs" with the Jews to heaven, members of the same mystical body, the Church, sharers in the same high destiny "in Christ" (i.e., in vital union with Him), which was long ago promised to Abraham and his offspring (Gen. xii. 3; Gal. iii. 8, iv. 29; Rom. iv. 13, 16), and is now made manifest in the preaching of the Gospel.

His promise of the Douai should be "the promise," according to the best Greek and Latin texts.

7. The Apostle begins now to speak of the mission that has been entrusted to him, the dispensation spoken of above in iii. 2. He has been made a "minister" of the Gospel, not by his own choice or because of his merits, but by a gratuitous gift of divine grace, which made an Apostle out of a persecutor and gave him invincible strength to pursue his vocation. The grace here referred to was a *gratia gratis data,* a divine gift to be used for the benefit of others.

According to . . . according to. Note the parallelism: divine grace made him a minister of the Gospel, and divine grace sustains him in his work for the Gospel; his vocation was a divine gift, and his labors were the result of a divine operation, of God-given working power. Cf. Col. i. 29; Gal. ii. 8.

8. Here and in the following verse St. Paul will speak of the purpose of his preaching.

To me. The thought of the greatness of the mission confided to him by the grace of God reminds the humble Apostle of his personal unworthiness and insignificance.

The least in the Greek is a word probably coined by the Apostle himself, which literally means "leaster," or "more least."

Of all the saints, i.e., of all the Christians (cf. 1 Cor. xv. 8, 9).

9. And to enlighten all men that they may see what is the dispensation of the mystery which hath been hidden from eternity in God, who created all things:

10. That now the manifold wisdom of God may be made known to the principalities and powers in heavenly *places* through the church,

St. Paul never forgets his past life as a persecutor, and the more he realizes the greatness of the grace of God bestowed on him, the more clearly his own unworthiness appears.

To preach, etc. Behold the grace and the mission vouchsafed to Paul, to announce to the Gentile world the infinite treasures of divine truth, love and power, which God has provided for mankind through Jesus Christ.

Unsearchable, literally, "untrackable by footprints," untraceable, a word found only here and in Rom. xi. 33 in all the New Testament; it means *incomprehensible.* So vast are the treasures of grace hidden in the Gospel and confided to the Church that they utterly transcend our powers of understanding.

9. **To enlighten,** etc. Such was the further effect of Paul's preaching of the Gospel, to make known to all men the divine plan, hidden from eternity, of saving the whole world by means of the human life, labors, sufferings, death, and glorious resurrection of the eternal Son of God made man.

All men. The Greek word is omitted by some ancient MSS. and good authorities, but the weight of authority favors its retention.

Hidden from eternity, etc. Not until the coming of Christ, the Messiah, was the divine economy relative to the salvation of men actually and completely made known; till then it was known in its fullness only to the Godhead.

Who created all things. The Apostle adds this to remind his readers that He who was able to create all things through the Son in the beginning is now able to redeem all through the Son. Some lesser authorities add, "by means of Jesus Christ," which may be rejected as a gloss. Cf. Col. i. 25-27 for a parallel passage to verses 8 and 9 here.

10. As it was the purpose of the preaching of Paul to make known to the nations the revelation of the mystery hidden in God from eternity (ver. 8-9), so in turn was it the purpose of that revelation to make known to the world the unsearchable riches of

11. According to the eternal purpose, which he made in Christ Jesus, our Lord:

the Messiah and His stewardship, hidden from the beginning in the Creator (ver. 10-11), that is, "that now" (in contrast to the ages that preceded the coming of the Christ) "the manifold wisdom of God, etc." (i.e., the many-sided and infinitely varied wisdom of God in providing for the salvation of man through the Incarnation of the Son of God) might be made known through the Church to the world of angelic intelligences, including both the good and the evil angels.

Now (Vulg. *nunc*), omitted in the Douai, is expressed in the Greek.

Manifold. Literally, "much variegated." The word is found here only in the New Testament.

Principalities and powers, i.e., good and bad angels, according to St. Chrysostom and the evidence of vi. 12 below (cf. also i. 21 above).

In the heavenly places. See on i. 3.

Through the church, in which the divided human family has been united, and which contains and dispenses the treasures of grace, thus continuing the work of the Redeemer till the end of time in the sight of men and angels. "It is by no means repugnant that through the work of Christ, which the Church continues and carries out to the end of the present world, the infinite riches of the wisdom and mercy of the Redeemer should be successively manifested to the angels themselves" (St. Thomas, *h. l.*).

11. **According to the eternal purpose,** etc., literally, "according to the purpose of the ages, etc." The manifold wisdom of God was hidden in the eternal purpose; and that purpose, running through the whole course of the ages, has now been "made" (i.e., realized) in "Christ Jesus, our Lord," sacrificed, risen, and enthroned forever as the center and Sovereign of the universe; and with the realization of the purpose the multifarious wisdom of God has been made known in part already, and is continually being unfolded to men and angels down to the end of the world. It is disputed whether the words, "which he made," refer to the decree which God made from eternity regarding future ages, etc., or to the execution of that decree in time; but the context seems to favor the latter explanation.

12. In whom we have boldness, and access with confidence by the faith of him.

13. Wherefore I pray you not to faint at my tribulations for you, which is your glory.

12. St. Paul has just discussed the purpose of God's revelation made known through the preaching of that revelation, which was to disclose to heavenly intelligences the manifold wisdom of God, as realized in Christ. Now, in verses 12-13, he will treat of the consequences of that same revelation. The first of these consequences is that in Christ, that is, by reason of our mystical union with Him, "we have boldness, etc.," i.e., we now enjoy freedom of speech and communication with the Father, "and access" (i.e., introduction) to Him, not in fear, but in confidence (Rom. viii. 38 ff.), and this through the faith we have in Christ.

The faith of him means the faith we have "in Him," as we know from similar constructions in Mark xi. 22; Gal. ii. 16, iii. 22; Rom. iii. 22, 26; Phil. iii. 9.

13. Another consequence of the revelation preached by Paul is the sufferings it brought upon him; but here he prays that his readers may not grow remiss and faint-hearted as a result of the afflictions he has to endure for preaching the Gospel to them; for his sufferings are their glory, inasmuch as they are an evidence of God's love for them, since God was willing to permit His Apostle to endure so much for their sakes: the privileges they enjoy and the afflictions Paul has undergone that they might have those privileges indicate how dear they are to God.

Wherefore, i.e., in view of your dignity and privileges, resulting from God's eternal decree realized in Christ.

I pray. This is more probably to be understood of a real prayer to God for the Apostle's readers, as we gather from the similar use of the verb in Eph. iii. 20 and Col. i. 9.

Not to faint should not be interpreted as applying to the Apostle himself, who gloried in his tribulations and declared that nothing could separate him from the love of Christ (Rom. v. 3, viii. 38, 39; 2 Cor. xii. 10; Col. i. 24), but to his readers, to whose glory it was that he had to suffer, and who therefore should not be discouraged.

14. For this cause I bow my knees to the Father of our Lord Jesus Christ,

15. Of whom every paternity in heaven and earth is named,

16. That he would grant you, according to the riches of his glory to be strengthened by his Spirit with might unto the inner man.

17. That Christ may dwell by faith in your hearts; that being rooted and founded in charity,

ST. PAUL PRAYS THAT HIS READERS MAY BE STRENGTHENED IN FAITH AND IN THE PRACTICE OF VIRTUE, 14-19

14-19. Having considered his ministry among the Gentiles, St. Paul now continues his prayer interrupted in ver. 1b. Prostrating himself in mind before the Father of all, from whom all fathership in heaven and on earth derives its name and its nature, he asks that his readers may be interiorly strengthened by the Divine Spirit; that Christ by faith may dwell in their hearts; that, being rooted and founded in charity, they may be able to comprehend with all the faithful the full scope and extent of His love for us, which surpasses all our understanding; and that, finally, they may come to embody in their own lives the full content of plenitude of God.

14. The Apostle resumes the prayer begun in verse 1, but interrupted by the long parenthesis of verses 2-13.

For this cause, i.e., in view of the grace given the Gentiles, which makes them equal sharers with the Jews in Messianic benefits.

I bow my knees, etc., words denoting a humble and fervent attitude of prayer, not necessarily expressed by the physical posture. The "Father" is addressed because He is the creator and source of all things. The words, "of our Lord Jesus Christ," should be omitted, according to the evidence of the Greek MSS. and the best Patristic authority.

15. Of whom every paternity, etc. St. Paul is stressing the common Fatherhood of God. Every paternity (πᾶσα πατριά) is named from the father (πατήρ), and all created fatherhood is but a reflection at best of the Fatherhood of God.

In heaven and on earth, i.e., among the angels in heaven and the different nations of the earth; every possible family derives its name and has its being from the Father above. The angels are said to be divided into different families according to their different orders (Estius).

16-19. The Apostle comes back to the purpose for which he has

18. You may be able to comprehend, with all the saints, what is the breadth, and length, and height, and depth:

19. To know also the charity of Christ, which surpasseth all knowledge, that you may be filled unto all the fullness of God.

figuratively bent his knees in prayer, and asks God to give his readers strength, and this "according to the riches of his glory," i.e., in a manner beyond measure, or according to His infinite power and goodness. In i. 19 St. Paul had prayed that his readers might know "what is the exceeding greatness of his power towards us who believe," and here he prays that they may be made mighty with that power; and his prayer now is a positive supplication corresponding to the negative petition, "not to faint," of iii. 13.

By his Spirit, etc., i.e., that they may be strengthened by the grace of the Holy Ghost in the higher or spiritual faculties of their souls, in their conscience, understanding, imagination, and will—for all of which the *heart* in Scripture is regarded as the seat. In further and more determinate words, he prays "that Christ may dwell by faith in their hearts" (i.e., that the presence of Christ in their minds and wills may, by means of a faith which operates by charity, become ever more perfect), so that "being rooted, etc." (i.e., being firmly fixed in love of God), they "may be able to comprehend" (i.e., mentally to perceive) "with all the saints" (i.e., in union with the whole assembly of the faithful) "what is the breadth, etc." (i.e., the measurement or full extent of the Messiah's love for us Christians); that is to say, that they may even know how great is the love of Christ towards us, so that, as far as it is possible for created intelligences, they may have the strength at length to grasp in Beatific Vision the fullness of the divine nature, that is, that they, the members of Christ's mystical body, may be able to take in of the divine nature, according to their capacity, as much as their Head, in whom dwells the fullness of divinity corporally (iv. 13), perceives according to His capacity.

It is obvious that the Christian perfection of his readers for which St. Paul here prays can be attained in its fullness only in the life to come beyond the grave, though the progress towards it should go on here continually; and even in that other life of Beatific Vision the soul, while perceiving and knowing in an ever-increasing measure the love of Christ for it, can never fully grasp its divine object through all the ages of eternity, simply because the object is infinite; the created knowledge can never be commensurate with the increate object; the goal is ever being attained, but is never attained or attainable; and hence the Apostle says it "surpasseth all knowledge."

At first sight it sounds paradoxical that St. Paul should pray that his readers may "be able to comprehend" and "to know" that which he afterwards says "surpasseth all knowledge," but his meaning is clear: he is praying for such a perception and such a knowledge of the love of Christ for them and such a grasp of the divine nature on their part as will be commensurate with their finite capacities, which can ever be increased and extended, but which, in the nature of things, can never equal and exhaust their divine and infinite object. Forever the redeemed soul will find in God more to know, more to love, more to adore; and even at the farthest stretch of the eternal years it will still be as far away from completely comprehending or exhausting the overflowing ocean of God's infinite being as it was at its entrance into bliss. Here indeed is a revelation that provides the only philosophy of life that has a clue for the otherwise hopeless riddle of our present existence; that rescues our poor life from its littleness and miseries and links it with the tides of the Eternal; that promises an ultimate and adequate satisfaction to the endless reachings of the human mind and the boundless longings of the human heart.

A further explanation of some words in these verses (16-19) may be needed. Thus, "unto the inner man" is paralleled by "in your hearts" in the following verse, and it means the higher spiritual faculties of the soul—the domain of reason, thought, conscience, will, etc., as said above.

By faith, i.e., by means of an implicit trust in all that has been revealed, and this, not merely by a speculative adhesion of the mind to revealed truth, but by a practical exercise in works of what one believes, by a faith that lives by charity: "If any one love me, he will keep my word, etc." (John xiv. 23 ff.).

Being rooted, like a tree of the Lord in the rich soil of the love of God, **and founded,** like stones of the Temple on the same love.

In charity. It is disputed whether these words should go with what precedes or with what follows; and also whether there is question of God's love for Christians or of the love Christians have for

God. As to the first point, it seems that the participles "rooted" and "founded" need determination, and therefore that the phrase "in charity" should go with them. As to the second point, since the Apostle is praying that his readers may understand Christ's love for them, and since love is perceived by love and the more Christ is loved the better He is understood, it would seem that the words "in charity" ought to refer to the love Paul's readers have for Christ.

May be able to comprehend, as far as a finite being can comprehend.

With all the saints, may be taken disjunctively or collectively, as implying what each one of the faithful may be able to do, or what all of them together can do, the knowledge and experience of each individual soul adding to and enriching the knowledge and experience of every other soul.

What is the breadth, etc., is probably an accumulation of terms to express exhaustive measurement; the Apostle wishes his readers to perceive the love of Christ for them to the full extent of their capacity. The object is not expressed after this clause, but we have taken it to be love of Christ for the faithful, which will be named just below. See Rom. viii. 39 for similar terms of measurement relative to divine love: "Neither height nor depth, nor any other creature, will be able to separate us, etc." Others, with the Greek Fathers, take the object of the foregoing dimensions to be the mystery of the salvation of all nations through Christ, treated before in this and in the preceding chapters. Such, we are told, is the meaning, because the words, "to know also," that follow indicate an addition to the thought that precedes, and have their own object distinctly expressed, namely, "the charity of Christ." But, we may ask, is not that great mystery of the union of all peoples in Christ the effect or the fruit of divine love, and therefore ultimately to be resolved into that love? Moreover, the phrase, "to know also," may be correctly rendered from the Greek, "and even to know," which intensifies the thought just previously expressed, without adding to it something new.

That you may be filled, etc. The fullness here intended may be understood of God's own fullness, which is poured into our souls according to our capacity to receive it: "Be ye perfect, as your

20. Now to him who is able to do all things more abundantly than we desire or understand, according to the power that worketh in us;

21. To him be glory in the church, and in Christ Jesus, unto all generations, world without end. Amen.

heavenly Father is perfect, etc." (Matt. v. 48) ; or it may be taken, as in i. 23, of the fullness which is given to God through the Church. We prefer the first meaning, which is that understood by St. Thomas, St. John Chrysostom, and many others among modern expositors.

DOXOLOGY, CLOSING THE DOGMATIC PART OF THE EPISTLE, 20-21

20-21. As in the Epistle to the Romans (xi. 33-36), so also here St. Paul terminates the Dogmatic Part of his letter with a solemn ascription of praise to God. He has considered the great mystery of the union of all nations in Christ, and his own ministry in the revelation of that mystery; he has asked much for his readers, but he has done so with all confidence, because the Almighty Father is able to do all things more abundantly than we can know or understand. It is fitting, therefore, to bring these sublime considerations to a close with words of praise to Him who has done so much for us, and who is able to do infinitely more than we can conceive or desire; neither God's gifts nor His power can we fully comprehend.

20. **According to the power,** etc., i.e., according to the grace of the Holy Spirit within us (cf. Rom. viii. 26; Col. i. 29).

21. **To him,** etc., i.e., to God all-powerful and our supreme benefactor be the external praise due to His wondrous works.

In the church, i.e., in the mystical body of Christ, which is the theatre wherein are manifested principally the grace and mercy of God.

And in Christ, the Head of the Church, from whom all graces come to us.

Unto all generations, etc. Throughout all time and all eternity the redeemed shall praise God for the graces and mercies He has bestowed upon them in Christ.

Amen, so be it.

CHAPTER IV

1. I therefore, a prisoner in the Lord, beseech you that you walk worthy of the vocation in which you were called,

iv. 1—vi. 20. The precepts of Christ follow from the doctrine of Christ as conclusions from premises, so that rightly lived the Christian life is nothing more than a vivid reflection of Christ's teachings. So far in this Epistle the Apostle has spoken of Christians as predestined members of Christ's mystical body, as living stones in God's temple, and as units in the divine household, destined to a glory beyond all our imaginings. High, therefore, is their calling; and he would have them walk worthy of it. To this end he describes first in this Moral Part the general character of the Christian life as lived in mutual charity and holiness (iv. 1-24); then he treats of particular duties, whether pertinent to all or to individual members of the Christian family (iv. 25—vi. 9); and finally he illustrates the life of Christians as a warfare (vi. 10-20). See *Introduction*, No. VIII, B.

CHRISTIANS MUST WALK WORTHY OF THEIR VOCATION IN ALL UNITY, iv. 1-16

1-16. The Christian life imposes on its members the obligation of preserving, by means of humility and loving forbearance, the spirit of unity which has been given them in the Holy Ghost. All have the same hope; all acknowledge one and the same Lord as their head; the same faith is common to all, expressed in one and the same Sacrament of Baptism; and finally, all have the same heavenly Father. There is a great diversity of gifts and functions in the Christian society, but the Ascended Christ is the Source of them all; and all have the one purpose, which is growth into perfect

2. With all humility and mildness, with patience, supporting one another in charity,

3. Careful to keep the unity of the spirit in the bond of peace:

corporate unity, so that the Church will come to express in its own life and maturity the life of Christ its divine Head.

I therefore. The Apostle is now going to deduce practical conclusions from what he has been saying in the first part of the Epistle; and hence he means to say that, in view of all the blessings and privileges they enjoy as a result of their call to the faith, they ought to do what he is about to exhort.

A prisoner in the Lord, or, as he said above in iii. 1, "the prisoner of Jesus Christ," for having preached the Gospel.

Beseech you, etc. Better, according to the Greek, "exhort you, etc." In view of the blessings they have received and of all Paul has suffered for them and other Christians, they ought to lead lives in conformity with their high dignity.

2. He now shows them practically what they must do to live lives worthy of their calling as Christians, recommending four principal virtues. They must practise: (a) "humility," which is opposed to pride, a source of discord and the enemy of the peace of society; (b) "mildness," which implies gentleness and submission under trial, as opposed to anger and injurious conduct; (c) "patience," which means long-suffering and forbearance with the defects of others and with injuries received from others; (d) "charity," or love of neighbor, the root and supernatural spring of all the other virtues, which makes easy the practice of all the others, and without which no other virtue can be perfect.

3. **Careful,** etc. Behold the end to which is ordained the practice of the four virtues just mentioned, namely, "the unity of the spirit, etc.," i.e., concord of mind and heart, of thoughts and feelings; and this unity of souls is effected by the "bond of peace," which is the tranquillity of order. This "bond (or *co-bond*) of peace" means the peaceful union of souls, united by Christian love. It is the peace of which our Lord spoke at the Last Supper: "Peace I leave with you, my peace I give unto you, etc." (John xiv. 27). Compare the present passage with its parallel in Col. iii. 13-15 (cf. Hitchcock, *h. l.*). It is more probable that "spirit" here is to be understood of concord of minds and hearts rather than of the Holy Ghost (so St. Thomas, Estius, and others).

4. One body and one Spirit; as you were called in one hope of your calling:

5. One Lord, one faith, one baptism:

6. One God and Father of all, who is above all, and through all, and in all.

4. After commending the foregoing concord of souls, the Apostle goes on to consider the elements from which the unity of the Church results objectively. There are three intrinsic elements: one body, one Spirit, one hope or end of our calling; there are three extrinsic factors: one Lord, one faith, one baptism; and finally, there is one transcendent element or factor, whose universal action is exercised in three ways: one God and Father of all, who is above all, and through all, and in us all (ver. 4-6). Cf. Vosté, *h. l.*

Where there is "one body" (which is Christ's mystical body, the Church), "one Spirit," which animates the Church (namely, the Holy Ghost), and "one hope of your calling" (which is eternal beatitude), there surely ought to exist oneness of mind and heart, as said above. Some expositors take "Spirit" in this verse to mean concord or harmony among the members of the Church; but it is more likely that it means the Holy Spirit, because there is question now of the essential constitution of the Church and of that which unites it objectively, from which subjective harmony among its members should result, as an effect from its cause.

5. In the preceding verse the Apostle considered the intrinsic elements of unity. Now he will treat of the extrinsic elements. The faithful have one leader, Christ, whom they all obey and in whom they are all united; they have the same objective law or faith in Christ, by which they accept the same truths and observe the same precepts; they have one and the same divine seal by which they are made members of the one mystical body of Christ, namely, Baptism.

6. Here we have the transcendent element of unity, "One God" (from whom we all have the same nature) "and Father of all" (uniting us all in one common brotherhood through adoption in Christ), "who is above all" things (as governing all), "and through all" (as pervading all), "and in all" (as sustaining all). It is better to understand the adjective "all" here as neuter rather than masculine (so Westcott, Robinson, Vosté) ; and hence the Vulg. is arbitrary in varying from the one gender to the other. The *nobis* of the Vulg. is not represented in the best Greek.

7. But to every one of us was given grace, according to the measure of the giving of Christ.

8. Wherefore he saith: *Ascending on high, he led captivity captive; he gave gifts to men.*

7. So far the Apostle has considered the unity of the Church as to its common elements; and now he will consider that which is proper and special to individual members of the same mystical body, namely, their different gifts and functions, all of which should tend to the good of the whole (ver. 7-16).

To every one of us (i.e., to each one of the faithful who make up the unity of the Church, and not to the ministers only) **was given grace** (i.e., the special divine help to discharge certain duties and offices in the Church, and this was done, not haphazardly confusedly, but) **according to the measure,** etc. (i.e., according to the work each one was to do in the Church in fulfillment of the purpose of Christ, the Giver of that grace).

8. In this and in the two following verses the Apostle shows that our Lord is indeed the distributer of the gifts spoken of in verse 7; and to prove it he quotes in the present verse Psalm lxvii. 19, which, in its literal sense, refers to a temporal victory of the Jews over their enemies through the help of Jehovah, but in its spiritual meaning refers to the triumphal Ascension of our Lord into heaven after achieving our redemption by His victory over sin and Satan. The Psalmist is picturing Jehovah as ascending to His Sanctuary on Mt. Sion after the victory of His people, and there accepting spoil from His vanquished foes; and this is a figure of the Ascension of Christ into heaven, following the completion of the work of our redemption, and thence distributing His gifts to the faithful on the Day of Pentecost. The munificence of Jehovah to Israel prefigured the bounty of Christ bestowing His gifts on men. The Apostle is probably quoting the Psalm from memory, and so does not give the exact words either of the Hebrew or of the LXX of the Psalm.

He saith. Better, "It saith" (i.e., the Scripture says).

Captivity means "captives," the Hebrew abstract standing for the concrete. But who are the captives in the application? If we need to seek an application for this phrase, they are (a) mankind wrested from the captivity of the evil one, Satan, or (b) the conquered evil spirits who had enslaved man until the coming of Christ.

9. Now that he ascended, what is it, but that he also descended first into the lower parts of the earth?

10. He that descended is the same also that ascended above all the heavens, that he might fill all things.

He gave. In the Psalm we have "Thou didst receive," a different person and a different verb; but St. Paul, speaking in the third person of our Lord, is using the words which the Psalmist addressed to Jehovah in the second person. As Jehovah received spoil from Israel's enemies, so did our Lord receive gifts to be distributed "to men" (i.e., to the faithful).

9. The Apostle means to say here that the Ascension of Christ into heaven presupposes His descent from heaven to this earth at the time of His Incarnation; or to the lower parts of the earth, to the Limbo of the dead, after His crucifixion; or, if we take the ascent to be previous to the descent, the meaning is that after our Lord ascended into heaven, He later descended at Pentecost through the Holy Spirit with His special gifts of grace to the faithful, or in general to take up His dwelling in the souls of the just. But St. Paul is saying that the descent was previous to the ascent, and hence we must reject opinions that suppose the contrary. We should hold, then, that the descent in question was either at the time of the Incarnation when our Lord first came to this earth (so Knabenbauer, Cajetan, and many non-Catholics), or when He visited the abode of the dead between His own death and glorious Resurrection (so St. John Chrysostom, St. Jerome, Estius, Vosté, etc.). The latter opinion is thought to be more in harmony with: (a) Pss. lxii. 10, cxxxviii. 15; Rom. x. 7; Acts ii. 27; 1 Peter iii. 19, iv. 6; (b) the context of St. Paul, for in the following verse it is said that our Lord "ascended above all the heavens," the contrary of which would be to descend to the lowest parts of the earth: He ranged from the lowest to the highest, thus visiting all, "that he might fill all things" (ver. 10).

What is it? That is, "What does it imply?" The word "first" agrees with the context, but is of doubtful authenticity.

10. **He that descended** (from heaven to earth, and even to the lower parts of the earth, though His Incarnation) **is the same also that ascended,** etc. (on Ascension Day, and took His seat on the right hand of the Father), **that he might fill all things** (by the

11. And he gave some apostles, and some prophets, and other some evangelists, and other some pastors and doctors,

exercise of His power and rule, and the influence of His grace, especially in His Church). The person that ascended is the same as the person that descended. The Son of God descended from heaven, taking upon Himself our human nature; and the Son of man ascended according to His human nature to the sublimity of immortal life (St. Thomas, *h. l.*).

Above all the heavens. These words contain no approval by St. Paul of the opinion of the Rabbins that there were seven heavens; the Apostle is merely emphasizing the supreme exaltation of the Lord. It is true that in 2 Cor. xii. 2, St. Paul himself speaks of the "third heaven," but there he is most likely only referring to the immediate presence of God.

11. Returning to the thought of ver. 7, after the parenthesis of ver. 8-10, the Apostle is now going to speak about the various gifts bestowed by our Lord on certain ones among the faithful, and the end to which these gifts are ordained (cf. also Rom. xii. 4-6; 1 Cor. xii. 4 ff.). It is to be noted that the various names here designate offices or functions rather than persons. Therefore, "apostles" are those who had the gift of the apostolate, and most likely included others besides the Twelve, like Paul, Barnabas, etc. (Rom. xvi. 7).

Prophets are those who taught, instructed, and exhorted others (1 Cor. xiv. 1-5), as well as foretellers of future events, like Agabus (Acts xi. 27, 28, xxi. 10, 11).

Evangelists are not necessarily those only who wrote the Gospels, but missionaries and preachers of the word among strangers and infidels (John xxi. 15 ff.; Acts xxi. 8; 2 Tim. iv. 5; 1 Peter ii. 25).

Pastors and doctors. Before these two names in Greek there is but one article; whereas the article precedes each of the names given before in this list. From this fact St. Jerome, St. Thomas, and others have concluded that the care of souls and the office of teacher go together, that he who is a pastor ought also to be a teacher. But other commentators hold that there is question of separate functions here not necessarily to be found in the same person, just as there was above, and that St. Paul omitted the article

12. For the perfecting of the saints, for the work of the ministry, for the edifying of the body of Christ;

13. Until we all meet into the unity of faith, and of the knowledge of the Son of God into a perfect man, unto the measure of the age of the fullness of Christ;

14. That henceforth we be no more children tossed to and fro, and carried about with every wind of doctrine by the wickedness of men, by cunning craftiness, by which they lie in wait to deceive;

before the last word here in his hurry to close the list (so Vosté).

12. Here the Apostle points out the end or purpose of the ministry just detailed. All those gifts and offices were "for the perfecting of the saints" (i.e., for the purpose of equipping or fitting out those on whom they were bestowed) "for the work of the ministry" (i.e., for the fulfillment of the duties they were to discharge among the faithful), thus enabling all the members of the Church to do each his full share by word, work and example towards "the edifying of the body of Christ" (i.e., towards building up and perfecting the Church, and spreading its work and influence over the world). The word rendered "perfecting" occurs here only in the New Testament, and most probably means "equipment," "preparation." Those who translate it in the sense of "perfection" reverse the order of the words in the verse and make "the perfecting of the saints" the end and purpose of "the work of the ministry" and "the edifying of the body of Christ."

13. Until does not here refer so much to time as to the ultimate purpose or end to which all the charisms in question are ordained, which end or purpose is "unity of faith" and a supernatural "knowledge of the Son of God"; so that by individual and corporate spiritual growth, effort and influence the Church may come to realize and express in her own life that mature and full-grown perfection which is in Christ her divine Head. Christ is the standard or "measure" of perfection toward which the individual Christian and the Church as a whole must tend, and which, individually and collectively, the faithful must, in so far as possible, endeavor to express here on earth. Hence "age" here refers not to the years but to the perfection of Christ.

14. The Apostle here states negatively what he said in a positive manner in the preceding verse; there he showed how the Church was to attain its perfection, and now he shows how it should avoid

15. But doing the truth in charity, we may in all things grow up in him who is the head, *even* Christ:

16. From whom the whole body, being compacted and fitly conjoined together, by what every joint supplieth, according to the operation in the measure of every part, maketh increase of the body, unto the edifying of itself in charity.

what is opposed to its perfection. We must not henceforth exhibit the mental weakness and ignorance of children, who are fickle and inconstant, subject to the influence of all the false opinions and changing novelties by which wicked, cunning, and crafty men try to lead the unwary astray.

Tossed to and fro, etc. Better, "tossed about on the waves, and carried round and round by every wind of doctrine," as so many non-Catholics are, which is not a very safe way to reach the port of salvation. "What St. Paul deprecated as the waywardness of an undisciplined child, is now glorified as free thought" (Rickaby). The Vulgate, *fluctuantes et circumferamur,* should read *fluctuantes et circumlati,* to agree with the best Greek; and *in nequitia* should be *in fradulentia* (the Greek word being a metaphor from cheating at dice).

15. Instead of being deceived and led into error by evil and cunning men, we must be followers of "the truth," i.e., we must confess, love, and practise the truths made known to us by our faith; and not only so, but our faith and works must be vivified by "charity," or the love of God, so that "in all things," or better, "as to all things" (i.e., as to our whole being, our entire Christian perfection), we may "grow up in him, etc.," i.e., increase and solidify our union with Christ, our divine Head. The more we grow in perfection, the more we come to resemble in all things Jesus Christ who is the Head of the mystical body of which we are the members.

16. Having just spoken of Christ, the Head of the mystical body which is the Church, the Apostle now goes on to describe the growth and increase of that mystical body as it is united in charity to Christ its Head.

The words "being compacted" down to "every part" inclusive should be regarded as parenthetical, so that the main sentence reads: "From whom the whole body maketh increase, etc." This verse affords a typical example of St. Paul's compressed and pregnant style, where in a few words a multitude of ideas are contained. It is extremely obscure, as St. Chrysostom says, because the Apostle wants to say everything at once. We find a parallel in Col. ii. 19.

From whom, i.e., from Christ, the fountain whence flows the whole spiritual life of "the whole body," which is the Church, the members of which "being compacted, etc.," i.e., being closely and harmoniously connected, one with the other, and vitally conjoined so as to form one organic whole and act as a unit. The words "compacted" and "conjoined" are expressed by present participles in Greek, and therefore convey the idea of a living, progressive process of growth by which the Church is ever moving on in development, strength, and perfection to its final consummation in heaven.

By what every joint supplieth. Passing over several different and less likely opinions about the exact meaning of the Greek word ἁφῆς (here rendered "joint") and ἐπιχορηγίας (rendered "supplieth"), we may hold the most probable meaning of the Apostle to be that help descends from Christ the Head into the whole mystical body through the joints by which the various members are connected one with the other. As in the physical organism help comes from the head to the different members through the joints or connecting physical links, so in the mystical body of Christ, the Church, help is communicated from Christ the Head to the various members (to the faithful) through the joints, i.e., through the various ministries, gifts and functions spoken of above in verse 7; but the help thus supplied is not the same for each member, but is "according to the operation, etc."—that is, it is in proportion to the power or supply of help given it by the Head, which supply or power is itself proportioned to the capacity of each member and to the work each particular member is given to perform. And all the members being thus assisted and thus operating, it happens that the whole body "maketh increase, etc." (i.e., grows in unity, strength, and effectiveness), and all this through the vitalizing principle and power of "charity."

CHRISTIANS MUST PUT OFF THE OLD MAN ACCORDING TO THE FLESH AND PUT ON THE NEW MAN ACCORDING TO GOD, 17-24

17-24. At the beginning of the present Chapter St. Paul, starting with the words "I therefore," proposed to deduce practical consequences in conduct from the doctrines he had just previously laid

17. This then I say and testify in the Lord: that henceforward you walk not as also the Gentiles walk in the vanity of their mind,

18. Having their understanding darkened, being alienated from the life of God on account of the ignorance that is in them because of the blindness of their hearts.

down; but after an exhortation to unity his intention was diverted into a description, more dogmatic than moral, of principles fundamental to the unity of the Christian commonwealth, the Church (ver. 4-11), and to a consideration of the ideal Church as a whole (ver. 12-14) and the harmonious interrelation of its members (ver. 15-16). Now resuming his original intention, expressed at the beginning of the Chapter, he will take up the question of the personal holiness of individual members of the Church, and explain it (a) negatively, in reference to the Gentile life of ignorance and impurity which they have discarded (ver. 17-19), and then (b) positively, in regard to the new life of enlightenment and purity which they have embraced as Christians (ver. 20-24).

17. **This then I say,** etc. The Apostle now resumes in a more solemn manner the exhortation begun in verse 1 of this Chapter, that his readers should lead lives worthy of their exalted vocation as members of Christ's Church. The word here translated "testify" occurs elsewhere in the New Testament only in Acts xxii. 26, and in Gal. v. 3; it is a term of solemn appeal.

In the Lord, in whom we are all united, and from whom the Apostle got his mission and authority.

That henceforth, etc., i.e., that you no longer live as you did before your conversion, and as the pagans still live, "in the vanity, etc.," i.e., in the state of intellectual and moral perversity wherein they were unable to distinguish between moral good and moral evil. For a description of this condition of the pagans see Rom. i. 18-32; 1 Peter iv. 1-4. The Greek for "mind" here (νοῦς) embraces not only the abstract theoretical faculty of thinking and reasoning, but also the practical moral judgment of good and evil, as is evident from the following verse.

18. In this verse St. Paul says that the "blindness"—or better, "hardness" or "dullness"—of the hearts of the Gentiles, which made them impervious to the divine overtures, was the cause of their culpable "ignorance" of the will and law of God, and this ignorance left their understanding darkened, with the result that they were

19. Who, being bereft of feeling, have given themselves up to lascivious-ness, unto the working of all uncleanness, unto covetousness.
20. But you did not so learn the Christ;
21. If at least you have heard of him, and have been taught in him, as the truth is in Jesus:
22. To put off, according to former conversation, the old man, who is corrupted according to the desire of error.

"alienated from the life of God," i.e., they lived lives not in con-formity with the divine precepts, and far removed from the centre and source of all spirituality and holiness. Thus, their willful sins caused their hardness or dullness of heart, their hardness or dullness of heart caused their ignorance and mental darkness, and this in turn caused their alienation from the central source of grace and spiritual life.

19. It is not surprising that the moral and intellectual state de-scribed in the preceding verse should have left the pagans "bereft of feeling" (ἀπηλγηκότες), i.e., without remorse and indifferent, so that they gave themselves up without restraint to all manner of impurity and to the commission of all kinds of uncleanness "unto covetousness," i.e., with a greediness (πλεονεξία) never to be satiated. Some expositors understand πλεονεξία here to mean sexual excess. The *desperantes* of the Vulgate should be *indolorii* or *indifferentes* to agree with the best Greek (St. Jerome).

20. In verses 17-19 the Apostle has shown his readers what their life must not be as Christians; now in verses 20-24 he will set before them what the Christian life demands of them in a positive way.

But you did not, etc., i.e., you were not so instructed in the teachings of the Gospel of Christ at the time of your conversion that you will allow yourself now to live as you lived as pagans.

21. **If at least,** etc. See above on iii. 2.

Have been taught, etc., i.e., have been taught in Christ's school, according to the doctrine revealed by Him.

In Jesus, i.e., in the historical Jesus who was the prophesied Christ. Only here in this Epistle does the name of Jesus appear alone.

22. This and the two following verses in Greek begin with an infinitive, "to put off," "to renew," "to put on," all of which go back to what the readers of this Epistle "have been taught, etc.," in verse 21. They have been taught—or rather, they were taught at the

23. And be renewed in the spirit of your mind;

24. And put on the new man, who according to God is created in justice and holiness of the truth.

time of their conversion—to put off the old sinful man inherited from Adam, whose principles and mode of life were theirs as pagans, and living according to which they became ever more and more plunged into sin and error.

According to the desire of error, i.e., according to the dictates of the passions, which are always false and deceitful, promising joy and pleasure but ending in sorrow and pain.

23. **To put off the old man** (ver. 22) and **to put on the new man** (ver. 24) are really one act, and therefore they are expressed by the aorist infinitive in Greek, signifying one definite act; but **to be renewed in the spirit,** etc., is a progressive process, and as such it is expressed by the Greek present infinitive (Westcott).

In the spirit of your mind. The meaning of this expression, which occurs nowhere else, is not quite certain, though it is clear that it refers to the human spirit or the mind, and not to the Holy Ghost. It seems to indicate that mind, or part of the mind, which through grace is subject to God, and which in justice and truth lives according to God, in contrast to the vanity and perversity of mind of the Gentiles (Vosté).

24. It is not sufficient to put off the old man of sin which you have inherited from Adam, but you must also "put on the new man, etc.," i.e., the man who has been regenerated by the grace of the Holy Ghost, and who having been created "according to God, etc." (i.e., having been created in the beginning in the image and likeness of God), imitates God in his new life of grace by keeping the commandments which reflect the divine will and therefore God Himself. This new man, or creation of grace, "is created in justice and holiness," i.e., he lives a life faithful to the obligations he owes to his neighbor (justice) and to the duties he owes to God (holiness)—that is, a life which is in entire conformity with "the truth" of the Gospel, as revealed in the Gospel.

THE VIRTUES CHRISTIANS MUST PRACTISE AND THE VICES THEY MUST AVOID, iv. 25–vi. 9

iv. 25—vi. 9. The Apostle is now going to show in a practical way just what it means for Christians to have put on the new man;

25. Wherefore putting away lying, speak ye the truth every man with his
neighbor, for we are members one of another.

26. Be angry, and sin not. Let not the sun go down upon your anger;

27. Give not place to the devil.

that is, he is going to apply more in detail to Christian life and
conduct the principles he has laid down. He will treat first of precepts that are pertinent to all Christians, to Christian society in
general (iv. 25—v. 21), and then of precepts that regard particular members of the Christian family, that regulate the Christian
home (v. 22—vi. 9). In the remaining verses of the present Chapter
he speaks of some of the principal vices which the mutual charity
of Christians forbids, and of some of the virtues which that same
charity enjoins upon the members of the Church.

25. **Wherefore**, i.e., since you have put off the old man and put
on the new man who is characterized by justice and holiness, you
must be on your guard against falling back into the sins of your
former life; and first of all, you must put "away lying," because
this is so injurious to the neighbor, whom we are bound not to
injure but to assist, as being all members of the one mystical body
of Christ. Lying injures not only the neighbor, but oneself also, because we are all members of the same body, and that which injures one part of the body is felt in all the parts; the injury of the
part reacts on the whole.

26-27. Another sin to be avoided is unreasonable anger, that is,
anger which springs from wounded personal feelings rather than
from repugnance at something objectively wrong, or which is out
of proportion to the objective harm done.

Be angry, and sin not. These words are from Ps. iv. 5, cited
according to the LXX. The meaning is: "If you have occasion to
be angry, be careful that your anger does not become sinful."

Let not the sun, etc. This is a proverbial expression, and it
refers not to the anger but to that which caused the anger in question. The meaning is that the cause of anger should be removed
and the offence given should be repaired as soon as possible. The
Jewish day closed with the sunset.

Give no place to the devil. Excessive and prolonged anger
affords an opportunity for the devil to act, and to excite in the soul
feelings of hatred, revenge, and the like. To agree with the Greek,

28. He that stole, let him now steal no more; but rather let him labor, working with his hands the thing which is good, that he may have something to give to him that suffereth need.

29. Let no evil speech proceed from your mouth; but that which is good, to the edification of faith, that it may administer grace to the hearers.

30. And grieve not the Holy Spirit of God: whereby you were sealed unto the day of redemption.

there should be no full stop at the end of verse 26, and verse 27 should read: "Neither give place, etc."

28. The next prohibition is not to steal; on the contrary, let those who through idleness or laziness were accustomed to steal as pagans, or are now stealing as Christians, do some good manual work as a remedy against this vice and as a means of earning something to be given to those in need, in reparation for goods ill-gotten in the past.

Stole is present tense in Greek, as if to imply that some among the Christians had not yet given up their pagan habit of stealing.

29. The Apostle now turns to the conversation of Christians, prohibiting foul speech of every kind, and enjoining "that which is good, etc." (i.e., that which is calculated to edify the neighbor), so "that it may administer, etc." (i.e., that it may be an occasion of grace to those who hear it).

Evil. Literally, "rotten," which fitly described much of the talk that was common in heathen society.

To the edification of faith. Better, according to the authority of the best MSS., "to the building of the need," i.e., as necessity requires, according to the demands of place, time, and person (St. Jerome).

Grace here is understood by Theodoret to refer to that talk which is agreeable and acceptable to the hearers; but it is better to understand it in the ordinary Pauline sense of supernatural grace, which will also include the other meaning.

30. Another reason for avoiding foul speech is that the Holy Ghost may not be grieved, "whereby" (i.e., in whom and by whom) both the speaker and the hearer of polluting speech "were sealed" at the time of their conversion, when they received the Sacraments of Baptism and Confirmation, both of which were usually conferred together in the early Church.

Unto the day of redemption, i.e., until the general resurrection,

31. Let all bitterness, and anger, and indignation, and clamor, and blasphemy, be put away from you, with all malice.
32. And be ye kind one to another; merciful, forgiving one another, even as God hath forgiven you in Christ.

when we shall take full possession of our redemption. See on i. 14.

31. In this final prohibition St. Paul strikes at the root of the different vices he has been enumerating: this root is "malice," of which those other sins were the manifestations.

Bitterness is an aversion arising from prolonged anger; it is akin to sulkiness.

Anger is a transient outburst of passion, whereas **indignation,** or wrath, is a settled or chronic condition including the purpose of revenge.

Clamor, as here meant, is a violent and angry assertion of one's real or supposed rights and wrongs.

Blasphemy is taken literally from the Greek, but it would be better to translate it in this passage by "reviling," since there is question now of evil speech, not against God but against man.

Malice, i.e., malevolence or the desire to injure, is the root of the sins just mentioned. Compare the parallel passage in Col. iii. 8.

32. The Apostle has just given some of the sins by which charity is wounded; so now he will mention some of the opposite virtues by which charity is preserved and exercised, adding the motive for the practice of these virtues. He would have his readers be "kind" (i.e., sweet and courteous to one another), "merciful" (i.e., tenderhearted), "forgiving" (i.e., ready to pardon one another's offences), and all this because "God hath forgiven" (or better, "did forgive") them at the time of their conversion, "in Christ" (i.e., through the merits of Christ). See parallel passage in Col. iii. 12-13.

CHAPTER V

PRECEPTS FOR CHRISTIANS IN GENERAL, 1-21

1-21. This Chapter continues the thought of the preceding Chapter, and verses 1-2 here really belong at the end of Chapter IV, with which they are so intimately connected. The Apostle has just been saying that his readers, in forgiving one another, should imitate

1. Be ye therefore followers of God, as most dear children;

2. And walk in love, as Christ also loved us, and delivered himself for us, an oblation and a sacrifice to God for an odor of sweetness.

3. But fornication, and all uncleanness, or covetousness, let it not so much as be named among you, as becometh saints:

God who has pardoned them for the sake of Christ; and now he continues that thought, and makes the further plea that in their relations with one another they should imitate the charity of Christ who gave Himself as a sacrifice to God for us all.

Verses 1-21 here, apparently having in view pagan pleasures and festivities, contain five commands mainly for self-guidance regarding Christian love, light, wisdom, gladness and submission, as Chapter iv. 25-32, contained five prohibitions regarding others.

1. God is our Father and we are His adopted children, and so we ought to imitate Him in forgiving others as He has forgiven us; the more we imitate our Father, the more we become like Him, and consequently the more we are loved by Him.

Therefore connects this verse with the preceding Chapter.

2. The example of our Lord is now given as a motive for the exercise of fraternal charity.

Walk in love, i.e., let charity be the animating and governing principle of your lives, after the example of Christ who out of love for us delivered Himself up to the death of the cross for our salvation.

Loved us. The versions read thus, but a number of Greek MSS. have: "Loved you."

An oblation and a sacrifice. The first word is more general, the second more particular in meaning. The term "sacrifice" can also stand for a bloody or an unbloody offering, and certainly the former is not to be excluded here where the sacrifice of our Lord is in question. The purpose of St. Paul here is to show the completeness of our Lord's sacrifice, as being the antitype of both the bloody and the unbloody sacrifice. Very probably the Apostle is alluding in this passage to Ps. xxxix. 7, which is Messianic, and which is explicitly cited in Heb. x. 5.

An odor of sweetness is a sacrificial phrase taken from the Old Testament (Gen. viii. 21; Lev. i. 9, 13, 17, etc.), and it simply means that the sacrifice was pleasing and acceptable to God.

3. From the sublime thoughts just enunciated the Apostle now

4. Or obscenity, or foolish talking, or scurrility, which is to no purpose; but rather giving of thanks.

5. For know you this and understand, that no fornicator, or unclean, or covetous person (which is a serving of idols), hath inheritance in the kingdom of Christ and of God.

6. Let no man deceive you with vain words. For because of these things cometh the anger of God upon the children of unbelief.

descends to practical matters, and in verses 3-14 warns his readers against sins of the flesh and works of darkness, so characteristic of the pagan world. He has just been speaking of Christian love in a positive way, and now he will speak of it negatively, by forbidding sinful love, whether sensual or avaricious. Impurity and grasping self-assertion were central sins of paganism, and they are condemned by the Apostle in all their forms; not only are they not to be practised, they are not even to be named among Christians, who by their profession are consecrated to the God of holiness, purity, and justice.

4. Likewise the "saints" are to avoid all obscene and filthy language, all foolish talk about immoral things, all jesting in the sense of depraved pleasantry, which serves no good purpose and is unbecoming; on the contrary, the mouths and tongues of Christians should be filled with the praises of their Creator and Redeemer, in thanksgiving for all His benefits.

5. **For know you this,** etc., is according to the best Greek reading here, which may be translated as imperative or indicative. The Apostle is going to speak of something his readers know very well.

Fornicator, as here used, means also adultery and every illicit sexual union.

Unclean refers to private impurity.

Covetous person, i.e., inordinate lover of material wealth, a person who makes a god of his money.

Which is a serving of idols. There are other Greek readings of this clause, but that followed by the Vulgate is the most probable. Covetousness is a kind of real idolatry.

Hath inheritance, etc. Since the foregoing sinners serve illicit and perishable things in preference to the true God, they must perish with them, instead of sharing in the rewards of the elect of heaven.

6. The Apostle warns his readers not to be deceived and led into error by any "vain" (i.e., empty and false) words or talk, regarding the sins he has just condemned; for because of those very sins

7. Be ye not therefore partakers with them.

8. For you were heretofore darkness, but now light in the Lord. Walk then as children of the light.

9. For the fruit of the light is in all goodness, and justice, and truth;

10. Proving what is well pleasing to God:

the punishment of God "cometh," i.e., visits now and will continue to visit in the future those rebellious ones who disobey and disregard His teachings as contained in the Gospel. Cf. Col. iii. 6.

7. Be not. Literally, "Become not," sharers in their sins, else you will be sharers in their punishment.

8. The Apostle now gives other reasons to show why the faithful ought to avoid the sins mentioned above. Before their conversion they were "darkness," i.e., the very embodiment of moral ignorance and corruption; but now as Christians they embody "light," possessing the truth of Him and living in union with Him who said: "I am the light of the world, etc." (John viii. 12 ff.). Their lives, therefore, ought to be in conformity with the knowledge and grace they have received. This and the two following verses constitute a parenthesis in which the Apostle is again contrasting (as in ii. 11-22 and iv. 17-24) the new condition of his readers with their old condition.

9. **Fruit of the light.** The *Textus Receptus* and some other lesser MSS. have: "fruit of the Spirit," which is certainly not the best reading, as the context shows. It was doubtless introduced from Gal. v. 22.

Is in, etc., i.e., consists in, etc.

Goodness is the quality by which a person is good in himself and shows himself benevolent to others: it is opposed to anger (iv. 31).

Justice, as here used and in general, is the rectitude of moral acts, and in particular it is understood as the virtue which regulates our dealings with our neighbor; it is opposed to avarice (v. 3).

Truth is the supreme rule of life, governing our obligations to ourselves, our neighbor, and God; it is opposed to lying (iv. 25). This verse is a parenthesis within the parenthesis of ver. 8-10. Cf. Vosté, *hoc loco.*

10. **Proving,** etc., i.e., testing all things by the touchstone of God's will and good pleasure, and conforming in our actions to the results thus ascertained.

11. And have no fellowship with the unfruitful works of darkness, but rather reprove them.

12. For the things that are done by them in secret, it is a shame even to speak of.

13. But all things that are exposed are made manifest by the light; for all that is made manifest is light.

14. Wherefore he saith: *Rise thou that sleepest, and arise from the dead; and Christ shall enlighten thee.*

To God should be "to the Lord," according to the Greek. Thus, our Lord is here supposed to be God, because He is made the judge and norm of our actions: the judgment of the Lord is the judgment of God. The parenthesis closes with this verse, and the thought goes back to that of verse 7.

11. Here the Christians are warned not only to have no part in the sinful works of the pagans, but by their own good lives and example they are to register their disapproval of them. Perhaps their disapproval is to be expressed also in words, if necessary; but from the following verse it seems they are not even to speak of those works, if this can be avoided. The sinful practices of the pagans are said to be "unfruitful," as being devoid of all merit for eternal life and deserving of eternal damnation; they are the opposite of the fruits of the light (ver. 9).

12. The dark deeds here referred to are mentioned in Rom. xiii. 13. St. Paul is alluding to certain nocturnal feasts and mysteries which the pagans celebrated with an idolatry and an immorality that were unspeakable.

13. The Apostle is telling his readers that, whereas they were formerly moral darkness because of their sins, they are now moral light in the Lord (ver. 8), and that the spiritual radiance now emanating from their good lives and example is able to convert the moral darkness of the gross paganism around them into moral light like themselves. Nothing can resist the influence and light of a truly holy life; spiritual light makes manifest sin and works of darkness, and turns them from darkness to light; everything that is thus made manifest becomes light in its turn.

14. **Wherefore he saith.** Who saith? It is difficult to determine. Many moderns think the Apostle is here referring to some ancient hymn or baptismal formula of the early Church, which was well known to the faithful. Others think he is citing some apocry-

15. See therefore how you walk circumspectly, not as unwise,
16. But as wise: redeeming the time, because the days are evil.
17. Wherefore become not unwise, but understanding what is the will of the Lord.
18. And be not drunk with wine, wherein is luxury; but be ye filled with the Spirit,

phal work. With greater probability still others hold that we have here a free citation of Isa. lx. 1: "Arise, be enlightened, O Jerusalem: for thy light is come, etc." The application is clear: Let those who are asleep and dead in sin, arise, and they shall be enlightened by Christ, and thus enabled in their turn to shed their light on the pagan darkness around them.

15-17. The Apostle here tells his readers seriously to consider and watch what kind of life they lead in the midst of the pagans around them, that it may be, not the life of the unwise, but of the wise, as becomes those who are enlightened and instructed by divine grace and the light of the Gospel.

The *fratres* of the Vulgate is not represented in the Greek.

Circumspectly. Better, "accurately" or "carefully." Whether we connect this adverb with "see" or with "walk" makes little if any difference as to the meaning of the verse, which is clear.

Redeeming the time, i.e., letting no opportunity slip by them of doing and saying what they could to further the cause of God (Lightfoot). This they were to do because of the evils and temptations and of the evil days in which they lived. They should make "the will of the Lord" their standard and their guide in all things.

The *voluntas Dei* of the Vulgate should be *voluntas Domini* to agree with the Greek. Thus, the will of Christ is here made the supreme rule and norm of our actions, and consequently our Lord's divinity is presupposed.

18. Another great sin of paganism was drunkenness, and St. Paul often speaks of it in his letters (see Gal. v. 21; 1 Cor. v. 11, vi. 10; Rom. xiii. 13; 1 Tim. iii. 3). An admonition against this sin was opportune after the warning against impurity in the first part of the Chapter; for drunkenness is a fruitful source of immorality of all kinds. St. Jerome says: "In vino luxuria, in luxuria voluptas, in voluptate immunditia est." Of course, *per se*, it is the excess in the use of wine that is sin and that causes sin, but from use to abuse in such matters the way is broad and easy, and many enter thereat.

19. Speaking to yourselves in psalms, and hymns, and spiritual canticles, singing and making melody in your hearts to the Lord;
20. Giving thanks always for all things, in the name of our Lord Jesus Christ, to God and the Father,
21. Being subject one to another, in the fear of Christ.

Instead of being filled with wine, the Apostle counsels his readers to be filled with the Holy Ghost and His graces, from which there will result a pure delight that leads, not to grief and sorrow, but to enduring joy and happiness.

The *sancto* of the Vulgate, though supposed by the context, is not in the Greek. That the Holy Ghost is here meant, and not merely man's spiritual nature, is further made plain by referring to the other passages in this Epistle where this same phrase occurs (i. 22, iii. 5, vi. 18), and to the still more certain passages in other Epistles (1 Cor. xii. 3, 13; Rom. xv. 16). See also the parallel passage in Col. iii. 15-17.

19. If the Holy Spirit fills the souls of the faithful, it will be natural that the sacred exhilaration within them should burst forth "in psalms, and hymns, and spiritual canticles," i.e., in instrumental and vocal music, arising not only from their lips, but also from their "hearts to the Lord." This musical expression of fervor among the assembled early Christians is spoken of in Acts iv. 24, 31, xvi. 25, and was referred to by Pliny in his letter to the Emperor Trajan, written between 108 and 114 A.D., when he said: "They [the Christians] are accustomed to meet before dawn on a stated day, and to chant to Christ, as to a God, alternately together" (*Epist.* x. 97). Of course, St. Paul here seems to be speaking of social gatherings rather than of liturgical services.

20. According to his own custom, the Apostle now exhorts his readers ever to thank God "for all things," both good and bad, because all have been ordained or permitted for the eternal good of the elect by the God who created us and the Father who sent Christ to redeem us; and this they were to do "in the name of our Lord Jesus Christ," our Mediator, through whom all our blessings come.

21. In this verse the Apostle inculcates Christian submission. In grammatical form the verse goes with the preceding, but in substance it belongs to what follows, because with these words the Apostle turns to the discipline of the home, assigning as the motive of our submission, one to another, "the fear of Christ" (i.e., rever-

22. Let women be subject to their husbands, as to the Lord:
23. Because the husband is the head of the wife, as Christ is the head of the church. He *is* the saviour of the body.

ence for Christ), who is to be our future judge. At the end of verse 20 there should be only a comma in the Vulgate.

PRECEPTS FOR DOMESTIC LIFE; THE WIFE AND THE HUSBAND,
22-33

22-33. So far in this Chapter the Apostle has been giving general precepts regarding all Christians, but here he begins to treat of those that pertain to particular states, taking up the duties of wives and husbands in the remaining verses of this Chapter, and continuing in the first nine verses of the following Chapter with a consideration of the duties of children and parents and servants and masters respectively. It is worthy of note that in each class the Apostle starts with the weaker member and concludes his admonition with a precept or precepts for the stronger member, speaking first to wives and then to husbands, first to children and then to parents, first to servants and then to masters. In each particular case the spirit of Christ is to be the ruling principle; all precepts are to be obeyed in Christ and for Christ, who is the head of the mystical body of which Christians are the members. Thus, wives are to be subject to their husbands as to the Lord (v. 22), children are to obey their parents in the Lord (vi. 1), servants are to obey their temporal masters in the Lord (vi. 5). On the other hand, husbands should love their wives as Christ has loved the Church (v. 25, 28, 33), parents are to bring up their children in the discipline and correction of the Lord (vi. 4), masters must remember that there is the same Lord for all (vi. 9). See Vosté, *op. cit., hoc loco.* This section of our Epistle on domestic duties has a close parallel in Col. iii. 18—iv. 1.

It was a revolutionary doctrine that St. Paul taught in this section of the present letter, as also in the corresponding section of the Epistle to the Colossians. He was writing to a strange mixture of Greeks, Phrygians, Romans, Jews, and the like—all converts to Christianity, but subject to and influenced by Roman rule. Up to then women had been in a state of subordination and subjection little better than dire servitude. In the Roman family the father

24. Therefore as the church is subject to Christ, so also let the wives be to their husbands in all things.

was the head who ruled with absolute and often tyrannical authority over the wife, the children, and the slaves. His power was practically unlimited in the domestic circle, and he exercised it at times by punishing, torturing, and even putting to death his children and slaves, often for only trivial reasons; the wife fared but little better than her children. Nor did Christian teaching effect much change for the better in this severe discipline, generally speaking, until long after the time of St. Paul. Under Antonius Pius (138-161 A.D.) masters were made liable to accusation for the death of their slaves; the *potestas manus* of the husband over his wife finally ceased under Constantine and the other Christian emperors; and under Valentinian and Valens (about 364-375 A.D.) the chastisement of children was restricted. Therefore, in asking consideration for wives, children, and slaves, St. Paul had to proceed very cautiously, reminding them of their duties first, so as not to produce an unfavorable reaction to the teaching he wanted to give also to husbands, fathers, and masters. These latter had to be weaned away gradually from their pagan principles and customs, and imbued slowly with the new and lofty doctrines of Christianity, illustrated by the example of Christ. See Hitchcock, *op. cit., hoc loco,* 22-23.

Be subject. These words are not in the best Greek MSS., but they are to be supplied from the preceding verse to complete the sense. If St. Paul requires wives to be obedient to their husbands, he is not less insistent on the husband's duty to love and protect his wife (ver. 25, 28, 33), and on the perfect spiritual equality between wife and husband (Gal. iii. 28). The wife is to be obedient to the husband in Christ, and the husband's headship is to be one of love, modeled on the headship of Christ over the Church.

The saviour, etc. Christ is not only the head of the Church, but He is also its "saviour," i.e., literally its "deliverer," "preserver," by His passion and death. In like manner, therefore, the husband is bound to love, govern, protect and defend his wife.

The *eius* of the Vulgate in verse 23 is not expressed in the Greek, but is required by the sense. See 1 Cor. xi. 3.

24. **In all things.** The Apostle is speaking to Christians, and he is supposing the husband's relation to his wife to be like the rela-

25. Husbands, love your wives, as Christ also loved the church, and delivered himself up for it,

26. That he might sanctify it, cleansing it by the laver of water in the word,

27. That he might present it to himself a glorious church, not having spot or wrinkle, or any such thing; but that it should be holy, and without blemish.

tion of Christ to the Church; and consequently he is supposing the husband will not command or require of his wife anything that is not right and according to the law of God.

25. Verses 22-24 were addressed mainly to wives, but in verses 25-33 St. Paul speaks directly of the obligations of the husband. Having treated first, though briefly, of the obligations of the wife, he is now in a better position to dwell on the duties of husbands, and this at greater length, as it was more needed. To the wife he proposed the Church as a model, and now to husbands he will hold up Jesus Christ as a model and a pattern according to which they should regulate their treatment of and their dealings with their wives. Husbands are to love their wives as Christ has loved His Church, and they are to prove their love for their wives by sacrifice as Christ proved His love for the Church by delivering Himself up in sacrifice for it. The Church as a whole is here substituted for its members.

26-27. The Apostle will now give the effect and purpose of Christ's love and sacrifice for the Church, which were that He might cleanse and sanctify it by the washing of Baptism, that He might present it to Himself as a glorious spouse, and that it might live and continue holy and without blemish in His sight.

Sanctify . . . cleansing. Both these verbs are in the aorist in Greek, and hence do not signify distinct intervals of time; cleansing from sin and sanctifying are one and the same act and process, or rather the negative and positive aspects respectively of the same act.

The laver of water refers to the water of Baptism, "the laver of regeneration, etc." (Tit. iii. 5), the figure being taken from the bath of the bride before marriage among the Greeks.

In the word. Better, "accompanied by the word," i.e., accompanied by the verbal formula which gives specific meaning to the water. The water thus becomes the matter, and the word or utterance becomes the form of the Sacrament of Baptism. With less

28. So also ought men to love their wives as their own bodies. He that loveth his wife, loveth himself.

29. For no man ever hated his own flesh; but nourisheth and cherisheth it, as also Christ doth the church:

30. Because we are members of his body, of his flesh, and of his bones.

probability of correctness some interpret "word" here of the preaching of the Gospel, or of faith, or of the profession of faith. The *vitæ* of the Vulgate is not expressed in Greek.

That he might present, etc. Our Lord cleansed and purified the Church as a bride for Himself, and arrayed her in a glory which St. John exhausts symbolism to describe in Apoc. xix. 7 ff., xxi, xxii. This sanctification of the Church is going on here on earth, but its completion and perfection are reserved for the life to come.

28-29. The Apostle now applies to husband and wife what he has just said about Christ and the Church.

So, i.e., in the same manner; as Christ loved the Church in order "that He might present it to Himself holy and without blemish," so should the love of husbands for their wives have in view their sanctification; and as Christ loves the Church as His mystical body, so husbands should love their wives as being one flesh with them, as constituting one body with them, of which the husband is the head. The Apostle does not say: "Let husbands love their wives *as* they love their own bodies, but *because* wives are to husbands as their own bodies" (Vosté).

He that loveth his wife loveth himself, and the reason is that the wife is one with the body of the husband. From this it naturally follows that a man should love his wife as he loves himself, as another self; and since it would be unnatural for anyone under normal conditions to hate his own body and to be wanting in love and care for it, so would it be unnatural for a man not to love and care for his wife. Again the analogy of Christ enforces the argument.

No man ever hated, etc. The body is not to be hated or neglected, except when it gets in the way of a higher good.

30. Here the Apostle passes from the impersonal to the first person plural, showing that the Church of which he has been speaking means its members, the Christians themselves; and hence the reason why Christ so loves the Church is that we Christians constitute it, as members of His mystical body.

31. *For this cause shall a man leave his father and mother, and shall cleave to his wife, and they shall be two in one flesh.*

32. This is a great sacrament; but I speak in Christ and in the church.

Of his flesh, etc. These words are wanting in the best MSS., and are doubtless a gloss introduced from Gen. ii. 23.

31. This verse repeats Gen. ii. 24 according to the LXX, and shows the intimate union that exists between married persons, and how intimate consequently the love between them ought to be (cf. Matt. xix. 5, 6). The verse is a Scripture proof of what the Apostle has just said above in verses 28 and 29.

The *suam* of the Vulgate has no support in the Greek; and *in carne una* should be *in carnem unam,* as in the Greek, meaning "unto one flesh," i.e., as one flesh.

32. **This is a great sacrament.** Better, "This mystery is great," i.e., a secret of the divine plan beyond the reach of unaided natural powers. What is this mystery or divine secret? It is the mystical or spiritual signification implied in conjugal union as created by God, by which marriage became a type and figure of the union between Christ and His Church. The mere union of man and woman in marriage is no mystery; the mystery is in what that union, as created by God, signifies and typifies, and that is the union between Christ and His Church. Therefore the Apostle says, "but I speak, etc.," i.e., I speak with reference to Christ and His Church. Thus, the intimate union of Christ with the Church was prefigured by the union of man and woman in marriage; and hence in a *wide sense* matrimony, according to the intention of the Holy Ghost, has always been, from the very beginning of human kind, a sacrament, i.e., a *sign of a sacred thing.* But while from the union between Adam and Eve were born children of man according to nature and in sin, from the mystical union of Christ and His Church are born children of God in grace; the human race is regenerated in the Holy Ghost. There is not, then, question in this passage of a Sacrament of the New Law in the *strict sense* (so Vosté, *hoc loco*). The most we can say, therefore, is that the sacramental doctrine of marriage is implied in the Apostle's argument, though it is not explicitly taught; and this is what the Council of Trent (sess. XXIV) means by the word *innuit,* which it employed to express St. Paul's sacramental teaching in this passage.

33. Nevertheless let every one of you also in particular love his wife as himself: and let the wife reverence her husband.

33. Nevertheless. Better, "For the rest." In conclusion the Apostle summarily repeats the precepts given above, asking each married man to love his wife as his other self (ver. 28) and each wife to reverence her husband in Christ (ver. 21).

CHAPTER VI

1. Children, obey your parents in the Lord, for this is just.

1-9. In these verses the Apostle continues his instruction on Christian submission, begun at verse 21 of the last Chapter. Having spoken of the mutual duties of husbands and wives, he now goes on to consider those of children and parents (ver. 1-4), and of servants and masters (ver. 5-9). Children must obey their parents (ver. 1-3), and parents must lovingly instruct their children in the discipline of the Lord (ver. 4). Similarly, let servants be obedient to their masters as to Christ, remembering that they will receive a reward from God (ver. 5-8) ; and, on the other hand, let masters be kind to their servants, reflecting that they themselves are servants of Christ, and that there is in heaven one Lord of all who will judge all in justice and equity (ver. 9).

1. Obey your parents, etc. The Apostle is speaking to Christian children and parents, but of course his words have a wider application.

In the Lord. These words restrict the obedience of the children and the commands of the parents to things in harmony with the law of God, and they also indicate that the obedience of children should be prompted by a supernatural motive. From this we may infer the practice of infant baptism in the Apostolic Church, because the Apostle seems to take it as understood that the children of Christian parents were already baptized, therefore "in the Lord." The supreme example and model of such obedience was given by our Lord Himself (Luke ii. 51): "For this is just," i.e., dictated by nature and in conformity with the divine commands.

2. *Honor thy father and thy mother,* which is the first commandment with a promise:

3. *That it may be well with thee, and thou mayest be long-lived upon earth.*

4. And you, fathers, provoke not your children to anger; but bring them up in the discipline and correction of the Lord.

2. The first part of this verse and verse 3 are from Exod. xx. 12, and Deut. v. 16, verbatim according to the LXX.

Which is the first, etc., i.e., (a) the first in the Second Table of the Law, for the First Table contains the commandments that pertain to God, the Second those that pertain to men (Ambrosiaster) ; or (b) the first in dignity or the principal commandment, having a promise annexed, which is immediately given. This is the principal commandment for children, as comprehending the rest (Vosté). The clause, therefore, simply means: this is the principal commandment for you children, and it has a promise attached to it, as you can see from the words that follow.

3. These words of the Old Law refer directly to the promised land of Palestine, but indirectly to heaven, of which Palestine was a figure. It is to be observed regarding this promise that, since our earthly life is subordinated to the good of life eternal, even obedient children are sometimes taken away by premature death lest they should be contaminated by a wicked world (Wis. iv. 10-11), while bad children not infrequently enjoy length of days in order that they may turn from an evil life and be saved.

4. **And you, fathers,** etc. The "you" here and in ver. 9 (Vulgate, *vos*) is not expressed in the Greek. The father is mentioned as head of the family, but the mother's authority is included with that of the father because of the oneness of husband and wife, as explained above. The Apostle means to say that, while children should be obedient to parents, the latter ought to show themselves worthy of obedience, not by rigorous domination but by just and gentle persuasion. And this applies to all superiors, who should be guided in the control of others by justice and charity, instead of being blinded by authority, which they at times unjustly exercise, ignorant or forgetful of this full-meaning verse of St. Paul.

The discipline, etc., refers to moral formation in general according to the will of Christ, and not according to one's own ideas, regardless of the expressed divine will. Parents are stewards of Christ as regards their children, and therefore are seriously bound to exer-

5. Servants, be obedient to them that are your lords according to the flesh, with fear and trembling, in the simplicity of your heart, as to Christ:

6. Not serving to the eye, as it were pleasing men, but, as the servants of Christ doing the will of God from the heart,

7. With a good will serving, as to the Lord, and not to men.

8. Knowing that whatsoever good thing any man shall do, the same shall he receive from the Lord, whether he be bond, or free.

9. And you, masters, do the same things to them, forbearing threatenings, knowing that the Lord both of them and you is in heaven; and there is no respect of persons with him.

cise in this capacity a faithful stewardship by word and example. See Col. iii. 20-21 for a parallel passage.

5-8. In these verses St. Paul is admonishing "servants" (literally, "slaves") to render to their human masters a conscientious and respectful service which has its motive, not in personal or outward advantage, but in a sincere desire to please their spiritual Lord and Master, Christ, to whom their earthly lords are subordinated; and which further looks forward with the eyes of faith to the heavenly reward which Christ, the supreme Master and just Judge of us all, will render to each one, "whether he be bond, or free."

9. The Apostle now admonishes masters to be animated by the same supernatural motives toward their servants, seeing in them the person of Christ and being kind and merciful to them, mindful at all times that there is in heaven one Judge of all, slaves and masters, Jesus Christ, who cares nothing for the titles and positions of men, but will reward or punish according to the works each one has done while in the flesh: we are all slaves of Christ, our common divine Master, and all must appear before His judgment seat.

In this section, verses 5-9, it is worthy of note that St. Paul is not speaking of the rights of slaves and masters respectively, but of the obligations incumbent on each class of doing their respective duties, one to the other: it is duties, not rights, that the Apostle is emphasizing. For parallel passages see Col. iii. 22—iv. 1; 1 Cor. vii. 20-24.

THE SPIRITUAL COMBAT AND THE MEANS OF VICTORY, 10-20

10-20. After giving particular precepts for the home circle, St. Paul now passes to the outer world and admonishes all Christians to be ready for the warfare which must be waged against the enemies

10. Finally, brethren, be strengthened in the Lord, and in the might of his power.

11. Put you on the armor of God, that you may be able to stand against the deceits of the devil.

12. For our wrestling is not against flesh and blood; but against principalities and powers, against the rulers of the world of this darkness, against the spirits of wickedness in the high places.

13. Therefore take unto you the armor of God, that you may be able to resist in the evil day, and to stand in all things perfect.

of their salvation. He first exhorts his readers to prepare for the conflict (ver. 10-13); then describes the armor of the Christian warrior (ver. 14-17); and finally reminds them of the necessity of continual prayer and vigilance as the means of vanquishing Satan and his hosts, and asks in particular that they would pray unceasingly for himself and the spread of the Gospel (ver. 18-20).

10. **Finally.** Literally, "For the rest," i.e., as to what remains to be said regarding necessary precepts.

Brethren is wanting in the best MSS., and is probably not authentic, as it does not occur elsewhere as here used in this Epistle.

In the Lord, the one source of spiritual strength.

And in the might of his power, i.e., in His omnipotent power.

11. **The armor of God,** i.e., the spiritual panoply which God has provided for our spiritual warfare and by which the necessary strength is given us to win the combat against the secret attacks of the devil.

To stand, i.e., to resist his wiles and temptations.

The devil. See on ii. 2.

12. It is necessary that our armor be strong, for our struggle "is not against flesh and blood," i.e., against weak mortal men, "but against principalities, etc.," i.e., against the evil spirits of darkness; "against the rulers of the world, etc.," i.e., against the demons who are the leaders of the world of sin and moral darkness; "against the spirits of wickedness," i.e., evil spiritual beings and forces, "in the high places," i.e., in the place where these evil spirits dwell and where our battle with them is waged (see on i. 3, ii. 2). For other allusions to the Evil One and his mysterious authority over the world of men, see Luke iv. 6; John xiv. 30, xvi. 11; 2 Cor. iv. 4; 1 John v. 18.

13. **Therefore,** i.e., since our fight is so unequal, being against evil spiritual forces and powers, the Apostle urges that we take up

14. Stand therefore, having your loins girt about with truth, and having on the breastplate of justice,
15. And your feet shod with the preparation of the gospel of peace:
16. In all things taking the shield of faith, wherewith you may be able to extinguish all the fiery darts of the wicked one.
17. And take unto you the helmet of salvation, and the sword of the Spirit (which is the word of God).

"the armor of God," i.e., that we make use of grace and the spiritual resources at our disposal, so as to be "able to resist in the evil day," i.e., at the time and moment of temptation and hostile attack, with the result that when the struggle passes we may be able "to stand in all things perfect," i.e., firm and immovable in grace and virtue, ready for the next attack.

14. The Apostle now begins to describe the various parts of the Christian soldier's equipment, and his imagery is drawn partly from the dress of the Roman soldiers who in turn had charge of him in prison, and partly from two passages in Isaias where the Messiah is described as a warrior (Isa. xi. 4, lix. 17). He speaks first (ver. 14-17) of defensive and then of offensive arms, giving a spiritual meaning to each of the arms and each article of dress of the Roman soldier. The Christian soldier must "stand" (i.e., be ready for the conflict), having "truth" (i.e., sincerity and moral rectitude) for belt, and "justice" (i.e., loyalty in word and action to the law of God) as breastplate; for shoes he must have readiness and alacrity of soul to affirm "the gospel of peace"; "faith" must be his shield, and the inspired "word of God" his sword.

15. **Preparation.** The Greek for this word occurs here only in the New Testament, and it most probably means readiness and alacrity of soul to preach the Gospel. Spiritual *equipment* gives the meaning of the term as well as anything. St. Chrysostom says: "The preparation of the gospel is nothing else than the best life."

16. **In all things**, etc. A lesser reading has "above all things, etc.," which would mean that, besides all that has been just said, we should take the shield of faith, etc. But "in all things, etc." is the better reading; and it means that in all the circumstances of our life of warfare faith is our shield, the heavy armor of our souls, by which we can ward off "the fiery darts of the wicked one," i.e., of Satan.

17. "The helmet of salvation" means our salvation, the salvation offered us by Christ (Cajetan), or the hope of salvation (1

18. By all prayer and supplication, praying at all times in the spirit, and in the same watching with all instance and supplication for all the saints:

19. And for me, that speech may be given me, that I may open my mouth with confidence, to make known the mystery of the gospel.

20. For which I am an ambassador in a chain, so that therein I may be bold to speak according as I ought.

21. But that you also may know the things that concern me, *and* what I

Thess. v. 8). The helmet protects the head, and the salvation offered us by our Lord is the pledge of our eternal inheritance. The "sword of the Spirit" is "the word of God," i.e., the utterance of God; the two phrases are in apposition here, and they explain each other: "The word of God is living and effectual, and more piercing than any two-edged sword" (Heb. iv. 12).

18. Here the Apostle admonishes that we must pray at all times, in all places, and for all persons, as a means of making really effectual the foregoing helps in the battle for salvation. All our help comes from God, and prayer opens the door to God's treasure-house of graces.

Prayer and supplication are perhaps used together here for the sake of emphasis, though the former word can be distinguished from the latter as meaning a general offering of our thoughts and desires, while the latter has reference to our special petitions.

The Spirit. Literally, "in spirit," i.e., in the fervor of our souls as animated and inspired by the Spirit of God.

For all the saints, as all are members of the same mystical body whose head is Christ.

19-20. The Apostle now asks a part in the prayers of his readers that he may be able courageously and efficaciously to preach "the mystery of the gospel," i.e., the perfect equality of Jews and Gentiles in the Messianic kingdom, the universality of the salvation of Christ. It was for preaching this equal salvation for all men in Christ that the Apostle was cast into prison; and this made him, though a prisoner, the representative of Christ the King in the imperial city, "an ambassador in a chain," i.e., coupled by a chain around his right wrist to the left of a Roman soldier in his hired lodging in Rome.

THE MISSION OF TYCHICUS, 21-22

21-22. These verses occur almost verbatim in Col. iv. 7-8.

You also. This phrase is understood to imply that Tychicus had visited others before delivering this letter to its readers, namely, the

am doing, Tychicus, my dearest brother and faithful minister in the Lord, will make known to you all things:

22. Whom I have sent to you for this same purpose, that you may know the things concerning us, and that he may comfort your hearts.

23. Peace be to the brethren and charity with faith, from God the Father, and the Lord Jesus Christ.

24. Grace be with all them that love our Lord Jesus Christ in incorruption. Amen.

Colossians, and consequently it is concluded that the letter to the Colossians was written before this one.

Tychicus was a native of Asia Minor, perhaps of Ephesus (Acts xx. 4; 2 Tim. iv. 12). His name is found in inscriptions of Asia Minor and Rome, on coins of Magnesia, thirteen miles from Ephesus, and of Magnesia by Mt. Sipylus, where the Bishop of Ephesus now resides, thirty-eight miles from his titular see (see Hitchcock, *Ephesians*, p. 506; Lightfoot, *Colossians*, p. 234).

Whom I have sent, an epistolary aorist.

Concerning us, i.e., Paul and his companions in Rome.

That he may comfort your hearts, distressed by my imprisonment, and perhaps impending death.

BLESSING, 23–24

23-24. Contrary to his custom St. Paul gives his benediction to third persons, "brethren," instead of second persons, "you."

With faith goes back to "charity," by which it is informed, and to "peace," which is its fruit, as a gift from the Holy Ghost. The single preposition before "God the Father and the Lord Jesus Christ" shows that both constitute the common source of supernatural peace and charity.

With all them that love is a circumlocution for "saints," and it occurs only here.

In incorruption. Literally, "in incorruptness," i.e., with an enduring, immortal love; the expression refers back to "love." The weight of evidence seems to be against the retention of "Amen" here, though it makes a fitting close to so glorious an Epistle.

THE
EPISTLE TO THE PHILIPPIANS

INTRODUCTION

I. Philippi. Philippi was a city in Eastern Macedonia on the borders of Thrace, some eight or nine miles inland and to the north-west from ancient Neapolis, its seaport on the Ægean Sea. Its original name was Crenides, or Little Fountains, so called from the springs which fed a great marsh to the south of the town. About the middle or latter part of the fourth century B.C. it was taken, enlarged, and fortified by Philip of Macedon, the father of Alexander the Great; and from him it received its later name.

Philippi was situated on a hill dominating a large and fertile plain which stretched to the north and northwest of the city, and it was cut off from the sea by a line of hills on its east and south-east. It was, however, easily accessible from Neapolis through the Via Egnatia, the great Roman highway, which ran through a depression in the hills from Neapolis to Philippi and connected the Ægean on the east with the Adriatic on the west.

In the neighborhood of Philippi were rich gold and silver mines which offered the chief attraction to Philip of Macedon in his re-founding of the city, and from which he drew the vast wealth needed for his victorious military career. The city and the rest of the dominions of Perseus, King of Macedonia, fell into the hands of the Romans in 168 B.C., and in 42 B.C., on the plain of Philippi, Mark Antony and Octavian (afterwards Augustus) in a decisive battle defeated Brutus and Cassius, the assassins of Julius Cæsar, thus bringing to an end the party that had hoped by the death of Cæsar to restore the old Roman republic. In commemoration of this victory the Emperor Augustus made Philippi a Roman military colony, calling it after himself *Colonia Julia Augusta Victrix Philippensium,* and conferring upon it the *jus Italicum,* which gave its colonists the right of constitutional government, independent of the provincial governor, the right of proprietorship according to Roman law, and exemption from poll and land taxes. As a Roman colony Philippi had its own duumviri, or two supreme magistrates, the στρατηγοί of Acts xvi. 20, 22, 35-38. Thus, the city became a center of Roman influence, and with its public baths and theatres, its worship of Diana, Sylvanus and Dionysus, its cosmopolitan character (combining as it did the life of Asia and the life of Europe), it was like another Rome in miniature. St. Luke (Acts xvi. 12) called it the chief city of the district, but its rank was seriously disputed by Amphipolis, about thirty miles to the southwest, with the precedence inclining to the latter city. The inhabitants of Philippi in St. Paul's time were mostly Latin in origin, with a strong minority of Macedonian stock and a sprinkling of other nationalities attracted by the military and commercial importance of the place. There were Jews also, but so few in number that they had not even one synagogue. The town was destroyed by the Turks in later centuries, and nothing remains of it now but some ruins.

II. **The Church of Philippi.** St. Paul came to Philippi from Troas during the first part of his second missionary journey, around 51 A.D. (cf. Acts xvi. 11 ff.). His companions were Silas from Antioch (Acts xv. 40), Timothy from Lystra (Acts xvi. 1), and very likely Luke from Troas—as we gather from Acts xvi. 10, where the first person plural begins to appear in the narrative. The Apostle was accustomed to begin his preaching in the houses of Jewish worship, but Philippi seems to have had no synagogue, so few and unimportant were the Jews there. On the Sabbath day a little company of worshippers gathered for prayer beyond the city gates on the bank of the River Gangites, and when St. Paul appeared to address them he found that only a few devout women made up the assembly. Of these the first to respond to his preaching was a Gentile lady by the name of Lydia, a seller of purple from Thyatira in Asia, who was living in Philippi for commercial purposes. She was soon followed by the whole family of which she was the mistress, and her house became the home of St. Paul and the centre of the Christian community of the town (Acts xvi. 13-15). Among the other women attracted by the new preaching was a slave girl, who, for the profit of her masters, discharged the functions of an oracle, giving answers to questions under a kind of inspiration or faculty of divining. As she annoyed Paul by acclaiming him as he daily passed by to the place of prayer, the Apostle finally turned and exorcised her; and the spirit of divination left her, and she became a devout Christian. But the girl's masters, stirred by their pecuniary loss, brought Paul and Silas before the magistrates of the city, and had them scourged and cast into prison. The innocence of the two prisoners, however, was vindicated the first night by an earthquake which nearly destroyed the prison and was the occasion of converting the Roman jailer and his whole family. The magistrates also learning that Paul and Silas were Roman citizens, whom it was unlawful to scourge, sent their lictors to the prison to release the prisoners. At St. Paul's demand they acknowledged their error, but besought him and his companions to leave the town. This they consented to do after a meeting of the brethren in the house of Lydia (Acts xvi. 16-40), while leaving Luke behind to look after the newly founded but flourishing Church of Philippi.

It is worthy of note that the Philippian Church was composed mostly of Gentile converts, and that the earliest of these were women. The female element seems to have continued strong there, as we may gather from Phil. iv. 2, 3; and this may account for the absence of doctrinal disputes in the Church, and especially for the great kindness the Philippians always manifested toward St. Paul. They were poor themselves, but at Paul's request they collected money for the poor saints in Jerusalem (2 Cor. viii. 3), they sent gifts to Paul when he was in Thessalonica and in Corinth (2 Cor. viii. 9; Phil. iv. 15, 16), and again when he was a prisoner in Rome (Phil. iv. 18).

St. Paul's next visits to Philippi were some years later, while on his third missionary journey. The first was doubtless when passing through Macedonia on his way from Ephesus to Corinth, perhaps in the early summer of 57 A.D. (1 Cor. xvi. 8; Acts xix. 23 ff., xx. 1 ff.), though we are not told explicitly of this visit. It is very probable that it was at Philippi that St. Paul waited in anxiety for the arrival of Titus from Corinth, and there wrote 2 Cor. after the arrival of Titus (2 Cor. ii. 12, 13, vii. 5, 6, viii. 1, ix. 2, 4). The third visit occurred the next spring when St. Paul, returning from Corinth through Macedonia, arrived at Philippi in time for the Passover, there joined Luke again (as we conclude from the resumption of the "we passages" in Acts), and then continued his journey to Jerusalem (Acts xx. 5 ff.). This is the last recorded visit of the Apostle to the Philippian Church, but we may pretty safely assume from the Pastoral Epistles that he paid a subsequent visit there during his eastern travels, after being released from his first Roman captivity, when journeying from Ephesus to Macedonia (1 Tim. i. 3). In fact, 2 Tim. iv. 13 seems to point to another and still later visit to Philippi.

The next time we hear of the Church of Philippi is in the first part of the second century, when St. Ignatius, Bishop of Antioch, having been condemned to death as a Christian, passed that way on his journey to Rome, where he was to be thrown to the wild beasts. We know from his Epistles that his route lay through Philadelphia, Smyrna, and Troas. From the last town, like St. Paul, he must have passed over to Neapolis, and thence by the Via Egnatia to Philippi. On his departure the Philippians wrote a letter to the faithful of Antioch, consoling them for the loss of their Bishop, and another letter to his friend Polycarp of Smyrna, asking him for as many of Ignatius' letters written in Asia Minor as could be spared. Our knowledge of these events is derived from St. Polycarp's reply to the Philippians, which is still extant. The subsequent history of the Church of Philippi is unimportant, especially for our purpose here.

III. **Occasion, Purpose, and Character of This Letter.** As said above, the Philippians possessed and always retained a particular affection for and interest in St. Paul, due perhaps to the influence from the beginning of devout women in the Church there. Although not at all well-to-do themselves, they sent the Apostle money on different occasions, as we have seen, and when they learned of his imprisonment in Rome they sent Epaphroditus to him with gifts and instructions to minister to his needs (Phil. ii. 25-29, iv. 18), and to report on the condition of the Church at Philippi. Paul was naturally very much delighted at the arrival of the beloved envoy and the practical testimony he conveyed of continued devotion and love on the part of the Philippians for their Apostle and founder —affection which had already been shown repeatedly by the same community. The report given of the Church at Philippi seems also to have been pleasing and generally satisfactory.

Not long after his arrival in Rome Epaphroditus fell seriously ill, much to the distress of St. Paul as well as the Philippians, but fortunately recovered in due time. As soon as he was well again, the Apostle hastened to send him back to his home (Phil. ii. 26-30), giving him at the same time this letter to the faithful and heads of the Church at Philippi. The letter is an intimate expression of joy and gratitude for the help given the Apostle by the Philippians and for the loving sentiments that prompted it. But intermingled with these familiar outpourings of the heart are a number of moral reflections and exhortations, based on the example of Christ and in conformity with the teachings of the Gospel, particularly with regard to charity and concord among all the faithful (Phil. i. 9-11, 26 ff., ii. 1-8, 13, 14, 16). St. Paul seemed especially disturbed over the misunderstandings between Evodia and Syntyche, two prominent women in the Church (Phil. iv. 2 ff.), and this is a distinct indication of the influence of the female element among the faithful at Philippi. He warns also against the evil influence, actual or possible, of Judaizers, and of those whose life is a scandal, and who make a god of their belly (Phil. iii. 2-4, 18, 19). There is still another passage in this Epistle which seems to point to some keen disappointment at the lack of zeal and self-sacrifice manifested by some of the Apostle's co-workers; Timothy appears to be the only one that comes up to the high standard of his requirements (Phil. ii. 19-23).

Since the letter is so very personal and familiar, these observations and counsels do not follow any particular order, but are set down just as they occur to the Apostle as he writes. This Epistle is one of the most intimate of St. Paul's writings. Here he addresses his tried and trusted friends, and we get an idea of the overflowing affection which was natural to him and one of the secrets of his genius for friendship. He is deeply grateful for the gifts and the love of the Philippians, but his acknowledgment is restrained by his sense of duty as their Apostle and counsellor (Phil. iv. 10-20).

IV. **Date and Place of Writing.** This aspect of the present Epistle has been sufficiently discussed under the similar heading in the *Introduction* to Ephesians. It is enough to say here that the weight of argument and of authority shows that this letter was written from Rome during Paul's first captivity there (61-63 A.D.), either before or after the writing of the other Captivity Epistles— Ephesians, Colossians and Philemon. Whether this letter preceded or followed those other Captivity Epistles is earnestly disputed, but without any convincing conclusion one way or the other. For a summary of the arguments on both sides see Moule, *Introd. to Philippians,* pp. 15 ff.

V. **Authenticity and Integrity.** All antiquity is unanimous in accepting the authenticity and integrity of this Epistle. Apart from quotations from it or references to it in the writings of Clement of Rome, Ignatius of Antioch, *The Shepherd of Hermas,* etc. (cf. Cornely, *Introduction,* vol. IV, p. 491; Toussaint, *Philippiens* in *Dict. de la Bible*), we have St. Polycarp early in the second century writing to the Philippians and speaking explicitly of the letter or letters (ἐπιστολαι) St. Paul had sent them, some passages of which Polycarp quotes in his own letter. Marcion included it in his Canon, and the Muratorian Fragment, Irenæus, Clement of Alexandria, and Tertullian expressly attribute it to St. Paul. After Tertullian the testimonies are still more numerous and incontestable. As regards modern scholars, the great majority concede without hesitation that the Epistle as we have it is the work of St. Paul. In fact, its authenticity and integrity were never questioned until the nineteenth century when Baur, followed by others of the German rationalistic school, denied that Philippians was the work of Paul. The arguments, however, on which these critics have essayed to ground their claims are of so little value now as to be rejected by all the best rationalistic and Protestant scholars (cf. Jacquier, *Histoire,* etc., tom. I, pp. 349 ff.; Vigouroux, *Dict. de la Bible, Philippiens*).

The language and style of the Epistle are also thoroughly Pauline. Although there occur in it some forty strange expressions not found elsewhere in St. Paul, that proves nothing, since the same phenomenon is true of the admittedly authentic letters of the great Apostle; and over against this we can cite the presence of many words, expressions, figures, and characteristics of writing which are acknowledged to be peculiar to St. Paul.

Nor can any difficulty be found in the doctrine of this Epistle. The theology is again Pauline throughout, as even so rationalistic a writer as Holsten readily concedes. Attempts to find differences between the Christology of this Epistle and that of 1 Corinthians and other Epistles, or between the doctrine of justification taught here and that of Romans, have proved groundless and futile.

Some authors have felt there is a break in the unity of the Epistle at iii. 2, which extends to iv. 1, where Jews or Judaizing Christians suddenly fall under the Apostle's severe censure. It is suggested that this may be a fragment from some other letter of St. Paul's, perhaps to the Romans, which somehow found its way into this Epistle. But, in the first place, it is very hard to see how a part of one letter could get into the middle of the roll of another letter (for these letters were copied on rolls of parchment); and, in the second place, to deny the integrity of one of Paul's Epistles because of some sudden interruptions in the style or breaks in the continuity of the thought is to betray essential ignorance of the Apostle's character and literary habits. Again, repetitions, like the double conclusion in iii. 1 and iv. 4, instead of being difficulties against the oneness of the document are only natural in a letter so familiar and personal as is this one. It is little wonder, therefore, that small success has attended the efforts made against the unity and integrity of the Epistle to the Philippians; and we may well conclude this section of our *Introduction* to this letter with the following testimony concerning it of the Protestant scholar, McGiffert: "The Epistle deserves to rank alongside of Galatians, Corinthians, and Romans as an undoubted product of Paul's pen, and as a coordinate standard by which to test the genuineness of other and less certain writings" (*The Apostolic Age*, p. 393).

VI. **Analysis of Contents.** We have observed above that this Epistle does not follow any very orderly plan, owing to its essentially personal and intimate character. Dogma is not absent from the letter, though it is not prominent, and when it does occur it is intermixed with the moral exhortations, counsels and effusions which constitute the bulk of the Epistle. We may, however, distinguish in Philippians three main divisions: (a) an introductory part (i. 1-11); (b) a body (i. 12—iv. 9); (c) a conclusion (iv. 10-23).

A. INTRODUCTION (i. 1-11). Paul first addresses himself to the faithful, bishops and deacons of Philippi, wishing them the grace and peace which are from God the Father and from the Lord Jesus Christ (i. 1, 2). He then gives thanks to God for the many benefits bestowed on the Philippians, who by their alms have had part in the work of the Gospel and in the merits of his imprisonment (i. 3-8). Finally, he prays for their continual progress in sanctity and Christian perfection (i. 9-11).

B. THE BODY OF THE LETTER (i. 12—iv. 9). The Apostle gives his readers an account of his condition and that of the Church in Rome: his bonds are a means for the spread of the Gospel. Some indeed are preaching it out of envy and contention, others out of charity; but it makes no difference to Paul so long as Christ be preached (i. 12-18). As for himself, he knows not whether to prefer life to work for the good of souls, or death which will unite him to Christ (i. 19-26).

As regards the faithful, he exhorts them to live lives worthy of the Gospel he has preached to them, and in conformity with the example he has given them (i. 27-30). He urges them especially to unity and charity based on humility and self-denial (ii. 1-4), first, in imitation of Christ who emptied Himself, assuming the condition of a slave for our sakes and thereby meriting supreme exaltation (ii. 5-11) ; and secondly, for the sake of their advancement in sanctity and the glory they will thus give to him who labored for them and is willing to die for their sakes (ii. 12-18).

St. Paul next tells the Philippians that as soon as his situation will permit he will send Timothy to them, who is so reliable and so devoted to them (ii. 19-24). Meanwhile he is returning Epaphroditus, their trusted legate to him, whose recent illness, occasioned by his work for Christ, has been a source of much anxiety both to him and to them (ii. 25-30).

The Apostle, it seems, was about to close his letter—"as to the rest, etc." (iii. 1)—when suddenly, perhaps because of news just brought him or because he has just recalled an important point, he interrupts his thought and warns his readers against Judaizers, citing again his own example. He has all the reasons for glorying that these have, and more ; but he has despised all these things for the sake of that justice and perfection which are secured, not by the works of the Law, but by faith in Christ (iii. 2-11). Not that he has attained this perfection, but that he is ever pressing on towards it (iii. 12-14). Let the Philippians imitate him, looking to the glory that is to come, and fly those who seek the goods of this world (iii. 15-21). He closes the body of his letter with a series of short exhortations to steadfastness and concord, and recommends joy, peace and prayer, briefly recapitulating the duties of a Christian life (iv. 1-9).

C. CONCLUSION (iv. 10-23). The Apostle terminates his Epistle with renewed thanks for the gifts sent him, while stressing his detachment from all earthly conditions and things and his total resignation to God's will (iv. 10-19), with a doxology (iv. 20), and with salutations and a blessing (iv. 21-23).

BIBLIOGRAPHY

Among the Greek Fathers three commentators on this Epistle are of premier importance: St. Chrysostom, Theodore of Mopsuestia, and Victorinus (see Migne, *P. G.*). St. Thomas ranks next among the Latins, as combining with his own acute genius the best of Patristic lore. See Bibliography for Ephesians.

Since the Council of Trent the best commentators on this Epistle down to modern times were Cornelius a Lapide and Maldonatus. In recent times, besides those commentators on all the Pauline letters and on the Captivity Epistles in particular already recommended in the Bibliography for Ephesians, the following among Catholics are deserving of special attention: Beelen, *Comm. in Epist. S. Pauli ad Philipp.* (Louvain, 1852); Cornely, *Introd. specialis in singulos N.T. libros* (Paris, 1897); Müller, *Der Ap. Paulus Brief an die Philipper* (Freiburg, 1899); Sales, in *La Sacra Bibbia,* vol. II (Turin, 1914); Jones, *The Epistle to the Philippians,* in *The Westminster Series* (London, 1918).

Non-Catholic Commentators: Ellicott, *A Critical and Grammatical Comm. on St. Paul's Epistle to the Philippians* (London, 1888); Moule, *The Epistle to the Philippians,* in *The Cambridge Bible for Schools and Colleges* (Cambridge, 1895); Vincent, *Philippians and Philemon,* in *The International Crit. Comm.* (1897); Lightfoot, *St. Paul's Epistle to the Philippians* (16th ed., London, 1908); Du Buisson, in *A New Comm. on Holy Script.* (New York, 1928); Robertson, in *The Abingdon Bible Comm.* (New York, 1929).

The Epistle to the Philippians

CHAPTER I

1. Paul and Timothy, the servants of Jesus Christ; to all the saints in Christ Jesus, who are at Philippi, with the bishops and deacons.

1, 2. St. Paul together with Timothy, his trusted companion and probably his amanuensis at this time, addresses in artless and affectionate terms the beloved faithful of Philippi and their spiritual leaders, wishing them, in combined Greek and Hebrew forms, grace and peace from God the Father and from Christ Jesus, their Saviour.

1. **Paul**, the author of this letter. He omits the title "apostle" here because there is no reason to require insistence on his divine authority and mission. See on Rom. i. 1.

Timothy, who was with Paul at this time and perhaps wrote down the present Epistle, and who had helped the Apostle in founding the Church at Philippi (Acts xvi. 1 ff). For further particulars about Timothy, see *Introduction* to 1 Timothy in this volume.

Servants. Literally, "slaves," but in a redeemed and figurative sense of that degrading word.

Jesus Christ. There is more evidence for the reverse order of these terms, "Christ Jesus." This title of our Lord is peculiarly Pauline, occurring in the two orders about 165 times in his Epistles.

All the saints, i.e., all those who by their religious profession have separated themselves from the world and consecrated themselves to God. The Apostle says "all," showing no distinction, and no cause of distinction, such as factions or sects.

Philippi. See *Introduction*, No. I.

With the bishops, etc. This is the only time St. Paul mentions the clergy in the inscription of a letter. In early times the title "bishop" was given to the heads of the various local churches,

2. Grace be unto you, and peace from God our Father and from the Lord Jesus Christ.

3. I give thanks to my God in every remembrance of you,

4. Always in all my prayers, making supplication for you all, with joy,

5. For your communication in the gospel of Christ from the first day unto now,

whether they were bishops in the strict sense of the word or only priests; the term here being in the plural doubtless means priests or presbyters. See Acts xxi. 17, 28; Tit. i. 5-7; 1 Tim. iii. 1-13, v. 17, where the terms "bishops" and "presbyters" are interchanged. St. Paul names the bishops and deacons most likely because they took the principal part in sending gifts and helps to him.

2. **Grace . . . peace.** See on Eph. i. 2.

God our Father, etc. The Father is the ultimate source of all blessings, and Christ, His co-equal Son, is the medium and channel. See also on Eph. i. 2.

THANKSGIVING AND PRAYER FOR THE PHILIPPIANS, 3-11

3-11. Here the Apostle begins to speak in the first person singular, showing that the letter is his own, and not a joint work between him and Timothy. He thanks God for the part the Philippians have had in the work of the Gospel and in the merits of his sufferings (ver. 3-8), and he prays that they may continually progress in spiritual knowledge and in the grace of Him to whom they owe their spiritual life, so as to be perfect when the heavenly Bridegroom comes to call them to their eternal rewards (ver. 9-11).

3-4. The Apostle assures his readers that in all his remembrance of them he thanks God, who is the source of all their spiritual blessings, and that in all his petitions it is a cause of joy to him to make requests for them.

In all my prayers. Better, "In every request of mine."

5. He assigns the reason for his supplication with joy in their behalf, namely, their "communication in the gospel, etc.," i.e., their co-operation with him in the work of spreading the Gospel from the first day they heard it preached up to the time this letter was written. The reference is to the devotedness, labors, sufferings, gifts, etc., by which they had participated with the Apostle in the propagation and furtherance of the Gospel.

6. Being confident of this very thing, that he, who hath begun a good work in you, will perfect it unto the day of Christ Jesus.

7. Indeed it is right for me to be so minded in regard of you all, for that I have you in my heart; that in my bonds, and in the defence and confirmation of the gospel, you all are partakers of my grace.

8. For God is my witness, how I long after you all in the heart of Christ Jesus.

6. The Apostle now tells the Philippians that he feels certain that God the Father who began in them the work of their redemption and sanctification will complete the process, bringing it to perfection against the day of their deliverance from the present life. Thus, he teaches the necessity of grace, not only to begin a good work in the supernatural order, but also to continue it and to persevere in it until death (cf. *Conc. Trid.*, sess. VI, cap. 13).

A good work, i.e., their conversion to Christianity, which was followed by their labor and zeal in behalf of the Gospel and St. Paul.

The day of Christ Jesus is a frequent expression with St. Paul, and refers to our Lord's coming in judgment, whether at the death of the individual or at the end of time to judge the world. The similar expression of the Old Testament, "the day of the Lord," meant the day of God's visitation of the earth in judgment and redemption.

7. He gives the reason for the confidence expressed in the preceding verse. It is perfectly right and natural that he should feel thus toward the Philippians, because of his intimate and tender love for them, and because, through the help they have given him, they are sharers in the "grace" of his apostolate, whether exercised in "bonds," i.e., in prison, or in "defence" of himself and of his preaching against the accusations and calumnies of the Jews, or "in confirmation of the gospel," i.e., in explaining and proving the truth of the Gospel before Jews and Gentiles (Acts xxviii. 23 ff.). "For that I have you in my heart" may also be rendered "for that you have me in your heart," i.e., he is mindful of them because they also remember him.

The *gaudii mei* of the Vulgate should be *gratiæ meæ*, to agree with the Greek.

8. As a proof of his ardent love for the faithful of Philippi St. Paul now invokes God, who reads the heart, as his witness; he loves

9. And this I pray, that your charity may more and more abound in knowledge and in all discernment,

10. That you may approve the better things, that you may be sincere and
without offence unto the day of Christ,

11. Filled with the fruit of justice, through Jesus Christ, unto the glory
and praise of God.

them all with the love wherewith Christ loves them; his heart is
one with the heart of his Master.

In visceribus of the Vulgate means with the most ardent love,
the Greek of which is properly rendered in English by "heart," as it
refers to the seat of tender and noble affections. The Greek also
reverses the order of *Jesu Christi* of the Vulgate here.

9. In verse 4 the Apostle told his readers that he prayed for them
all with joy. Now he tells them what he requested for them, namely,
that their "charity" (i.e., their love of God and their neighbor)
might continually increase and become ever more perfect "in knowledge," i.e., in full, developed understanding (ἐπίγνωσις) of Christian
virtues, and "in all discernment," i.e., practical judgment (αἴσθησις)
as to the application of those virtues in dealing with their neighbor.

10. This full knowledge and judgment St. Paul requests for the
Philippians in order that they may be able to appraise things according to their true worth; that, distinguishing between the moral
values of their actions, they "may approve, etc.," i.e., that they may
test and choose those which are more excellent, with the result that
they "may be sincere" (i.e., pure and innocent in the sight of God)
"and without offence" (i.e., that their conduct may be no obstacle
or stumbling block to their neighbor).

In the day of Christ, i.e., when the Lord comes to judge and
reward them according to their works. See on verse 6 above.

11. The Apostle wishes the faithful not only to be innocent and
blameless, but also to be "filled with the fruit of justice," i.e., with
good works, which can be done only through the grace of Christ.
"Justice" here is better rendered "justness" or "righteousness,"
which implies a complete harmony between the soul and God; it is
given through Christ. "Only so far as the life of the believer is
absorbed in the life of Christ, does the righteousness of Christ
become his own" (Lightfoot). Hence our Lord said: "I am the
true vine, etc." (John xv. 1 ff.).

Unto the glory, etc. The glory and praise of God is the last end and true goal of all our charity, justice, good works, etc., as the Apostle here reminds us.

THE BODY OF THE EPISTLE, i. 12–iv. 9

i. 12—iv. 9. The Apostle explains his personal situation and the progress of the Gospel in the Eternal City, in spite of rivalry and opposition (i. 12-26); and then, as if in response to news received, he goes on to exhort his readers to be true to their calling in doing and suffering for the sake of the Gospel, stressing the need of unity and humility (i. 27—ii. 4). In the practice of humility and in bearing their sufferings they have the supreme example of Christ Himself, who thus merited His exaltation to supreme Lordship (ii. 5-11). It is therefore Christ that they should copy; and in so doing they will reflect glory on their Apostle who has not labored in vain and who is willing to die in their behalf (ii. 12-18). He is sending to them at once Epaphroditus, Timothy will follow soon, and shortly he hopes to come himself (ii. 19-30). Beginning his final injunctions (iii. 1), he digresses to warn against Judaizers, citing his own career (iii. 2-16), and against pagan self-indulgence and a spirit of worldliness among Christians (iii. 17-21). Some final exhortations close the body of the letter (iv. 1-9). See *Introduction*, No. VI, B.

THE APOSTLE'S IMPRISONMENT HAS BEEN USEFUL FOR THE SPREAD OF THE GOSPEL IN ROME, i. 12-26

12-26. It seems the Philippians had made known to Paul their anxiety regarding the welfare of the Gospel, as a result of his imprisonment; they feared the Gospel was suffering while he was enchained. But the Apostle informs them here that the contrary is the case, inasmuch as the success of his preaching in prison has excited the jealousy of other preachers and thus stimulated them to greater efforts. This is a cause of great rejoicing on his part. As for his own prospects of release, he is confident that all will turn out for the best. Personally he is torn between the alternatives of dying and being with Christ, on the one hand, and living for the sake of the Philippians, on the other hand. He seems to be confident of the latter; he will again be with them to assist them and give them joy in Christ Jesus.

12. Now, brethren, I desire you should know that the things which have happened to me have fallen out rather to the furtherance of the gospel:

13. So that my bonds are made manifest in Christ, in all the court, and in all other places:

14. And many of the brethren in the Lord, *growing* confident by my bonds, are much more bold to speak the word without fear.

12. St. Paul wishes the brethren of Philippi to know that his imprisonment, with all its circumstances and consequences, instead of being a damage to the spread of the Gospel and a knowledge of its teachings, has had rather the opposite effect; it has made the Gospel better known, as he will now explain.

13. In the first place, the Apostle's imprisonment has become known in its true significance, as the result of preaching Christ as the promised Messiah and the Saviour of the whole world; he is a prisoner not on account of any crime that he has committed, not out of politics in which he has been implicated, but on account of his identification with the cause of Christ. And this real cause of his imprisonment has become known "in all the court" (better, "throughout the whole prætorian guard"), through the many soldiers who successively relieved one another in guarding the Apostle and to each of whom he and his cause became well known and advertised "in all other places" (better, "to every one else besides," i.e., to the whole imperial city, generally speaking).

We have taken "in Christ" to mean in the cause of Christ, for the sake of Christ; but it can also mean "through Christ," i.e., by the counsel and provision of Christ. Taken in this latter sense, the meaning would be that it was by Christ's divine intervention, though all unseen, that the real cause of St. Paul's imprisonment became widely known, and through this a knowledge of the Gospel spread abroad. Other explanations of "in all the court" are less likely.

14. Another salutary effect of the Apostle's chains was the infusion of fresh energy into "many" (better, "the majority") of the Christians in Rome who, having become timid and remiss in their preaching and work for the Evangel, now beholding the zeal and intrepitude of their fettered Apostle were exhibiting more energy and fearlessness than ever before in behalf of the Gospel's saving truths.

Brethren in the Lord means Christians, as distinguished from Paul's brethren in the flesh, the Jews.

15. Some indeed, even out of envy and contention; but some also for good will preach Christ.

16. Some out of charity, knowing that I am set for the defence of the gospel;

17. And some out of contention preach Christ not sincerely, supposing that they raise affliction to my bonds.

There is sufficient MSS. evidence for omitting *Dei* of the Vulgate, as a gloss explanatory of *verbum.*

15. Not all these preachers, however, were animated by the same spirit.

Some may refer to Christian Judaizers, who, while not denying at this time at least any point of revealed doctrine, were nevertheless contending that the Mosaic observances were the necessary gateway to the full benefits and perfect blessings of Christianity, and who, witnessing the greater fame and success of Paul, were moved with "envy" to emulate his influence and his preaching from prison. But more likely these "some" were just certain members of the Christian community of Rome who were ambitious and jealous of Paul, a stranger who in so short a time had so great an influence (cf. Lemonnyer, *Ep. de S. Paul*, II partie, pp. 10-11). Certainly, whatever these preachers were contending for, there was no question at this time of a preaching of false doctrine on the part of St. Paul's opponents, otherwise he could never have rejoiced over their work for Christ (ver. 18); the Apostle had not forgotten what he had previously written to the Galatians, i. 6-9, iii. 1 ff.

But there were other preachers who were altogether in sympathy with the Apostle, and who were inspired by the zeal and influence of his prison labors in behalf of the Gospel to greater efforts in their own respective fields, thus affording added joy and consolation to the Apostle's heart.

Good will here means sympathy for the things of God.

16-17. In these two verses the Apostle explains the motives by which the two classes just mentioned were moved, the one to support and the other to oppose his preaching. The order of these verses, 16 and 17, is inverted in some MSS., but the great weight of authority favors the order of the Vulgate.

Some out of charity, etc., i.e., some of those preachers proclaimed the Gospel out of love for St. Paul, knowing the divine commission he had received, etc.; but the others had a bad motive, being moved

18. But what then?   So that by all means, whether by occasion, or by truth, Christ be preached: in this also I rejoice, yea, and shall rejoice;

19. For I know that this shall fall out to me unto salvation, through your prayers, and the supply of the Spirit of Jesus Christ,

by a spirit of partisanship or intriguing (ἐξ ἐριθείας), and so tried to lessen the Apostle's popularity and influence and keep hearers away from him, thus adding to his "affliction," i.e., the distress of being in prison, and so unable to go out and seek his audience and refute his opponents.

18. **But what then?**   That is, what difference does it make whether those preachers were moved by good or by bad motives in their preaching of the Gospel, so long as Christ was preached? The Apostle was not seeking his own glory, but the glory of Christ; and therefore it made little difference to him whether or not those who promoted the cause of Christ liked or disliked him personally.

By occasion, or by truth, i.e., whether the Gospel was only a secondary or the primary reason of their preaching.   "Per occasionem annunciat Christum, qui non intendit hoc principaliter, sed propter aliud, puta lucrum vel gloriam" (St. Thomas).

I rejoice, etc.   If those opponents of the Apostle had been preaching false doctrine of any kind, he could never have rejoiced over their preaching in any sense of the word (see Gal. i. 6-9).

19. Besides the fact that Christ is being preached by Paul's enemies, which is the primary cause of his rejoicing, the Apostle finds a secondary cause for joy, now and in the future, in the thought that his sufferings and afflictions, through the help of the prayers of the faithful and the grace of the Holy Ghost, will contribute to his eternal salvation and his greater blessedness in heaven.

It is worthy of note that, notwithstanding all his vast labors for the Gospel, St. Paul rests the hope of his salvation, not on his own merits, but on the prayers of others and the abundant supply of grace of the Holy Spirit.   That "salvation" here refers to his eternal reward, and not to liberation from prison, or any lesser spiritual good along the way to heaven, is clear from the usual meaning of σωτηρία elsewhere (i.e., Rom. xiii. 11; 1 Thess. v. 8; Heb. ix. 28; 1 Peter i. 5).

Through your prayers.   St. Paul often manifested his confidence in the power and efficacy of intercessory prayer (e.g., Rom. xv. 30; 2 Cor. i. 11; 1 Thess. v. 25; 2 Thess. iii. 1; Col. iv. 3).

20. According to my expectation and hope; that in nothing I shall be confounded, but with all confidence, as always, so now also shall Christ be magnified in my body, whether *it be* by life, or by death.

21. For to me, to live is Christ: and to die is gain.

22. But if to live in the flesh, this is to me the fruit of labor, and which I shall choose I know not.

23. But I am straitened between two: having a desire to be dissolved and to be with Christ, a thing by far the better:

24. But to abide still in the flesh, is more needful for you.

The supply. The Greek carries the idea of ample, abundant supply.

The Spirit of Jesus Christ is none other than the Holy Ghost, who proceeds equally from the Father and the Son, and who is called sometimes the Spirit of the Father and sometimes the Spirit of the Son (cf. Rom. viii. 9; Gal. iv. 6; John xiv. 16, 26, xv. 26, etc.). Whether we are to understand here the Holy Spirit Himself or His grace, makes little difference, since the two ideas would come to the same thing. These final words are also a proof of the divinity of our Lord, the Holy Spirit being His Spirit.

20. Through the prayers of the faithful and the grace of Christ the Apostle is *ardently hoping* (such is the meaning of the Greek) for eternal salvation, but on his own part he is going to see that in nothing shall he be found wanting, that he will continue in the future as in the past to preach the Gospel "with all confidence" (i.e., freely and fearlessly), so that the glory of Christ shall continue to be manifested "in my body, etc." (i.e., by spending his body and his energies for Christ, if he lives, or by the sacrifice of his life in the cause of Christ if he is put to death). Why he will not "be confounded" (i.e., disappointed), whether he lives or dies, he explains in the following verses.

21. St. Paul had already told the Galatians: "I live, now not I; but Christ liveth in me" (Gal. ii. 20). He was totally identified with Christ; Christ was the soul and centre of his life, the prime mover in all his actions, the goal and term of all his aspirations; to the Apostle "to live" was to labor for Christ and in union with Christ, and thus augment his merits for heaven, while "to die" was to be with Christ in glory and to enjoy his eternal reward.

22-24. The Apostle is confronted by the alternatives of dying and being with Christ in glory, on the one hand, and of remaining in this earthly life for a time and thus serving the interests of the

25. And having this confidence, I know that I shall abide, and continue
with you all for your furtherance and joy of faith:
26. That your rejoicing may abound in Christ Jesus in me by my coming
to you again.

Gospel and the Church, on the other hand; and he knows not which
to choose, as there is great profit in either choice. So he is torn
between conflicting emotions, desiring the former, knowing that it
would be far better "to be dissolved" (or better, "to depart"), and
thus be forever with Christ in paradise, but feeling that the Philippians need him, and that consequently he ought to remain on earth
a while longer.

This is to me the fruit of labor. The Greek is concise and
therefore somewhat difficult, but the meaning is clear: To continue
in this life would mean to the Apostle an occasion of *fruitful labor*
(καρπὸς ἔργου) for the cause of Christ on earth.

Far the better, literally, "much more better," a phrase indicative
of St. Paul's strong preference to die and be with Christ. From
ver. 23 it is evident that the souls of the saints are admitted to the
presence of God immediately after death.

The *necessarium* of the Vulgate (ver. 24) is a comparative in
Greek, *more necessary.*

For you, better, "on account of you."

25-26. And having this confidence. The Greek means that the
Apostle is firmly persuaded, that he enjoys a feeling of personal
certainty. But with regard to what? That he is going to live and
see the Philippians again? If this is the meaning, it would seem
to be out of harmony with the uncertainty expressed just above in
verses 20-23, and also with what he says below in ii. 17. The best
explanation seems to be that of St. Chrysostom and others, who
say that St. Paul is speaking above about the uncertainty of life
or death in his case, whereas here he is stressing the utility and
profit of the event, whichever it turns out to be: if he dies, he will
be with Christ in glory; if he lives, he will be a help and a source
of joy to the Philippians; in any case the result will certainly be
good, of this he is firmly persuaded. In this explanation verse 25
is to be understood, in the light of the whole context, as conditional. "This confidence" refers to what follows: if he continues
to live, he knows that he will be of great spiritual profit to the
Philippians, and will thus give joy to their faith.

27. Only let your conduct be worthy of the gospel of Christ; that, whether I come and see you, or, being absent, may hear of you, that you stand fast in one spirit, with one mind laboring together for the faith of the gospel. 28. And in nothing be ye terrified by the adversaries: which to them is a sure sign of perdition, but to you of salvation, and this from God:

In me. The meaning is that St. Paul will be the occasion of their rejoicing, all the more so because the Apostle's adversaries have been trying to discredit him while he has been in prison.

AN EXHORTATION TO LIVE GOOD LIVES AND TO CONTINUE THE GOOD FIGHT FOR THE GOSPEL, 27-30

27-30. At the close of the previous section St. Paul seemed to express the likelihood of seeing the Philippians again; but here he exhorts them to be good citizens and live worthily of the Gospel whether he sees them again or not. He wants them to be united in mind and action in their fight for the saving truths they profess and not to fear their adversaries, being assured that final victory will be theirs. They are suffering for Christ's sake, and are waging the same conflict which they beheld in their Apostle when he was in Philippi and which still is his in Rome, as they know.

27. Just above the Apostle has spoken of his own condition and prospects. Now he turns to the Philippians and tells them there is only one thing that will trouble him, and that is if he should hear something bad about them and their conduct. Wherefore he says: "Let your conduct be worthy, etc.,"—literally, "let your citizenship be worthy, etc.," i.e., conduct yourselves in a manner worthy of the Gospel of Christ, as citizens of heaven (iii. 20).

In one spirit, i.e., in unity of mind, heart, and way of acting, as a result of the grace of the one Holy Spirit dwelling within you. Some take "spirit" here to mean the Holy Ghost directly, and refer to 1 Cor. xii. 13, Eph. ii. 18, where the identical phrase here used is doubtless to be understood of the Holy Spirit. The effect will be the same in either opinion, as St. Paul is speaking of religious conduct.

Laboring, better, "striving" or "contending." The metaphor is drawn from the prize-seeking contests in the amphitheatre.

28. The Apostle now tells the Philippians not to be "terrified by the adversaries," i.e., the idol-worshippers and Jews of Philippi who

29. For unto you it is given for Christ, not only to believe in him, but also to suffer for him;

30. Having the same conflict as that which you have seen in me, and now hear to be still mine.

persecute them, but to face them with courage and steadfastness. Their calm fortitude, he says, since they are contending for the eternal truth of the Gospel, will be, in the nature of things, "a sure sign" of the ultimate overthrow of their foes and of their own spiritual triumph.

Others explain "a sure sign" thus: the persecutions which they inflict on you will be for them a cause of perdition and for you a source of profit and salvation. The first explanation seems preferable, and appears to imply that the opponents themselves are inwardly persuaded of the final loss of their cause. At best the passage is obscure.

And this refers to the whole idea previously expressed, namely, their constancy in the face of opposition, which is not from their own strength, but "from God," i.e., the gift of God.

29. In the preceding verse St. Paul encouraged the faithful by saying that their very constancy in fighting and enduring for the Gospel was an evident token of their eternal salvation; and here he bids them be reassured in the great privilege they enjoy as a gift of God, not only in believing in Christ, but in having the high honor "also to suffer for him," i.e., in His behalf. If they suffer for Christ and with Christ, they will also be crowned with Him.

30. Finally, the Apostle encourages his readers by reminding them that in their sufferings they are sharing the lot experienced by him, the founder of their Church, when he first preached the Gospel in their city (Acts xvi. 20 ff.), and which he has been enduring in Rome, as they "now hear," very likely from Epaphroditus, the bearer of this letter.

CHAPTER II

AN EXHORTATION TO UNITY AND HUMILITY, 1-11

1-11. In verse 27 of the preceding Chapter St. Paul exhorted the Philippians to unity of thought and action in their efforts for the spread of the Gospel, and here (ver. 1-4) he goes back to that

1. If there be therefore any comfort in Christ, if any consolation of charity, if any fellowship of the spirit, if any bowels of commiseration,

2. Fulfill ye my joy, that you be of one mind, having the same charity, being of one accord, agreeing in sentiment.

3. Let nothing be done through contention, neither by vain glory: but in humility, let each esteem others better than himself;

thought and appeals to his readers in still more earnest tones that they should make full his joy by the practice and cultivation of complete unity and harmony among them. This relationship of concord among brethren, he goes on to say, must be grounded on humility, on lowliness of mind. And since in the pagan world humility was despised as a sign of degradation, as an abject and groveling state suited only to the condition of slaves, he cites (ver. 5-11) the supreme example of Christ who, though He was the Son of the eternal God Himself, took on Himself for our sakes the form of a lowly servant, even that of an outcast dying the most ignominious of deaths; and who in return for His extreme self-humiliation merited an exaltation above all other names, whether in heaven, on earth, or under the earth, that, namely, of supreme Lordship of the world.

1-2. It seems St. Paul must have learned that there were at Philippi some discordant elements among the Christians, arising from ambition, pride, vainglory, self-seeking, and the like; and hence he appeals to them by the deepest spiritual sentiments and relationships between him and them to complete his happiness and joy by exhibiting towards one another a spirit of concord and mutual charity. He piles up his reasons of appeal in rhetorical fashion, introducing each member by "if," not as though he doubted their state of mind and heart, but only to strengthen his exhortation. He means to say: "If there be any comfort in the fact that you are Christians, if there be any consolation which charity can inspire, if there be any reality in the common spiritual benefits and blessings we enjoy in the Holy Ghost, if there be in you any tender feelings of mercy and compassion; then complete the joy I have in you by thinking alike, by exercising mutual charity towards one another, by having one soul and mind in all you do." Of the phrases in verse 2 inculcating unity, Vaughan says St. Paul has multiplied them in a "tautology of earnestness."

3. Here the Apostle indicates the obstacles to unity and concord

4. Each one not considering the things that are his own, but also those that are other men's.

5. Let this mind be in you, which was also in Christ Jesus,

of spirit, namely, "contention," i.e., a spirit of partisanship or faction, and "vain glory," i.e., the inordinate seeking of one's own interests and self-praise. Instead of being moved by such unworthy impulses in their dealings with their neighbor, the Apostle urges that they be guided by the Christian virtue of "humility," which will teach them to see the good that is in everybody else while making them conscious of their own defects, and will thus lead each one of them to "esteem others better than himself." There is no one so good as not to have some defects, and no one so bad as to be devoid of all good qualities; and hence if we keep in mind our own faults, on the one hand, and the good traits of our neighbor, on the other hand, it is easy to esteem others better than ourselves (St. Thomas, *h. l.*).

4. The Apostle gives another means of exercising fraternal charity, and thus of promoting unity, namely, sympathy and a kindly interest in the affairs of others.

The Vulgate *sed ea, quæ*, etc., should read, *sed et ea, quæ*, etc., to agree with the Greek; which shows that, while looking after our own affairs with due attention, we should also take a helpful interest in things that concern others.

5. In verses 5-11 St. Paul will illustrate and enforce the doctrine he has been inculcating by the supreme example of the Saviour in His voluntary incarnation, humiliation, and exaltation. Though issuing from a practical exhortation, the passage is profound in its doctrinal teaching and unsurpassed in its theological importance. In these few verses we have summed up the whole history of Christ— His nature and eternity as God, His incarnation with its humiliating consequences, and His glorious triumph and exaltation. The fact that St. Paul, in order to enforce some of the simplest moral duties, makes an appeal to such profound mysteries shows, on the one hand, the natural and intimate connection between Christian theological teaching and practical Christian life; and, on the other hand, how thorough and profound must have been the instruction given the early Christians by the Apostles and how these great doctrines of the divinity, incarnation, etc., of Christ formed a part of that in-

6. Who being in the form of God, thought it not robbery to be equal to God,

struction, and were, at the writing of this letter, apparently so well understood as to need only to be stated in their broad outlines to be grasped in their meaning and application.

Let this mind, etc. The *enim* of the Vulgate at the beginning of this verse is not represented in the best Greek. The Apostle wishes to say that, if his readers will have the same attitude of mind and soul which our Lord had at the time of His incarnation, all that he has requested in the verses just preceding will be easily and readily complied with.

In Christ Jesus, i.e., in the Divine Person who was God from eternity, who was eternally predestined by the Eternal Father as the Christ to be, and who became incarnate in time to save mankind from their sins.

6. Jesus Christ is here described in His eternal, pre-existent life as God.

Who refers to the single Personality, who is one and the same both in His pre-existence and in His earthly life.

Being (ὑπάρχων). The Greek participle emphasizes the pre-existence of Christ.

In the form of God, i.e., having the nature, essence, inward being of God; for such is the meaning of "form" (μορφή) here. Thus, before His incarnation Christ, or the Divine Person who became the Christ, pre-existed in the Divine Nature, as the eternal Son of the eternal Father.

Thought. This is a human way of expressing the Son's attitude regarding the surrender of His position of equality with God in order to become man; not that He actually gave up anything that belonged to Him as God, but that His Divine Person in the incarnation took upon Himself the lowly form of human nature.

Robbery. The Greek word for "robbery" (ἁρπαγμός) occurs only here in the Greek Bible, and may mean (a) the act of robbing or seizing by force; or (b) the matter of robbery, or thing to be seized. The latter is the meaning here, and it conveys the idea of holding to a thing with a tenacity and jealousy that would make one unwilling to surrender it. There is no question here of unlawful possession, but only of anxiously clinging to what rightfully

7. But emptied himself, taking the form of a servant, being made in the likeness of men, and in habit found as a man,

belongs to one. The sense of the whole phrase is that the eternal Son, at the prospect of His becoming man, did not so cling to His dignity and equality with God the Father in His divine nature as to be unwilling to become incarnate, thus assuming an inferior state as man.

Fr. Rickaby says the phrase "equal to God," or "on equality with God," does not regard the relation of the Son to the Father, but the relation of the Word to the nature which He chose as man; and he explains οὐχ ἁρπαγμόν as (He) "made no hurry." In his view the passage means that our Lord did not at once insist on appearing as man in His glorified human nature, but delayed it till after His Resurrection (*Further Notes on St. Paul, h. l.*).

Having spoken of the divine nature and dignity of the Son, the Apostle will speak in the two following verses of His humiliation in His earthly life.

7. **But emptied himself,** by becoming man, by taking for a time an external human form which veiled, as it were, the Divinity that He possessed as God, and deprived Him of the external prerogative of glory to which as God He always retained His right. On this phrase, "he emptied himself," St. Thomas says: "Hoc est intelligendum secundum assumptionem eius quod non habuit; sicut enim descendit de cœlo, non quod desineret esse in cœlo, sed quia incepit novo modo esse in terra, sic etiam se exinanivit, non deponendo divinam naturam, sed assumendo naturam humanam." How the Son "emptied himself" (*kenosis*), the Apostle describes in the three phrases that follow:

(a) by "taking the form of a servant," literally, "of a slave," i.e., taking the nature of man. With regard to God all creatures are servants or slaves, even the angels. The word "form" here is the same as in verse 6 above, and hence means nature, essence, etc.;

(b) by "being made in the likeness of men," i.e., appearing like other men, since He had the same nature as other men. The Divine Word, without ceasing to be God, assumed human nature, uniting the natures of God and of man in the one Divine Person, and appeared externally just like other men;

(c) by "being in habit found as a man," i.e., being recognized as

8. He humbled himself, becoming obedient unto death, even to the death of the cross.

9. For which cause God also hath exalted him, and hath given him a name which is above all names:

a man in His outward form and manner of acting by all His compatriots and associates (e.g., by eating, drinking, etc., like other men). In the preceding verse the Apostle affirmed the Divinity of Jesus Christ, and here he affirms the true humanity of the same Divine Person, showing that Christ was both true God and true man. Cf. Sales, *h. l.*

8. Having described the way in which the Divine Word emptied Himself, the Apostle will now show the extreme humility and self-abasement to which He subjected Himself in the human nature which He assumed: He became "obedient" to the will of His heavenly Father "unto death," and that, not an ordinary death, but one of shame and horror, namely, "the death of the cross." The expression "unto death" expresses the degree of His obedience. St. Paul wishes his readers to learn from this example of full and supreme self-abnegation on the part of their Master the humility, charity, and self-denial that will bring them peace and concord.

9. In verses 9-11 we have a description of the exaltation of our Lord, corresponding to His *kenosis*. We have already seen the extreme degree to which He emptied and humiliated Himself in obedience to the will of His eternal Father, and now we shall see what recompense He received.

For which cause, etc., i.e., as a reward for our Lord's extreme and voluntary abasement He was exalted by the Eternal Father to a dignity beyond any that exists or can exist below the Divinity Itself. That our Lord merited this supreme exaltation, He Himself declared on the day of His resurrection: "Ought not Christ to have suffered these things, and so to enter into his glory?" (Luke xxiv. 26). His own great saying was fulfilled in His case: "He that shall humble himself shall be exalted" (Matt. xxiii. 12; Luke xiv. 11, xviii. 14).

Hath exalted him, above all other creatures, placing Him in the highest position of honor and authority next to the Godhead (cf. Eph. i. 21 ff.; Col. iii. 1; Heb. i. 13; Rom. viii. 34, xiv. 19; etc.).

Name stands here for power, dignity, majesty; and therefore a name "above all names" means a dignity and a majesty greater than anything that is possible below the Divinity Itself. By "name" here

10. That in the name of Jesus every knee should bow, of those that are in heaven, on earth, and under the earth,

11. And that every tongue should confess that the Lord Jesus Christ is in the glory of God the Father.

the Apostle does not refer to our Lord's proper name, Jesus, which was given Him long before His exaltation and was recognized by men, and which was common to many other men (Estius).

10. The purpose of the exaltation of Jesus is now given.

That in the name of Jesus, etc., i.e., so great a dignity and honor was bestowed on our Lord in order that all creatures might bow before His revealed majesty and adore Him as Lord of the world and Saviour of mankind.

Every knee should bow is a phrase signifying supreme adoration (cf. Isa. xiv. 24; Rom. xiv. 11; Eph. iii. 14). The human nature of Christ, as being hypostatically united to the Word, deserves the same adoration as the Divinity of the Word Itself.

Of those that are in heaven, etc., i.e., of angels in heaven, of men on earth, and of those who are in their graves (Theodoret), and even of the demons (St. Chrysostom). Most likely all created things are in view here. See Apoc. v. 12 ff., James ii. 19, for references to all creatures, including the demons. The phrase "under the earth" means the underworld, the realm of the dead, of discarnate spirits. The pious custom of bowing the head at the mention of the name Jesus has at least indirect sanction from this verse.

11. The same thought is continued and developed.

That every tongue, etc., i.e., that all nations and peoples shall praise and honor the Son as they do the Father, recognizing the same glory in the Son as in the Father, as is said in John v. 23. But the Greek of this passage is as follows: "That every tongue should confess that Jesus Christ is Lord, to the glory of God the Father." In this reading the direct object of the confession is the universal sovereignty and therefore the Divinity of our Lord, and such a confession or recognition of the Son is ordained to the glory of the Father as to its last end: it is to the glory of the Father to have a Son to whom all things are subjected (Theophylact), the praise of Christ the Lord is to the glory of the Father (Estius). Thus, our Lord Himself said: "Father, the hour is come, glorify thy Son, that thy Son may glorify thee" (John xvii. 1).

In verses 5-11 here we have the following clear teachings: (a)

12. Wherefore, my beloved (as you have always obeyed, not as in my presence only, but much more now in my absence), with fear and trembling work out your salvation.

the Divinity of Jesus Christ and His consubstantiality with the Father; (b) the true humanity of Christ; (c) the union of two natures in the one Divine Person; (d) the merit of our Lord's sacrificial obedience and death. In consequence we also have here the refutation of the following errors: (a) Arianism, which denied the consubstantiality and equality of the Son with the Father; (b) Sabellianism, which denied the plurality of persons in God; (c) Nestorianism, which held that there were two persons in Jesus Christ; (d) Eutychianism, which taught only one nature in Christ; (e) Docetism, which attributed to our Lord a fantastic and not a real body; (f) Apollinarism, which said the body of Christ was not like our bodies. Cf. St. Thomas, *h. l.*

EXHORTATION TO PERSEVERANCE IN HOLINESS, 12-18

12-18. With the example of Christ's humility to guide them, and the example of Christ's exaltation to encourage them (Lightfoot), the Apostle appeals to the Philippians obediently and reverently to work out their salvation in co-operation with God, the source of all their graces. Keeping themselves blameless in a world of sin, they must be as a light to others on the way to heaven, thus shedding glory on their Apostle in the day of Christ's coming. Even if he is to be poured out as a libation in the sacrifice for their faith, the Apostle says he rejoices, and he bids them also to rejoice with him.

12. **Wherefore.** The Apostle deduces a practical conclusion from what he has been saying about the self-denial and obedience of Christ. He first praises his beloved Philippians for the obedience they have always shown in being faithful to his teachings and the precepts of the Gospel, and then goes on to exhort them to still greater faithfulness and efforts in his absence, because their perils are increased by the very fact that he is not present to warn them of dangers and to prescribe remedies and helps as he did when with them. They must work out their salvation "with fear and trembling," i.e., with great solicitude for their own spiritual welfare and a reverential fear of offending God. In thus admonishing his read-

13. For it is God who worketh in you, both to will and to accomplish, according to *his* good will.

ers the Apostle was only prescribing what he practised in his own case, as we see in 1 Cor. ix. 27, x. 12. From this exhortation it is clear that we can co-operate with the grace of God in effecting our salvation, and also that no one can be absolutely sure, without a special divine revelation, of persevering to the end in God's favor.

13. The Apostle now adds the reason why they are to work out their salvation with fear and trembling, namely, because the business of their salvation is not simply a matter of their own strength, but depends on God both as to its wish and accomplishment, so that without the grace of God they can neither desire nor do anything in the way of supernatural salvation. Thus it is the grace of God that produces in us "to will" (i.e., the efficacious determination to perform supernatural good) and "to accomplish" (i.e., the execution of that determination) ; and this grace God gives, not because He is obliged to give it, but because it is His "good will" (i.e., it is an act of pure benevolence on His part). It follows, then, that God can withdraw this grace if we are unfaithful to it.

And this efficacious movement on the part of God, far from destroying our liberty, presupposes it, otherwise the Apostle could not have just told his readers to work out their salvation with fear and trembling. On this subject St. Augustine says: "Certum est nos velle cum volumus, sed ille facit ut velimus bonum. . . . Certum est nos facere cum facimus, sed ille facit ut facimus præbendo vires efficacissimas voluntati . . . et ipse ut velimus operatur incipiens, qui volentibus cooperatur perficiens. . . . Ut ergo velimus sine nobis operatur, cum autem volumus et sic volumus ut faciamus nobiscum cooperatur, tamen sine illo vel operante ut velimus vel cooperante cum volumus, ad bona pietatis opera nihil valemus" (*De gratia et lib. arb.*, 16, 17).

In these two verses, 12 and 13, the Apostle teaches the following: (a) that of ourselves we cannot be sure of persevering in good; (b) that faith without works is not sufficient for salvation; (c) that good works can merit salvation; (d) that these good works are done by our free will; (e) that free will is not sufficient of itself to perform good works, but must be moved by grace, without which we can do nothing useful for eternal life (see *Conc. Trid.*, sess. VI, *De justificatione*). Cf. Sales, *h. l.*

14. And do ye all things without murmurings and disputings;

15. That you may become blameless, and sincere children of God, without reproof, in the midst of a crooked and perverse generation; among whom you shine as lights in the world,

16. Holding forth the word of life to my glory in the day of Christ, because I have not run in vain, nor labored in vain.

17. Yea, and if I be made a victim upon the sacrifice and service of your faith, I rejoice, and congratulate with you all.

18. And for the selfsame thing, do you also rejoice, and congratulate with me.

14-16. As contributing to the work of their salvation, therefore, the Apostle now admonishes his readers to avoid all "murmurings" against God because of their lot as Christians, and all "disputings" and wranglings with one another about the ways of divine providence; so that their lives may be an example to the pagans among whom they live and a shining light in the moral darkness that surrounds them. Thus they will be living as becomes their dignity as "children of God" (i.e., as Christians), and will be "holding forth the word of life" (i.e., the teachings of the Gospel) as the sure and safe guide to the true and only real life (John vi. 6, 9; Acts v. 20; 1 John i. 1); and this will redound to the glory of their Apostle, showing that he has not labored for them in vain, when Christ comes to judge all mankind at the end of the world.

17-18. St. Paul expected to see the Philippians again, but he speaks here as if he considered his execution a possibility; and in that event he says that, even if he is to "be made a victim, etc." (better, "to be poured out" as a libation over the "sacrifice and service" of their faith), he will rejoice, and he assumes that they will also rejoice with him, as sharing his spirit of martyrdom. St. Paul is picturing the Philippians, in their character as Christian believers, as a "sacrifice"; he regards their lives as a "service" or sacerdotal ritual; and he is looking upon his own life-blood, in his possible martyrdom, as an accompanying libation. His figurative language may refer to the Jewish sacrifices or to the pagan sacrifices, with both of which his converts must have been familiar.

ST. PAUL IS GOING TO SEND TIMOTHY AND EPAPHRODITUS TO PHILIPPI, 19-30

19-30. In this familiar letter the Apostle has given his readers advice, he has written about himself—what he hopes and fears as

19. And I hope in the Lord Jesus to send Timothy unto you shortly, that I also may be of good comfort, when I know the things concerning you.

20. For I have no man so of the same mind, who with sincere affection is solicitous for you.

21. For all seek the things that are their own, not the things that are Jesus Christ's.

22. And ye know the proof of him, that as a son with the father, so hath he served with me in the gospel.

regards his future—and now he speaks of the two faithful disciples whom he is sending to Philippi. Timothy, his most reliable co-worker, who is also deeply interested in the Philippians and well known to them, will come as soon as St. Paul learns how things are going to turn out in his own case; and then he himself hopes to come before long (ver. 19-24). He is sending to them at once Epaphroditus, who has been so kind and helpful to him, and who for the sake of the Gospel has been seriously ill, as they know to their sorrow. May they be cheered by his coming, may they receive him with gladness, and honor all such self-sacrificing workers for God (ver. 25-30)!

19. **In the Lord.** All Paul's hopes, thoughts, emotions, activities, etc., repose in divine help.

Timothy, who had helped to found the Church at Philippi (Acts xvi. 3 ff.).

Shortly, i.e., as soon as Paul knows the outcome of his trial.

20. He now gives the reason why he will send Timothy, namely, because he has no one "so of the same mind, etc.," i.e., no one who can equal Timothy in zeal and solicitude for the welfare of the Philippians. Paul is not comparing Timothy with himself, at least directly, but with his other workers; Timothy excels them all in interest for the faithful of Philippi, and in that respect of course he more closely resembles his great master.

21. A further reason is given for sending Timothy.

For all seek, etc. The Apostle is referring to his immediate circle of workers, most of whom apparently had not always shown the spirit of utter self-denial and self-forgetfulness which his own invincible character demanded: they were inclined at times to seek their personal ease and safety. Perhaps he had Demas and those like him in mind (2 Tim. iv. 10; cf. Col. iv. 14; Phlm. 24).

22-24. **And ye know the proof of him,** i.e., they know his worth

23. Him therefore I hope to send unto you immediately, as soon as I see how it will go with me.

24. And I trust in the Lord, that I myself also shall come to you shortly.

25. But I have thought it necessary to send to you Epaphroditus, my brother and fellow-laborer, and fellow-soldier, but your apostle, and he hath ministered to my wants.

26. For indeed he longed after you all: and was sad, for that you had heard that he was sick.

27. For indeed he was sick, nigh unto death; but God had mercy on him; and not only on him, but on me also, lest I should have sorrow upon sorrow.

28. Therefore I am sending him the more speedily: that seeing him again, you may rejoice, and I may be less sorrowful.

29. Receive him therefore with all joy in the Lord; and treat with honor such as he is;

from his zealous labors with St. Paul at Philippi (Acts xvi. 3, xvii. 14, 15).

As soon as I see, etc., i.e., as soon as he knows the issue of his Roman trial. He expects to be released, and then he will follow Timothy to Philippi.

25. The Apostle begins here to speak of Epaphroditus, whom the Philippians had sent to Rome with gifts (iv. 18), and whom he now considers it "necessary" to send back to Philippi for the reasons given below in verses 26-27.

Epaphroditus is mentioned only here and in iv. 18. St. Paul speaks of him as a "fellow-soldier," i.e., a companion in the battle against the enemy of souls and the faith. He was the Philippians' "apostle," i.e., their messenger to St. Paul in Rome.

26-27. These verses assign the reason for the return of Epaphroditus to Philippi. He desires to return for he knows the Philippians are anxious about him, and St. Paul wishes him to go back for the same reason. Had death taken him in his illness, another great sorrow would have been added to the sorrows of the Apostle's imprisonment.

28. **Less sorrowful.** His soul was never free from sorrow. Hence he says "less sorrowful," not "without sorrow." St. Paul is more concerned over the happiness of the Philippians than over his own; to add to their joy will mean more to him than to retain the presence and helpfulness of their messenger to him, much as he desires the latter.

29. **Treat with honor,** etc., i.e., hold in high esteem all such zealous and loyal Gospel-workers.

30. Because for the work of Christ he came to the point of death, hazarding his life, that he might fulfill that which on your part was wanting towards my service.

30. The work of Christ, i.e., the long journey to Rome and the labors and fatigue endured at Rome in behalf of St. Paul and the Gospel.

Hazarding, etc. Literally, "gambling, etc.," i.e., he risked his life in order to supply by personal effort what it was impossible for the Philippians to do for St. Paul in the eternal city, and which in their enforced absence they required him to discharge in their name.

CHAPTER III

THE DIFFERENCE BETWEEN THE TRUE AND A FALSE GOSPEL, 1-16

1. As to the rest, my brethren, rejoice in the Lord. To write the same things to you, to me indeed *is* not wearisome, but to you *is* necessary.

1-16. Before bringing his letter to a close St. Paul wishes once more to remind his readers of the dangers of the Judaizers. Those self-appointed seducers go about with their insolent ways, evil practices, and false doctrines, boasting of their fleshly, hereditary privileges, while lacking all true spirituality. If it were a question, he says, of trusting in the flesh, he could surpass them all; but he has renounced those perishable privileges, along with every other impediment, in order that he might gain Christ and know Him, that he might attain to that justness which is through faith in Christ, and that, by imitating the life of His master here below, he might be crowned with Him hereafter. He says he has not yet attained to that desired perfection, but he is pressing on towards it; and he exhorts those of his readers who are likewise minded to do the same, keeping faithful to the standard they have attained.

1. As to the rest. This is a formula which St. Paul often uses to bring his letters to a close, or to introduce a new topic or the last topic of a series. Very likely he was about to terminate this Epistle, bidding his readers "rejoice in the Lord," the fountain of all true joy, when he remembered the Judaizers, who were disturbing the peace of the Church at Philippi and becoming more audacious because he was in prison. Therefore, he takes pains to warn the faith-

2. Beware of dogs, beware of evil workers, beware of the concision.

3. For we are the circumcision, who in spirit serve God; and glory in Christ Jesus, not having confidence in the flesh,

4. Though I might also have confidence in the flesh. If any other thinketh he may have confidence in the flesh, I more;

5. Being circumcised the eighth day, of the stock of Israel, of the tribe

ful against them, repeating the "same things" (i.e., the same admonitions) which he had given before, very probably in other letters he had written them that have not come down to us.

Necessary. Better, "advantageous," "useful."

2. Beware of dogs. More literally, "Look at the dogs," i.e., Look out for them. With great emphasis and indignation the Apostle now turns to denounce the Judaizers, describing them as "dogs," to indicate their insolent, barking, and unclean character; as "evil workers," whose conduct would destroy the work of Christ; as those "of the concision," ironically alluding to their false notion of circumcision which consisted in mere physical mutilation devoid of spiritual significance. It is more probable that we have here three distinct descriptions of one class of persons than an indication of three different classes, representing respectively Gentiles, self-seeking Christian teachers, and unbelieving Jews.

3. In contrast to these boasters of mere physical mutilation, the Apostle says "we are the circumcision," i.e., the truly circumcised, having the circumcision of the heart (Rom. ii. 28-29), of which he proceeds to give the three characteristics.

Who in spirit serve God. Better, "who worship by the Spirit of God," i.e., who, moved by God's own Spirit, render to God a service that is worthy of Him.

And glory in Christ Jesus, the source of all justification and the sole author of salvation.

Not having confidence in the flesh, i.e., in carnal rites and observances which were given only for a time, until Christ should come.

4-6. In verses 4-11 the Apostle will show the Judaizers that he opposes their carnal privileges, not because he himself did not possess them, and indeed in the highest degree, but because they were unable to effect justification—a state of soul which could be obtained only through Jesus Christ.

If any other, etc. He means to say that, if it were of any use, he has more reason to put his trust in hereditary privileges than

of Benjamin, a Hebrew of the Hebrews; according to the Law, a Pharisee;

6. According to zeal, persecuting the church; according to the justice that is in the law, conversing without blame.

7. But the things that were gain to me, the same I have counted loss for Christ.

8. Furthermore I count all things to be but loss for the excellent knowledge of Jesus Christ my Lord; for whom I suffered the loss of all things, and count them but as dung, that I may gain Christ,

9. And may be found in him, not having my justice, which is of the law, but that which is of the faith of Christ, which of God, justice in faith:

any of those false teachers, as the following will show. He was "circumcised" in infancy, as the Law required; he was "of the stock of Israel," the true covenant race; "of the tribe of Benjamin," i.e., a descendant of that beloved son of Jacob whose tribe gave Israel her first king and remained faithful to Juda at the disruption of the kingdom; he was a "Hebrew of Hebrews," having always retained the language and customs of his race, whereas the Hellenists spoke Greek and largely adopted the customs of the Gentiles; he was by choice "a Pharisee," and therefore a zealous and rigorous observer of the Law of Moses; he went so far in his zeal for Judaism that he actually persecuted "the church of God"; he gave such scrupulous attention to the observance of the Law that his life was "without blame" in so far as the Law could make it so.

The *Dei* of the Vulgate in verse 6 should be omitted, according to the best Greek.

7. But all those Jewish prerogatives, which meant so much to him among the Jews, he has come to regard as "loss," i.e., as useless, and even a hindrance to the possession of Christ, in whom alone justification and salvation are to be found.

8. The Apostle augments his statement. Not only those Jewish privileges, but also all similar things of the flesh, he has considered as useless and damaging in comparison with the surpassing spiritual benefits that have come to him through knowing his Lord and Saviour Jesus Christ, for whose sake he "suffered the loss of all things," at the time of his conversion, counting them all as "dung" (better, as "refuse," i.e., as of no value) in order that he might "gain Christ," the secret and source of all graces and benefits. The present tense, "may gain," is used only because the past experience is projected into the present.

9. The same truth is stated in another way.

10. That I may know him and the power of his resurrection, and the fellowship of his sufferings, being made conformable to his death,

May be found. Again the past experience is spoken of as present, so vividly is it realized.

Not having my justice, etc., i.e., a justice which is acquired from the works of the Law and by one's natural powers; "but that which is of the faith, etc.," i.e., that justice which God gives on account of the faith one has in Jesus Christ; faith is the foundation of this justice or justness, and God is its author and giver.

The *Jesu* of the Vulgate here is not according to the best Greek.

10. Returning to the thought of verse 8, the Apostle further explains the reasons and advantages of his rejection of Judaism with all its privileges.

Here in verse 10 he assigns a threefold end or purpose he had in seeking to "gain Christ" and to "be found in him," having that justice which is through faith in Christ: (a) "that I may know him," i.e., that he might have an intimate, practical knowledge of Christ, God and man, the source of all knowledge and the model of all virtues; (b) that he might know "the power of his resurrection," i.e., the power of the risen, glorified, immortal Christ, by whom we have been reconciled with God (Rom. iv. 24-25), who is the earnest of our own resurrection (1 Cor. xv. 20; 1 Thess. iv. 14), and who has sent us the Holy Spirit with his manifold graces, thus uniting us intimately to Himself (John vii. 39, xx. 22; Acts ii. 33); (c) that he might have "the fellowship of his sufferings, etc.," i.e., that he might bear his own afflictions and sufferings for the sake of Christ, and with the help of Christ's Holy Spirit, as his Master had borne His cross for him, and this he desires as a means of entering into a full, practical and fruitful knowledge here on earth of the risen, glorified Christ. The way to the living Christ is that marked out by Christ Himself: "If we suffer with him, that we may be also glorified with him" (Rom. viii. 17); "Ought not Christ to have suffered these things, and so to enter into his glory?" (Luke xxiv. 26).

Sufferings, patiently borne for Christ and in union with Christ, are the royal way that leads to Christ now reigning in glory after His triumph over sufferings and death through the power of His resurrection; and it is by thus entering upon and continuing in this

11. If by any means I may attain to the resurrection which is from the dead.

12. Not as though I had already attained, or were already perfect: but I follow after, if I may by any means apprehend, wherein I am also apprehended by Christ.

13. Brethren, I do not count myself to have apprehended. But one thing

way of suffering that one's life becomes "conformable" to the death of the Master: "Always bearing about in our body the mortification of Jesus, that the life also of Jesus may be made manifest in our bodies" (2 Cor. iv. 10).

11. The end and purpose of this fellowship with Christ's sufferings and conformity to the Master's death, and indeed of all that the Apostle has related from verse 7 to now, was that he might, by all his sacrifices and sufferings, attain to the glorious "resurrection which is from the dead," by which in body and soul he would be made like to his glorified Redeemer and thereafter forever associated with Him.

The resurrection here in question is the General Resurrection of all the just at the end of time, of which Christ's resurrection was the pledge. St. Paul's hypothetical manner of speaking in this verse, "if by any means, etc.," indicates the great difficulty of attaining to that blessed state and the consequent uncertainty connected with it, apart from the help of God.

12. In verses 12-17 the Apostle cites his own example as an exhortation to his readers that they should increase their efforts to attain Christian perfection. It might be concluded from all he has said (ver. 7-11) about his sacrifices in order to acquire justice before God, and about his sufferings in union with Christ in order to reach the supreme goal of life, that he had reached a state of perfection in which further effort is unnecessary. Hence he hastens to observe in this present verse that he has not yet attained to this perfection, that much remains to be done, that, far from resting on his merits, he is bending every effort, like the runners in the Greek stadium, to win his prize, which is fully and perfectly to possess Christ, who took strong and lasting possession of him at the time of his conversion on the road to Damascus (Acts ix. 3 ff.).

I follow after. Better, "I press on."

The *Jesu* of the Vulgate is not in the best MSS.

13-14. The thought of the preceding verse is amplified, again

I do: forgetting the things that are behind, and stretching forth myself to those that are before,

14. I press towards the mark, to the prize of the supernal vocation of God in Christ Jesus.

15. Let us therefore, as many as are perfect, be thus minded; and if in anything you be otherwise minded, this also God will reveal to you.

16. Nevertheless whereunto we are come, that we be of the same mind, let us also continue in the same rule.

under the figure of the runners in the stadium. The Apostle tells the Philippians that, instead of considering himself perfect or to have reached his goal, he is using every energy, like an athlete in a contest, to press on to the mark and to win the prize, which for him is eternal life with Christ in heaven.

Forgetting the things, etc., i.e., not stopping to think of his labors, his virtues, his merits; and "stretching forth, etc.," i.e., ever seeking new opportunities for growth in the grace and the knowledge of our Lord and Saviour Jesus Christ (2 Peter iii. 18). The Greek word for "prize" is found only here and in 1 Cor. ix. 24, in the New Testament; and it means eternal glory in both places. The "vocation" or call to this "supernal" or heavenly prize is from God the Father "in Christ," i.e., through the merits of Christ.

15. From the two preceding verses it may be inferred that there were some at Philippi who thought they had arrived at perfection, and that consequently they had nothing further to do in spiritual ways. If this was the case, we can see a touch of irony in the term "perfect" here; and the Apostle wishes to say: "Let those who think themselves perfect remember that religious perfection consists in a holy dissatisfaction with one's present state, combined with a constant effort to press on."

And if in anything you be otherwise minded, etc. He means to say that, if there were those who sincerely disagreed with him in this matter, God would yet enlighten them, either directly through the Holy Ghost, or through the teaching of their spiritual leaders.

16. **Nevertheless,** etc., i.e., as to what we have already attained about divine things (Estius), or as to the standard of life we have so far reached, let us continue according to it, and press on. There is a slight difference between the Vulgate and the best Greek reading of this verse. According to the latter, the sense is: "While some of you may be in need of further light on certain points, I recom-

17. Be ye united followers of me, brethren, and observe them who so walk even as you have our model.

18. For many walk, of whom I have told you often (and now tell you weeping), that they are enemies of the cross of Christ;

19. Whose end is destruction; whose God is their belly; and *whose* glory is in their shame; who mind earthly things.

mend that you order your lives in accordance with the truth you have so far attained, avoiding dissensions of any kind." Of course, the Apostle uses the first person plural to soften his words.

Ut idem sapiamus of the Vulgate, while according to some less important Greek MSS., may be regarded as a gloss. Likewise the word *regula*. Our ordinary English version follows the Vulgate.

A WARNING AGAINST BAD EXAMPLE, 17–21

17–21. St. Paul feels obliged to place before his readers as a standard of life and conduct his own example and that of his companions. He has warned them before with sorrow of those whose worldly excesses are a contradiction of their profession, who are enemies of the cross of Christ, and whose end is destruction. As a safeguard against such debasing influences, he reminds the Philippians of their high destiny as to their bodies as well as their souls; for their home is in heaven, whence in due time their Saviour will come to transform by His almighty power their present fleshy tabernacles into spiritual and imperishable bodies like His own.

17. **And observe them who so walk,** etc., i.e., take note of those Christians who live according to the model we have given them. The Apostle is referring to the example he and his companions and associates have given.

In the Vulgate *imitatores* should be *co-imitatores,* to agree with the Greek.

18–19. **For many walk,** etc. It is disputed whether the "many" here means Judaizers or bad Christians, but most probably the latter are in question. Both indeed would be "enemies of the cross of Christ"—the former, by insisting on legal observances, for if justice is from the Law then Christ died in vain (Gal. ii. 21), and the latter, by their moral excesses, for those who are Christ's have crucified the flesh with its vices and evil desires (Gal. v. 24). But it is much more natural to understand St. Paul to be moved to tears over those who had once been good Christians and had de-

20. But our conversation is in heaven: from whence also we look for the Saviour, our Lord Jesus Christ,

21. Who will reform the body of our lowness, made like to the body of his glory, according to the operation whereby also he is able to subdue all things unto himself.

generated, than over those like the Judaizers who had never been true to Christ.

I have told you often, when at Philippi.

Whose end is destruction, i.e., for whom final and eternal ruin and loss is reserved. "Destruction" or perdition (ἀπώλεια) here is the same as in Phil. i. 28. It means the utter loss of blessedness, the very antithesis of salvation (σωτηρία); and as blessedness or salvation is eternal, so must be this "destruction" or perdition of the damned: "And these shall go into everlasting punishment; but the just, into life everlasting" (Matt. xxv. 46). See on 2 Thess. i. 9.

Whose glory is in their shame, i.e., who glory in the very things of which they ought to be ashamed. Those who think the Judaizers are meant here take "shame" to be circumcision (St. Augustine); St. Chrysostom thinks "shame" refers to sins of uncleanness.

20. Having mentioned the characteristics of bad Christians, the Apostle will now give the marks of those who are faithful.

But. The Greek has γάρ here; but since St. Paul is contrasting the lives of good and bad Christians, the sense requires a particle of contrast, like "but" or "whereas"; the thought of this verse goes back to verse 17.

Our conversation, literally means "our manner of living," but the Apostle means "our home," "our country"; the true Christian walks the earth, but his thoughts, aims, hopes, and desires are in heaven and in things that lead thereto.

We look for. Better, "we eagerly expect," as with "outstretched neck and upturned eyes" (Rickaby).

21. The true Christian looks forward to the glorious time of his complete deliverance, both of body and of soul; when Christ will come at the end of the world and transform our present miserable, suffering bodies into glorious, immortal temples like His own glorified body (1 Cor. xv. 40-49); when the risen Saviour will exercise that power in our regard by which, as God, He will rule and dominate all things (1 Cor. xv. 25-27).

CHAPTER IV

EXHORTATION TO VARIOUS VIRTUES AND HOLY THOUGHTS, 1-9

1. Therefore, my beloved brethren, and my desired; my joy and my crown, so stand fast in the Lord, beloved.
2. I beg of Evodia, and I beseech Syntyche, to be of one mind in the Lord.

1-9. After all the Apostle has said in the last part of the preceding Chapter, his exceeding love for the Philippians manifests itself in endearing terms, asserting that they will be his garland of victory and joy in the day of Christ's coming to judge the world. He exhorts them to steadfastness; he entreats Evodia and Syntyche, especially, to have no dissension, asking his loyal comrade to assist these latter, since they, like Clement and his other fellow-workers, have been so faithful to him in labors for the Gospel. Then to all he recommends joy in the Lord, forbearance towards all men, freedom from anxiety, prayerfulness and thankfulness; and he assures them that, if they practise these virtues, the peace of God will take up its abode in their hearts and minds in Christ Jesus (ver. 1-7). Finally, recapitulating, he begs them to feed their minds on all that is true and good, wherever it may be found, asking them in practice to obey his precepts and imitate his example as a sure way to heavenly peace (ver. 8-9).

1. **Therefore.** This verse concludes what the Apostle has been saying in the preceding Chapter, most probably in verses 17-21.

My beloved . . . my desired. The corresponding words in the Vulgate here should be in the positive, instead of the superlative degree, to harmonize with the Greek. The Apostle is exhorting the Philippians to steadfastness in Christian life and conduct as inculcated by him and his companions, for he wishes to present them to Christ as his achievement in the final judgment.

2. This verse seems to show that the two ladies mentioned occupied a prominent place in the work of the Philippian Church, and

3. And I entreat thee also, my sincere companion, help those women who have labored with me in the gospel, with Clement and the rest of my fellow laborers, whose names are in the book of life.

4. Rejoice in the Lord always; again, I say, rejoice.

5. Let your modesty be known to all men. The Lord is nigh.

that some dissension had arisen between them. They are not mentioned elsewhere.

3. **Companion.** Literally, "yoke-fellow," i.e., fellow-worker. It is unknown who he was. Perhaps he was Epaphroditus; or possibly the Greek word here (σύζυγος) is a proper name, and should be rendered "Syzygus."

Those women. Literally, "them" (αὐταῖς), i.e., the two ladies spoken of in the preceding verse.

Clement, perhaps a resident of Philippi, though he is identified with Clement of Rome by many of the Fathers.

The book of life, i.e., God's eternal register in heaven (Apoc. xiii. 8, xx. 12); it is God's certain knowledge of those who are predestined (St. Thomas). The metaphor is taken from the custom in antiquity of keeping in a register the names of all the people of a country or town (cf. Exod. xxxii. 32; Isa. iv. 3; Dan. xii. 1).

4. Speaking to all, the Apostle repeats his exhortation of iii. 1, bidding his readers "rejoice in the Lord always," on account of the many spiritual blessings they now enjoy and that are promised them both here and hereafter by the Saviour who has redeemed them; there is never wanting to them a motive of spiritual joy.

5. As an effect of their spiritual joy, they are to manifest their "modesty" (i.e., their gentleness and sweetness of character) "to all men," even to those whom he had before called enemies of the cross of Christ (St. Chrysostom); with all they are to deal in a kindly manner, thus showing the value and loveliness of the religion they profess.

The Lord is nigh. This assigns the great cause of their joy; "a man rejoices at the coming of a friend" (St. Thomas). Hence this phrase is to be connected with what precedes, and the Greeks understood it of the General Judgment. Others think it refers to the ever-present grace and help of God (so St. Thomas). The former opinion is more probable: Christ is coming to judge and crown us for our patience and spirit of sweet endurance; the Apostle often speaks of the final judgment as if it were close at hand, **in**

6. Be nothing solicitous; but in every thing, by prayer and supplication, with thanksgiving, let your petitions be made known to God.

7. And the peace of God, which surpasseth all understanding, will keep your hearts and minds in Christ Jesus.

8. For the rest, brethren, whatsoever things are true, whatsoever modest, whatsoever just, whatsoever holy, whatsoever lovely, whatsoever of good report, if there be any virtue, if any praise—think on these things.

order that his readers might keep it ever in their minds (a Lapide, Knabenbauer, etc.).

6. Anxious solicitude is an impediment to joy, and hence the Apostle now admonishes, "be nothing solicitous" (i.e., have no anxieties) either as regards goods you lack or evils you bear, but in every work and condition have recourse to God "by prayer and supplication" (i.e., with fervor and perseverance), not forgetting prayers of "thanksgiving," for God is ever ready to hear your worthy "petitions," and will always grant what you ask, or something better. God never fails to answer in some way prayers that are properly made, though He will not give us what is not for our good; and gratitude for favors received disposes God to grant more favors.

7. The effect of prayer that is properly made is peace of mind and soul.

The peace of God, i.e., the peace whose author and giver is God.

Which surpasseth all understanding, i.e., which is supernatural, and therefore cannot be produced by human means or understood by those who have not experienced it.

Will keep. Literally, "will guard," like a sentinel at a gate, "your hearts and minds" (i.e., your feelings and thoughts) "in Christ Jesus," our spiritual citadel. St. Paul is speaking in military terms.

8. Coming now to the end of the body of his letter, St. Paul summarizes the things he wishes his readers seriously to consider and meditate on. The subjects indicated are quite general, pertaining to pagan morality as well as Christian virtues.

True, i.e., genuine, sincere.

Modest, i.e., becoming, seemly.

Just, i.e., according to the norms of right dealing.

Holy, i.e., pure, elevated, free from debasing elements.

Lovely, i.e., lovable, gracious.

9. The things which you have both learned, and received, and heard, and seen in me, these do ye, and the God of peace shall be with you.

10. Now I rejoice in the Lord exceedingly, that now at length your thought for me hath flourished again, as you did also think; but you were busied.

Of good report, i.e., winning the esteem and approval of men, in the sense of 1 Tim. iii. 7: "He must have a good testimony of them that are without"; and of 2 Cor. viii. 21: "We forecast what may be good not only before God, but also before men."

Virtue, a very general term summing up the first four qualities just named, and found only here in St. Paul. It embraces all that is virtuous in any way.

Praise, also a very general term summing up the last two qualities named above, and meaning, worthy of approbation, praiseworthy. The last two qualities are paraphrased as follows by Lightfoot: "Whatever value may reside in your old heathen conception of virtue, whatever consideration is due to the praise of men."

The *disciplinæ* of the Vulgate is not according to the best Greek MSS.

9. St. Paul has just given his readers ample food for meditation; and, before telling them to put these lofty thoughts into practice, he calls attention to his own example, to what they have seen in him and heard about him from others, in order to make it plain that he is not asking them to do what is too hard or impossible. If they will follow his advice, "the God of peace" will be with them, to help them and to enable them to relish the possession of true tranquillity of soul.

CONCLUSION, 10-23

10-23. Having closed the didactic part of his letter, St. Paul now turns to personal matters. He thanks the Philippians for the gifts they sent him, recalling the privilege they have had in sharing, through their charity, in his labors and afflictions ever since they first had the Gospel preached to them, assuring them that he needs nothing further and that God will repay them in glory. Offering greetings from himself and his companions, he then imparts his blessing.

10. The Apostle rejoices with a holy joy at the gifts the Philip-

11. I speak not as it were for want. For I have learned, in whatsoever state I am, to be content therewith.

12. I know both how to be brought low, and I know how to abound: everywhere, and in all things I am instructed both to be full, and to be hungry; both to abound, and to suffer need.

13. I can do all things in him who strengtheneth me.

14. Nevertheless you have done well in communicating to my tribulation.

pians have sent by Epaphroditus, not so much because they have succored him, but because by their charity they have profited spiritually.

That now at length, etc. Some see in these words a slight rebuke, as if the faithful at Philippi had been guilty of neglect in the Apostle's regard; but the real meaning is that a change for the better in their temporal circumstances or opportunities had enabled them to assist the Apostle once more as they had done in the past; they had the will to help all along, but they had been impeded.

As you did also think, etc., i.e., they did continue to care for him, they wanted to come to his assistance, but opportunity was lacking.

11-13. In these verses the Apostle tells the Philippians that the gladness he experienced over their gifts was not due to his want or to the relief they gave him; for he has learned in the school of Christ to be content wherever he is, or with whatever he has, be it little or much, be he in need or in affluence. He has arrived at this state of spiritual peace and equanimity, not by his own efforts, but by reason of his union with Jesus Christ and the supernatural power given him by his Master: all his strength is from Christ.

I am instructed. Better, "I have been initiated," a phrase often used with reference to pagan mystery cults, initiation into which was a slow and difficult process. It means here that St. Paul through faith, and perhaps by divine revelation, had learned the secret of the peace and contentment of mind which he describes in these verses. The Apostle was well aware of the great truth that it is what a man *is* that he carries into the future life, and that he leaves behind what he *has* here.

14. **Nevertheless.** From what the Apostle had just said the Philippians might conclude that he was not pleased with their gifts, and hence he now praises their liberality.

15. And you also know, Philippians, that in the beginning of the gospel, when I departed from Macedonia, no church communicated with me as concerning giving and receiving, but you only:

16. For unto Thessalonica also you sent once and again for my use.

17. Not that I seek the gift, but I seek the fruit that abounds to your account.

18. But I have all, and abound: I am filled, having received from Epaphroditus the things you sent, an odor of sweetness, an acceptable sacrifice, pleasing to God.

In communicating, etc., i.e., in taking a share in his affliction; because they thus made themselves worthy to have a share also in his rewards.

15-16. He recalls their liberality of the past, which began with the first preaching of the Gospel at Philippi. And this singular honor belongs to the Philippians alone of all the Churches evangelized by St. Paul.

No church communicated with me, etc. The Apostle is here using commercial language, and his meaning is that no other Church gave him material aid in exchange for his spiritual benefits (cf. 1 Cor. ix. 11).

For unto Thessalonica, etc. Scarcely had the Apostle left the Philippians on his way to Greece than they sent him gifts, and that several times, while he was yet in Macedonia (Acts xvii. 1-5). From no other Church, however, did he ever accept aid, as he tells us himself (2 Cor. xi. 7-9).

17. While praising the prompt liberality of the faithful of Philippi, St. Paul here, as in verse 11, is careful to remind them that he is not seeking help for himself, but rather the spiritual benefit of the Philippians; he rejoices at the merits they are gaining by their kind charity.

18. Again he forestalls a possible misunderstanding. In saying that he seeks in the gifts of the Philippians abundant spiritual fruit for them, it might seem to be implied that he wanted them to send him more. Therefore he here assures them that he has all that he needs, and more than he needs.

An odor of sweetness. The alms of the Philippians were not only acceptable to the Apostle, but were also pleasing to God, like a sweet-smelling sacrifice (cf. Gen. viii. 21; Exod. xxix. 18; Ezech. xx. 41).

19. And my God will supply all your want, according to his riches in glory in Christ Jesus.

20. Now to God and our Father be glory world without end. Amen.

21. Salute ye every saint in Christ Jesus.

22. The brethren who are with me, salute you. All the saints salute you; especially, they that are of Cæsar's household.

23. The grace of our Lord Jesus Christ be with your spirit. Amen.

19. The Apostle now assures the Philippians that, in return for their material gifts to him, God will repay them with spiritual treasures; and this, not according to their merits, but "according to his riches," which He will lavish on them "in glory," i.e., in their heavenly home above. "His riches in glory" are the fruit of "the riches of his grace" (Eph. i. 7).

In Christ Jesus, i.e., by reason of their union with Christ.

The *impleat* of the Vulgate should be *implebit*, to agree with the Greek.

20. The words just spoken about the rewards of the Philippians cause the Apostle to break into a doxology in gratitude to the Giver of all good things, who is also "our Father."

Glory. Better, "the glory," as in the Greek, meaning the glory which belongs to God.

World without end is a Hebraism, meaning for all eternity.

Amen, so be it.

21-22. St. Paul sends first his personal salutations to each Christian of the Church at Philippi; then subjoins those of his immediate circle; and finally, those of all the Roman Christians, especially those of "Cæsar's household," who were "probably slaves and freed men attached to the palace" (Lightfoot). The mention of these last personages shows how widespread and powerful was the influence of the Gospel, which had penetrated even into the royal palace.

23. The Apostle concludes his Epistle with his accustomed blessing, which was very likely an autograph.

THE
EPISTLE TO THE COLOSSIANS
INTRODUCTION

I. Colossæ. Colossæ was an ancient city of southwestern
Phrygia in the Roman Province of Asia. It was situated in the valley of the Lycus River about one hundred and twenty miles east
from Ephesus and on the great highway of trade between the East
and the West of the ancient world. At one time it enjoyed considerable importance, but declined with the foundation and growth of
Laodicea, some ten miles to the west, about the middle of the third
century B.C. Besides the wealth and prosperity which developed
in the closely adjacent Laodicea, other factors which contributed to
the decline and ruin of Colossæ were the earthquakes that repeatedly
shook it and the fame and attractiveness of Hierapolis, the Sacred
City, situated only thirteen miles to the northwest. Hierapolis, the
birthplace of the Stoic philosopher Epictetus and the later residence
of the Apostle Philip of Bethsaida, was a pleasure and health resort
and a centre of pagan worship.

In the time of St. Paul Colossæ was but a small town or mere
village, lacking any special industry or commercial importance. Its
inhabitants, therefore (largely Phrygian, intermingled with Greeks
and some Jews), had more leisure time than was wholesome for their
spiritual welfare: they talked and speculated too much, and so developed some erroneous doctrines by attempting to express Christian
ideas in the terms and forms of philosophic and religious thought
then current in Phrygia and in Asia Minor generally. Repeated
raids and devastations by the Saracens during the seventh and eighth
centuries completed the destruction of Colossæ and the town became a heap of ruins. Nothing remains of it now. The Lycus
still flows through the valley, but the city once overhanging it on
the upper part of its course, and forever distinguished by the letter
of St. Paul, has long ago ceased to exist.

II. The Church of Colossæ. Since in the time of St. Paul the town of Colossæ was far inferior in wealth, population and general importance to the neighboring cities of Laodicea and Hierapolis, one may naturally ask why he addressed an Epistle thither. It was doubtless the least important place to which the Apostle ever wrote any of his letters that have come down to us. Nor had he ever been there himself, as seems clear from Col. i. 4, 6-8, ii. 1. In his journeys from the East through Asia Minor to the West it appears that he always kept to the "upper coasts" (Acts xix. 1), following the Cayster route, which was shorter, and so easier for foot travellers like himself. Why, then, this Epistle to Colossæ, and not to Laodicea or Hierapolis? The obvious and chief explanation seems to lie in the fact that Colossæ was the home of Epaphras, Philemon and Onesimus, three special friends of St. Paul. Political and commercial relations were close between Colossæ and Ephesus, and it must be that Epaphras and Philemon had come in contact with Paul and had been converted by him early during the Apostle's sojourn in the latter city. These two then carried the faith back to Colossæ, their own city. In fact, it seems clear from Col. i. 7, 8 that Epaphras became the founder of the Church in his native town; and from Phlm. 2, 3 it is plain that Philemon actively co-operated in propagating the new religion, even lending the use of his own house for the gatherings of the faithful. Onesimus, Philemon's runaway slave, met St. Paul in Rome, and was converted by him shortly before the writing of this Epistle.

Moreover, the errors combated in this Epistle, though doubtless not confined to Colossæ, appear to have been especially prevalent there, owing to its situation on the great highway of trade, and in particular to the comparatively leisurely life of its people. It is true that Laodicea was similarly situated, but its much greater population and intensive life of business allowed less time for the simmering of new thoughts and new ideas and the development of fanciful theories in religious matters. But the letter to Colossæ and the ministry of Epaphras were by no means to be confined to the one town, but were to be extended to Laodicea and to the whole Lycus valley. It is reasonably certain that Epaphras evangelized that entire district, for St. Paul expressly says of him: "I bear him testimony that he hath much labor for you, and for them that are at Laodicea, and them at Hierapolis" (Col. iv. 13). St. Paul also expressly ordered that this letter be read in the Church of Laodicea (Col. iv. 16).

Another reason why this letter was sent to Colossæ, rather than to the larger and more important city of Laodicea, is that very probably our Epistle to the Ephesians was in reality sent to the Laodiceans, and that St. Paul was referring to it in Col. iv. 16. This probability we have already discussed in the *Introduction* to Ephesians, No. IV.

III. The Occasion and Purpose of This Letter. From what has been said already, we can see how the new religion was likely to spread apace in Colossæ, and how, owing to the character of its mixed population, there might be dangers to the purity and integrity of the faith there. And so it happened, as a matter of fact. Conditions became in a few years so serious that, when St. Paul was a prisoner in Rome the first time, Epaphras, the founder and head of the Church of Colossæ (Col. i. 7, 8, iv. 12, 13), deemed it necessary to go all the way to the Eternal City for the purpose of explaining the situation to the great leader and master.

Of course, the report given by Epaphras of Colossian conditions was not at all one of entire complaint and apprehensiveness; for the charity and faith of the Church as a whole were sufficiently encouraging to evoke St. Paul's express commendation (Col. i. 8, ii. 5). But false teachers had appeared and were sowing the seeds of doctrines which, if not checked, would imperil the faith they had received in its purity from their founder and his co-workers.

Just who these false teachers were and what their doctrines were in detail it is extremely difficult to determine; a multitude of conflicting opinions have been advanced. From the Epistle (Col. ii. 8-23), however, we can gather the main outlines of the errors in question. In the first place, there were Judaizers who, perhaps claiming a higher way of perfection, wished to introduce the observance of the Law of Moses and rabbinical traditions, such as the ordinances regarding Sabbaths, new moons, etc., and the prohibition to eat, drink, taste, or even touch certain things, on the assumption that matter is evil. On the other hand, there were errors of a semi-Gnostic type tending to detract from the dignity of Christ, holding that the angels were superior or at least equal to Him, and that we must have access to God through them. All these errors were of Jewish origin, as the best Catholic and non-Catholic scholars agree, and as is plain from the allusions to Jewish observances, feasts, regulations, and the like.

Now, St. Paul wrote the present letter to correct such pernicious teachings and to give the faithful of Colossæ a true conception of Christian life and practice, based on a correct understanding of the relation of Christ to God, to the universe, and to the Church. This he does first by a clear presentation of the true doctrine about Christ, which robbed the false teachers of the very foundation of their errors. Christ, he says, is our Redeemer and Saviour; He is the image of the invisible God; all things have been made in Him and by Him, and all consist in Him; He is the first-born from the dead, the head of the Church, and He exercises primacy over all things; He is the universal Mediator through whom alone peace and recon- ciliation have come to all; He is the explanation and the consum- mation of all God's dealings and mysterious dispensations and the hope of our future glory (Col. i. 14-27); in Christ, finally, are hid all the treasures of wisdom and knowledge (Col. ii. 3-7). Thus, by a positive teaching of the truth does St. Paul attempt, in the first place, to correct the false doctrines that were spreading among the faithful of Colossæ. His method of correction, in the second place, is by attacking more directly their errors, showing the futility and emptiness of a false ethical system which they vainly tried to dignify as a "philosophy" (Col. ii. 8-23). All this will more clearly appear from an examination of the contents of the Epistle.

IV. **Analysis of Contents.** The Epistle to the Colossians is divided into four parts: an introduction (i. 1-8), a dogmatico- polemical part (i. 9—ii. 23), a moral part (iii. 1—iv. 6), and a conclusion (iv. 7-18).

A. INTRODUCTION (i. 1-8). Following his customary form of salu- tation (i. 1, 2), St. Paul assures his readers of his prayers of thanks- giving to God upon the report he has received of their Christian virtues of faith in Christ, of love towards one another, and of hope arising out of the Gospel preached to them (i. 1-5). The world- wide message has come to them, as to others, and has borne fruit, following the preaching of it by Epaphras, the Apostle's faithful minister, who has now brought this good news to Rome (i. 6-8).

B. DOGMATICO-POLEMICAL PART (i. 9—ii. 23). The report given by Epaphras has enabled St. Paul to give his prayers for the Colossians the needed direction. Hence he begins by praying that they may receive a fuller knowledge of God's will and eternal purpose, in order that they may live more holy lives; for, as this knowledge deepens, their lives will become spiritually more fruitful (i. 9, 10). The strength to do this will come from God Himself (i. 11). For the children of God share the light that is every Christian's inheritance; and from the darkness in which once they lived God has transferred them into the kingdom of His own beloved Son, through whom we have been redeemed and delivered from our sins (i. 12-14).

The Apostle next speaks of the person of Christ and of His supreme dignity (a) with respect to the invisible God, of whom He is the eternal image, (b) with respect to all creation, of which He is the first-born, the source, the creator, and the head, and (c) with respect to the Church, His redeemed creation, of which He is the beginning and mystical head through His death on the cross (i. 15-20). May the Colossians, therefore, once dead in sin and enemies of God but now sharing in the graces of Christ's redemption, strive to lead blameless lives, which will be possible only if they hold fast to the faith they have received which is preached everywhere, and of which the Apostle is in a special sense the minister (i. 21-23) !

The reference to the share in Christ which the Colossians now enjoy induces St. Paul to explain to them his own part in this divine work. His very sufferings, united to those of Christ, help to further the work of the Church; and his relation to his readers is a part of God's plan for their salvation (i. 24, 25). This union of Christians with Christ is a mystery, before hidden but now revealed to all the faithful, and extended beyond the Jews to the Gentile world (i. 26, 27). This is the message which Paul is commissioned to preach, not to a privileged few, but to every man, to all the world; and it is for this that he labors through the power God gives him (i. 28, 29). St. Paul writes thus of his labors that the Colossians may understand his interest in them and in those that have never seen him, and to explain why he prays for their enlightenment (ii. 1-3). He warns them against a specious error (ii. 4) ; he is with them in spirit, and he rejoices too to know of the steadfastness of their faith in Christ (ii. 5). Let them, therefore, continue to advance in the faith they have been taught, fixed and unwavering, and be ever more thankful for it (ii. 6, 7).

So far the Apostle has been refuting the false teaching at Colossæ by a positive statement of the truth. Now he will attack more explicitly the errors that endanger them. These are partly dogmatic and speculative (ii. 8-15), partly practical (ii. 16-23). Let the Colossians not be deceived by systems which, claiming the plausible name of "philosophy," are wholly of this world, and not according to Christ, in whom dwells the fullness of divinity and from whom the Colossians have received all the spiritual benefits they enjoy (ii. 8-15).

False doctrines at Colossæ have naturally been followed by false practices. The new teachers have been insisting on Jewish legal observances, which have no longer any value for Christians (ii. 16, 17) ; they have been teaching a false humility and a wrong cult of angels, forgetting that Christ is the head of all (ii. 18, 19) ; and the practical asceticism they have been inculcating is useless and vain (ii. 20-23).

C. MORAL PART (iii. 1—iv. 6). Basing his teachings on the principles just laid down in the dogmatic part of his letter, St. Paul now begins to treat of the duties of the Christian life in general (iii. 1-17) and in particular (iii. 18—iv. 1), after which follow some leading precepts addressed to all the faithful (iv. 2-6).

Those who have become Christians ought to live for heaven, in union with their risen Lord, awaiting His second coming in glory (iii. 1-4). They should, therefore, put off the old man of sin with his evil deeds, and put on the new man of grace, growing more and more into the likeness of Christ, and into a state where there is no longer any distinction of nationality or class, but where Christ is supreme over all (iii. 5-11). This new man includes the practice of the gentler virtues, and especially of charity and a good intention in all we do (iii. 12-17).

In the next place the Apostle gives particular directions for various relationships of life—for wives and husbands (iii. 18, 19), for children and parents (iv. 20, 21), for servants and masters (iii. 22—iv. 1). Some general counsels addressed to all the faithful, especially as regards prayer and prudence, terminate the moral part of the Epistle (iv. 2-6).

D. CONCLUSION (iv. 7-18). The letter closes with a commendation of Tychicus and Onesimus, the messengers by whom it was sent to Colossæ (iv. 7-9), a number of personal salutations (iv. 10-15), some recommendations (iv. 16, 17), and a blessing (iv. 18).

V. **Authorship and Integrity of Colossians.** The genuineness of the Epistle was never questioned until Meyerhoff and Baur in the first part of the nineteenth century began to raise objections to it. Antiquity was unanimous in its favor. It was expressly attributed to St. Paul by the Canon of Muratori, and was quoted by Justin Martyr, by St. Irenæus, by Clement of Alexandria, by Origen, and by Tertullian. It is found in the first collections of St. Paul's Epistles, and in the early versions, like the Itala and the Peshitto. Marcion included it in his Canon, and the Valentinians and other early heretics quoted it as Scripture. There are traces of it in Clement of Rome, in the Epistle of Barnabas, in St. Ignatius and St. Theophilus of Antioch, in Polycarp, etc.

As to later and recent writers, it can be said that the authenticity of this Epistle has been admitted, not only by all Catholics, but also by the best Protestant and rationalistic scholars, such as Weiss, Godet, von Soden, Jülicher, Harnack, Zahn, Lightfoot, Sanday, Moffatt, Adeney, etc. In short, the external arguments in favor of Colossians are so strong, and they are so thoroughly supported by the internal evidence, that the objections brought forward by a few critics, like Meyerhoff, Holtzmann and Baur, have found scant favor even in the most radical circles. For example, to attempt to find difficulties against the authorship of this letter on the ground that its style differs in certain places and in some respects from that of earlier Epistles, or that it contains certain terms not found elsewhere in St. Paul, or that the Christology is here more highly developed, or that the errors dealt with must have been of later date, or that this letter is too similar to Ephesians to have been written by the same author—to advance these and such like objections is to ignore or to set at naught all the facts in the case as disclosed to us by everything we know about St. Paul himself, with his rich and versatile character and command of language, about the occasion and purpose of this letter, about the development and history of

Gnosticism in its Judaic and Greek forms, and about the time, place of composition, circumstances, etc., of the Epistles to the Ephesians and the Colossians.

In this connection the student may read what we have said on the authorship of Ephesians, for there things have been discussed that are pertinent here.

Nothing of any great moment can be said against the integrity of this letter, though Dr. Hort believes that Chapter II has not come down to us entirely uncorrupted; and this seems likely, especially with regard to ii. 18, 23, where the readings are so many and so difficult. In conclusion, therefore, we may say with Dr. Sanday and the best modern authorities that Colossians is distinguished by an unbreakable unity and a genuine Pauline character.

VI. **Date and Place of Composition.** These questions have been sufficiently treated under the same heading in our *Introduction* to Ephesians. As said there, the connection between the Ephesian Epistle and those to the Colossians and Philemon is extremely close. The literary affinity between the first two is remarkable. Tychicus is the bearer of both of them, and he is accompanied by Onesimus, who is carrying the letter to Philemon (Eph. vi. 21; Col. iv. 7-9). The same persons send greetings in Colossians and Philemon, namely, Aristarchus, Mark, Epaphras, Luke and Demas. In fact, all the proper names that occur in the letter to Philemon are found also in the Epistle to the Colossians, with the exception of Philemon himself and Appia, most probably his wife. Philemon is not greeted in Colossians because a separate letter had been addressed to him at the same time. Hence it seems beyond doubt that these three letters must have been written from the same place and about the same time, that is, from Rome, while St. Paul was in prison there, 61-63 A.D. See *Introduction* to Ephesians.

BIBLIOGRAPHY

Besides the commentaries on this Epistle already mentioned in the Bibliography for Ephesians, we call attention to the following among Catholics: Messmer, *Erklärung des Kolosser-briefes* (Brixen, 1863) ; Henle, *Kolossa und der Brief des Apostels Paulus an die Kolosser* (Munich, 1887) ; Sales, in *La Sacra Bibbia*, vol. II (Turin, 1914).

Among non-Catholics we have those already given in the Bibliography for Ephesians and Philippians, namely, von Soden, Abbott, and Shaw; and in addition we have Bleek, *Vorlesungen über den Briefe an die Kolosser, Philemon* (Berlin, 1865) ; von Hofmann, *Die Briefe Pauli an die Kolosser und an Philemon* (1870) ; Klopper, *Der Brief an die Kolosser* (Berlin, 1882) ; Maclaren, *The Epistle to the Colossians* (London, 1887) ; Lightfoot, *St. Paul's Epistles to the Colossians and to Philemon* (8th ed., London, 1892) ; Moule, *The Epistles of St. Paul the Apostle to the Colossians and to Philemon,* in *The Cambridge Bible for Schools and Colleges* (Cambridge, 1906) ; Williams, *The Epistle to the Coloss.* (Cambridge, 1907) ; Crafer, *Colossians and Philemon,* in *A New Comm. on Holy Script.* (New York, 1928) ; Dodd, *Colossians and Philemon,* in *Abingdon Bible Comm.* (New York, 1929).

The Epistle to The Colossians

CHAPTER I

1. Paul, an apostle of Jesus Christ, by the will of God, and Timothy the brother,
2. To the saints and faithful brethren in Christ, who are at Colossæ.
3. Grace be to you and peace from God our Father and from the Lord Jesus Christ. We give thanks to God, and the Father of our Lord Jesus Christ, praying always for you,

1-8. Following his customary form, St. Paul, in company with Timothy, salutes the faithful of Colossæ, assuring them of his constant prayers of thanksgiving to God in their behalf on account of their faith in Christ, their charity towards one another, and the consequent reward awaiting them hereafter. This hope of future blessedness came to them with the preaching of the Gospel truth; and with them as elsewhere, from the time of its first preaching, this worldwide message of salvation has yielded a great spiritual harvest. It was Epaphras, Paul's beloved comrade, who preached the Gospel to the Colossians, and who has now brought news of them to him in Rome.

1-2. For a nearly identical greeting see Eph. i. 1.

Timothy. See *Introduction* to 1 Tim., No. I. Timothy was associated with Paul at this time in Rome, and probably he wrote down this letter as the Apostle dictated it.

Faithful brethren, i.e., fellow-Christians, who were full of active, living faith.

Colossæ. See *Introduction*, No. I.

In the Vulgate of verse 2 *Jesu* should be omitted, as in the Greek.

3. **Grace be to you and peace,** etc. See on the same sentence in Eph. i. 2.

4. Hearing your faith in Christ Jesus, and the love which you have towards all the saints,

5. For the hope that is laid up for you in heaven, which you have heard in the word of the truth of the gospel,

6. Which is come unto you, as also it is in the whole world, and bringeth forth fruit and groweth, even as it doth in you, since the day you heard and knew the grace of God in truth.

7. As you learned of Epaphras, our beloved fellow-servant, who is for you a faithful minister of Christ,

8. Who also hath manifested to us your love in the Spirit.

And from the Lord Jesus Christ. There is nearly equal MSS. evidence for the omission or the retention of this phrase here, which is found in Eph. i. 2.

We give thanks, etc. The meaning is that, as often as he and Timothy prayed, they gave thanks to God for the Colossians' life of faith and love; or that, as often as they prayed for the Colossians, they thanked God for the spiritual benefits the latter enjoyed.

4. The reason for his prayer of thanksgiving is now assigned, namely, the Colossians' faith in Christ and their charity to their brethren.

Hearing, from Epaphras (ver. 8).

5-6. **For the hope,** etc., i.e., on account of the hope, etc. There is question here, not of *hope,* but of the *object* of hope, of the thing hoped for, the reward awaiting the faithful life hereafter; and so it is disputed whether St. Paul is thanking God for the reward in store for the virtues and good works of the Colossians, as well as for their faith and love, or whether this hoped-for reward is the basis and motive of their active faith and love. The former explanation seems to be the meaning here (cf. Knabenhauer, *hoc loco*).

Which you have heard, etc. Better, "whereof you have heard, etc."

In the word, etc., i.e., in the announcement or preaching of the Gospel which was given them (ver. 6), and which everywhere in the whole Roman world is a growing and fruit-bearing seed, as it has been with them ever since they first "heard and knew" (i.e., understood and recognized) "the grace of God" (i.e., the contents of the Gospel) "in truth" (i.e., as it is in reality).

7-8. **Epaphras,** a resident and perhaps also a native of Colossæ;

and, if not the founder of the Church there, at least one of the chief workers in it. He is mentioned below in iv. 12 and in Phlm. 23. Tradition makes him the first Bishop of Colossæ. It is unlikely that he is to be identified with Epaphroditus, spoken of in Phil. ii. 25, iv. 18, though his name is an abbreviation of the latter's.

Fellow-servant, i.e., companion in the service of Christ, who preached the Gospel at Colossæ, and who now has brought to Paul and his companions in Rome a report of the love the Colossians have for them.

The *Jesus* of the Vulgate (ver. 7) is not in the Greek.

DOGMATICO-POLEMICAL PART OF THE EPISTLE, i. 9—ii. 23

i. 9—ii. 23. The Apostle prays that the Colossians may grow in knowledge of God's will and purpose in their regard, so as to be able to increase correspondingly the spiritual fruitfulness of their lives, aided by the strength He gives them. They must thank the Eternal Father who has made them members of His kingdom through the redemption wrought by His Son (i. 9-14).

He next describes the person and work of Christ, who is the image of the unseen God, the Creator of all things, the Head of the Church, and the Saviour by whose redemptive merits all things have been reconciled to the Father (i. 15-20). May the Colossians show in their conduct the benefit of the redemption they have received by leading holy and blameless lives, which will be possible only if they hold fast to the faith preached to them, of which Paul is the minister (i. 21-23)!

The Apostle then explains his sufferings for Christ and his commission to preach to the whole world God's age-old mystery, now made manifest to Christians through Christ, of uniting Jews and Gentiles in the one Church of Christ (i. 24-29). This is why he prays for the unity, charity, and purity of faith of the Colossians, Laodiceans, and all who have not seen his face (ii. 1-7).

Let the Colossians be on their guard against false teachers among them, whose erroneous speculations will lead them away from Christ, their true head and redeemer (ii. 8-15), and will plunge

9. Therefore we also, from the day that we heard it, cease not to pray for you, and to beg that you may be filled with the knowledge of his will, in all wisdom, and spiritual understanding:

10. That you may walk worthy of the Lord in all things pleasing: being fruitful in every good work, and increasing in the knowledge of God:

11. Strengthened with all might, according to the power of his glory, unto all patience and long-suffering with joy,

12. Giving thanks to the Father, who hath made us worthy to be partakers of the lot of the saints in light:

them into practices that are useless, false, and vain (ii. 16-23). See *Introduction*, No. IV, B.

THE APOSTLE'S PRAYER FOR THE COLOSSIANS, 9-14

9-14. The report of the Colossians given to St. Paul by Epaphras has enabled the Apostle properly to direct his prayers for them. Accordingly he prays that they may receive a clearer knowledge of the divine will and purpose, to the end that they may lead lives more pleasing to God and more fruitful in good works, thus manifesting the results of the blessings of redemption they have received.

9. **Therefore,** i.e., in view of the report given by Epaphras in the preceding verses 4-8.

We heard it, i.e., heard of their faith in Christ (ver. 4).

Cease not to pray, etc., means to pray frequently, as in Rom. i. 9; 1 Thess. i. 2, ii. 13, v. 17; 2 Tim. i. 3.

Wisdom is such an illumination of the mind as to enable the judgment to go back to the supreme cause of things, and, thus enlightened, to direct particular things to their proper ends (Cajetan).

Understanding is that perception of things which enables us rightly to grasp their nature and character, and thence to formulate rules for action. The term "spiritual" here qualifies both wisdom and understanding, showing the Spirit of God to be the source of both.

10. This verse gives the purpose of the gifts just requested for the Colossians.

The *Deo* of the Vulgate should be *Domino*, according to the Greek.

11. Besides a deeper knowledge of God's will and divine mysteries, the Apostle asks that the Colossians may also be strengthened

13. Who delivered us from the power of darkness, and translated us into the kingdom of the Son of his love,

14. In whom we have redemption, the remission of sins;

from on high, so as to be able to resist all their temptations and bear all their trials.

According to the power of his glory, i.e., in a manner worthy of His supreme nature as manifesting itself.

Unto all patience, etc., i.e., the effect of the divine power implored is to enable the faithful to bear their suffering and trials with a spirit of holy endurance and perseverance, and with a joyful heart. The phrase "with joy" more properly belongs to what immediately precedes than to what follows.

In the Vulgate we should read *in omnem patientiam et longanimitatem,* to agree with the Greek.

Giving thanks to the Father, etc., as becomes dutiful and grateful children whom the heavenly Father, the fountain and source of all blessings, has admitted to a share in the glorious inheritance of the saints, which is a life of grace here and eternal beatitude hereafter. This kingdom to which we are admitted in Baptism is "in light," as opposed to the kingdom of darkness over which Satan presides (Eph. v. 8, vi. 12; I Thess. v. 5; Rom. xiii. 12).

The *Deo* of the Vulgate is not in the Greek.

13-14. These verses show how the Father has made us Christians "worthy to be partakers of the lot of the saints in light." It was by delivering us from the power of sin and Satan and making us members of the kingdom of His beloved Son, through the redeeming blood of that same divine Son.

Power of darkness, i.e., the dominion of Satan who rules that part of the world which has not been regenerated by Christ.

Delivered . . . translated. These verbs are aorist in Greek, the first expressing the negative and the second the positive aspect of the one and same process of regeneration and sanctification.

Kingdom means the Church Militant.

Son of his love is a Hebraism meaning beloved Son.

Per sanguinem eius of the Vulgate is not according to the best Greek MSS.; it was perhaps introduced here from Eph. i. 7, which see.

15. Who is the image of the invisible God, the first-born of every creature:
16. For in him were all things created in heaven and on earth, visible and invisible, whether thrones, or dominations or principalities, or powers—all things were created by him and unto him.

THE SUPREME DIGNITY OF CHRIST, 15-23

15-23. In the preceding verses St. Paul has shown, against the false teachers who were trying to pervert the Colossians, what great blessings we owe to our Lord. And now in this section he goes further, and shows that Christ is the image of the invisible God, anterior to all creation; the Son in whom and by whom all things were created and are sustained. And not only is the Son the head of the universe, but He is also, in a very special manner, the head of the Church; in Him dwells the fullness of Divinity, and through His sacrificial death on the cross all things have been reconciled to the Father (ver. 18-20). The Colossians are included in this redemption, for they were formerly enemies of God, but have now been reconciled to the Father through the atoning death of the Son. The goal of this reconciliation was that they might be spotless before God here and now; and this they will continue to be, if only they hold fast to the faith which they have received, which is the same everywhere, and of which Paul is the minister (ver. 21-23) .

15. Verses 15-20 here are the most important part of the present Epistle. They constitute a compendium of Christology, and, taken in conjunction with Eph. i. 20-23, Phil. ii. 6-11 and Heb. i. 1 ff., they represent St. Paul's most sublime writings relative to the person and dignity of Christ (Sales, *hoc loco*).

Who is the image, etc., i.e., the inward utterance and perfect expression of His Father, the Word of God (Rickaby, *h. l.*). Christ is the substantial and perfect image of the Eternal Father, having the same divine nature and essence and having been begotten as the Eternal Son of the Father from eternity: "Philip, he that seeth me, seeth the Father also" (John xiv. 9).

The first-born of every creature, i.e., born of the Eternal Father from eternity, as is clear from the two following verses.

16. That the Son was begotten before all ages, before anything was created or made, is now proved; "for in him," as effects are in their cause, "were all things created," i.e., produced and brought

17. And he is before all, and in him all things consist.

18. And he is the head of the body, the church, who is the beginning, the first-born from the dead; that in all things he may hold the primacy;

into being; which shows that He existed prior to and above all creation, all succession, all becoming.

In heaven and on earth, etc., i.e., everything in the whole created universe was made by the Son. To emphasize his doctrine against the false teachers who were denying Divinity to the Son and maintaining a chain of angelic mediators between God and the world, the Apostle repeats at the end of the verse that "all things were created by him," as by their first cause, "and unto him" (εἰς αὐτόν), i.e., for Him, as their final cause and goal.

Thrones, dominations, etc. See on Eph. i. 21.

17. To stress the pre-existence and pre-eminence as well as the creative power of Christ, the Apostle here repeats against the false teachers that the Son was prior and superior to all created things, and that all were not only created by Him, but are maintained in their existence by Him.

Consist. Better, "stand together," hang together, cohere; all things were created by the Word, and all continue in existence and are conserved by Him.

The Vulgate *ante omnes* should be *ante omnia*, denoting all creation, as in the Greek.

18. Christ is not only the creator and conserver of all things in the universe, but He is also the creator of the new spiritual order of things inasmuch as He has repaired and redeemed all things; for He is the Founder and Head of that mystical body which is His Church (see on Eph. i. 22).

Who is the beginning, i.e., the efficient cause and creator of that organization which is the Church; He is the fountain and author of grace and glory.

The first-born from the dead, i.e., the first in time to be raised from death to a glorious and immortal life, thus becoming the principle and model of the final resurrection of all who belong to Him. Just above, in ver. 15-16, it was said that Christ was the "first-born" of all things in general, that is, the creator of all, and here it is said that He is the "first-born" of His redeemed creation. In both orders, the natural and the supernatural, He holds "the primacy" of power and dignity; He is the creator of all things in the natural

19. Because in him, it hath well pleased *the Father,* that all the fullness should dwell;

20. And through him to reconcile all things unto himself, making peace through the blood of his cross, both as to the things that are on earth, and the things that are in heaven.

order, and He is the redeemer and saviour of all in the supernatural order of grace and glory.

19. Here and in the following verse the Apostle further shows how the Word holds the primacy in all things. First, "because in him, etc.," i.e., at the time of the Incarnation it pleased the Father, or God, that "all the fullness" of Divinity, and consequently of grace and truth (John i. 14), through the hypostatic union of the divine and human natures in the one Person of the Word, should take up its permanent abode in Christ.

The Father is not expressed in Greek, but it is most natural to take it as the subject of the verb "hath well pleased" in view of the subject in verses 12 and 13 and the context of verses 15-18.

Fullness, i.e., plenitude, totality—"the fullness of the Godhead," as it is expressed in ii. 9 below. See on Eph. i. 23.

Should dwell. The Greek implies permanency of dwelling.

20. In the second place, it has pleased God the Father "through him" (i.e., through Christ) "to reconcile all things unto himself" (cf. Rom. v. 10; 2 Cor. v. 18, 19). These references to Rom. and 2 Cor. show that we should understand εἰς αὐτόν here to mean the Father rather than the Son.

Making peace through the blood of his cross. The meaning is that through the sacrificial death of the Son on the cross peace was effected with the Eternal Father (cf. Rom. v. 1).

Both as to the things that are on the earth, etc. See on Eph. i. 10. The Apostle is stressing the point here, against the false teachers at Colossæ, that Christ is the one and only medium of reconciling with the Father all things, spiritual and material, human and angelic. Men, indeed, needed reconciliation in the strict sense of the word; but as regards the material creation and the angelic world see on Eph. i. 10. Here, however, there is no question of reconciling men and angels with one another, but of reconciling all with God the Father. Therefore, to explain how the sacrificial death of Christ effected reconciliation and peace between the angelic world and the Father some have had recourse to the meaning of

21. And you, whereas you were some time alienated and enemies in mind in evil works,

22. Yet now he hath reconciled you in the body of his flesh through death, to present you holy and unspotted, and blameless before him:

23. If so ye continue in the faith, grounded and settled, and immovable from the hope of the gospel which you have heard, which is preached in all the creation that is under heaven, whereof I Paul am made a minister.

Eph. iii. 10, and explain the difficulty in the sense of that passage. Thus, men are really cleansed and restored to divine favor, while angels acquire greater knowledge and joy as a result of man's salvation (so Knabenbauer, *h. l.*). Others think that reconciliation, as applied here to angelic beings, must be taken in a wide sense, meaning that Christ's propitiation brought the world of angels into closer union with God, thus making them less alien than they had been before that august event (so Alford, Moule, etc.).

21-22. In verses 21-23 St. Paul applies to the Colossians what he has been saying in general regarding the redemptive work of Christ. Formerly, in their pagan state, they also had been alienated from God; their mental attitude was hostile to Him, as was proved by their evil deeds. But now they have been reconciled to the Father through the atoning sufferings and death on the cross of God's only Son.

In the body of his flesh, etc., i.e., in His own mortal, passible body, as distinguished from His mystical body, the Church: "For God indeed was in Christ, reconciling the world to himself, etc." (2 Cor. v. 19).

To present you holy, etc. The purpose of this reconciliation was the sanctification of the Colossians, so that they might appear in the sight of God here and now free from vice of every kind and adorned with all virtues.

23. Here the Apostle tells the Colossians that they will continue in their holy state only if they preserve unsullied the faith which they have received from Epaphras, and which is the same as that preached everywhere else by St. Paul and his disciples.

Grounded and settled, etc. See on Eph. iii. 17.

The hope of the Gospel, which is eternal salvation.

Which is preached, etc. St. Paul wants to assure the Colossians that the Gospel they have heard is the same as the authentic Gospel preached elsewhere.

24. Now I rejoice in my sufferings for you, and fill up those things that are wanting of the sufferings of Christ, in my flesh, for his body, which is the church,

Whereof I am made the minister. Some think these words were added to show the identity between the Gospel preached by Paul and that delivered by Epaphras; but it is more likely that they were intended as a link between what the Apostle has been saying and what he is about to say regarding his work in behalf of the pagans.

THE APOSTLE'S COMMISSION, 24-29

24-29. Paul tells the Colossians that he is suffering on their account, but that this is a source of joy to him since his afflictions help the Church to contribute her part toward the sufferings of Christ; for God has commissioned him a servant of the Church for the purpose of making known the long-hidden mystery that Gentiles, as well as Jews, are to be embraced in the one Church of Christ, thus becoming heirs of heavenly glory. This is the universal doctrine St. Paul proclaims, laboring and striving with the help of divine power.

24. The *qui* of the Vulgate at the beginning of this verse is not supported by the best Greek MSS. St. Paul will explain in the verses that follow (up to ii. 3 inclusive), why he is writing to a Church he has not founded, nor ever visited.

Now I rejoice, etc. The Apostle is in prison for preaching to pagans the same Gospel that the Colossians have received, and he rejoices on their behalf, because of the spiritual benefits his afflictions bring to them and to the Church.

Fill up those things, etc. Better, "fill up on my part ($\dot{a}\nu\tau a\nu a\pi\lambda\eta\rho\hat{\omega}$) those things, etc." The Apostle does not mean to say that his labors and sufferings on behalf of the Gospel added anything to the efficacy and satisfactory value of Christ's atoning sacrifice and death on the cross, which, being superabundant and infinite, were more than sufficient for the redemption of all mankind, and of many more worlds than ours (St. Thomas). But by "the sufferings of Christ" he means here the fatigue, labors, persecutions, and the like, endured by our Lord in His public life and ministry, which, as they were the lot of Christ, the head, during His brief mortal

25. Whereof I am made a minister according to the dispensation of God, which is given me towards you, that I may fulfill the word of God,

26. The mystery which hath been hidden from ages and generations, but now is manifested to his saints,

existence, must also be the lot of His mystical body, the Church, till the end of time; it is these sufferings of Christ's mystical body that must be supplied by the Apostles and their true followers throughout the history of the Church. Our Lord labored, preached and suffered for a time for the spread of the Gospel, and His Church must continue through its ministers to labor, to preach and to suffer for all time for the same purpose, thus vicariously supplying to the ministry of Christ what was not possible for our Lord in person to supply. This is the obvious and natural meaning of this great passage. But the Greek Fathers explain it otherwise. Admitting that the passion of our Lord was entirely sufficient to save all mankind, they hold that its fruits are not applied to all except through the sufferings of the saints; and hence what is "wanting of the sufferings of Christ" is their application through the trials and tribulations which the Apostles and the faithful endured and continue to endure for Christ's sake and in union with Him.

In my flesh, i.e., in St. Paul's own body. The Apostle endured in his own body and person many grievous sufferings and afflictions for the sake of the Gospel and the Church.

25. **Whereof,** i.e., on behalf of which, namely, the Church, he has been "made a minister," or servant, "according to the dispensation," or stewardship, committed to him by God Himself for the benefit of the Colossians, as of all other pagans. The Colossians were embraced by Paul's ministry, for to him it was given to "fulfill the word of God," i.e., to spread the teachings of the Gospel, to found Churches etc. everywhere, especially among the Gentiles (Rom. xv. 19; 1 Cor. xiv. 36; 2 Cor. ii. 7), that he might "present every man perfect in Christ Jesus" (ver. 28).

26. **The mystery,** i.e., the "word of God," or the teaching of the Gospel, spoken of in the preceding verse. This mystery, or secret, undiscoverable by natural means, was the salvation of all men, Gentiles as well as Jews, through Christ and the revelation made by Him, and the union of all men in the one Church of Christ. See on Eph. iii. 2-9.

To his saints, i.e., the faithful, both of Jewish and pagan origin.

27. To whom God hath willed to make known the riches of the glory of this ministery among the Gentiles, which is Christ in you, the hope of glory.

28. Whom we preach, admonishing every man, and teaching every man in all wisdom, that we may present every man perfect in Christ Jesus.

27. To whom God hath willed, etc. These words show that the revelation of the great secret was a free and gratuitous act on the part of God.

The riches of the glory, etc., i.e., the wealth of divine goodness and mercy which has been manifested in the conversion of the Gentiles even more than in that of the Jews, for the latter had a revelation of the Messiah to come and of a future life.

Which is Christ, i.e., this mystery or the riches of this mystery is all in Christ, in whom are contained all the divine counsels regarding human salvation and all the blessings promised to man.

In you, i.e., among you, and in your hearts by faith (Eph. ii. 12 ff.).

The hope of glory, i.e., Christ is their and our hope of glory and eternal beatitude; He is the author and source of all good for time and eternity.

In the Vulgate there should be no comma after *Christus,* but one may be placed after *vobis.*

28. Such is the Christ whom St. Paul and his companions preach, the sole and all-sufficient author and means of salvation here and of future blessedness hereafter, whose hidden mystery has been made known to all men for the salvation of all. The Apostle is criticizing the false teachers at Colossæ who were insisting on the necessity of legal prescriptions, on an exaggerated cult of angels, and on an initiation into perfection which was confined to a select few.

Every man. St. Paul repeats these words three times in this verse in order to stress the universality of salvation for all, Gentiles as well as Jews.

In all wisdom may mean, (a) that St. Paul and his helpers corrected faults and explained doctrine with all the knowledge with which they were endowed, or (b) that they disciplined and instructed every man in a perfect knowledge of God, so as to enable each one to live a life worthy of God.

That we may present, etc. The scope of Apostolic discipline

29. Wherein also I labor, striving according to his working which he worketh in me in power.

and teaching was to make every man perfect in the faith and love of Christ.

29. Here the Apostle tells us that the end and purpose of all his labors and struggles, like those of an athlete in the arena, was to render every man perfect in Christ, and that the secret of his endurance and success was to be found, not in his own strength and merits, but in the grace of Christ which was efficacious in him.

Striving. The Greek of this word contains a reference to the contest of the athletes in the arena. Cf. 2 Tim. ii. 9; iv. 7.

CHAPTER II

WHY PAUL WRITES TO UNKNOWN CHURCHES, 1-7

1. For I would have you know, what manner of care I have for you and for them that are at Laodicea, and whosoever have not seen my face in the flesh:

1-7. St. Paul writes to the Colossians and their neighbors of Laodicea, though he has never seen them, in order that they may be united in charity and have a full understanding of that divine secret of which he has been speaking. The secret is to know God and Jesus Christ whom He has sent (John xvii. 3). The Apostle is anxious about his unknown readers, because of the specious errors that are abroad among them. Though absent in body, he is spiritually present with them, and he rejoices at the solid battle front their faith is presenting to the enemy. They have learned the truth about Christ, and may they show it in their lives, and ever abound in thanksgiving!

1. The first three verses of this Chapter are intimately connected with the end of the preceding Chapter, and they explain St. Paul's "labor" and "striving" in behalf of the Colossians and their neighbors whom he had not seen. The Apostle's zeal and solicitude went out to all Christian communities, and especially those of Gentile origin (2 Cor. xi. 28).

Care means rather "struggle," according to the Greek.

Laodicea. See *Introduction* to this Epistle, No. II.

2. That their hearts may be comforted, being instructed in charity, and unto all riches of fullness of understanding, unto the knowledge of the mystery of God the Father and of Christ:

3. In whom are hid all the treasures of wisdom and knowledge.

4. Now this I say, that no man may deceive you by loftiness of words.

2. The Apostle here tells the purpose of his solicitude and prayers for his unknown correspondents, namely, "that their hearts may be comforted," i.e., that they may be admonished and strengthened in faith, as there is question of doctrine and of guarding against errors; that "being instructed in charity," or rather, "being bound together in charity" (i.e., in Christian love), they may attain to a full understanding of the mystery which God the Father has revealed to us in Christ. The phrases "unto all riches, etc." and "unto the knowledge of the mystery, etc." are parallel, one to the other, and explain each other.

The last words of this verse, "of God the Father, etc.," are variously read in the MSS., versions, and Fathers; but the sense is clear in any reading. Perhaps the best reading is that of the Vatican MS. and St. Hilary: τοῦ θεοῦ, Χριστοῦ.

Christ is in apposition with "mystery."

3. The Mystery of God which St. Paul would have his readers grasp is none other than Christ, in whom are contained all the riches of divine and human wisdom and knowledge. As God, Christ possessed infinite wisdom and knowledge, and as man His knowledge was superior to that of men and angels. The faithful, therefore, need not go to other teachers or masters, nor give heed to the doctrines preached by the false teachers in the name of angels; let them hear and follow in all things Jesus Christ, who is the way, the truth, and the life. "Jesus Christ is a great Book. He who can indeed study Him in the word of God will know all he ought to know. Humility opens this Divine Book, faith reads in it, love learns from it" (Quesnel, quoted by Moule, h. l.).

4. The Apostle comes now to the case of the Colossians, showing that what he has been saying was intended to put them on their guard against the false teachers, who have been trying to deceive them by plausible arguments.

Now this I say, doubtless refers to what he has said in the verses just preceding about the mystery and wealth of knowledge which are in Christ.

5. For though I be absent in body, yet in spirit I am with you; rejoicing and beholding your order, and the steadfastness of your faith which is in Christ.

6. As therefore you have received Christ Jesus the Lord, walk ye in him,

7. Rooted and built up in him, and confirmed in the faith, as also you have learned, abounding in it in thanksgiving.

In place of *in sublimitate,* other good MSS. of the Vulgate have *in subtilitate*; the Greek has, "in persuasiveness of speech."

5. St. Paul knows the state of things at Colossæ, and, though absent in body, he is present with the faithful in mind and heart; and he rejoices at the resistance they are offering to the false teachers.

Order . . . steadfastness. Better, "orderly array . . . solid front." These are military terms, perhaps suggested by the soldiers of the Prætorian Guard by whom in their turn the Apostle was surrounded at this time.

6. **As therefore,** referring to what he has just said about their firm faith. In this and the following verse the Apostle is stressing the need of continuing united to Christ, or persevering in the faith which the Colossians received from Epaphras, their apostle and master, and of shaping their lives according to its teachings.

The Lord. This expression shows that the historic Jesus was also the Christ, the Messiah, and the sovereign and universal Master. See on Eph. iii. 11; Phil. ii. 11.

7. **Rooted . . . built,** two metaphors—one taken from a tree firmly fixed in the ground and the other from a house strongly constructed—to enforce again the necessity of adhering to Christ, the sole principle of the supernatural life; and the means of this union is the faith, as they "have learned" it from Epaphras. See on Eph. iii. 17, ii. 22.

In it, i.e., in faith, producing the full fruit of faith.

The Vulgate *in illo* should be *in ea,* to agree with the Greek, though some MSS. have simply, "abounding in thanksgiving." It was entirely becoming that the faithful should be abundantly grateful for the gift of faith and for the rich blessings it brought them.

THE PHILOSOPHY OF THE FALSE TEACHERS IS OPPOSED TO CHRIST, 8-23

8-23. St. Paul now directly considers the so-called philosophy of the false teachers among the Colossians, and he finds it is in oppo-

8. Beware lest any man cheat you by philosophy, and vain deceit: according to the traditions of men, according to the elements of the world,
and not according to Christ:

sition to Christian principles in doctrine and in practice. It is based
on human traditions and worldly elements, instead of following
Christ, in whom dwells the fullness of the Godhead, in whom the
Colossians will find all they need for salvation, and who is superior
to all powers. In Christ they have received the true circumcision,
which is of the heart, having been buried with Him in Baptism and
risen with Him through faith to a new life. Yes, when they were
dead in their sins, God gave them new life in Christ, pardoning
them their offences and liberating them from the burdens of the
Law. It was the victory of the cross that cast off the principalities
and powers, and led them away in triumphal defeat (ver. 8-15).
Therefore, the Colossians must not be judged by regulations and
observances which were only shadows of the reality which is Christ.
Nor let them be cheated of their prize by a wrong asceticism and
worship of angels which would lead away from Christ, the head
of all; for it is through Christ alone that the Church attains that
full growth which is of God. Since, then, the Colossians have died
to the elements of the world, they should pay no need to those
things which perish in the using. These precepts and doctrines of
men have an outward appearance of value, but they are really
impotent against sensual indulgences (ver. 16-23).

8. **Cheat you.** Better, "make you his spoil," or "spoil you."

Philosophy here is to be understood in a wide sense, as embracing a system of teaching in religious matters. Thus it was often
used in antiquity, as when Philo speaks of the Jewish religion and
the Law of Moses as a philosophy (*Leg. ad Caium*, 23, 33); and
Josephus applies the same name to the doctrines of the Pharisees,
Sadducees, and Essenes (*Ant.*, xviii. 1, 2). There is no thought
in this passage of belittling true philosophy, which is the fruit of
correct reasoning from sound principles.

Vain deceit. The false teachers pretended to have a superior
wisdom to communicate, but which in reality was empty and far
removed from truth. Instead of coming from God, or divine revelation, or the use of right reason, their so-called philosophy was
based on "the traditions of men" (i.e., mere human opinions) and

9. For in him dwelleth all the fullness of the Godhead corporally;

10. And you are filled in him, who is the head of all principality and power:

11. In whom also you were circumcised with a circumcision not made with hands, in the despoiling of the body of the flesh, in the circumcision of Christ:

"the elements of the world" (i.e., certain Jewish rites and institutions, which were regulated by the Jewish calendar, such as new moons, sabbaths, and other recurring festivals). See below, on ii. 16. Other authorities think the term "elements" here is used in a technical sense "for spiritual beings supposed to animate and preside over the elements of the physical universe, and generally conceived as resident in the heavenly bodies" (so Dodd, in *Abingdon Bible, h. l.*). It seems best to say with Fr. Rickaby that "it was not the mere observance of Jewish festivals, but beyond that the positive cultus of the heavenly bodies or of angels as controllers of those bodies, that displeased St. Paul" (*Further Notes on St. Paul, h. l.*).

9. The faithful must not seek spiritual knowledge and help outside of Christ, for in Him dwells the "fullness of the Godhead," i.e., the totality of deity.

Corporally, i.e., corporally, totally, entirely. See on i. 19 above. Others explain "corporally" to mean, not figuratively, but substantially and personally; or with a bodily manifestation (Lightfoot).

10. As the fullness of deity is in Christ, making Him all-perfect, the faithful can find in Him all they need for their salvation and religious perfection; they need not seek elsewhere. Christ is the "head of all principality, etc.," i.e., all angels are subject to Him and inferior to Him.

11. The false teachers were advocating circumcision of the body as a means to spiritual perfection; but St. Paul reminds the Colossians that in virtue of their union with Christ they have already received the real, interior, spiritual circumcision, which is of the heart, and which alone counts before God. This spiritual circumcision consists "in the despoiling, etc.," better, "in the stripping off of the fleshy body," i.e., in the cutting away of the lower instincts and appetites in man, in the putting off of the old man of sin (Rom. vi. 6).

The word *sed* in the Vulgate should be omitted.

12. Buried with him in baptism, in whom also you are risen again by faith in the operation of God, who raised him up from the dead.

13. And you, when you were dead in your sins, and the uncircumcision of your flesh, he quickened together with him, forgiving us all offences:

14. Blotting out the handwriting of the decree that was against us, which was contrary to us. And he hath taken the same out of the way, fastening it to the cross:

12. The Apostle explains when and how the Colossians received the circumcision of Christ. It took place at the time of their Baptism, when their immersion in the water signified their death and burial to sin, and their coming out of it represented their resurrection to a new life of grace. See on Rom. vi. 4 ff.

By faith, etc. In order that Baptism may confer spiritual life, faith in the power of God who raised Jesus to life is required in adults who have the use of reason (Rom. i. 17).

Who raised him, etc. The Apostle mentions the resurrection of Jesus, because this mystery is fundamental to Christianity.

13. Such is the circumcision of Christ, which is conferred through Baptism; and now the Apostle will apply to the Colossians what he has been saying on this subject, recalling first to their minds their former miserable condition of soul as pagans.

The uncircumcision of your flesh means their unregenerate state, in which they obeyed the promptings of the flesh (Eph. ii. 3).

He quickened, etc., i.e., God the Father raised you to new, spiritual life, "with him" (i.e., with Christ), when by faith you became united to Christ in Baptism. According to the best Greek MSS., the Vulg. should read *donans nobis*; the forgiveness of sins was something common to all converts, Jewish and Gentile.

14. Blotting out, etc., is parallel to the preceding phrase, "forgiving us all offences" (ver. 13), and means that God had cancelled the indebtedness which our sins had caused to be registered against us.

Handwriting of the decree. Better, as in R. V., "the bond written in ordinances," i.e., the signature of obligation to observance, whether expressed in the "ordinances," or "orders," or "decrees" of the Mosaic Law for the Jews (Deut. xxvii. 15-26); or in the dictates of the natural law and conscience for the pagans (Rom. ii. 12, 14, 15).

The reference then is primarily to indebtedness incurred by the

15. And despoiling the principalities and powers, he hath exposed them confidently in open shew, triumphing over them in him.

Jews in violating the decrees and prescriptions of the Law of Moses, but secondarily also to that incurred by the Gentiles in violating the law written on their own hearts. Therefore, when the Apostle says, "which was contrary to us," all are included, all were under the curse of law, Gentiles as well as Jews. See on Eph. ii. 15. Now God, through Christ, has destroyed this account that stood against us, taking it "out of the way," in which it stood between us and God; and this He did by "fastening it to the cross" of Christ, on which our Lord suffered and atoned for all our sins and transgressions.

The Vulgate *chirographum decreti* should be made to agree with the Greek, which has τοῖς δόγμασιν (dative) ; hence we should read *decretis,* and understand a *chirographum* which was expressed in or based on "decrees," or "orders," or "ordinances."

15. As God through Christ has quickened us, forgiving our offences and blotting out the handwriting that was against us (ver. 13-14), so has He spoiled, exposed to contempt and derision, and triumphed over the hostile powers that had held man captive. It was through the Law that those principalities and powers were able to enslave man (Gal. iii. 19, iv. 9, 10) ; and hence those agencies met their defeat when our Lord by His death on the cross abolished the Law, bringing it to an end.

Principalities and powers. These two terms are used above (i. 16, ii. 10) in a favorable sense for good angels, but here they are taken in an evil sense for demons, as in Eph. vi. 12.

Exposed them confidently. Better, "made a show of them with outspokenness," i.e., exposed them publicly to ridicule and contempt, leading them as captives in triumphal procession (θριαμβεύσας αὐτούς).

The Latin *confidenter* and *palam* are a rendering of the Greek ἐν παρρησίᾳ; and *in semetipso* should be *in eo* (ἐν αὐτῷ), i.e., in Christ, or in the cross. It is not certain whether the subjects of the verbs in verses 13-15 should be understood to be God or Christ, but it seems better, in the light of the context, to take God as the subject. God triumphed over the enemies of man through Jesus Christ by means of the cross of Christ.

16. Let no man therefore judge you in meat or in drink, or in respect of a festival day, or of the new moon, or of the sabbath,

17. Which are a shadow of things to come, but the body *is* of Christ.

18. Let no man seduce you, willing in humility and religion of angels, walking in the things he hath seen, in vain puffed up by the sense of his flesh,

19. And not holding the head, from which the whole body, by joints and bands, being supplied with nourishment and compacted, groweth unto the increase of God.

16-17. So far, in verses 8-15, St. Paul has been opposing the erroneous speculations of the false teachers, and now, in verses 16-23, he will attack their false asceticism. He warns his readers not to be disturbed about their neglect of outworn Mosaic observances regarding food and drink, the Jewish festivals, such as the New Moon, the Sabbath, and the like, the importance of which the false teachers were stressing and magnifying. All these things were good in their day, under the Old Law, as foreshadowing the reality to come, which was Christ; but now that Christ has come, these things are done away; they are a hindrance to be avoided.

The Vulgate *sabbatorum* is according to the Greek, but σάββατα, though plural in form, is singular in meaning (Matt. xii. 1; Mark i. 21, iii. 2; Luke iv. 16, etc.).

18-19. Here the Apostle admonishes the Colossians to beware of the pretentious humility and superstitious cult of angels advocated by the false teachers.

Let no man seduce, etc. Better, "let no one rob you of your prize," i.e., of eternal life (see Phil. iii. 14), by tempting you to forsake Christ.

Willing in humility, etc., i.e., delighting in an artificial, voluntary self-abasement and an obsequious service of angels. Those "heretics" taught that man was so miserable and far removed from God that intermediaries between him and God were necessary; and consequently to these intervening beings, whom they called angels, they attributed a part in the work of man's creation and redemption which was as absurd as it was untrue.

Walking in the things, etc. More literally, "taking his stand on things he has seen," i.e., preferring his alleged visions and revelations to the Apostolic Gospel. Such is the best reading of this passage, though other good authorities think a "not" has dropped out

20. If then thou be dead with Christ from the elements of this world, why are you under decrees as though living in the world?

21. Touch not, taste not, handle not;

22. Which are all unto destruction by the very use, according to the precepts and doctrines of men.

of the text before "seen," and that we should read, "taking his stand on things he has not seen," i.e., pretending to a knowledge of angels and of the spirit world which has no real basis. This is the reading followed by the Vulgate.

In vain puffed up, etc. Better, "foolishly puffed up with his fleshly mind." The false teachers were full of pride, and, while alleging superior knowledge about spiritual things, their thoughts in reality were low and carnal, mere earthly dreams.

And not holding the head, etc., i.e., not keeping intimately united to Christ, the head of the Church, from whom the members derive their organic unity, power and growth.

From whom the whole body, etc. Better, "from whom the whole body, being supplied and knit together through the joints and ligaments, grows with the increase that is of God." The meaning is that all vital unity and spiritual growth among the members of the Church must come from Christ, who is the head of the Church and the only source of spiritual supply. See on Eph. iv. 16.

20-22. In verses 20-23 the Apostle shows the futility of the ascetical practices preached by the "heretics" at Colossæ.

If then you are dead, etc. The connective "if" here, as later in iii. 1, does not express doubt or conjecture, but rather assumption; it assumes the death in question to be a fact. Since the faithful in Baptism have mystically died with Christ and so have been freed "from the elements of this world" (see above, on ii. 8), why should they still continue to live as if subject to these ancient rites and ceremonies, which enjoined that they should "touch not, taste not, etc." (Lev. xi. 4 ff., xv. 1 ff.) ? These prohibitions, which the false teachers were endeavoring to enforce, did not affect permanent moral principles, but rather things material that perished with the using; and now that the Law of Moses has been abrogated, they have no divine authority or sanction, but are "according to the precepts and doctrines of men," i.e., according to human opinions and human traditions.

23. Which things have indeed a shew of wisdom in superstition and humility, and not sparing the body; not in any honor to the filling of the flesh.

Which are all unto destruction by the very use. This sentence is best treated as a parenthesis.

The *quid decernitis* of the Vulgate (ver. 20) is passive in Greek; hence we have rendered, "why are you under decrees?" The precepts of verse 21, *ne tetigeritis,* etc., are singular in Greek, which better expresses the ridiculousness of the practices for each individual.

23. **Which things, etc.** These precepts and doctrines of the false teachers had an external appearance of wisdom by reason of the worship of angels, humility, and bodily rigor, which they superstitiously and pretentiously implied; but they were of no value with God, and rather tended to serve than to curb the full gratification of the passions of man, since they were only external and separated from the true source of all genuine spirituality, which is Christ.

Not in any honor, etc. Far better in the R. V., which reads: "Not of any value against the indulgence of the flesh." Such seems to be the meaning of a difficult verse, the text of which has probably been corrupted in transmission. See Knabenbauer, *h. l.*; also Sales, Moule, and Crafer in *A New Com. on Holy Script., h. l.*

CHAPTER III

MORAL PART OF THE EPISTLE, iii. 1—iv.16

iii. 1—iv. 6. In the Moral Part of the Epistle to the Colossians St. Paul, arguing from the principles he has laid down in the Dogmatic Part, takes up the duties of the Christian life in general, showing what life in union with the Risen Lord demands, first in a negative and then in a positive way (iii. 1-17). Next he treats of relative duties, pertinent to particular states (iii. 18—iv. 1), concluding with some precepts addressed to all Christians (iv. 2-6). See *Introduction,* No. IV, C.

1. Therefore, if you be risen with Christ, seek the things that are above; where Christ is sitting at the right hand of God:

2. Mind the things that are above, not the things that are upon the earth.

3. For you are dead; and your life is hid with Christ in God.

4. When Christ shall appear, who is our life, then you also shall appear with him in glory.

CHRISTIANS MUST EXHIBIT NEWNESS OF LIFE, iii. 1-17

iii. 1-17. After having directly attacked the errors of the pseudo-doctors and shown their baneful and futile consequences (ii. 8-23), the Apostle now returns to the positive teaching of ii. 6, 7, pointing out that Christians share in the risen life of their Lord, and that consequently new and higher motives should dominate their activities. Being dead to the lower things, they are now centred in Christ, and will appear with Him hereafter in glory (ver. 1-4). This new life requires in a negative way a breaking with all the sins of their pagan past (ver. 5-9), and on its positive and practical side an ever fuller growing into the likeness of Christ, and into a state where Christ is supreme for all mankind (ver. 10-11). Moreover, this new life involves a practice of those virtues which Christ's example has taught, especially charity, which is the bond of perfection, and unity, which couples the members of the Christian society with their divine Head. May the message of Christ be fruitful in them, making itself vibrant in their hearts and vocal in their music! All their undertakings must be performed in their Master's name, and thus they will be rendering continual thanks to God the Father who has conferred all blessings on us through Christ (ver. 12-17).

1-2. As an antidote to the doctrines of the false teachers who were imposing material things as a means of spiritual progress, St. Paul here tells his readers to lift their thoughts above where Christ their Head is seated, as a king on his throne, ready to dispense His gifts and graces to His subjects.

If. See above, on ii. 20.

Be risen, etc. See on ii. 12.

At the right hand, etc., i.e., the place of power and authority.

3-4. The Apostle now gives the reason why all the thoughts and desires of the faithful should be above. In Baptism they died to the world and things of earth, and their supernatural life, like the life of their Risen Saviour, is hidden from the sight of men; but

5. Mortify therefore your members which are upon the earth; fornication, uncleanness, lust, evil concupiscence, and covetousness, which is the service of idols.

6. For which things the wrath of God cometh upon the children of unbelief,

7. In which you also walked some time, when you lived in them.

8. But now put you also all away anger, indignation, malice, blasphemy, filthy speech out of your mouth.

at the end of time when Christ appears in glory to judge the world, then their hidden life shall also be made manifest.

In verse 4 of the Vulgate we should have *vita nostra,* instead of *vita vestra,* according to the best Greek.

5. The faithful must master and hold at bay those evil tendencies of their nature which would destroy their hidden life and lead them away from Christ. The Apostle mentions here, as in Eph. v. 3, 5, some of the sins and vices to which they were most inclined, and which therefore they must especially guard against. See on Eph. v. 3, 5.

Your members which are upon the earth most likely refers to the vices which he proceeds to enumerate, and which are all in the accusative or objective case following "mortify" (Knabenbauer, *h. l.*).

Covetousness . . . the service of idols. Lightfoot says that "covetousness" here is to be taken in its ordinary sense, as greed for material gain, and that the Greek word of itself never denotes sensual lust. But that the word lends itself to a connection with sensual ideas appears from a comparison of this passage with Eph. iv. 19, v. 3, 5; 1 Thess. iv. 6; 1 Cor. v. 11. "Service of idols" would then refer back to all the sins just enumerated. Cf. Moule, *h. l.*

6. The Apostle warns his readers of the punishment that is in store for the vices just spoken of.

Upon the children of unbelief is not in the best Greek, but is probably to be retained on good documentary evidence. See on Eph. v. 6.

7. **In which** can refer to the "children of unbelief" of the preceding verse (in which case we should translate "among whom"), or to the vices mentioned in verse 5; more probably the latter.

When you lived, etc., refers to the time before their conversion.

8. See on Eph. iv. 29, 31.

9. Lie not one to another: stripping yourselves of the old man with his deeds,

10. And putting on the new, him who is renewed unto knowledge, according to the image of him that created him.

11. Where there is neither Gentile nor Jew, circumcision nor uncircumcision, Barbarian nor Scythian, bond nor free, but Christ is all, and in all.

12. Put ye on therefore, as the elect of God, holy, and beloved, the bowels of mercy, benignity, humility, modesty, patience:

13. Bearing with one another, and forgiving one another, if any have a complaint against another: even as the Lord hath forgiven you, so do you also.

14. But above all these things have charity, which is the bond of perfection:

9. **The old man,** etc. See on Eph. iv. 22, 24, 25.

10. The Apostle has just been enumerating sins which Christians must avoid. But it is not enough to weed out vices; virtues must be planted in.

The new. See on Eph. iv. 24.

Who is renewed, etc. The regenerate life is one of progress, growing into ever fuller knowledge and more perfect love of God, of Christ, and of our duties as Christians (2 Cor. iv. 16).

According to the image, etc. As man in the natural order was made in the image and likeness of God (Gen. i. 26-28), so in his regeneration does he come to express that image, but in a far more perfect manner (Gal. vi. 15).

11. In this new state of regenerated humanity the old distinctions of races and conditions of men are wiped out, and all are united in one mystical body of which Christ is the head and the faithful the members.

Barbarian was a contemptuous term, applied in pre-Augustan times to all who did not speak Greek; later it signified all who were devoid of Roman and Greek culture.

Scythian meant the worst of barbarians. The Scythians were much like the modern Turks, and the Greeks and Jews regarded them "as the wildest of wild tribes" (Moule).

12-14. St. Paul has given just above a short list of sins illustrative of those to which the Christian has died; and now (ver. 12-17) he will mention some of the typical virtues which should characterize the life of grace. Since Christians are the chosen people of God and the recipients of His special graces and favors, they

15. And let the peace of Christ rule in your hearts, wherein also you are called in one body: and be ye thankful.

16. Let the word of Christ dwell in you abundantly, in all wisdom teaching and admonishing one another in psalms, hymns, and spiritual canticles, singing in grace in your hearts to God.

17. All whatsoever you do in word or in work, do all in the name of the Lord Jesus, giving thanks to God the Father by him.

18. Wives, be subject to your husbands, as it behooveth in the Lord.

ought to manifest in their lives those virtues which are in keeping with their privileged state.

Bowels of mercy, a Hebrew expression, means tenderness of heart, sentiments of compassion.

Charity is the queen of virtues, the silver cord which binds all the others together, and without which every other virtue is imperfect. See on Eph. iv. 2, 32; 1 Cor. xiii.

The *habete* of the Vulgate before "charity" is not expressed in the Greek, but some verb, like *have* or *put on*, is understood.

15. See on Eph. ii. 11-22, iv. 1-6.

Rule in your hearts. The Greek for "rule" here means a moderator, or an umpire in an athletic game. In place of *exultet*, the Vulgate should have *regnet*.

And be ye thankful, for the many divine benefits and graces of your vocation. Perhaps "grateful" would be a better word than "thankful" here.

16. **Word of Christ,** i.e., the message of the Gospel. The more the teachings of Christ penetrate the heart, the more will charity, peace, and gratitude abound among the faithful. The phrase "in all wisdom" more probably goes with what follows, and hence there should be no comma after *sapientia* in the Vulgate.

Admonishing, etc. See on Eph. v. 19.

17. Christians by their Baptism and consecration to God have become the property of their divine Master, they are one with Him; and consequently all they do and say should be in conformity with this holy relationship. This is the way to render continual thanks to God the Father.

ADMONITIONS FOR DOMESTIC LIFE, iii. 18—iv. 1

iii. 18—iv. 1. St. Paul speaks here of the mutual duties of wives and husbands, children and parents, slaves and masters. Though

19. Husbands, love your wives, and be not bitter towards them.

20. Children, obey your parents in all things; for this is well pleasing to the Lord.

21. Fathers, provoke not your children to indignation, lest they be discouraged.

22. Servants, obey in all things your masters according to the flesh, not serving to the eye, as pleasing men, but in simplicity of heart, fearing God.

23. Whatsoever you do, do it from the heart, as to the Lord, and not to men:

24. Knowing that you shall receive of the Lord the reward of inheritance. Serve ye the Lord Christ.

25. For he that doth wrong, shall receive *for* that which he hath done wrongfully: and there is no respect of persons with God.

briefer, his treatment is practically identical with what he has in Eph. v. 22—vi. 9, on which see commentary for an explanation of the present passage.

CHAPTER IV

GENERAL PRECEPTS ADDRESSED TO ALL CHRISTIANS, 2-6

1. Masters, do to your servants that which is just and equal, knowing that you also have a master in heaven.

2. Be instant in prayer, watching in it with thanksgiving:

3. Praying at the same time for us also, that God may open unto us a door of speech to speak the mystery of Christ (for which also I am bound);

2-6. In these concluding words of the Moral Part of the Epistle to the Colossians St. Paul first counsels prayer and thanksgiving in general for all, and in particular for himself, that he may be able to make the best of his opportunities (ver. 2-4). He then advises tactfulness in dealing with pagans, zeal in the use of time, and graciousness in speech (ver. 5-6).

2. **Be instant in prayer,** i.e., let your prayers be continual, for prayer is the very breath of the soul.

With thanksgiving. He does not deserve new benefits who is not grateful for those received, says St. Thomas.

3. The Apostle asks the faithful to pray for him that he may have opportunity to preach the Gospel.

A door of speech. Better, "a door for the word," i.e., the opportunity of preaching the Gospel.

4. That I may make it manifest as I ought to speak.

5. Walk with wisdom towards them that are without, redeeming the time.

6. Let your speech be always in grace seasoned with salt: that you may know how you ought to answer every man.

7. All the things that concern me, Tychicus, our beloved brother and faithful minister and fellow-servant in the Lord, will make known to you;

8. Whom I have sent to you for this same purpose, that he may know the things that concern you, and comfort your hearts,

The mystery of Christ, which was that the Gospel was to be announced to the Gentiles.

I am bound, i.e., imprisoned, chained to a Roman sentinel; and all because he had preached the Gospel. See on Eph. iii. 3-9.

4. The Apostle asks for help that he may discharge his obligation of preaching the Gospel as he is required by his divine commission: "Woe is unto me if I preach not the Gospel" (1 Cor. ix. 16).

5. Discretion in dealing with non-Christians was of the greatest importance, lest obstacles to preaching the Gospel should arise.

Redeeming the time, i.e., letting no opportunity pass of doing good.

6. The faithful should cultivate grace and tact in speaking with pagans, so as to give edification and be able to answer questions that may be put to them about the faith.

CONCLUSION OF THE EPISTLE, 7-18

7-18. Tychicus will bear this letter to the Colossians, accompanied by Onesimus, their fellow-townsman; and both will tell the faithful at Colossæ all the news about the Apostle and his companions in Rome (ver. 7-9). Those who are with Paul in the Eternal City join him in sending greetings to the Colossians and he asks that his greetings be extended to the faithful at Laodicea, to Nymphas, and to the church that is in his house (ver. 10-15). This letter should be read at Laodicea, and the one sent to the Laodiceans should be read at Colossæ. Archippus should be reminded of his duty. Paul pens the final words and his blessing with his own hand (ver. 16-18).

7-8. See on Eph. vi. 21-22. Tychicus was the Apostle's trusted messenger (Tit. iii. 12; 2 Tim. iv. 12).

That he may know the things that concern you. A better reading of this passage is: "That ye may know our condition."

9. With Onesimus, a beloved and faithful brother, who is one of you. All things that are done here, they shall make known to you.

10. Aristarchus, my fellow-prisoner, saluteth you, and Mark, the cousin german of Barnabas, touching whom you have received commandments; if he come unto you, receive him:

11. And Jesus, that is called Justus: who are of the circumcision; these only are my helpers in the kingdom of God; who have been a comfort to me.

9. **Onesimus,** a slave of Philemon at Colossæ, who deserted his master and fled to Rome, where he was converted by St. Paul. See *Introduction* to Philemon.

Brother, i.e., a fellow-Christian.

Who is one of you, i.e., a Colossian. Not all the Colossian Christians, however, were or had been slaves; many of them were freeborn.

10. Paul now includes the salutations of those companions who were with him in Rome (ver. 10-14). The first three—Aristarchus, Mark, and Justus—were of Jewish origin; the other three were Gentile helpers, that is, converts from paganism—Epaphras, Luke, and Demas. Aristarchus was a Thessalonian, who had been with Paul at Ephesus, and had accompanied him to Jerusalem, and afterwards to Rome (Acts xix. 29, xx. 4, xxvii. 2).

My fellow-prisoner perhaps means here only that Aristarchus was closely associated with Paul in the latter's imprisonment in Rome (Phlm. 24).

Mark, or John Mark, the companion of Paul and Barnabas on the first missionary journey, the cousin of Barnabas, and the author of the Second Gospel (Acts iv. 36, xii. 12, xv. 37, 39).

Touching whom, etc. Perhaps this means that Mark was unknown to the Colossians, or that his former estrangement from St. Paul had left him under some suspicion with the faithful.

11. **And Jesus,** etc. He is not otherwise known to us. The Hebrew form of his name was Jehoshua, or Joshua.

Who are of the circumcision, i.e., converts to Christianity from Judaism. Some think Aristarchus was of Gentile origin, on account of Acts xx. 4.

These only are my helpers, etc. Probably he means the leaders among the Jewish Christians, or those only of his own nationality who gave him special help.

12. Epaphras saluteth you, who is one of you, a servant of Christ Jesus, who is always solicitous for you in prayers, that you may stand perfect, and full in all the will of God.

13. For I bear him testimony that he hath much labor for you, and for them that are at Laodicea, and them at Hierapolis.

14. Luke, the beloved physician, saluteth you; and Demas.

15. Salute the brethren who are at Laodicea, and Nymphas, and the church that is in his house.

16. And when this epistle shall have been read with you, cause that it be read also in the church of the Laodiceans: and that you read that which is of the Laodiceans.

17. And say to Archippus: Take heed to the ministry which thou hast received in the Lord, that thou fulfill it.

12-13. **Epaphras** was the Apostle of the Colossian Church, and perhaps the founder of the other two Churches of the Lycus Valley also.

And full. Another and better reading here gives "fully assured," i.e., with a conscience that is entirely and certainly illuminated regarding the will of God.

Laodicea . . . Hierapolis. See *Introduction* to this Epistle, No. I.

14. **Luke,** the writer of the Third Gospel.

Demas was probably a Thessalonian. He is mentioned here without affection, and later forsook St. Paul for love of the world (Phlm. 24; 2 Tim. iv. 10).

15. **Nymphas** was a Laodicean, who was doubtless well-to-do, and had a large house where the faithful were accustomed to gather for worship. His name is probably an abbreviation of Nymphodorus.

His house. Another good reading has "their house," referring to Nymphas and his family.

16. See *Introduction* to Ephesians, No. IV.

17. **Archippus** was probably the son of Philemon (Phlm. 2), and likely assistant to Epaphras in the Church at Colossæ. He must have been in sacred orders, as St. Paul speaks of "the ministry" he had "received in the Lord." The Apostle's word of admonition to him seems to indicate either that he was just beginning, or that he was not sufficiently attentive to his duties. Cf. 2 Tim. iv. 5.

18. The salutation of Paul with my own hand.   Be mindful of my bonds. Grace be with you.   Amen.

18. The Apostle affectionately closes the letter with his own hand. He asks the Colossians to remember the imprisonment he is suffering for having preached the Gospels to the Gentile world.   His blessing is short, as in 1 and 2 Tim.   Perhaps the "Amen" should be omitted.

THE EPISTLE TO PHILEMON

INTRODUCTION

I. Philemon. This correspondent of St. Paul's, to whom the Apostle addressed the shortest but one of the most beautiful of his letters, was most probably a native of Colossæ. It is very likely that he owed his conversion to St. Paul, some time during the latter's long residence at Ephesus (Phlm. 19; Acts xix. 26). The Apostle speaks of him as his dear and intimate friend, and calls him his "fellow-laborer" (Phlm. 1, 13, 17, 22). That he was a man of means appears from the facts that he owned slaves, that he was charitable and hospitable to his fellow-Christians (Phlm. 2, 5-7), that he was able to give a part of his house for the use of the faithful (Phlm. 2), and that St. Paul could feel free to ask him to prepare a lodging for him on his forthcoming visit to Colossæ (Phlm. 22).

According to tradition Philemon became a Bishop of Colossæ (*Apost. Const.*, vii. 46), and was martyred there in company with Appia, Archippus, and Onesimus during the Neronian persecution (*Menæa* of Nov. 22). It is most probable that Appia was his wife, and Archippus his son or brother, since only these three are addressed by name in this purely personal and private letter (Phlm. 1, 2). It would seem that Archippus was employed in some ministerial capacity in the Church of Colossæ (Col. iv. 17).

II. Occasion and Purpose of This Letter. As we have just seen, Philemon was an intimate friend of St. Paul's who was likely converted by the Apostle during the latter's long residence in Ephesus, and who had subsequently done much for the Gospel. Being evidently a rich man, he doubtless had many slaves, one of whom, Onesimus, perhaps after robbing his master (Phlm. 18), had fled away to Rome. It is highly probable that Onesimus had met St. Paul in Ephesus, having accompanied his master thither from his home in Colossæ, or that at least he had heard of the

Apostle from his master, and perhaps from others. At any rate, this fugitive to Rome somehow got in touch with St. Paul there, and was converted to the faith by him (Phlm. 10, 11).

Observing the fine qualities of his new convert, the Apostle would have gladly retained him for service in Rome (Phlm. 10, 13), but he knew the fugitive's first duty was to his master; and he also knew that death was the ordinary punishment for a runaway slave. St. Paul therefore sends Onesimus back to Philemon, accompanied by Tychicus and bearing this letter in which he very gracefully and tactfully pleads pardon for the offender and requests that he be taken back in kindness by his master. This the Apostle asks both as a personal favor to himself (Phlm. 9, 11, 14), and on the ground that Onesimus is now a brother in Christ, a fellow-Christian (Phlm. 16). He even hints at the emancipation of the fugitive, fearing to request it openly and directly (Phlm. 21).

III. **Date and Place of Composition.** This letter was written in Rome during St. Paul's first captivity there, between 61 and 63 A.D. For arguments, see under the same heading in the *Introductions* to Ephesians and Colossians.

IV. **Authenticity of This Epistle.** Because of the non-doctrinal contents of this letter, its brevity, and its personal and private character, we should not expect it to be quoted by the Apostolic Fathers, nor widely recognized in public at an early date. And yet the external evidence in favor of its genuineness is relatively strong. It is found in the Muratorian Fragment and in the Old Latin and Syriac Versions; it was recognized by Origen, by Tertullian, by Eusebius, by St. Jerome and St. John Chrysostom; Marcion included it in his Canon; and it is found in the oldest collections of St. Paul's Epistles.

The internal evidence is also above all serious questioning. In vocabulary, phraseology and style, it is remarkably like the other letters of St. Paul and, in particular, like the three other Captivity Epistles, written about the same time. All the best non-Catholic scholars of today ascribe the letter to St. Paul without hesitation.

V. **Slavery.** This was a universal institution in all ancient nations. It was a marked feature of Græco-Roman civilization, where slaves constituted the vast bulk of the population, especially in the later centuries of Greece and Rome. In fact, the social standing of

Roman masters was rated according to the number of their slaves. The slave's condition in both Greece and Rome was that of a piece of property, like a horse, an ox, or a tool of any kind, only with this degrading difference in Rome that the slave was often made to serve the immoral and unnatural desires and purposes of his wicked master. Thus, behind a thin veneer of culture and civilization, which was confined comparatively to a few, the condition of mankind in antiquity was for the most part unnatural, degrading, and horrible.

This was the situation that confronted our Lord and the Apostles, and, while internally they were uncompromisingly opposed to slavery and all its attendant evils, they adjusted themselves to it politically and externally for the time being, lest by attacking the evil directly they should bring upon themselves and the Gospel the fierce wrath of the existing powers to the utter destruction of rising Christianity and the loss of all hope of future betterment and the emancipation which the preaching of the Gospel was sure to effect in the oncoming centuries. The Gospel was a leaven, it was a vitalizing seed which, if planted among the nations, was sure to work and grow and bear its fruit in due time. Hence it was all-important not to do anything which would prevent or limit the planting of this transforming seed among mankind everywhere; but in this submission to existing conditions over which they had no immediate control we must never attempt to see any approval of slavery by our Lord or the Apostles. That institution, as it existed in the pagan world, was diametrically opposed to the equal rights to life, liberty, grace, pursuit of happiness, etc., which the Gospel message guaranteed to all men without distinction; and hence it was only necessary that the Gospel be preached, understood and practised in order to bring about the eventual doom of human slavery. That such has actually been the case in all civilized countries where Christianity has penetrated and exerted its influence, the testimony of mankind and history are our witnesses.

For a longer and more satisfactory discussion of this question of slavery in ancient times and the attitude of the Gospel and the Church towards it, see Lightfoot, *Colossians and Philemon*, pp. 317-327; Moule, *Introd. to Philemon*, Chap. IV, in *Cambridge Bible For Schools and Colleges*.

VI. Analysis. Short as this letter is, it may be divided, like the other Epistles of St. Paul, into (a) an introduction (ver. 1-7), (b) a body (ver. 8-22), and (c) a conclusion (ver. 23-25).

The introduction consists of a salutation (ver. 1-3) and thanksgiving for Philemon's love and faith (ver. 4-7). In the body of the letter St. Paul requests Philemon to receive back the runaway with kindness (ver. 8-17), assuring him that this will greatly please the writer, who hopes to visit him soon in Colossæ (ver. 18-22). The conclusion contains final salutations and a benediction (ver. 23-25).

BIBLIOGRAPHY

The chief Patristic commentaries on Philemon are those by Theodore of Mopsuestia (edited by Swete, vol. II), St. Chrysostom and St. Jerome, as found in Migne. For other Catholic commentators consult those cited in the Bibliographies for Ephesians and Colossians, Toussaint in Vigouroux, *Dict. de la Bible,* Camerlynck, in *The Catholic Encyclopedia.*

Non-Catholic commentators on this Epistle will also be found in the Bibliographies for Ephesians and Colossians.

Other general works are: H. Wallon, *Histoire de l'esclavage dans l'antiquité* (Paris, 1897); P. Allard, *Les esclaves chrétiens* (Paris, 1900); Vigouroux, *Esclavage,* in *Dict. de la Bible.*

The Epistle to Philemon

ONE CHAPTER

1. Paul, a prisoner of Christ Jesus, and Timothy, a brother: to Philemon, our beloved and fellow-laborer;
2. And to Appia, our sister, and to Archippus, our fellow-soldier, and to the church which is in thy house:
3. Grace to you and peace from God our Father, and from the Lord Jesus Christ.
4. I give thanks to my God, always making a remembrance of thee in my prayers,
5. Hearing of thy charity and faith, which thou hast in the Lord Jesus, and towards all the saints:
6. That the communication of thy faith may be made evident in the acknowledgment of every good work, that is in you in Christ.

1-7. Paul, a prisoner in Rome, addresses Philemon, a well-to-do Colossian, and his household, wishing them grace and peace, and thanking God for the charitable manifestation of Philemon's faith in behalf of the poor Christians. May the Christians derive from their practical experience of the fruits of faith as produced by Philemon a fuller appreciation of the power of the Gospel! The report of it all has rejoiced the Apostle.

1-2. **Timothy.** See *Introduction* to 1 Tim., No. I.

Philemon . . . Appia . . . Archippus, etc. See *Introduction* to this letter, No. I.

3. See on Eph. i. 2.

4. Thanksgiving and intercession were a part of the epistolary convention of St. Paul's time, but they have a deeper meaning in his Epistles. See on Eph. i. 15, 16.

5. Philemon's active faith in behalf of the Christians at Colossæ explains St. Paul's thanksgiving to God.

Charity and faith embrace the whole Christian life.

6. The Apostle here explains what he asks in prayer for Philemon,

7. For I have had great joy and consolation in thy charity, because the bowels of the saints have been refreshed by thee, brother.

8. Wherefore though I have much confidence in Christ, to command thee that which is to the purpose,

namely, "that the communication, etc.," i.e., that the fellowship or share the faithful have had in the charitable distribution of material and spiritual goods on the part of Philemon, may produce around him a true appreciation or recognition of the power of the Gospel in "every good work" (i.e., in practical results) "in Christ Jesus" (i.e., for the glory of Christ).

Evident is according to the Vulgate, but the Greek requires "effectual." The *operis* of the Vulgate is not expressed in Greek, but may be retained as implied.

In you. Perhaps a better reading is "in us," and the meaning then is "in us Christians, in our relation to Christ." A better reading also omits "Jesus" here.

7. The report of Philemon's charity was another reason for the Apostle's prayers of thanksgiving.

The word "bowels" among the Hebrews represented the seat of tender feeling; hence "hearts" is a better translation of the sense here and in similar passages of Scripture.

BODY OF THE LETTER, 8-22

8-22. Paul pleads with his friend Philemon to receive back his runaway slave who has become a Christian while in Rome (ver. 8-21), and asks that a lodging be made ready for himself in preparation for his forthcoming visit to Colossæ (ver. 22).

8-12. St. Paul is commending the faith and charity of Philemon, which are well known and highly appreciated; and in view of so fine a reputation he makes his plea for the fugitive slave, Onesimus.

Wherefore though I, etc. The Apostle means to say that, in virtue of his authority as an Apostle of Christ, he could command Philemon to do his Christian duty by Onesimus and pardon him, but, relying on the faithful charity of which Philemon has given so much proof, he prefers to exhort him to receive back the runaway, who now as a Christian is profitable, not only to his master, but to Paul also.

8. **Confidence.** Better, "boldness."

9. For charity sake I rather beseech since I am such an one as Paul, an old man, and now a prisoner also of Christ Jesus.

10. I beseech thee for my son, whom I have begotten in my bonds, Onesimus,

11. Who hath been heretofore unprofitable to thee, but now is profitable both to me and thee,

12. Whom I have sent back to thee. And do thou receive him as my own heart:

13. Whom I would fain retain with me, that in thy stead he might have ministered to me in the bonds of the gospel:

14. But without thy counsel I would do nothing; that thy good deed might not be as it were of necessity, but voluntary.

To command. More literally, "to command in plain speech."

Which is to the purpose. Better, "what is fitting."

9. **Charity** may refer to the deeds of charity which Philemon has been performing, or to the love of friendship existing between him and St. Paul.

Beseech. Better, "exhort."

An old man. Paul's age and afflictions will appeal to Philemon. The Vulgate *cum sis talis* ought to be *cum sim talis,* as in the Greek, referring to Paul as "an old man," or as "an ambassador" (R. V. Margin), i.e., an envoy of Christ in prison, which would mean that he is no ordinary man who is petitioning Philemon for mercy to Onesimus.

10. **I have begotten,** in Baptism.

11. **Unprofitable.** Onesimus means "Useful" or "Helpful." But when he deserted his master, and perhaps robbed him besides, Philemon considered him "unprofitable," to say the least. Now, however, by his conversion he has greatly benefited St. Paul, and will be of great profit in his future faithfulness to Philemon.

12. **I have sent back,** an epistolary aorist, as also in ver. 19.

And do thou receive. These words are wanting in some of the best MSS.

My own heart. See above, on ver. 7.

13-14. St. Paul says Onesimus was so useful to him in Rome that he would have liked to retain him, but that he would not presume to do so without the free consent of Philemon.

Thy good deed. The reference may be to Philemon's wellknown kindness, on which Paul could have presumed in retaining Onesimus; but more likely to the pardon which Paul hoped Philemon would freely grant Onesimus.

15. For perhaps he therefore departed for a season from thee, that thou mightest receive him again for ever:

16. Not now as a servant, but instead of a servant, a beloved brother, especially to me, but how much more to thee both in the flesh and in the Lord.

17. If therefore thou count me a partner, receive him as myself.

18. And if he hath wronged thee in any thing, or is in thy debt, put that to my account.

19. I Paul have written it with my own hand: I will repay it: not to say to thee, that thou owest me thy own self also.

20. Yea, brother. May I enjoy thee in the Lord: refresh my heart in Christ.

21. Trusting in thy obedience, I have written to thee: knowing that thou wilt also do more than I say.

15-16. **He departed.** Better, "he was parted," i.e., ran away.

For a reason. The Apostle suggests that perhaps it was providential that Onesimus left his master, since that was the occasion of his conversion to Christianity, and his consequent usefulness to St. Paul as a helper in the work of the faith, and his double usefulness to Philemon "in the flesh" (i.e., as a member of Philemon's family) "and in the Lord" (i.e., as a Christian).

17. St. Paul now asks Philemon, in virtue of the faith and charity that are common between them, to take Onesimus back as if he were the Apostle himself.

A partner, i.e., a sharer in the same faith and charity.

18-19. **If he hath wronged thee,** etc. This would seem to imply that Onesimus had in some way caused his master a loss, for which Paul is willing to compensate the latter.

I have written it, etc. St. Paul for the moment takes the pen into his own hand, as a sign of the earnestness of his promise to make up any loss sustained by Philemon on account of Onesimus; but in doing so he does not forget that he is the Apostle Paul to whom Philemon owes his conversion to Christianity—a debt which he can never pay.

Not to say to thee, etc. Better, "to say nothing of thine owing me thy very self."

20. **May I enjoy thee in the Lord.** Better, "let me have this profit from thee in the Lord." There is a play on the words here, for Onesimus means *profitable*.

My heart. See above on verse 7.

The Vulgate *in domino* should be *in Christo,* as in the Greek.

21. St. Paul appeals to the Christian obedience of Philemon to

22. But withal prepare me also a lodging. For I hope that through your prayers I shall be given unto you.

23. There salute thee Epaphras, my fellow-prisoner in Christ Jesus;

24. Mark, Aristarchus, Demas, and Luke my fellow-laborers.

25. The grace of our Lord Jesus Christ be with your spirit. Amen.

grant his request in behalf of Onesimus, and "more"—hinting, perhaps at the latter's liberation from the state of slavery.

22. Philemon can hardly refuse what St. Paul asks, since their relations are so intimate, and to stress this intimacy at this psychological time, the Apostle asks Philemon to be ready to give him hospitality on his forthcoming visit to Colossæ.

CONCLUSION OF THE LETTER, 23-25

23-25. St. Paul in closing includes the greetings of his companions in Rome, who are the same as those mentioned at the close of Colossians (iv. 10-14), with the exception of Jesus who was called Justus. The blessing is for Philemon and his household, as in verse 2.

THE TWO EPISTLES
TO THE THESSALONIANS

INTRODUCTION

I. Thessalonica. Thessalonica, the modern Saloniki, in ancient times was called Thermæ, from the hot mineral springs found in its vicinity. It was situated on the northwestern part of the Thermaic Gulf, and the Via Egnatia, the great Roman highway of trade, ran through it from East to West. The Athenians occupied and destroyed it during the Peloponnesian War in 421 B.C., but about a century later (circa 315 B.C.) it was rebuilt by Cassander, who gave it the name of his wife, Thessalonica, the half-sister of Alexander the Great. After the Battle of Pydna on the plains of Philippi in 168 B.C., Thessalonica surrendered to the victorious Romans, and it was made the capital of the second of the four districts into which Macedonia was then divided. Later, when these four districts were united into one province, Thessalonica became the capital and metropolis of all Macedonia. In 42 B.C. the Romans made it a free Greek city with the privilege of electing its own magistrates, whom St. Luke, with noteworthy historical exactitude, called by the unusual and technical name of politarchs, or rulers of the city (Acts xvii. 6).

In the time of St. Paul, Thessalonica was the most flourishing and populous city of Macedonia. Its inhabitants were chiefly Greeks, but the Romans were also there in large numbers, besides a numerous colony of Jews, who had their own synagogue (Acts xvii. 1, 4).

II. The Church of Thessalonica. St. Paul with Silas, and perhaps Timothy also, came to Thessalonica during the first part of his second missionary journey, following his expulsion from Philippi (Acts xvii. 1 ff.). On the Sabbath he entered the synagogue there, and began to preach to the Jews that Jesus was the Messiah as foretold in their Scriptures. Though his efforts were largely unavailing, he continued thus to reason with them for three weeks, winning some of them over to the faith, and converting a large number of Greek proselytes and not a few leading ladies. But the majority of his fellow-countrymen were steadfast in resisting him, and, being moved with jealousy, they finally compelled him to leave the synagogue. He then continued his ministry in private homes and through personal interviews, and it seems that the house of one Jason (Acts xvii. 5) became the chief place of worship and instruction for the Gentiles who desired to hear him.

How long the Apostle remained at Thessalonica, we do not know. But from the Epistle we can see that his stay there must have been longer than the three weeks implied in the narrative of Acts (xvii. 2). Some few months, at least, must have been required for the establishment of a Church so flourishing as this afterwards proved to be. He could not devote all his time to preaching either, because he and his companions, by personal manual labor, had to earn their own living besides (1 Thess. ii. 9; 2 Thess. iii. 8). And his preaching was thorough and effective, as we shall see from the analysis of the Epistle. So fruitful, indeed, was the ministry of Paul and his fellow-workers in that Macedonian capital that the envy of the Jews forced them out before their work was finished. These enemies of St. Paul accused him to the magistrates of the city of preaching a king contrary to Cæsar, and nothing was left the Apostle and his co-workers but to withdraw. This they did under cover of darkness, proceeding to the neighboring town of Berea.

III. **Occasion and Purpose of These Letters.** (a) 1 THESSALONIANS. St. Paul's ministry at Berea was short but rich in results (Acts xvii. 10-13), and he left Silas and Timothy there to continue the work he had begun, as he proceeded to Athens. In the latter city his preaching was nearly a failure. He therefore soon sent word to Silas and Timothy to come to him at once (Acts xvii. 15). They came without delay, bringing news of continued or fresh persecutions at Thessalonica, so that both Paul and his two companions had a mind to return there forthwith to console and encourage the faithful, but they could not (1 Thess. i. 6, iii. 3, ii. 17, 18). So Paul and Silas decided to send Timothy to the troubled Church, while Paul passed on to Corinth and Silas returned, perhaps to Berea or some other part of Macedonia (1 Thess. iii. 2; Acts xviii. 1).

Not long after St. Paul had arrived at Corinth, he was rejoined by Timothy, who brought a report of conditions in Thessalonica. On the whole the news was favorable. Notwithstanding persecutions, the faith had continued strong, so that the brethren there were an example to all that believed in Macedonia and Achaia (1 Thess. i. 4 ff.). But there were also some errors and abuses that needed correcting. It seems that the Apostle's authority and the methods of his ministry had been questioned in certain quarters (1 Thess. ii. 1-12). Some were in danger of lapsing back into their pagan vices, while others were idle and restless, waiting for the Parousia (1 Thess. iv. 1-12). Still others were troubled over the fate of relatives and friends who had died before the Coming of the Lord; and certain ones had grown careless as a result of the Parousia being too long delayed (1 Thess. iv. 13—v. 11). It seems there was also some disorder or lack of respect for those in authority (1 Thess. v. 12-15).

It was upon receipt of such news as the foregoing that St. Paul, in company with Silas and Timothy, wrote the present letter. He and his two associates hope to come to Thessalonica soon; but in the meantime they send this letter to express their satisfaction at the good news reported, to defend their own conduct and authority, and to correct the existing abuses and errors.

(b) 2 THESSALONIANS. Shortly after the receipt of the first letter to the Thessalonians word was brought St. Paul at Corinth, perhaps by the bearer of that Epistle, about the most recent conditions in Thessalonica and the effect in that city of the letter just received. Persecution had continued to rage more furious than ever, and yet faith and charity were increasing (2 Thess. i. 3-5). But the Parousia was still a disturbing question, and in this respect the first letter seems to have made matters worse, instead of better. Some of the faithful had become so convinced of the imminence of the "Day of the Lord" that they had abandoned their daily duties, and had given themselves over to prayer and meditation, living on the charity and bounty of others. In their assemblies there were excitement and disorder, and there was danger that the whole Church would be thrown into confusion. These misguided members claimed the authority of St. Paul for their beliefs and teachings, and it seems there was in circulation a forged letter, purporting to be from the Apostle himself (2 Thess. ii. 2, iii. 6-14). In view of these conditions, St. Paul, with Silas and Timothy, writes this second letter to the Church at Thessalonica to comfort and encourage the faithful there, to clear up misunderstandings regarding the Second Coming of the Lord, to strengthen discipline, and to recall the idle to their accustomed daily duties and labors.

IV. **Date and Place of Writing.** All authorities, ancient and modern, are pretty well agreed that these two letters were written at Corinth during the Apostle's long stay in that city of over eighteen months on his second missionary journey (Acts xviii. 1 ff.). The precise dates will depend on the system of chronology one adopts. But in our *Introduction* to Philippians we have said that Paul founded that Church around 51 A.D. He then passed on to Thessalonica, where, as observed above, he must have tarried for several months in order to establish so flourishing a Church. Being forced to leave, he next went to Berea and thence to Athens, spending but a short time in each of those cities, and finally came to Corinth. His arrival, therefore, in this last-named city was not very long after he had left Thessalonica. But before he would write this first letter we must allow time for Timothy's mission to Thessalonica and his return to Paul at Corinth, for the spread of the faith of the Thessalonians to various parts of Macedonia and Achaia and their manifestation of charity to all the brethren in all Macedonia, for the occurrence of a number of deaths in the Thessalonian Church, etc. (1 Thess. i. 7-8, iii. 6, iv. 10, 13). All this would require some time. But, on the other hand, we cannot make the writing of this first letter too late, as sufficient time must be allowed for the dispatching of the second letter also from Corinth during the Apostle's same sojourn there. Of course, it is clear that no great length of time intervened between the composition of the two letters, and this is admitted by all authorities who concede the genuineness of the second letter. Thus, Paul had the same associates in writing the second as in writing the first letter, and the situation at Thessalonica was about the same. It seems reasonable, therefore, to conclude that 1 Thess. was written some time during 52 A.D., and 2 Thess. in the latter part of the same year or in the first part of the following year. These dates fit in with the chronology we have adopted, and they are as likely as any others that might be given, if not a little more so. At any rate, these are the oldest of St. Paul's letters, unless we hold the rather doubtful opinion that Galatians was his first Epistle. See *Introduction* to Galatians in vol. I.

The opinion of some ancient authorities and codices that 1 Thess. was written from Athens is based on a misunderstanding of 1 Thess. iii. 1-6, and is contradicted by the express statements of Acts xviii. 1, 5. Equally unfounded is the view of Baur, Ewald, Bunsen, and certain other non-Catholics, who hold that our second letter preceded the first to the Thessalonians. A simple examination of the two letters is sufficient to refute such a theory; for it is plain that the first letter treats of the foundation of the Church at Thessalonica while the second is dealing with its development, and the teachings of the latter presuppose those of the former.

V. Authenticity. (a) 1 THESSALONIANS. The external and the internal evidence in favor of the genuineness of this Epistle is so strong as to place it beyond all question; and consequently among modern exegetes there is now practically no one who has any difficulty on this point.

The first and oldest testimony for 1 Thess. is 2 Thess., which presupposes it, and which was written not long after it. Next come the Apostolic Fathers and early Christian documents, such as Ignatius Martyr, Polycarp, *The Teaching of the Twelve Apostles,* and *The Pastor of Hermas*—in all of which can be found citations from or pretty certain allusions to this Epistle (cf. Funk, *Patres apostolici,* pp. 640 ff.). After these, we find explicit reference to it in the Muratorian Fragment; Marcion included it in his Canon; it is frequently cited by Irenæus, Clement of Alexandria, St. Justin Martyr, and Tertullian; and Eusebius, the faithful witness of primitive tradition, included it among the fourteen Epistles of St. Paul (cf. Cornely, *Introd.,* III., pp. 480 ff.). This Epistle is also found in the best ancient MSS., and in the old Latin and Syriac versions.

Internal evidence is not less conclusive in establishing the authenticity of this letter. The style and doctrine are Paul's throughout, and the Apostle's character, as known from his other Epistles, is clearly manifested here. It is true that Baur and his followers of the Neo-Tübingen School rejected this letter on purely internal grounds; but the reasons they brought forward in support of their position are not worthy of any serious consideration. For example, they said it was lacking in doctrine; that ii. 14-16 was an exaggeration, or else referred to the destruction of Jerusalem in the year 70; that the eschatological teaching given here was not to be found in the Epistles that are admittedly Pauline, etc.

As to the first objection, we need only look at the Epistle to see that just the contrary is true. For here all the leading doctrines are characteristic of St. Paul, such as the death and resurrection of Jesus (i. 10, iv. 14, v. 10), His Divinity and Sonship (i. 9, 10), the resurrection of the body (iv. 15-18), sanctification by the indwelling Holy Spirit (iv. 8), the call of the nations to the kingdom of Christ, the Church (ii. 12), the mediatorship of Christ (v. 10), etc.

In ii. 14-16 St. Paul is simply saying that the converts in the Thessalonian Church are suffering the same things from their fellow-countrymen as the converts in Judea suffered from their compatriots, and that the blindness and perfidy of the latter have brought upon them the curse of God for time and eternity. There is nothing un-Pauline in this method of argumentation.

If eschatology occupies a larger place in this and in the following Epistle than in the other later Epistles of St. Paul, it is simply because there was a need for it in the Thessalonian Church which did not exist to the same degree elsewhere, or that, since his hearers and readers so grossly misunderstood him in these Epistles, he thought it best to say less about it in later times. The Apostle always adapted his letters to the needs and conditions of the particular Church to which he was writing and to the requirements of circumstances. These difficulties, therefore, are purely subjective and worthless; and they are rightly disregarded by modern scholarship.

(b) 2 THESSALONIANS. The external evidence in favor of the authenticity of this letter is even stronger than that in support of the first one. The testimony of the MSS. and of the versions is the same, but the early Fathers and apologetic writers are clearer and more explicit in regard to this Epistle. The internal evidence here is also very strong; so strong, indeed, that such critics as Harnack and Jülicher have admitted the letter to be Paul's on purely internal grounds. Thus, the contents of the Epistle is closely linked with 1 Thess.; the vocabulary, style, and structure are remarkably similar; the transitions, outbursts of prayer, and other characteristics are unmistakably Pauline. In fact, the similarity between these two Epistles is so marked that certain critics, like Holtzmann, Weizacher, Schmiedel, and others have denied the genuineness of 2 Thess. for that very reason, maintaining that it is the work of some clever forger of the second century. But, as there is no other support for such an opinion, it can be simply set aside as unwarranted.

The greatest objection to the authenticity of this letter is based on the difference in its teaching regarding the Parousia. The objectors tell us that the two Epistles are in contradiction on this question—that 1 Thess. teaches the imminence of the Parousia, whereas 2 Thess. makes it far removed. To this we reply, in the first place, that St. Paul had no definite revelation regarding the time of the Second Coming of the Lord, and hence did not and could not teach anything definite about it. In the second place, there is no contradiction in what he has to say on the subject in the two Epistles: he merely makes clearer in the second letter what was misunderstood in the first.

Another difficulty is that 2 Thess. is more Jewish than 1 Thess., and so must either be the product of a forger, or it was written first. Even if we grant the reason for this objection, it proves nothing more than that there were Jews at Thessalonica, which we admit, and that Paul had them more in mind in writing the second letter than when he wrote the first one; perhaps they were causing more trouble. Harnack explains this difficulty by saying that 1 Thess. was directed more expressly to the Gentile section and 2 Thess. to the Jewish group in the Thessalonian Church. But it seems hardly necessary to say so much; for, on the one hand, the Jewish element in 2 Thess. is only slightly more pronounced than in 1 Thess., and we know, on the other hand, that the Thessalonian Church was predominantly Gentile from the beginning.

We conclude, therefore, by accepting the verdict of all the best modern scholars that the authenticity of these two Epistles to the Thessalonians can be admitted without hesitation. They stand among the best attested letters of St. Paul. And this we can hold in spite of the fact that in certain notable respects these Epistles are the least Pauline of all the letters that have come to us from the great Apostle. For here we search in vain for such characteristic Pauline doctrines as justification by faith, the propitiatory death of Christ, the abrogation of the Law by grace, the relation of the Law to grace, and the like. Personal and historical elements abound in these letters, especially in 1 Thess., as we shall see from the following analysis.

VI. **Division of Contents.** (a) 1 THESSALONIANS. Besides a salutation (i. 1) and a conclusion (v. 25-28), we may divide this Epistle into two main parts, one personal and historical (i. 2—iii. 13), and the other hortatory and doctrinal (iv. 1—v. 24).

A. The salutation here (i. 1) is unusually familiar and friendly, omitting all titles and references to controversy. The Apostle and his companions are addressing friends.

B. In the personal and historical section (i. 2—iii. 13) the writers first give thanks for the good condition of the Church in Thessalonica (i. 2-10), and then in a general way defend the character of their ministry in Thessalonica against certain charges that have been circulated to their discredit (ii. 1-12). After that follow renewed thanks for the success of their preaching among the Thessalonians, who have withstood persecution as boldly as did the Christians of Judea (ii. 13-16). Having been obliged to leave their new converts, the Apostles would have gladly returned to them, had that been possible (ii. 17-20); and in their anxiety they did send Timothy, who, on his return, brought most consoling news (iii. 1-10). The Apostles, therefore, pray that God may soon grant them a visit to the Thessalonians, and that in the meantime the faithful there may increase in spiritual perfection (iii. 11-13).

C. In the hortatory and doctrinal part (iv. 1—v. 24) the Apostles warn the faithful against all forms of impurity, and exhort them to brotherly love and to an active, industrious life which will secure them independence and respect (iv. 1-11). They need not worry about their friends who have died before the Coming of the Lord, for all good Christians are united with their Risen Saviour, and those who have died first will meet Him ahead of those who are alive when He comes (iv. 12-17). The time of the Parousia is uncertain, and so it behooves all to hold themselves ready (v. 1-11). Let all, subjects and superiors, be faithful in the fulfillment of their respective duties (v. 12-15). Finally, some various injunctions regarding joy, prayer, and other spiritual matters, with a special prayer for the Thessalonians, terminate this part of the Epistle (v. 16-24).

D. The conclusion contains a request for prayers, a final salutation, a special recommendation, and a benediction (v. 25-28).

(b) 2 THESSALONIANS. This Epistle has only three short Chapters, and these are so divided in our Bible as fitly to represent the thought.

A. Again the Apostle and his companions first salute the faithful of Thessalonica (i. 1, 2). Then follow thanksgiving for the faith and love of the Thessalonians, and an assurance that God will reward them for their patient endurance of suffering and punish their persecutors in His own good time (i. 3-10). The Apostles assure their converts that they are always praying for their spiritual progress and perfection (i. 11-12).

B. The Second Chapter is doctrinal, and deals with the Parousia, which is the main subject of this letter. Let the faithful not be deceived into thinking that the Day of the Lord is at hand (ii. 1, 2); for certain extraordinary signs must precede, and until these appear there is no reason for alarm (ii. 3-11). Meanwhile, let the Thessalonians continue steadfast in their faith and in the performance of good works (ii. 12-16).

C. The Third Chapter contains first a request for prayers, and an expression of confidence in the spiritual progress of the Thessalonians (iii. 1-5). Then the Apostles warn the brethren against certain disorderly members who were indulging in idleness; and they support their censure by appealing to their own contrary conduct of laboring for their living while preaching the Gospel in Thessalonica (iii. 6-12). Let the brethren, therefore, continue in well-doing, and endeavor to correct the disorderly (iii. 13-15).

D. The Epistle closes with good wishes, a final salutation written by Paul with his own hand, and a blessing (iii. 16-18).

BIBLIOGRAPHY

As always among the Greeks, St. Chrysostom is the leading commentator also on these Epistles. After him, and dependent upon him, we have Theodore of Mopsuestia (edited by Swete), Theodoret, St. John Damascene, Theophylact, etc., as given in Migne, *P.G.* The ancient Latin Fathers did not write express commentaries on these two letters, and hence what they have given us is confined to particular texts. In fact, there is no Latin commentary of first rank on Thessalonians before St. Thomas Aquinas, who, as everywhere on the Epistles of St. Paul, has bequeathed to us here a wealth of profound erudition and marvelous insight. After St. Thomas Cardinal Cajetan doubtless comes first among all ante-Tridentine Latin commentators. Cajetan, however, as Dr. Vosté remarks, was greater as a theologian than as an exegete.

After the Council of Trent down to modern times the leading Catholic commentators on these Epistles were Estius, S.J. (1613), Justinianus, S.J. (1622), and Calmet, O.S.B. (1757). Following these in more recent years we have many fine works on Thessalonians, such as those by Drach (1871), Schäfer (1890), Padovani (1894), Lemonnyer (6th edit., 1908), Toussaint (1910), Knabenbauer (1913), Sales (1914), Vosté (1917).

Recent non-Catholic writers on these Epistles are also numerous. The best among them are the following: Lightfoot, *Biblical Essays*, vi, vii, and *Notes on the Epistles of St. Paul* (1895); Milligan, *St. Paul's Epistles to the Thessalonians* (1908); Findlay, in *The Cambridge Greek Test.* (1911); Frame, in *The International Crit. Comm.* (1912); Plummer, *Comm. on 1 Thess.* (1917); Jones, in *A New Comm. on Holy Script.* (1928); McCown, in *Abingdon Bible Comm.* (1929).

The First Epistle to The Thessalonians

CHAPTER I

1. Paul and Silvanus and Timothy to the church of the Thessalonians, in God the Father, and the Lord Jesus Christ:

1-10. With the briefest salutation found in all his Epistles St. Paul, in company with Silvanus and Timothy, greets the Thessalonian Church according to his usual manner. He then stresses his continued interest in them, recalling their faith and love, the circumstances of their conversion, their exemplary conduct, and their well-known and widespread reputation as outstanding Christians.

1. The form of address which St. Paul adapted in this, the earliest of his letters, was afterwards observed in all his Epistles, though he later enlarged and varied it according to conditions and circumstances.

Paul. In the two Epistles to the Thessalonians, as in the letters to the Philippians and Philemon, St. Paul omits his title of "apostle," because there was no reason to assert his authority in messages so friendly and personal. He also omits here "servant of Jesus Christ," out of reverence for Silas or Silvanus who, after the Council of Jerusalem, was called one of the chief brethren (Vosté).

Silvanus, always so called by St. Paul, but spoken of in Acts as "Silas" (Acts xv-xviii). He joined St. Paul at Antioch (Acts xv. 22, 23), accompanied him on his second missionary journey, and helped in the foundation of the Church at Thessalonica (Acts xv. 22 ff., xvi. 19, 29 ff., xvii. 1-10).

Timothy. See *Introduction* to 1 Tim., No. I.

The Church of the Thessalonians. See *Introduction* to this letter, No. II.

2. Grace be to you and peace. We give thanks to God always for you all; making a remembrance of you in our prayers without ceasing,

3. Being mindful of the work of your faith, and labor, and charity, and of the enduring of the hope of our Lord Jesus Christ before God and our Father:

4. Knowing, brethren, beloved of God, your election:

In God the Father, etc. The single preposition "in" here shows that to Paul's mind there was perfect equality in divine nature between the Father and our Lord.

2. For an analysis of the first main part of the Epistle (i. 2—iii. 13), see *Introduction,* No. VI, B.

Grace . . . peace. See on Eph. i. 2.

We give thanks, etc. See on Eph. i. 16.

Without ceasing, i.e., continually. Some connect this phrase with the following, but it makes better sense to join it to what goes before, as in our version.

3. The Apostle now tells why he "gives thanks to God" for the Thessalonians, namely, because of the practical manifestations of their faith, love, and hope—the three theological virtues which constitute the essence of the Christian life (cf. 1 Cor. xiii. 13). Here in his first Epistle St. Paul teaches what he teaches always elsewhere, that faith must be conjoined with works, it must be active: "Faith without good works is dead" (James ii. 17). The faith of the Thessalonians was manifested in labors of love and in endurance of temporal losses in view of eternal rewards for which they hoped.

4. The call of the Thessalonians to the faith and to membership in the Church of Christ is another reason why St. Paul gives thanks to God. These great spiritual benefits are a sure proof that they are "beloved of God," i.e., specially favored by God in being selected from among others for faith in Christ. With St. Paul *call* or *vocation* and *election* really mean the same thing, namely, admission to the faith and privileges of the Gospel, but *call* regards rather the *terminus ad quem,* and *election* the *terminus a quo;* the faithful were *elected* by God to be *called* to the faith. In St. Paul, therefore, both terms have reference to a supernatural gift of God; and in the present text the word "election" has to do with membership in the Church. The question of final salvation is, then, only indirectly touched upon in this place, inasmuch as one who is elected and called is on the way to final salvation. See Vosté, *Thessalonians, h. l.*

5. For our gospel hath not been unto you in word only, but in power also, and in the Holy Ghost, and in much assurance, as you know what manner of men we have been among you for your sakes.

6. And you became followers of us, and of the Lord; receiving the word in much tribulation, with joy of the Holy Ghost:

7. So that you were made a pattern to all that believe in Macedonia and in Achaia.

8. For from you was spread abroad the word of the Lord, not only in Macedonia, and in Achaia, but also in every place your faith which is towards God is gone forth, so that we need not to speak anything.

9. For they themselves relate of us, what manner of entering in we had unto you; and how you turned to God from idols, to serve the living and true God,

5. St. Paul here gives a reason for his conviction that the Thessalonians have been admitted to the privileges of faith and grace in the Church of Christ, recalling the circumstances of their conversion; for he and his companions preached the Gospel to them with a "power" and efficacy which only the Holy Ghost could supply, and with an "assurance" that was characteristic of the Apostolic preaching everywhere. This his readers know.

6. The election of the Thessalonians was also made manifest in the generous way they received the preaching of the Apostles, in the persecutions they steadfastly endured for the Gospel, and in the holy joy they exhibited amid their trials.

7. The result of the whole-hearted response of the Thessalonians to the preaching of the Gospel was that they became an example and a model in faith to all the other Greeks.

Macedonia and Achaia were the two provinces into which the Romans had divided Greece.

8. **For from you,** etc., i.e., from your city. The international character of Thessalonica made it easy for the faith of the Christians there to become widely known; and this is what Paul means by the somewhat hyperbolical expressions, "in every place" and "so that we need not to speak anything."

9. **For they themselves,** etc., i.e., those Christians from "every place" are full of the report of the preaching of Paul and his companions among the Thessalonians, and of the consequent success of that preaching.

How you turned, etc., from the service of pagan gods to that of the true God.

10. And to wait for his Son from heaven (whom he raised up from the dead), Jesus, who hath delivered us from the wrath to come.

10. The purpose of the conversion of the Thessalonians, like that of all others, was that they might be in readiness for the coming of Christ, our Redeemer and Judge, whether at the hour of death or at the end of the world.

Who hath delivered. Better, "who delivereth." The present tense indicates that the work of salvation is continuous.

The wrath to come, i.e., God's chastisement for sin.

CHAPTER II

THE APOSTLES' MINISTRY AT THESSALONICA IS DEFENDED, 1-12

1. For yourselves know, brethren, that our coming among you was not in vain,
2. But having suffered many things before and been shamefully treated (as you know) at Philippi, we had courage in our God, to speak unto you the gospel of God in much carefulness.
3. For our exhortation was not of error, nor of uncleanness, nor in deceit;
4. But as we were approved by God that the gospel should be committed

1-12. After recalling the abundant spiritual fruit of the Apostles' preaching at Thessalonica, which was due to the grace of God, St. Paul now turns to a defence of his own and of his companions' motives and conduct while there. His Jewish opponents, who had driven the missionaries from Thessalonica, had doubtless circulated calumnies and stories about them; and so the Apostle in these verses replies to their charges. He tells how he and his helpers labored there in spite of persecution, how free they were from self-interest, and how tenderly they cared for their converts.

1-2. St. Paul recalls the fearless manner in which he and his companions, Silvanus and Timothy, after having been scourged and imprisoned at Philippi (Acts xvi. 22-40) came and preached the Gospel at Thessalonica.

In much carefulness. Better, "with much solicitude," or, as the Old Latin has it, "amid much conflict."

3-8. In these verses the Apostles' preaching at Thessalonica is further explained. Their appeal arose not from "error" or delu-

to us: even so we speak, not as pleasing men, but God, who proveth our hearts.

5. For neither have we used, at any time, the speech of flattery as you know; nor taken an occasion of covetousness, God is witness:

6. Nor sought we glory of men, neither in you, nor of others,

7. Whereas we might have been burdensome to you, as the apostles of Christ; but we became little ones in the midst of you, as a nurse cherishing her children:

8. So desirous of you, we would gladly impart unto you not only the gospel of God, but also our own souls, because you were become most dear unto us.

9. For you remember, brethren, our labor and toil: working night and day, lest we should be chargeable to any of you, we preached among you the gospel of God.

10. You are witnesses, and God *also,* how holily and justly and without blame we have been to you that have believed:

sion; nor was it prompted by "uncleanness," i.e., unworthy and sordid motives and purposes, as was often the case with the worship of the heathen (e.g., the worship of Aphrodite at Corinth, where St. Paul was now writing) ; nor was "deceit" or fraud used to carry and enforce their message. The Apostles discharged their ministry as men "approved by God" and entrusted by Him with the preaching of the Gospel, who sought above all things to please God, the Judge of their hearts. They did not try to gain the favor of men by "flattery," nor make their ministry the occasion of material gain or of the praise of men, though they had a right to support for their labors and to respect and honor as "apostles of Christ." Instead of asserting their authority and making demands on the Thessalonians, the Apostles conducted themselves as children among them, and were desirous of communicating to their converts, not only the Gospel, but even their own lives, if that had been necessary. In verse 7 "little ones" (νήπιοι) is according to the best Greek reading, instead of ἤπιοι, which means "gentle." The sense is the same in either case.

9-10. Again St. Paul invokes the testimony of the Thessalonians themselves to prove the sincerity of purpose with which the Apostles preached the Gospel to them, how, namely, in addition to the fatigue of the ministry, they worked with their own hands for their temporal support, so as not to be a burden to their converts, and how blameless at the same time their conduct was.

11. As you know in what manner, entreating and comforting you (as a father doth his children),

12. We testified to every one of you, that you would walk worthy of God, who hath called you unto his kingdom and glory.

13. Therefore, we also give thanks to God without ceasing: because, when you received from us the word of the hearing of God you received it not as the word of men, but (as it is indeed) the word of God, which worketh in you that have believed.

11-12. In verse 7 above St. Paul compared his tender care of the Thessalonians to that of a nurse-mother, lovingly watching over her children; and now he likens the solicitude he had for them to the vigilance of a father, exhorting, encouraging, and adjuring each and all of them to live lives worthy of the God who has called them to membership in His Church here on earth and to a participation of His unveiled glory hereafter in heaven. Such conduct on the part of the Apostles while they were at Thessalonica should convince his readers of the sincerity and purity of their aims in preaching to them.

RENEWED THANKS FOR THE STEADFAST ZEAL OF THE THESSALONIAN
CONVERTS, 13-16

13-16. Having described the conduct of the Apostles at Thessalonica, St. Paul now thanks God for the manner in which the converts there received the Gospel message, and the courage and strength with which they endured the persecutions of their own countrymen, as their fellow-Christians in Palestine had stood up under the persecutions of the Jews. Knowing that the Jews were also at the bottom of the troubles at Thessalonica, the Apostle denounces them with a severity unparalleled elsewhere in his Epistles.

13. **Therefore we also,** etc. The Thessalonians were witnesses of the zealous labors of the Apostles, and now the Apostles thank God for the generous response to their preaching on the part of the converts at Thessalonica. They received the Gospel through the Apostles, but they recognized it as the "word of God" Himself, and this word or divine message produced the fruits of faith in their lives.

The word of the hearing of God, i.e., the Gospel message.

14. For you, brethren, are become followers of the churches of God which are in Judea, in Christ Jesus in that you have suffered the same things from your own countrymen, even as they have from the Jews,

15. Who both killed the Lord Jesus, and the prophets, and have persecuted us, and please not God, and are adversaries to all men;

16. Prohibiting us to speak to the Gentiles, that they may be saved, to fill up their sins always: for the wrath of God has come upon them to the uttermost.

In the Vulgate *qui operatur* should be *quod operatur,* to agree with the Greek, where the relative refers to "word" and not to "God."

14. The converts, therefore, must not become discouraged at their persecutions, as if the Gospel they had received was not divine, for they are only suffering from their own pagan townsmen what the Christians in Judea experienced at the hands of the Jews (Acts vi. 9 ff., viii. 1 ff., ix. 1 ff.). Paul was aware that the persecutions at Thessalonica were also instigated by the Jews (Acts xvii. 5, 13).

15-16. The unusual severity of these verses has led some critics to deny their authenticity, but without reason. St. Paul was simply citing facts, and his language is not so harsh as that used by the Lord Himself against the same people (Matt. xxiii. 3-37), and that employed by St. Stephen (Acts vii. 51 ff.). The persecutions at Thessalonica, for which the Jews were responsible, moved the Apostle to make this withering review of their principal crimes of the past. They had used the Romans as their instruments to kill "the Lord Jesus"; they had killed "the prophets," as our Lord had said (Matt. xxiii. 3-37; Acts vii. 51 ff.); they had "persecuted" Paul and his companions, driving him and them from place to place (Acts xii. 50 ff., xiv. 4 ff., xvii. 5 ff.); they were no longer God's beloved people, and had become the enemies of all men, trying to keep from them the saving Gospel of Christ, thus filling up the measure of their sins and calling down upon them the wrath of God to their own utter destruction.

To fill up, in a consecutive sense, as a result.

Always, i.e., now as in the past.

Has come, in their exclusion from the Messianic kingdom.

To the uttermost seems to refer to the exclusion from Messianic benefits and to the coming downfall of Jerusalem and the dispersion of the Jews as a nation in the year 70 A.D. If this latter event is

17. But we, brethren, being taken away from you for a short time, in sight, not in heart, have hastened the more abundantly to see your face with great desire.

18. For we would have come unto you, I Paul indeed, once and again: but Satan hindered us.

referred to here, St. Paul was speaking prophetically, of the future. Of course, Paul teaches in Rom. xi. 25-32 that Israel will finally return to the God of her fathers, but that will be just before the end of all things here below and the final judgment of the world.

THE APOSTLES' DESIRE TO REVISIT THE THESSALONIANS, 17-20

17-20. In the two preceding verses St. Paul has been led away from the main purpose of this part of his letter to a vigorous denunciation of the Jews who were persecuting the Christians and obstructing his work for the Gospel. Now he returns to the thought of the Thessalonians, and tells them how after his expulsion from their city he had desired to return, but had been variously impeded by Satan. The Thessalonians are his joy and will be his crown in the day of Christ's coming.

17. **Being taken away,** etc. Better, "being bereaved of you," as a parent that had lost his children.

Have hastened the more abundantly, etc. The meaning is: (a) the longer we were from you, the more we desired to see you (Lightfoot); or (b) the more we are impeded from seeing you, the more we strove to come to you (Milligan); or (c) the more we thought we should soon see you, the more ardent became our desire to see you (Vosté).

18. **We would . . . I, Paul,** etc. It is disputed whether St. Paul is here speaking for himself and his companions, or for himself alone. It seems better to take it that Paul and his companions were eager to visit the Thessalonians, and that Paul personally had made up his mind to do so more than once, but Satan prevented him (Findlay, *hoc loco*).

Satan, the Evil One, probably stands here for all the forces that resisted the Gospel. The reference in this instance may be to the Jews, or to physical illness, or to both.

19. For what is our hope, or joy, or crown of glory? Are not you, in the presence of the Lord Jesus at his coming?

20. For you are our glory and joy.

19-20. From the desire to see his converts St. Paul passes in transport to the great moment when he will render an account for them to the Supreme Judge. They are his hope, and at the coming of his Saviour and Judge they will be his joy and crown—his proud boast that he has not labored in vain (Phil. ii. 16, iv. 1). In this verse we have the first explicit mention of the Parousia, or Second Coming of Christ, which is uppermost in this and the next letter.

The *Christum* of the Vulgate (ver. 19) is not expressed in the Greek.

CHAPTER III

TIMOTHY'S VISIT TO THESSALONICA AND ITS RESULTS, 1-13

1. For which cause, forbearing no longer, we thought it good to remain at Athens alone,

1-13. This whole Chapter really belongs, by connection of thought and matter, to the last section of the preceding Chapter. In his anxiety St. Paul did send Timothy to visit and encourage the new converts at Thessalonica. When the Apostle was with them, he had foretold the trials to which they should be subjected, and he was fearing what effects these troubles may have had on their faith. But Timothy on his return gave a most comforting report, for which the Apostle thanks God from the bottom of his heart. Night and day he prays that he himself may be able to visit them, to make up what is wanting to their faith. May God grant him this favor, and may the Thessalonians meanwhile increase and abound in brotherly love towards all, so as to make ever greater progress in holiness, in preparation for the coming of the Lord!

1. In verses 1-5 St. Paul tells the Thessalonians that because of his great love for them and his anxiety about their spiritual welfare he sent Timothy from Athens to visit them, since he could not go himself.

2. And we sent Timothy, our brother, and the minister of God in the gospel of Christ, to confirm you and exhort you concerning your faith,

3. That no man should be moved in these tribulations: for yourselves know that we are appointed thereunto.

4. For even when we were with you, we foretold you that we should suffer tribulations, as also it is come to pass, and you know.

5. For this cause also, I, forbearing no longer, sent to know your faith, lest perhaps he that tempteth should have tempted you, and our labor should be made vain.

We thought it good, etc. The Apostle is most probably referring to himself and Silas, though some expositors think he is here using the epistolary plural. It is not likely that St. Paul ordered Timothy to go directly from Berea to Thessalonica before conferring with him, and probably Silas, also, at Athens. See *Introduction,* No. III.

2. Minister. This is according to the best Greek reading. Some lesser authorities have "co-worker."

In the gospel of Christ, i.e., in the Gospel that is from Christ.

3. That no man, etc. The purpose of the mission of Timothy was to strengthen the converts against their temptations.

In these tribulations, which they were suffering for the Gospel.

That we are appointed thereunto. These words have led some to think St. Paul was referring just above to his own "tribulations," which he feared would be a scandal to the new converts; but this is a less likely opinion, as appears from the following verse. He simply means that suffering is the lot of all who will follow Christ: "Through many tribulations we must enter into the kingdom of God" (Acts xiv. 21); "All that will live godly in Christ Jesus, shall suffer persecution" (2 Tim. iii. 12).

4. The knowledge and experience of the Thessalonians verifies St. Paul's prediction.

5. To show his anxiety about their tribulations, St. Paul here repeats that his personal interest in the Thessalonians caused him to send Timothy to them. He feared for their faith in the midst of sufferings, lest Satan may have prevailed against them, thus rendering his own labors in their behalf of no avail.

He that tempteth, i.e., Satan, who tempts to evil (Matt. iv. 3; I Cor. vii. 5).

Should have tempted you. Better, "had tempted you," referring to a past fact, of which St. Paul had little doubt.

6. But now when Timothy came to us from you, and related to us your faith and charity, and that you have a good remembrance of us always, desiring to see us as we also to see you;

7. Therefore we were comforted, brethren, in you, in all our necessity and tribulation, by your faith,

8. Because now we live, if you stand fast in the Lord.

9. For what thanks can we return to God for you, in all the joy where-with we rejoice for you before our God,

10. Night and day more abundantly praying that we may see your face, and may accomplish those things that are wanting to your faith?

11. Now God himself and our Father, and our Lord Jesus, direct our way unto you,

6-8. Being alone at Corinth and all uncertain about conditions at Thessalonica, St. Paul was in a state of great anxiety when Timothy joined him there, bringing glad tidings of the faith, charity, and personal affection for Paul of the new converts. This report of their faith was a source of comfort to the Apostle in his own trials and afflictions, and gave him new life to press on in his labors.

Related to us. Better, "brought us glad tidings," as if preaching the Gospel to him.

Now we live, i.e., he felt his tired and wearied life renewed.

9-10. St. Paul knows not how to thank God for the report about the Thessalonians, and he says his prayer is unceasing that he may be able to visit them in person and make up what may be wanting in their faith; his stay with them had not been long, and hence there was need on their part of more religious instruction, theoretical and practical. For a similar reason the Apostle at a later date wanted to visit the Church in Rome (Rom. i. 11).

11. Verses 11-13 conclude the first main part of the Epistle. In these verses St. Paul prays to God, first for the Apostles, that they may be enabled to visit the Thessalonians (ver. 11) ; and secondly, for the converts, that they may increase in charity (ver. 12), and may be found blameless in the day of Christ's coming (ver. 13). The second main part of the letter likewise closes with a prayer to God (v. 23-24). Cf. Vosté, *hoc loco*.

God himself and our Father, and our Lord Jesus. The *Christus* of the Vulgate is not in the Greek. Unity of action is here attributed to the Father and our Lord in directing the free actions of men for a supernatural purpose, and therefore their equality in divine nature is implied. See 2 Thess. ii. 16-17, where the same doctrine

12. And may the Lord multiply you, and make you abound in charity towards one another, and towards all men, as we do also towards you:
13. To confirm your hearts without blame in holiness, before God and our Father, at the coming of our Lord Jesus Christ, with all his saints. Amen.

is even more explicitly stated. How clear this doctrine was to the mind of St. Paul in these the first of his letters, and therefore in the earliest of New Testament writings!

Direct our way, etc. Better, "make straight our way," by removing all impediments.

12. **May the Lord multiply,** etc. Better, "may the Lord make you to increase, etc." Here again divine action is attributed to our Lord. As the Apostles are animated with charity towards the Thessalonians, so may the latter be towards "one another, and towards all men," for Christ died for all!

The *in vobis* of the Vulgate should be *in vos,* as in the Greek.

13. **To confirm your hearts,** etc. The reference is to the action and grace of the Lord spoken of in the preceding verse. The Apostle prays for the internal, as well as the external perfection of his readers.

Before God, etc., i.e., in the sight of God the Father.

At the coming, etc., i.e., when our Lord, accompanied by His holy angels, comes to judge the world. The Apostle wishes his converts to be arrayed with all the virtues of sanctity when the Lord comes in judgment.

With all his saints. What is the meaning of "saints" here? Some authorities, like Ambrosiaster, Flatt and Hofmann, referring the phrase back to "without blame in holiness," think all the faithful, living or dead, are meant; Findlay and others say only the holy dead are in question; Lightfoot and Milligan hold that we should understand both angels and the blessed dead; Knabenbauer, Vosté, and most modern commentators teach that only angels are to be understood in this passage.

The reasons for this last opinion are that in all the eschatological passages of the Old and New Testaments and in the apocryphal books only angels are mentioned as accompanying the coming Messiah. Moreover, the dead who have died in the Lord seem to be excluded from a part in the glorious coming of the Messiah, according to 1 Thess. iv. 15. It is true that certain New Testament

passages speak of "the saints" as having part in the judgment of
the world; but we must not confuse the judgment with the glorious
advent of the Christ, which is to precede the judgment. See Vosté,
hoc loco.

CHAPTER IV

THE HORTATORY AND DOCTRINAL PART OF THE EPISTLE, iv. 1—v. 24

1. For the rest therefore, brethren, we pray and beseech you in the Lord
Jesus that, as you have received from us how you ought to walk to please
God, as indeed you do walk, that you may abound the more.
2. For you know what precepts I have given to you by the Lord Jesus.

iv. 1—v. 24. In this second main part of his letter St. Paul first
exhorts his readers to flee different kinds of sin and to cultivate
various virtues (iv. 1-11). He next treats of the final appearance
of Christ (iv. 12—v. 11). Finally, he makes certain recommendations, and utters a prayer for the Thessalonians (v. 12-24). See
Introduction to this letter, No. VI, C.

EXHORTATION TO A CHRISTIAN LIFE, 1-11

1-11. In his prayer for the Thessalonians at the close of the
preceding Chapter St. Paul had prayed that his converts might
abound in charity and lead a blameless life (iii. 12-13). Now, after
calling attention to teachings he gave when founding their Church,
he comes to particulars, first admonishing them to avoid impurity
in all its forms (ver. 1-8), and then urging them to brotherly conduct, to industry, and to the need of giving good example to non-
Christians (ver. 9-11).

1. **For the rest** is a formula of transition often used by St. Paul,
directing attention to something else that is to follow.

We pray and beseech you, etc. The Apostle exhorts his readers
to continue to live according to the teachings he gave them when
he first evangelized them, and to strive for ever greater progress.

The Vulgate, *sic et ambuletis,* should read *sicut et ambulatis,* to
agree with the best Greek; in the ordinary Greek the phrase is
omitted.

2. St. Paul reminds the Thessalonians that the norms of life and
conduct which he gave them had as their ultimate authority and
sanction the "Lord Jesus," the divine Master of us all.

3. For this is the will of God, your sanctification; that you should abstain from fornication;

4. That every one of you should know how to possess his vessel in sanctification and honor:

5. Not in the passion of lust, like the Gentiles that know not God:

3. In verses 3-8 the Apostle exhorts the converts to chastity of life.

This is the will of God, i.e., this is what God wants in you, namely, that you sanctify yourselves. The Greek for "will" is without an article, and so means the will of God in particular, not in general.

Fornication was extremely common in the pagan world, and it was regarded generally with indifference by all classes. Hence the necessity of admonishing the new converts that God wished them to abstain from this vice, to which doubtless many of them had been addicted in their pre-Christian lives.

4. This verse states the positive side of what was stated negatively in the preceding verse. The Christians must know how to control themselves, so as not to degrade their own bodies by impurity. It is uncertain whether "vessel" here means one's own body or one's wife. The former meaning is held by Tertullian, St. John Chrysostom, Ambrosiaster, and many other ancients, and by Milligan, Findlay, the Westminster Version of Sacred Scripture and other moderns; while the second meaning is given by St. Augustine, St. Thomas, Estius, Le Camus, Knabenbauer, Vosté, and others.

The first opinion would seem to agree better with what is said in the preceding and in the following verse; but in favor of the second view it is maintained that σκεῦος usually means wife, that so it was used by St. Peter (1 Pet. ii. 7), and that the verb that follows it here (κτᾶσθαι) means *to acquire, to procure* and not *to possess.* In 2 Cor. iv. 7, however, σκεῦος is used for body. At any rate, St. Paul's exhortation is general, and has to do with every sort of personal purity, whether in or out of the married state. See on 1 Cor. vii. 2 in vol. I of this work.

5. Here St. Paul says the Christian must not be carried away by the unregulated impulses of his lower nature, like the Gentiles, whose ignorance of God led them into all manner of sexual excesses (Rom. i. 19 ff., ii. 14 ff.). Whether the Apostle is speaking in this verse of conduct in the married or in the unmarried state, depends on the meaning given "vessel" in the preceding verse.

6. And that no man overreach, nor circumvent his brother in business, because the Lord is the avenger of all these things, as we have told you before, and have testified.

7. For God hath not called us unto uncleanness, but unto sanctification.

8. Therefore, he that despiseth these things, despiseth not man, but God, who also hath given his Holy Spirit unto you.

9. But as touching the charity of brotherhood, we have no need to write to you, for yourselves have learned of God to love one another.

10. For indeed you do it towards all the brethren in all Macedonia. But we entreat you, brethren, that you abound more,

6a. Overreach. Better, "transgress," which in the original may be taken either as intransitive (in the sense of going beyond lawful bounds, and therefore of sinning) or as transitive (as governing "brother," and so of neglecting his rights). The context favors the first meaning in the sense of going beyond the limits of lawful matrimony, of invading the rights of another Christian's home by the commission of adultery.

Brother means Christian, for whom St. Paul is chiefly concerned, though his teaching does not exclude others.

In business. Better, "in the matter," i.e., the Christian is not to offend against his brother "in the matter" of purity, as the context shows. Great authorities, however, ancient and modern, are pretty equally divided in explaining *in negotio* of the Vulgate as referring to commercial matters—to business—and to matters of purity. The context favors the latter meaning.

6b-8. In these verses the Apostle gives three reasons on the part of God why Christians should avoid sins of impurity, namely, because God is the avenger of them, because He has called us to sanctification, and because He has given us the Holy Ghost, who is offended and outraged by impurity and injustice of every kind: "Know you not that you are the temple of God, etc." (1 Cor. iii. 16).

Despiseth these things, i.e., rejects or defies the call of God to "sanctification."

In nobis (ver. 8) of the Vulgate should be *in vos,* according to the best Greek MSS., thus referring to all Christians in general, rather than to the Apostles only, as the recipients of the Holy Spirit.

9-10a. St. Paul lauds the charity of the Thessalonians who, being taught in this matter by God's grace, need not his instruction. Indeed, their love for one another has been manifested by deeds of charity throughout all Macedonia.

10b-11. After praising the worthy for their charity, the Apostle

11. And that you use your endeavor to be quiet, and that you do your own business, and work with your own hands, as we commanded you; and that you walk honestly towards them that are without; and that you want nothing of any man's.

12. Now we will not have you ignorant, brethren, concerning them that are asleep, that you be not sorrowful, even as others who have no hope.

turns to another group who were abusing the hospitality of others, living on alms in idleness, in expectation of the imminent coming of the Messiah, going about disturbing others, and giving bad example to outsiders (2 Thess. ii. 1, iii. 11).

Do your own business, etc. This shows that many of the converts were of the working classes.

As we commanded you. When Paul was instructing the Thessalonians, he had said that, if anyone would not work, the same should not eat (2 Thess. iii. 10).

That you walk honestly, etc., i.e., that you conduct yourselves in an honorable manner before those who are not Christians, whether Jews or Gentiles.

In Greek a new verse begins at "and that you walk honestly, etc.," thus making 18 verses in this Chapter, instead of 17, as in the Vulgate. So it happens that verse 11 in the Vulgate equals verses 11 and 12 in the Greek.

THE FATE OF THOSE WHO HAVE DIED, 12-17

12-17. Following the moral exhortations of the preceding section, St. Paul now takes up some of the difficulties of the Thessalonians, as reported to him by Timothy. In this present section he discusses the condition of those of the faithful who have passed on before the advent of the Messiah. The converts must not worry about their beloved dead, thinking they will not have part in the glory of the Coming Lord. They will rise as Christ rose, and indeed will meet their Saviour before the living do. After that, the living will join them and be caught up together with Christ, to be forever with Him in glory. Let these thoughts be their comfort.

12. Now we will not have you ignorant, brethren, etc. This is a customary manner with St. Paul of introducing a subject of great importance. The Thessalonians had misunderstood the Apostle's teaching about the Second Coming of Christ; they thought they were to live to see it in their own time. And since some among

13. For if we believe that Jesus died and rose again; even so them who have slept through Jesus, will God bring with him.

14. For this we say unto you in the word of the Lord, that we who are alive, who remain unto the coming of the Lord, shall not prevent them who have slept.

them had recently died, they were profoundly grieved, thinking their loved ones would thus never witness or share in the glories of the Parousia. St. Paul bids them not to sorrow, as if they did not believe in the resurrection of the dead, as if they were pagans. Of course, he is condemning immoderate sorrow only.

Them that are asleep. This is "a characteristic, but not original Christian designation of the dead" (McCown, in *Abingdon Bible*, *hoc loco*).

13. The reason why the Thessalonians should not give way to inordinate sorrow is that the faithful dead are to rise again, and the proof of this is to be found in the Resurrection of Christ.

The sainted dead form one mystical body with Christ, of which He is the head. And since the head is risen, the members must also rise.

If we believe means "since we believe," as is evident from the context and from St. Paul's teaching elsewhere, especially in 1 Cor. xv. The Apostle is speaking only of the resurrection of the just, because he is consoling the Thessalonians for their dead who have died in Christ, and it is only these that shall have part in the glorious advent of the Saviour and enter into His kingdom of bliss. The unjust shall also rise, but only to be judged and die the second death.

14. St. Paul here tells the Thessalonians that, when Christ comes, those who are living at the time shall not enjoy any precedence over those who shall have died, and this he affirms "in the word of the Lord," i.e., as a doctrine communicated to him directly by Christ Himself.

That we who are alive, etc., i.e., those who survive, who are living at that time. The Apostle is speaking rhetorically in the first person plural, and so he is not to be understood as including himself and his companions among those who were to witness the Parousia. That he had no idea of teaching the imminent advent of Christ is clear from what he says below in v. 2, in 2 Thess. ii. 1 ff., and from the teaching of the Lord (Matt. xiii. 32 ff.; Acts i. 6 ff.)

15. For the Lord himself shall come down from heaven with commandment, and with the voice of an archangel, and with the trumpet of God:
and the dead who are in Christ, shall rise first.

16. Then we who are alive, who are left, shall be taken up together with
them in the clouds to meet Christ, into the air, and so shall we be always
with the Lord.

to which he was always faithful. And this is the explanation given
his teaching here by all the Greek and Latin Fathers, and after
them by St. Thomas, Estius, and all the leading Catholic commentators. In fact, to imply that St. Paul was in error in this
matter would be to destroy the nature of divine inspiration and
Biblical inerrancy. See Decision of Biblical Commission on this
subject, June 18, 1915.

15. **For the Lord himself,** etc. As the Lord ascended visibly
into heaven, so shall He appear at the end of the world (Acts i. 11).

With commandment, etc., as a general issuing orders to his
troops. These expressions are to be understood figuratively, as describing the conditions and phenomena that shall accompany the
Lord as He descends from heaven to call the dead to life. The
Apostle is using eschatological language common among the Jews,
and which was also employed by our Lord (Matt. xxiv. 30 ff.).
Cf. Knabenbauer and Vosté, *hoc loco.*

And the dead who are in Christ, etc., i.e., those who have died
in union with Christ shall first rise, so as to be on an equality with
those who are living, then will take place the transformation of the
living saints, and this will be followed by the rapture of all with
Christ, to be with Him evermore in glory (ver. 16). What a consoling doctrine for the bereaved Thessalonians! By the word "first"
St. Paul does not mean that the resurrection of the just will precede the general resurrection (about which he is not talking), but
that the resurrection of the holy dead will be prior to the transformation of the saints who are living at the time.

16. **Then we who are alive,** etc. St. Paul repeats with emphasis
the thought of verse 14. He seems to say plainly that those saints
who are alive at the time of the Parousia will not die, but will be
transformed and taken, together with the righteous dead already
raised to life, into glory with Christ. The Greek Fathers and many
modern interpreters so understand the Apostle; and this interpretation agrees with the correct reading and meaning of 1 Cor. xv. 51,

17. Wherefore, comfort ye one another with these words.

on which see commentary in vol. I of this series. To be consistent, we should explain "we who are alive" here as in verse 14, that is, as referring, not to St. Paul and his companions then living when the Apostle was writing nor to others then living with whom he compares those then dead, but to those just who will be living when the Lord comes in glory. Hence follows the conclusion that the righteous who are alive at the Second Coming of Christ to judge the world will pass to glory without dying, and this is what the Apostle was referring to in 2 Cor. v. 4. For further argument and a consideration of the opposing opinion on this subject, see vol. I of this series, on 1 Cor. xv. 51.

Shall be taken up together with them, etc. As Jesus ascended into heaven enveloped in a cloud (Acts i. 9), and as He shall come again "in the clouds of heaven" (Matt. xxiv. 30), so the just at the end of the world shall be transported by supernatural power beyond the clouds to meet the Lord in His regal majesty, and with Him to enter into glory for evermore.

17. In view of the consoling words he has just written (ver. 13-16), St. Paul bids his readers to take heart and be comforted in the loss of their dear ones.

CHAPTER V

THE DAY OF THE LORD IS UNCERTAIN, 1-11

1. But of the times and moments, brethren, you need not that we should write to you;

1-11. Behind the immoderate sorrow of the Thessalonians over their dead lay their false notion of the imminence of the Parousia. The Apostle, therefore, now reminds them of the teaching of the Lord Himself regarding the uncertainty of that august event, the coming of which will be like that of a thief in the night, "as the pains upon her that is with child" (ver. 1-3). Wherefore, it behooves us all to watch and to be ready to join Christ when He comes (ver. 4-10). Let the converts, then, comfort one another and edify one another (ver. 11).

1. **The times and moments.** These two expressions, taken from

2. For yourselves know perfectly that the day of the Lord shall so come as a thief in the night.

3. For when they say, peace and security; then sudden destruction comes upon them, as the pains upon her that is with child, and they shall not escape.

4. But you, brethren, are not in darkness, that that day should overtake you as a thief.

5. For all you are the children of light, and children of the day; we are not of the night, nor of darkness.

6. Therefore, let us not sleep as others do; but let us watch, and be sober.

7. For they that sleep, sleep in the night; and they that are drunk, are drunk in the night.

familiar Biblical phraseology, are most probably intended to signify the precise time of the Parousia. Cf. Acts i. 7; Matt. xxiv. 36; Mark. xiii. 32.

2. Yourselves know perfectly, etc., i.e., they had been well instructed on these points by St. Paul's preaching to them.

The day of the Lord, i.e., the time of His Second Coming in glory. The expression is a familiar one in St. Paul's writings, and also with the Prophets of the Old Testament. The visitation of Christ to judge the world will take place suddenly and unexpectedly, like the coming of a thief in the night, and none will escape (cf. Matt. xxiv. 43; Luke xii. 39, 40).

3. For when they say, i.e., when the unbelieving, those who are in darkness, say, etc. The punishment will fall when least expected. See Matt. xxiv. 36-39; Luke xxi. 34; Ezech. xiii. 10.

The *dixerint, superveniet,* and *effugient* of the Vulgate are all present tense in Greek.

4-5. In verses 4-10 the Apostle stresses the need of vigilance on the part of the faithful. In these two verses he tells the saints that they are no longer in moral darkness, as before their Baptism (Eph. v. 8), and as are the faithless; and therefore they need not fear the suddenness of the Lord's Coming or its consequences. Verse 5 but repeats in a positive way what is said negatively in verse 4.

We are not, etc. For a similar change of persons from the second to the first see Gal. iii. 25-26; Eph. ii. 2, 3, 13, 14, v. 2, etc.

6. Therefore introduces with emphasis the conclusion to be drawn from what has just been said.

Watch . . . be sober refer respectively to the performance of good works and abstention from evil.

7. Night is the normal time for sleep, and also for revelry; hence

8. But let us, who are of the day, be sober, having on the breastplate of faith and charity, and for a helmet the hope of salvation.

9. For God hath not appointed us unto wrath, but unto the purchasing of salvation through our Lord Jesus Christ,

10. Who died for us, that whether we watch or sleep, we may live together with him.

11. For which cause comfort one another; and edify one another, as indeed you do.

St. Paul's warning against the excesses of the pagans in either the one or the other.

8. **The breastplate.** The Apostle passes from the metaphor of the light to that of the armor of the soldier. For the application of this imagery, see on Eph. vi. 11-17. Here the Apostle speaks of only two defensive arms of the soldier, namely, the "breastplate" and the "helmet"; and he likens them to the virtues of faith, hope and charity, which are the foundation of the Christian life and of all perfection. Hope is the central thought in this Epistle.

Salvation (σωτηρία) here means eternal salvation of the soul, the enjoyment of God's eternal kingdom hereafter.

9-10. The Apostle now gives the reason for the certainty of our hope, namely, because God in calling us to Christianity has not destined us for damnation, but for eternal salvation through the merits of Jesus Christ, "who died for us," thus acquiring us as His property and making us His possession, so that whether "we watch or sleep" (i.e., whether we live or die), we belong to Him, by grace in this life and in glory hereafter. Therefore, whether we be living or dead at the time of the Parousia, we shall be Christ's. These last words show that St. Paul had no idea whether he and his companions should be alive or dead when the Parousia would take place; it might come while they were living and it might come after they were dead. Which it was to be, did not matter. The one thing that did matter was that they should be at all times one with Christ. See Knabenbauer, *hoc loco*.

11. In view of all that has been said about the Coming of the Lord from Chapter iv. 13 up to now, the Apostle exhorts his readers to "comfort one another," i.e., to continue to comfort one another, as they have been doing. He loves to praise his readers when they deserve it.

12. And we beseech you, brethren, to know them who labor among you, and are over you in the Lord, and admonish you;
13. That you esteem them more abundantly in charity, for their work's sake. Have peace with them.
14. And we beseech you, brethren, rebuke the unquiet, comfort the feeble-minded, support the weak, be patient towards all men.

12-24. Following the treatment of the dogmatic question about the Parousia, St. Paul now comes to various moral exhortations. Similar admonitions were given in Chapter iv. 1-11; but there they were for individuals, whereas here they are for the whole community. The first group are social, and have to do (a) with the duties of the faithful toward their ecclesiastical superiors (ver. 12-13), and (b) with the duties incumbent on those superiors as regards their subjects (ver. 14-15). The second class of admonitions is religious, relating (a) to joy, prayer and thanksgiving (ver. 16-18), and (b) to the use of charisms (ver. 19-22). A prayer for the Thessalonians closes this part of the letter (ver. 23-24).

12. In this verse the Apostle addresses the faithful of Thessalonica, admonishing them "to know," i.e., to recognize and appreciate the authority, and to obey the doctrine and instructions given them by their ecclesiastical superiors, who are their servants "in the Lord." We have here "a clear testimony, from the earliest writing of the New Testament, to the existence in the Church at the beginning of a ministerial order—a *clergy* (to use the language of a later age) as distinguished from the *laity*—charged with specific duties and authority" (Findlay).

13. Not only should the faithful recognize the authority and heed the teaching of their church superiors, but they should also esteem and love them highly on account of their labors in behalf of the faithful.

Have peace with them, i.e., with the clergy. This is according to the reading of the Vulgate and some of the best Greek MSS., but there is another and better Greek reading which has: "Have peace among yourselves."

14. In this and in the following verse St. Paul is addressing the bishops and priests of the Church at Thessalonica, as is evident from the admonitions he gives and as the best ancient and modern expositors admit.

15. See that none render evil for evil to any man; but ever follow that which is good towards each other, and towards all men.

16. Always rejoice.

17. Pray without ceasing.

18. In all things give thanks; for this is the will of God in Christ Jesus concerning you.

19. Extinguish not the spirit.

20. Despise not prophecies.

21. But prove all things; hold fast that which is good.

We beseech. Better, "we exhort."

The unquiet, i.e., those idle and restless ones who, in expectation of the imminence of the Parousia, were going about disturbing others.

The feeble-minded, i.e., those in anxiety about the coming of the Lord and the fate of their dead.

The weak, i.e., the infirm in faith.

15. This verse enunciates a cardinal Christian principle often emphasized by our Lord Himself (cf. Matt. v. 39 ff., 44 ff.; Luke vi. 27). It was especially needful for the Thessalonians, who were persecuted by the Jews and pagans both.

16-18. In these verses St. Paul gives three religious admonitions pertinent to all Christians. (a) They should always rejoice, even in adversity, because of the reward awaiting them in the hereafter; (b) they should pray continually, not only by the habit of making set prayers at specific times, but also by a spiritual intention and direction that should pervade all their activities; and (c) they should give thanks to God for all things, both good and bad, because all have been ordained for their spiritual welfare, and, if accepted in the right spirit, will redound to their greater good, at least in the life to come. Furthermore, thanksgiving for benefits received is one of the surest means of obtaining more favors.

For this is the will of God. It is uncertain whether these words refer to all three of the foregoing admonitions, or only to the duties of prayer and thanksgiving, or only to that of thanksgiving.

In Christ Jesus, etc. He means to say that such is the will of God in their regard as manifested in or through Christ Jesus; or, according to others, this is what God wishes from those who are in Christ, i.e., who are Christians.

19-21. The Thessalonians are not to suppress or despise the char-

22. From all appearance of evil refrain yourselves.

23. And may the God of peace himself sanctify you in all things; that your whole spirit and soul and body may be preserved blameless in the coming of our Lord Jesus Christ.

24. He is faithful who hath called you, who also will *do it*.

ismatic gifts, such as speaking with tongues and prophesying, which the Holy Ghost was wont to pour out on many of the converts in the Early Church; but all of them are to be tested by their fruits. It was easy for some to allege false revelations and visions, especially about the imminence of the Parousia.

The spirit is referred by some to all the gifts of the Holy Ghost, including sanctifying grace; but here the reference is more likely to the charisms spoken of at greater length in 1 Cor. xii-xiv.

Prove all things most likely refers not only to the gifts just spoken of, but to all actions of every kind, good and bad, as would be natural in an exhortation of this kind at the close of a letter.

22. Here the Apostle exhorts his readers to keep themselves from every kind of evil.

23-24. Again, at the end of this second main part of his letter, as at the end of the first main part (iii. 11-13), the Apostle prays to God that, by His grace, the Thessalonians may continually advance in holiness, and be found ready when the Lord comes.

God of peace, i.e., God who is the author and source of peace, and who will therefore be able to put at rest the Thessalonians disturbed by fear of the imminence of the Parousia.

Sanctify you in all things, i.e., as to all virtues.

Spirit, soul, body. The "body" is the seat of the senses, whose operations are to be directed in accordance with the law of God. The "soul" ($\psi\nu\chi\acute{\eta}$) is the principle of physical life and of sensible phenomena, and the seat of the passions. The "spirit" ($\pi\nu\epsilon\hat{\nu}\mu\alpha$) is the principle of the superior, spiritual life. As through the body we have contact with the material world, so through the spirit do we communicate with the invisible world of spirits and with God.

The Apostle's prayer for the Thessalonians rests on God who "is faithful" to the work He has begun. It was He who called and admitted them to the faith, and He will provide all that is necessary for their sanctification, so that they may be found worthy in the day of His coming.

25. Brethren, pray for us.
26. Salute all the brethren with a holy kiss.
27. I charge you by the Lord, that this epistle be read to all the brethren.
28. The grace of our Lord Jesus Christ be with you. Amen.

CONCLUSION, 25-28

25-28. In conclusion the Apostle asks the prayers of the faithful for himself and his companions, sends his salutations, directs that this letter be read in public for the benefit of all the Christians, and gives his blessing.

25. Pray for us. Some MSS. add "also," showing that, as he prayed for them, they in turn should pray for him.

26. With a holy kiss. It is possible that this was a liturgical practice in Judaism before St. Paul's time. Such it was, at any rate, in the Christian Church a century later (cf. Justin Martyr, *Apol.*, i. 65). See on Rom. xvi. 16; 1 Cor. xvi. 20.

27. Paul directs that this letter be read aloud in church, as the Law and the Prophets were read in the synagogue, so that all the faithful may benefit by it. This was the first Apostolic letter to be sent to a whole Church; and since many of the members were troubled about the Parousia, there was a special reason why all should know what their Apostle had to say on so momentous a question.

In the Vulgate the *sancti* before *fratres,* though supported by good MSS., seems strange in St. Paul as a designation for Christians used together with the term "brethren," and so should more probably be omitted.

28. The Apostle closes with his usual blessing, which varies in length in different letters. The Greeks used to terminate their letters with a wish for good health; but St. Paul is more concerned with the souls of his readers than with their bodies, and hence wishes them "grace." The "Amen" is probably liturgical.

The Second Epistle to the Thessalonians

CHAPTER I

THE APOSTLE GREETS THE THESSALONIANS AND CONSOLES THEM, 1-12

1. Paul and Silvanus and Timothy to the church of the Thessalonians in God our Father, and the Lord Jesus Christ.
2. Grace unto you, and peace from God the Father and the Lord Jesus Christ.
3. We are bound to give thanks always to God for you, brethren, as it is fitting, because your faith groweth exceedingly, and the charity of you all towards each other aboundeth:
4. So that we ourselves glory in you in the churches of God for your patience and faith and in all your persecutions and tribulations, which you endure,

1-12. After saluting the faithful at Thessalonica (ver. 1-2), the Apostle first thanks God for their faith, charity, and patient endurance of persecutions (ver. 3-4), and then describes the just judgment of God, which will reward them for their virtue and punish their oppressors (ver. 5-10). He concludes by assuring them that their Apostles are always praying for them, to the end that God may make them worthy of the call He has given them (ver. 11-12).

1-2. The greeting here is the same as in 1 Thess., save that the more intimate word "our" precedes "Father" in this inscription, and the added words "from God the Father and the Lord Jesus Christ" here designate the source of divine "grace and peace."

In the Vulgate of verse 2 *nostro* should be omitted, according to the best Greek.

3-4. **We are bound,** etc. The Apostles feel they are under a personal obligation of thanking God at all times for the great increase in the faith and charity of the Thessalonians, which remain steadfast and progress in the face of persecution.

So that we ourselves, etc. It was the patience of the Thessalonians in the midst of sufferings and afflictions—a patience that arose out of their firm faith—that gave St. Paul, Silvanus, and

228

5. A sign of the just judgment of God, that you may be counted worthy of the kingdom of God, for which also you suffer;

6. Seeing it is a just thing with God to repay tribulation to them that trouble you,

7. And to you who are troubled rest with us when the Lord Jesus shall be revealed from heaven, with the angels of his power

Timothy their reason for glorying; these Apostles had co-operated with God in giving them their glorious faith, which has become an example and a model "in the churches of God," i.e., throughout the whole Christian Church, "not only in Macedonia and in Achaia, but also in every place" (1 Thess. i. 8).

In the Vulgate of verse 4 *et* before *nos* should be suppressed.

5. **A sign,** etc. These words are in apposition to what has just been said about the sufferings of the faithful. The Apostle wishes to say that the patient sufferings of the Christians for their faith are a token "of the just judgment of God, etc.," i.e., they are a proof that present conditions are not the final order of things, that a day will come when goodness shall have its reward and sin its punishment.

The kingdom of God here means the kingdom established by Christ, with special reference to the hereafter.

The Vulgate *in exemplum* would better be simply *indicium* or *argumentum*. See on Phil. i. 27-28.

6. In verses 6-10 the Apostle shows that in the life to come God will give an eternal reward to those who have suffered for His sake, and, contrariwise, eternal punishment to unrepentant sinners. The general, solemn and liturgical character of these verses, consisting of parallel members, is thought to point to a primitive Christian hymn of which St. Paul was making use in this passage.

Seeing. Better, "indeed" or "since indeed," expressing not doubt but absolute certainty; the justice of God demands that He requite sinners for the sufferings they inflict on the just. It is an application of the *lex talionis*.

7. Affliction is in store for those who afflict the faithful (ver. 6b), and relief for those who are afflicted; sinners are to be paid in their own kind: "And Abraham said to him: Son, remember that thou didst receive good things in thy lifetime, and likewise Lazarus evil things, etc." (Luke xvi. 25; cf. Matt. xxvi. 52; Apoc. xiii. 10). And this is to take place "when the Lord Jesus, etc.," i.e., at the Second Coming of our Lord to judge the world.

8. In a flame of fire, giving vengeance to them who know not God, and who obey not the gospel of our Lord Jesus Christ:
9. Who shall suffer eternal punishment in destruction, from the face of the Lord, and from the glory of his power,

With the angels of his power, i.e., attended by angels as ministers of His power and executors of His will.

8. In verses 8-10 the judgment of the wicked is described in language and imagery which reflect the Old Testament, and, as said above, in a rhythmical structure which has led many scholars to think we may have here an adaptation of a primitive Christian hymn.

In a flame of fire, or as another good reading has it, "in a fire of flame." The sense is the same in either reading. It is better to join these words with what has just preceded, as descriptive of the manner in which our Lord will appear at the final judgment. In the Old Testament flaming fire often accompanied the manifestations of God as legislator and judge. Here it is a symbol of the divine majesty and anger, of His glory and power which nothing can resist.

Giving vengeance, etc., i.e., dealing out punishment to all wilful unbelievers in God and in the Gospel of Christ, whether Jews or Gentiles: "He that believeth not shall be condemned" (Mark xvi. 16); "He that doth not believe is already judged, etc." (John iii. 18-19). God's vengeance, or revenge, means nothing more than doing justice to sinners, who have wilfully brought on themselves all their woe. This is why God reserves revenge to Himself: "Revenge is mine, I will repay, saith the Lord" (Rom. xii. 19; Deut. xxxii. 35; Heb. x. 30). When we undertake to revenge a wrong, we are often influenced by passion, and so are more than likely to be unjust; not so God, whose essence is justice itself, and whose ways are altogether righteous.

9. **Who shall suffer,** etc. Better, "who will pay the penalty in eternal ruin." The Greek for "eternal punishment" ($\ddot{o}\lambda\epsilon\theta\rho os$ $a\dot{i}\omega\nu\iota os$) means "destruction without end." The term $\ddot{o}\lambda\epsilon\theta\rho os$ is found elsewhere only in the apocryphal work 4 Mach. x. 15, and it corresponds to the "everlasting fire" of Matt. xviii. 8, xxv. 41, and Jude 7; to the "eternal punishment" of Matt. xxv. 46; and to the "eternal judgment" of Heb. vi. 2. See Vosté, *hoc loco,* and on Phil. i. 28, iii. 19.

From the face of the Lord, words borrowed from Isa. ii. 10, 19, 21. The meaning, according to St. Chrysostom and others, is

10. When he shall come to be glorified in his saints, and to be made wonderful in all them who have believed (because our testimony among you
was believed) in that day.

that the appearance of the Lord will cause the destruction and punishment of the wicked: "The sight of their Judge and His Almighti-
ness, robed in fire and attended by His host of angels, will drive
these wicked men, terror-stricken, into ruin" (Findlay). But the
common opinion, which is that of St. Thomas, Bisping and many
others, understands the foregoing words to refer to the *pain of
loss* or exclusion from the divine presence: the wicked will suffer
everlasting punishment far removed from the presence of the Lord;
thus, their punishment will consist principally in the loss of God,
the source and fountain of every good that can contribute to man's
happiness and satisfy the ceaseless longings of his soul.

And from the glory of His power, i.e., the wicked shall be
removed far from that divine glory which has its source in God's
infinite power, and which Jesus Christ will communicate to His
elect according to their capacity to receive it.

10. **When He shall come,** etc. The punishment of the wicked
just described will take place when our Lord comes "to be glorified
in His saints," i.e., when, at the end of the world, He appears in
His glory and imparts that glory to those faithful souls who have
believed in Him and proved their faith by the performance of
good works, and who will be, as it were, the mirror of His own
glory: "I am glorified in them" (John xvii. 10) ; "But we all beholding the glory of the Lord with open face, are transformed into
the same image, etc." (2 Cor. iii. 18) ; at which same time He will
"be made wonderful in all them who have believed," i.e., the saints
at that glorious time, seeing with astonishment the undreamed-of
blessedness which their faith has brought them, will marvel at their
Saviour through whose grace they have attained their sanctity and
amassed their merits.

Because our testimony among you was believed, i.e., the Thessalonians will reap this great reward because they believed the Gospel which St. Paul and his companions had preached to them. This
sentence is a parenthesis, and it should be so indicated in the Vulgate.

In that day. With great emphasis these words are placed at the
end of the verse, in order again to remind the readers of the time

11. Wherefore also we pray always for you, that our God would make you worthy of his vocation, and fulfill with power all the good pleasure of his goodness and the work of faith;

12. That the name of our Lord Jesus may be glorified in you, and you in him, according to the grace of our God, and of the Lord Jesus Christ.

of the solemn manifestation of the Lord and the fulfillment of the events just described in this and in the preceding verses.

11. In verses 11-12 St. Paul says that his continual prayer for his readers is that they may be made worthy of their lofty vocation, and that Jesus Christ may be glorified in them and they in Him.

Our God, i.e., the God of us all.

Of his vocation, i.e., of the call He has given you, so that one day you will be found worthy of the reward of glory to which you have been chosen.

And fulfill with power all the good pleasure, etc., i.e., powerfully fill you with a desire of every good that a righteous will could wish for (St. Thomas) and that faith can effect.

12. The final purpose of the Apostle's prayer and of the sanctification of the faithful is that our Lord may be glorified in them, and that they in turn may be glorified in Him through the outpouring of His glory upon them in the beatific vision (cf. John xvii).

The name stands for the person, according to Semitic usage.

According to the grace, etc. The grace of God, communicated through Jesus Christ, is the source of the sanctification of the faithful.

CHAPTER II

THE PAROUSIA IS NOT YET, 1-11

1-11. The faithful must not be disturbed about the Coming of the Lord, for certain signs, yet far off, must first precede that grand event. There must come first a great religious revolt, and then the man of sin, Antichrist, must appear, as was explained before in the Apostle's preaching. This mystery of iniquity is already at work, but something holds back the full exercise of his power. He shall eventually be conquered by Christ coming in His glory, but he will first show great signs and wonders and seduce many.

1. And we beseech you, brethren, touching the coming of our Lord Jesus Christ, and of our gathering together unto him:

2. That you be not easily moved from your sense, nor be terrified, neither by spirit, nor by word, nor by epistle, as by us, as if the day of the Lord were at hand.

3. Let no man deceive you by any means, for unless there come the revolt first, and the man of sin be revealed, the son of perdition,

1. **Touching the coming of our Lord,** etc., i.e., on behalf of the Parousia, or Second Coming of Christ to judge the world.

And of our gathering together, etc. Better, "and of our being gathered together, etc.," referring to the reunion of the living and the dead at the coming of our Lord at the end of the world (1 Thess. iv. 17, v. 10).

The Vulgate *nostræ congregationis* should read *circa nostram congregationem.*

2. The Apostle asks the Thessalonians that they be calm and peaceful, that they do not lose their "sense" (i.e., their prudent and sober judgment), nor be greatly disturbed, as if the Parousia were at hand.

By spirit, i.e., by any pretended revelation or prophesy attributed to the Holy Ghost.

Nor by word, i.e., any utterance or teaching based on a pretended revelation or prophesy, or on some utterance of the Apostle, misinterpreted or falsely attributed to him.

Nor by epistle, as by us (ὡς δι'ἡμῶν), etc., i.e., any spurious letter circulated in the name of Paul, or false explanation of his first Epistle to the Thessalonians. Let none of these sources of error lead them to think the Second Advent is upon us.

The *missam* of the Vulgate is not expressed in the Greek.

3. There is nothing in the writings of St. Paul more obscure and difficult of explanation than verses 3-11 here. This is due partly to the eschatological events here described as going before the Parousia, about which the Apostle speaks nowhere else; partly to the fact that he assumes his readers to be thoroughly familiar from his oral teaching with the obscure points in discussion; and partly to the veiled terms in which those mysterious events are apparently of set purpose expressed. As a result, we cannot be too certain of the correctness of some of the expositions given.

The first warning is, "let no man deceive you," i.e., lead you into the mistake of thinking the Parousia is present.

4. Who opposeth, and is lifted up against all that is called God, or that is worshipped, so that he sitteth in the temple of God, shewing himself as if he were God.

By any means, whether by any of the three ways mentioned in verse 2, or in any other way; and the reason for this is immediately given by adding, "for unless there come a revolt first," i.e., a falling away from God (ἀποστασία), etc. That "revolt" or *apostasy* here means a religious defection or falling away from God is the opinion of St. Thomas and all modern interpreters. It will be the first of the great events that shall precede the Parousia. The Apostle, becoming absorbed in a description of the "man of sin," forgets to complete his sentence, "for unless, etc."; but it is clear that its completion would be, "the Day of the Lord will not come," or something similar. Such ellipses are frequent with St. Paul, who was accustomed to speak and to dictate his letters, as they are also common with many public speakers. The use of the definite article before "revolt" (ἡ ἀποστασία) shows that the Apostle was referring to a definite religious falling away known to his readers: "For many will come in my name, saying, 'I am Christ,' and they will seduce many, etc." (Matt. xxiv. 5 ff.).

And the man of sin be revealed. This is the second great event that shall go before the Parousia. The "man of sin" is doubtless to be identified with Antichrist (1 John ii. 18, 22, iv. 3; 3 John 7), whose other-world character is evident from the fact that he is to "be revealed." He is described: (a) as to his nature, "the man of sin"; (b) as to his fate, "the son of perdition"; (c) as to his ambition, which will be to take the place of God and to be worshipped as God (ver. 4).

In the best Greek MSS. "man of sin" is read as "the man of lawlessness," who is spoken of in verse 7 below as "the mystery of lawlessness," and in verse 8 as "the lawless one." This "man of sin," who will be the impersonation and personification of sin, this "man of lawlessness," in whom will culminate the lawlessness and godlessness of a godless world, is not Belial or Satan, but some emissary of Belial or Satan, as is clear from verse 9 below.

Son of perdition is a Semitic expression indicating the eternal destiny in final damnation of Antichrist (John xvii. 12).

4. **Who opposeth, and is lifted up,** etc. The verbs here are present participles in Greek, but the meaning is best expressed by

5. Remember you not that, when I was yet with you, I told you these things?

6. And now you know what withholdeth, that he may be revealed in his own time.

rendering with the Westminster Version, "who shall oppose and exalt himself against all, etc." The object of this opposition will be Christ (St. Jerome and many moderns), and hence St. John in his First Epistle styles the adversary in question as Antichrist (1 John ii. 18, 22, iv. 3). This archenemy of Christ will deny the true God and spurn false gods, so as to appropriate all worship to himself, pretending that he is the one and only God to whose adoration and service all sanctuaries are to be devoted, or rather prostituted. St. Paul's description of him recalls several similar characters of the Old Testament, namely, Antiochus Epiphanes (Dan. xi. 36-37), the prince of Tyre (Ezech. xviii. 2), and the king of Babylon (Isa. xiv. 13-14).

So that he sitteth, etc. Better, "so as to take his seat in the temple of God." The word "temple" here more probably is not to be understood literally of the Temple of Jerusalem nor of the Church of God, but should be taken as a mode of speaking by which the usurpation of all divine adoration and honor on the part of Antichrist is expressed (so Knabenbauer, Vosté and others): he will have it appear that he is God Himself, the only true God, therefore "showing himself as if he were God." On the deification of the Roman Emperors, see Findlay, *hoc loco,* in *Cambridge Bible.*

In the Vulgate *supra omne* would better be *contra omne,* and *ostendens se tanquam, etc.,* should be *gerens se ut Deus.*

5. By way of mild rebuke St. Paul asks the Thessalonians how it is that they have so soon forgotten what he told them relative to these matters when he was preaching to them in person.

These things, i.e., the great apostasy and the manifestation or appearance of Antichrist. Until these things occur, the Parousia will not take place.

6. In verses 6-7 the Apostle refers to what holds back the man of sin, and consequently the dawn of the last day. These verses are very obscure, because here again the Apostle is supposing his readers to be familiar with the instruction he had given them on this point.

Now is understood in a logical sense by some authorities, as if

7. For the mystery of iniquity already worketh; only that he who now holdeth, do hold, until he be taken out of the way.

to say: things being so, "now" you know, etc.; but it is better to take the term in its strict temporal meaning, as opposed to the future revelation and working of Antichrist (Vosté).

What withholdeth, i.e., what powerfully retards, or keeps back the appearance of Antichrist. What was this restraining influence (τὸ κατέχον)? In verse 7 it is spoken of as present and as masculine in gender, ὁ κατέχων ἄρτι; and so it would seem to be some personal force existing at the time this letter was written. St. Augustine confessed that he did not know what it was. According to the common opinion among the ancients, to which moderns are inclining, it was "the restraining power of law and order, especially as these were embodied in the Roman Emperor or Empire" (Jones, in *New Com. on Holy Script.*). In favor of this opinion it is said that the Apostle is assuming that his readers know well what he means from the instruction he had given them by word of mouth, and that here he only hints at it, refraining from open speech, so as not to compromise himself and his cause with the Imperial Government, which would be roused to persecution by any prediction of its downfall.

But if fear of Rome accounts for his veiled manner of speech in his letter, how could he have spoken more openly to the Thessalonians in oral discourse without being in danger of detection and exposure to the Roman authority? Theodoret thought the restraining agency was the Decree of God that Antichrist should not appear until the time appointed for him should arrive. Others have suggested the Holy Spirit as the restraining personal power. Fr. Prat in his *Theol. of St. Paul*, vol. I, pp. 114-117, thinks it is St. Michael, who, with his heavenly host, wages continual war against Satan on behalf of the elect, and who will be the herald of the resurrection and the final judgment. Still others think it is the preaching of the Gospel which must encompass the world before the end of time. Perhaps it is the living, fervent faith of Christians, which will decline and grow cold before the end (Matt. xxiv. 11-13).

That he may be revealed in his own time, i.e., that he may appear at the time decreed by God.

7. In this verse St. Paul says that Antichrist, here called "the mystery of iniquity," or according to the Greek "the mystery of

8. And then that wicked one shall be revealed whom the Lord Jesus shall kill with the spirit of his mouth; and shall destroy with the brightness of his coming, him

9. Whose coming is according to the working of Satan, in all power, and signs, and lying wonders,

lawlessness," is now operating in secret, and will continue to do so until the agency that restrains him be removed. His means of operation now are doubtless through heresies, errors, persecutions, and the like, which are but the preparation for his unbridled reign.

Only that he who now holdeth, etc. Far better, according to the Greek, "until he who now restrains be taken out of the way." In the Vulgate the phrase *tantum ut,* etc., should read, *tantum donec qui detinet adhuc de medio fiat* (Vosté).

8. In verses 8-11 St. Paul speaks of the coming of Antichrist, of his malevolent works, and of the reason why God will permit him so to harass the world.

And then, i.e., when the restraining influence has been removed.

That wicked one, i.e., "the man of sin," "the son of perdition" (ver. 3), Antichrist.

Shall be revealed, i.e., shall come forth from his mysterious concealment, from his other-world realm, whence now he works secretly.

Whom the Lord Jesus shall kill, etc. Again, as in verse 4, St. Paul reverts to the use of Old Testament language, referring now to the imagery of Isa. xi. 4 to describe the fate of Antichrist and the triumph of Christ over him. This powerful enemy of mankind the Lord Jesus will destroy by the issuance of a simple command, by a glance of his countenance; as in the beginning the Almighty spoke and creation leaped into being, so at the end He will need but to speak, but to appear in His majesty, and the great enemy will be laid low forever.

The brightness of his coming refers to the Parousia or Second Coming of Christ (1 Tim. iv. 14; 2 Tim. i. 10, iv. 1, 8; Tit. ii. 13).

9. The Apostle began to speak of the appearance of Antichrist in verse 8a, but immediately interrupted his description to portray his destruction by the command and presence of our Lord. Now he returns to the thought of 8a, and describes the coming and working of the great enemy. As Christ will have His glorious appearance, so will Antichrist have his contrary appearance, the operation of the latter being altogether opposed to that of the former: first, as to its principle, which will be "Satan"; secondly, as to its intimate nature,

10. And in all seduction of iniquity to them that perish; because they receive not the love of the truth, that they might be saved. Therefore God shall send them the operation of error, to believe lying:
11. That all may be judged who have not believed the truth, but have consented to iniquity.

which will be "lying"; and thirdly, as to its end or purpose, which will be "seduction" (cf. Vosté, *h. l.*).

Whose coming is according, etc. The present tense is used for the future. Antichrist will be the instrument of Satan, whom Satan will empower to produce all kinds of signs and wonders for the purpose of deceiving his victims.

Power, signs, wonders. A miracle is said to be a "power" (δύναμις), when considered as to its origin or cause; it is a "sign" (σημεῖον), when considered as to its purpose or end; it is a "wonder" (τέρας), when considered as to its extraordinary nature, which excites the admiration of men.

10. This verse describes the purpose of Antichrist and designates his victims. His activities will be directed to the deception and perdition of all men, but will be efficacious only with "them that perish," i.e., those whose lives and works have fitted them for perdition; "because they receive not the love of the truth," i.e., they refuse to accept and do not want the teachings of the Gospel; in punishment for which "God shall send them the operation, etc.," i.e., God shall punish them by permitting them to be led to put their faith in errors and lies; they did not want the truth of the Gospel; they refused to believe the miracles of Christ; so they will receive instead the wicked teachings and gross errors of powerful deceivers.

In the Greek, verse 11 begins with "Therefore God shall send, etc.," and there are thus 17 verses in this chapter in Greek, instead of 16 as in the Vulgate and our version.

11. The final reason is now given why God will permit the deception of the victims of Antichrist, namely, "that all may be judged, etc.," i.e., that all may be condemned who have preferred iniquity to the truth of the Gospel. According to St. Paul, sin leads in its train its own punishment (cf. Rom. i. 24-28). The wicked who have preferred sin, iniquity, lies, will receive like things in compensation; and God will employ Satan and Antichrist as instruments for their punishment; they will be made the dupes of their own wickedness.

12. But we ought to give thanks to God always for you, brethren, beloved of the Lord, for that God chose you firstfruits unto salvation, through sanctification of the spirit and faith of the truth

13. Whereunto also he called you by our gospel, unto the purchasing of the glory of our Lord Jesus Christ.

THANKSGIVING, EXHORTATION AND PRAYER, 12-16

12-16. St. Paul now turns away from the thought of the reprobate to think of the elect and the spiritual blessings of which they have been the willing objects, believing in the Gospel and consenting to the truth; and he says that for them who have been chosen by God and sanctified and ordained to eternal life, he and his companions ought always to give thanks to God (ver. 12-13). He exhorts his readers to steadfastness in what they have received from him, whether by preaching or by letter; and then offers a prayer that they may be comforted and strengthened in faith (ver. 14-16).

12. **But we,** i.e., Paul, Silas and Timothy.

Brethren, beloved of the Lord, as contrasted with the sad victims of delusion and unbelief.

For that God chose you, etc. The reading "firstfruits" here is according to the Vulgate, the Vatican, and some other good MSS., and means that the Thessalonians were among the first people in Europe to accept the Gospel (cf. Phil. iv. 15; Rom. xvi. 5; 1 Cor. xvi. 15). Instead of "firstfruits," we find in the Sinaitic, Alex., and other good MSS. the reading, "from the beginning," which means that God chose the Thessalonians for the Gospel and salvation from eternity (Eph. i. 4; Col. i. 20).

Unto salvation. This is the end to which God's eternal choice was ordained.

Through sanctification, etc. Behold the means of salvation, namely, the sanctifying grace of the Holy Ghost, on the part of God, and faith in the Gospel accompanied by good works, on the part of man. The expression "sanctification of the spirit" may be understood objectively, as meaning the sanctification of our souls; or it may be taken in a subjective and causal sense to signify the sanctification which is from the Holy Ghost. Both interpretations come to the same thing.

The *Dei* of the Vulgate should be *Domini*.

13. **Whereunto,** etc., i.e., to which faith and sanctification God

14. Therefore, brethren, stand fast; and hold the traditions which you have learned, whether by word, or by our epistle.

15. Now our Lord Jesus Christ himself, and God and our Father, who hath loved us, and hath given us everlasting consolation, and good hope in grace,

16. Exhort your hearts, and confirm you in every good work and word.

called the Thessalonians in time, through the preaching of the Apostles, "unto the purchasing, etc.," i.e., to the end that they might have a share in the eternal glory of our Lord Jesus Christ.

14. **Therefore, brethren,** etc., i.e., since you are called to so great a destiny.

Stand fast in the faith and practice of your religion.

And hold the traditions, i.e., the instructions, the dogmatic and moral teachings, which we have given you, "whether by word" of mouth, "or by our epistle," i.e., 1 Thess. In these last words we have a plain case against the teachings of Protestantism, that Scripture is the only source of divine revelation, to the exclusion of what has been passed down by word of mouth or tradition. On this passage St. Chrysostom says: "From this it is clear that the Apostles did not give everything through Epistles, but many things also not in writings; and these also worthy of faith. Wherefore, we also regard the tradition of the Church as worthy of faith. It is tradition, seek nothing further."

15-16. Since the Thessalonians could not of their own strength continue firm in their faith, St. Paul now prays God to give them the necessary grace.

Now our Lord Jesus Christ himself, etc. Our Lord is here mentioned before the Father, as in 2 Cor. xiii. 13 and Gal. i. 1, because He is the way to the Father. On these words St. Chrysostom remarks: "Where now are those who say that the Son is less than the Father, because He is named after the Father in the grace of washing?" St. Paul heartens his readers by reminding them that our Lord and God the Father have loved them from all eternity, and have given them "everlasting consolation" in the midst of tribulations through the "good hope" they have of possessing one day the joys of heaven; and this divine love God has for them, as well as the hope He has given them, is "in grace," i.e., is gratuitous, the result of pure mercy on His part. Therefore the Apostle prays that God would "exhort," i.e., comfort their hearts in the midst of tribulations, "and confirm," i.e., strengthen them in the pursuit of every good work. It is to be observed that the verbs "exhort" and "confirm" here are in the singular, following the mention of our Lord and God the Father, which shows that the action of our Lord is identical with that of the Father, and therefore that He is one with the Father in nature and substance.

CHAPTER III

MUTUAL INTERCESSION, 1-5

1. For the rest, brethren, pray for us, that the word of the Lord may run, and may be glorified, even as among you;
2. And that we may be delivered from perverse and evil men; for all men have not faith.
3. But the Lord is faithful, who will strengthen and keep you from evil.

1-5. The Apostle now requests prayers for himself and his companions (ver. 1-2). He assures the Thessalonians of God's faithfulness and of his own confidence in them (ver. 3-4), and prays once more for them (ver. 5).

1. **For the rest.** See on 1 Thess. iv. 1.

That the word of the Lord, etc., i.e., that the teaching of the Gospel may spread rapidly without impediment in the world.

And may be glorified, i.e., may be acknowledged and may produce the fruit of life among all men, as it has done "among you." The *Dei* of the Vulgate should be *Domini,* to agree with the Greek.

2. St. Paul's second request is that he and his companions "may be delivered from perverse and evil men," very likely referring to his Jewish opponents at Corinth at this time (Acts xvii. 13 ff., xviii. 6 ff.). It is not surprising that opposition should be encountered, "for all men have not faith," i.e., comparatively few embrace the faith, and this for two reasons, namely, because faith is first of all a free gift of God, and secondly, because men are indisposed and do not want faith.

3. After requesting their prayers, the Apostle now turns his thoughts to the Thessalonians themselves, assuring them that, however strong their enemies may be, "the Lord is faithful" to His promises (1 Cor. i. 9), and that, having called them to the Gospel, He will not be wanting in His grace to "strengthen" them in the

4. And we have confidence concerning you in the Lord, that the things which we command you both do and will do.

5. And the Lord direct your hearts into the charity of God and the patience of Christ.

6. And we charge you, brethren, in the name of the Lord Jesus Christ, that you withdraw yourselves from every brother walking disorderly, and not according to the tradition which they received of us.

pursuit of good and protect them against the incursions of "evil," or better, "the evil one," probably alluding to the last petition of the Lord's Prayer (Matt. vi. 13; Luke xi. 4).

Again, read *Dominus* for *Deus* in the Vulgate.

4. **We have confidence concerning you**, etc. The Apostle is speaking in the present tense, and seems to be preparing his readers for the more severe counsels he will give them in verse 6. He means to say that he is relying on their good will, assisted by God's grace which is never wanting to the well-disposed, for he adds, "in the Lord," the author of all grace.

5. After expressing his confidence in their good will to do all in their power, St. Paul now prays that God will make up to them whatever may be lacking on their part by moving and directing their hearts "in the charity of God, etc." It is not certain whether there is question here of the love which God has for us and the patience of which Christ gave us an example, or of the love we have for God and the patient expectation of the coming of Christ. The latter opinion is thought to be more probable (Cajetan, Vosté).

In charitate et patientia of the Vulgate should be *in charitatem et patientiam,* according to the Greek.

CORRECTION FOR DISORDERLY MEMBERS, AND EXHORTATION TO THE LOYAL, 6-15

6-15. Idleness at Thessalonica on the part of many who were looking for the early arrival of the Parousia had become worse since the reception of 1 Thess. These disturbers are now more sternly rebuked by the Apostles, with an appeal to their own example, who worked for their own living while preaching the Gospel (ver. 6-12). After rebuking the disorderly and troublesome, the Apostles address the good members, encouraging them to perseverance in works of faith and asking them to avoid the disobedient (ver. 13-15).

6. **We charge you, brethren,** etc. Speaking in the name and

7. For yourselves know how you ought to imitate us, for we were not disorderly among you;

8. Neither did we eat any man's bread for nothing, but in labor and in toil we worked night and day, lest we should be chargeable to any of you:

9. Not as if we had not power, but that we might give ourselves a pattern unto you to imitate us.

10. For also when we were with you this we declared to you: that, if any man will not work, neither let him eat.

with the authority of our Lord, the Apostles now command the Thessalonians to avoid all those whose moral conduct (ver. 11) is not according to the written and oral teaching which the Thessalonian Church has received. They therefore issue a species of excommunication against those idle and disturbing members of the Church, who, on pretext of the imminence of the Parousia, have given up their regular pursuits and are living on the charity of their neighbors. These directions, however, are to be executed in charity and for the spiritual benefit of the offenders (ver. 14-15).

The tradition, etc. See above, on ii. 14.

They received. This is the older reading; but some authorities prefer another good reading, "you received." There is little support for "he received," as in the Authorized Version. For a more real excommunication, see 1 Cor. v. 5; 1 Tim. i. 20.

7. In verses 7-9 the Apostles appeal to their own conduct and example while at Thessalonica as a model which the faithful should imitate.

Disorderly means idle, living on other people, as explained in the following verse.

8. **Eat any man's bread** is a Hebraism meaning "to partake of food," "to feast," "to live on." In order not to be any burden to the faithful the Apostle and his comrades worked day and night to make their own living. Cf. 1 Cor. ix. 15 ff.; 2 Cor. xi. 7 ff.; 1 Thess. ii. 9 ff.

9. It was not that the Apostles had not the right to demand temporal support for their spiritual services, but that they might give the faithful an example of self-denial in things legitimate for the sake of the Gospel.

10. These things St. Paul and his companions had inculcated, not only by example, but also by their express teachings while at Thessalonica.

11. For we hear there are some among you, who walk disorderly, working not at all, but curiously meddling.

12. Now we charge them that are such, and beseech them by the Lord Jesus Christ, that, working with silence, they would eat their own bread.

13. But you, brethren, be not weary in well-doing.

14. And if any man obey not our word by this epistle, note that man, and do not keep company with him, that he may be ashamed:

15. Yet do not esteem him as an enemy, but admonish him as a brother.

That, if any man will not work, etc.   This was probably a proverbial expression, based on the rule of Gen. iii. 19: "In the sweat of thy face shalt thou eat bread, etc." It is to be noted that the Apostle says "will not work," and not "can not work"; for the sick and disabled have a right to charity and care by others. Mere idleness for the sake of pleasure is here condemned authoritatively.

11-12. **We hear,** etc.   The tense is present in Greek, as it should also be in the Vulgate, which shows that the Apostle had recent news from Thessalonica regarding those disturbing persons who, instead of working and attending to their own affairs, were going about interfering with the affairs of others. In solemn words he admonishes them to be quiet and to earn their own living.

13. The Apostle now turns his attention to the faithful members of the Church at Thessalonica, and exhorts them to continue "in well-doing," which most probably means simply perseverance in virtuous living (so Vosté and moderns generally), though the older commentators, Knabenbauer and others think the Apostle is here referring to doing works of charity, giving alms, and the like.

14-15. In these verses, while enjoining social and religious ostracism for the contumacious Christians, St. Paul makes it clear that his purpose is for the good of the guilty persons, that they may be led to see the error of their ways and won to better behavior. Therefore, verse 6 is to be explained in the light of these verses.

CONCLUSION, 16-18

16-18. In closing his letter St. Paul wishes peace and the divine presence to all the faithful at Thessalonica; he salutes them in his own handwriting, as a sign of the genuineness of this Epistle, and embraces all in a final blessing.

16. Now the Lord of peace himself give you everlasting peace in every place. The Lord be with you all.

17. The salutation of Paul with my own hand; which is the sign in every epistle. So I write.

18. The grace of our Lord Jesus Christ be with you all. Amen.

16. In view of the disturbance which has upset the Thessalonian Church, St. Paul now asks our Lord, the author of peace, to give the faithful there lasting peace of mind and soul.

In every place. This is also the reading of the Gothic version and of the MSS., A,D,F,G; but the majority of the best Greek MSS. and the Syriac and Coptic versions have: "In every way."

The Lord be with you all, including the disorderly.

17. **The salutation of Paul with my own hand.** He means to say that he sends this greeting to them in his own handwriting, as a mark of the authenticity of the letter. It was the custom of the time to dictate letters to amanuenses, and this also seems to have been Paul's uniform practice. But here he writes the greeting at the end so that there will be no danger of falsification on the part of anyone at Thessalonica, where a false letter, pretending to be from him, appears to have been in circulation (ii. 2). It is probable that St. Paul wrote with his own hand the whole letter to Philemon (ver. 19), and perhaps that to the Galatians also (Gal. vi. 11). Cf. Vosté, *h. l.*

Which is the sign in every epistle. The reason for this precaution is probably to be found in the forged letter that was being circulated by misguided members of the Thessalonian Church, who claimed that it had come from Paul himself (cf. *Introduction*, No. III, b).

So I write, i.e., this is my handwriting.

18. The final benediction is the same as in 1 Thess. and in Rom. xvi. 20, save that the word "all" is added here, so as not to appear to exclude the well-intentioned but disorderly members of the Thessalonian Church.

THE PASTORAL EPISTLES

INTRODUCTION

I. Pastoral. For over two centuries now the two Epistles of St. Paul to Timothy and the one to Titus have been commonly known as "Pastoral Epistles." The term "pastoral" was, indeed, applied to the letters to Timothy by St. Thomas Aquinas in the thirteenth century; but its general currency as pertaining to these three letters seems to date from the time of Paul Anton (1726). The term is an appropriate one inasmuch as these Epistles were addressed by the great Apostle to the heads of Churches in their capacity of pastors of souls, whose duty it was to oversee, guide and instruct those committed to their care, to guard against error and preserve the purity of apostolic teaching, to set by example a high standard of Christian life and character, and to provide through careful selection, training, and ordination successors to carry on the glorious preaching and work of the Gospel when they themselves should be called to their rewards.

Though written for specific times and particular conditions pertinent to their own age, these Pastoral letters are invaluable to us and to all succeeding ages for the information they supply regarding primitive church organization and discipline, early heresies, the qualifications of Christian teachers and leaders, the duties of pastors, the ideals of zeal and devotion that should ever animate the bearers of the priestly office, and for the information they afford regarding the last years and activities of St. Paul. In a very special sense, therefore, these letters impress upon the Christian priest and bishop the necessity at all times of taking a spiritual view of his office, life and work, and of the weighty responsibility that rests upon him and the consequent necessity of keeping ever in close contact with his Master, to whom he must render an account of his stewardship, and from whom, if he is faithful, he may, like St. Paul, expect a crown of glory when his labors are over.

II. **Authenticity of the Pastorals.** Before beginning this discussion, "it will be convenient to remark in this place that these three Epistles are so closely linked together in thought, in phraseology, and in the historical situation which they presuppose, that they must be counted as having all come into being within a very few years of each other. The general consent of critics allows that they stand or fall together; and it is therefore not always necessary to distinguish the indications of the existence of one from those of the existence of another. We may speak generally, without loss of accuracy, of evidences of knowledge of the Pastoral Epistles if we come upon reminiscences of any one of them. And so, in investigating their literary history, we consider them not separately, but together" (Bernard, *Introd. to The Pastoral Epistles*, p. xii., in *Cambridge Greek Test.*).

For Catholics the question of the Pauline authorship of these letters is beyond dispute. In fact, no one ever doubted that Paul was their author until the beginning of the last century, when certain German and other scholars began to attack them, chiefly on internal grounds. Since that time the Pastorals have been under fierce fire, and they have been more generally rejected by non-Catholic critics than any other letters of St. Paul except Hebrews.

That prior to the last century the authenticity of these Epistles was universally accepted is admitted by all the best non-Catholic scholars. The following are some worthwhile testimonies: "There never was the slightest doubt in the ancient Church that the Epistles to Timothy and Titus were canonical and written by Paul" (Dean Alford). "Traces of their circulation in the Church before Marcion's time are clearer than those which can be found for Romans and Second Corinthians" (Zahn). "These Epistles are as well attested by external or historical evidence as the other Epistles of Paul" (De Wette). "The witness of the Early Church to their place in the New Testament canon and their Pauline authorship is as clear, full and unhesitating as that given to the other Epistles" (Findlay). "The work of no ancient classic author has such strong external and internal proof of its genuineness. . . . We may be sure that these Epistles are not a fraud" (Bishop Vincent). "The external attestation of the Epistles is quite on a par with that of the other Paulines" (Weiss).

Indeed, if we just briefly glance at the external evidence in the ancient Church in favor of these Epistles, we shall see that the foregoing testimonies are well founded. For allusions to their wording or quotations from them are to be seen in the writings of Clement of Rome and the Epistle of Barnabas (end of first century), of Ignatius, Bishop of Antioch (circa, 110 A.D.), of Polycarp (c. 117), of Justin Martyr (c. 140), of Heracleon (c. 165), of Hegesippus (c. 170), of Athenagoras of Athens (c. 176), of Theophilus of Antioch (c. 181), and St. Athenagoras (end of second century). Besides these authorities, we find many others at the same time or immediately following them who accepted the Pastorals without a sign of hesitation, such as Tertullian, Irenæus, Clement of Alexandria, Origen, etc. They are also found in the Muratorian Fragment, in the old Latin and Syriac versions, and in the list of Pauline Epistles accepted by Eusebius. Many other ancient witnesses might be added to this catalogue, but they would all be to the same effect, with the exception of a few early heretics—like Marcion, Valentine, Basilides—who, as Clement of Alexandria (*Strom.*, ii. 11) said, rejected these letters because they were contrary to their own false doctrines.

The internal evidence in support of the Pastoral Epistles, which is also very strong, will appear from an examination of the objections that are brought against their genuineness by modern non-Catholic scholars. For these objections, while not at all unanswerable, are of sufficient weight to demand our attention and serious thought. It is true, as has been said in part already, that many of the best non-Catholic authorities of the last as well as of the present century find nothing in these letters that can shake their Pauline authorship, so thoroughly established by external proofs from the beginning down to the first half of the last century. Among these authorities may be mentioned Adeney, Alford, Lightfoot, Hort, Findlay, Ramsay, Sanday, Plummer, Farrar, Godet, Gilbert, Schaff, Shaw, Lange, Weiss, Zahn, Wiesinger, and many more. Against the genuineness of the Pastorals we may mention the following: Baur, Davidson, Holtzmann, Meyer, Jülicher, Weizsacker, Hatch, Schwegler, Beyschlag, and Schenkel—all of whom believe these Epistles were written by some one who lived at a later date. But there is another large and increasing class of critics who take a middle position on this question. They are of the opinion that we have here documents containing genuine Pauline fragments and unpublished notes which a later writer incorporated into his own work and issued under Paul's name in order to give it greater influence and authority. Among these writers are: Ewald, Harnack, Bacon, Harrison, Hausrath, Deissmann, Moffatt, McGiffert, and others.

With this outline of the problem before us we may now proceed to examine the principal objections to the Pauline authorship of these letters.

III. **Objections to the Authenticity of the Pastorals.** FIRST OBJECTION. The historical and biographical data given in the Pastorals cannot be fitted into the life of St. Paul as detailed in the Book of Acts.

But they do not need to be so fitted. Who has said that the Acts ever pretended to give us a complete history of Paul or of anyone else? This objection proceeds from false suppositions, namely, that we have a complete account of St. Paul's life in the Acts of The Apostles, and that he was put to death at the end of his first Roman captivity. As a matter of fact, from St. Luke's record of the Apostle's arrest in Jerusalem and his later imprisonment in Rome and from the letters written by St. Paul during his first captivity there, we have every reason to accept the testimonies of Clement of Rome, the Muratorian Fragment, the *Acta Pauli*, etc., that the Apostle was not only released but that he actually afterwards visited Spain, as he had intended to do (Rom. xv. 24). St. Jerome, St. Chrysostom, Theodoret, and many other Fathers also tell us that Paul preached in Spain. Moreover, at his first arrest, there was no serious charge brought against him (Acts xxviii. 18 ff.), and in Rome he enjoyed great liberty (Acts xxviii. 30, 31), and seemed reasonably sure of being released and of being able to revisit the East (Phlm. 22; Phil. ii. 19-24). Harnack, Lightfoot, Weiss and others, therefore, rightly maintain that no proof can be given to show that the Apostle was not released from his first Roman captivity, and that, consequently, the historical data of the Pastoral Epistles (except II Tim.) can be referred to in the years following 63 or 65 A.D.

SECOND OBJECTION.   There is a large percentage of strange words and phrases in these Epistles that are not found in other letters of St. Paul, nor elsewhere in the New Testament.

This should cause no difficulty.   There are many words and expressions that are peculiar to every Epistle of this most versatile writer; and if the Pastorals have a greater number than the other letters, this can be quite satisfactorily explained by the difference of the persons addressed, the subjects treated, the Apostle's advancing years, his associates when writing, etc.

THIRD OBJECTION.   Great numbers of favorite Pauline words are absent from these letters.

But why should it be otherwise, if in later years he was treating of different subjects, writing to different persons, and subject to a different environment as he wrote?   But are these favorite words absent only from the Pastorals, or also from the other genuine Epistles of St. Paul?   Moffatt has made a list of these words; and Dr. Ahern, having examined every one of them, has found that with a single exception they are all absent from one or several of the admittedly genuine letters of St. Paul, and that the exceptional word occurs but once in some of them (cf. Ahern, *Timothy*, in *Catholic Encyclopedia*, vol. XIV, p. 728a).

Nor should we be disturbed at the absence in the Pastorals of many small words, like enclitics and prepositions; for it is conceded that the Apostle was not uniform in his use of them in his other letters, and that when treating practical matters, like those of the Pastoral Epistles, he was at all times sparing of these little words and particles.   Hence Jülicher says that no argument can be drawn from the absence of these words.

FOURTH OBJECTION.   The style of these Epistles is very different from St. Paul's usual manner of writing.

It is different from the argumentative and doctrinal parts of the Apostle's other letters, but it is so similar to the style of the practical sections of those other Epistles that not a few writers have jumped to the conclusion that we have in the Pastorals a composition of many authentic but unpublished Pauline fragments.   Bishop Lightfoot's study of the style of these Epistles led him only to the conclusion that they were all three written about the same time, and that a considerable period must have intervened between them and the other Epistles of St. Paul.

FIFTH OBJECTION. There are noticeable differences of theology here.

And this is what we should expect, since St. Paul is writing, not from an argumentative or controversial, but from a practical viewpoint. The Apostle is here giving Timothy and Titus practical directions and counsels; he is not discussing the deep problems of theology, nor giving instructions in Christian doctrine to his thoroughly schooled disciples. His former teachings are presupposed as the basis of the Christian life, and the moral instruction he now imparts differs from that of his earlier letters only in so far as new conditions and circumstances demand it.

SIXTH OBJECTION. The church organization implied in the Pastorals was not so advanced in the time of St. Paul.

If the organization and church discipline of these letters were an advance on those of the Apostle's earlier Epistles, this is again just what we should expect, for these were his last writings and things were moving rapidly in those formative days. But it is hard to find on this point anything in these letters which cannot also be found in the Acts and other Epistles. Thus, in the very beginning of their ministry we see that the Apostles, by prayer and the laying on of hands, set aside deacons who were to assist them in their work (Acts vi. vii). And Paul and Barnabas on their first mission, after they had preached and instructed, confirmed the souls of the disciples and ordained priests in all the Churches they had established (Acts xiv. 20-22). In Acts xi. 30 we see that priests (presbyters) were associated with the Apostles at Jerusalem, and that it was they to whom Paul and Barnabas sent the alms for the poor in Judea. In Acts xv. 2 we read that priests were assisting the Apostles at Jerusalem when Paul and Barnabas went up for the first Council of the Church, and they were with St. James at the reception of St. Paul in the Holy City (Acts xxi. 18). In Thessalonica and Corinth we know that definite arrangements were made for organization and discipline (1 Cor. v. 1-5; 1 Thess. v. 12). At Miletus at the close of his third journey St. Paul addressed bishops and priests (Acts xx. 28). To the Ephesians he spoke of "apostles, prophets, evangelists, pastors, and doctors" (Eph. iv. 11). Many other instances might be cited, but these are enough to show that the church organization and discipline implied in the Pastorals were found at an earlier date everywhere. Of course, it was only natural that, as time went on and the number of Churches and converts increased, there would be need for greater organization and a stricter and more detailed system of government and discipline.

SEVENTH OBJECTION. Timothy and Titus are addressed in these Epistles as if they were young, immature and untried disciples, whereas they were grown men of mature years who had been instructed by St. Paul and had long borne heavy responsibilities.

Our first reply to this apparent difficulty is that in the Roman world men were considered youths until they were forty-six years old. Until they were seventeen, boys were called children. But, in the second place, we should remember that Paul was an old man at this time, and he had known Timothy and Titus from their early years; they always seemed young to their old master. Moreover, they were comparatively young to undertake alone the weighty charges which were theirs at Ephesus and Crete, and were indeed youths in doctrine and experience as compared with Paul.

EIGHTH OBJECTION. The false teaching condemned in these Epistles seems to be the Gnosticism of the second century.

The most that can be said in support of this difficulty is that the developed Gnosticism of the second century had its beginning in St. Paul's time, and that he was warning against its incipient errors (1 Tim. iv. 1-5; 2 Tim. ii. 17, 18; 2 Tim. iii. 8, 13). But from 1 Tim. i. 7, and Tit. i. 14, iii. 9, it appears that the false teaching was Jewish, and that the "old wives' fables" condemned in 1 Tim. iv. 7, and in 2 Tim. iv. 4, were such as we find in Jewish Midrash and apocryphal books like the Jewish Haggadoth and the Book of Jubilees. We do not know any system of Gnosticism which corresponds with the errors condemned in the Pastorals, and the fact that St. Irenæus and others use these Epistles against the Gnostics of their time is no proof that St. Paul had them in mind when he wrote (cf. Ahern, in Catholic Encyclopedia, vol. XIV, p. 731 a; Hort, in Judaistic Christianity, pp. 130-146). The second-century Gnostics hated and despised the Old Testament, while the false teachers of the Pastorals were Judaizers who claimed to be authorities and right interpreters of the Law of Moses (1 Tim. i-7). Hence, it may be seriously doubted whether the Jewish ideas and teachings condemned in these letters had much, if anything, to do with the Gnosticism of the second century (cf. Gigot, *Introd. to The Pastorals*, in *Westminster Version of the Sacred Scripture*, p. xv).

NINTH OBJECTION. St. Paul in Acts xx. 25, said to the Ephesians: "I know that all of you shall see my face no more."

But St. Paul was not uttering an infallible prophecy at this time; he was simply expressing his own personal opinion as a man (Beelen).

TENTH OBJECTION. The writer of these Epistles was oblivious of Paul's teaching about the fatherhood of God, the union of the believer with Jesus, the power and witness of the Holy Spirit, etc.

But Timothy and Titus were perfectly familiar with these doctrines, and there was no need to discuss them at this time. The Apostle had other matters to deal with here. However, he had not forgotten these old subjects, even in the Pastorals, as we see from 1 Tim. i. 15, ii. 6; 2 Tim. i. 2, ii. 13; Tit. i. 4, iii. 4, 5, 7.

Other minor objections might be adduced against the authenticity of the Pastoral Epistles, but we think we have said enough to convince any unbiased mind that these letters are genuine. All external evidence is decidedly in their favor as authentic Pauline documents, and the internal evidence is all that could be reasonably required. Most of the objections that are raised can also be brought to a greater or less extent against the admittedly genuine Pauline letters, and very reasonable solutions can be given to the others.

We conclude, therefore, by affirming with the Biblical Commission of June 12, 1913, that both internal and external evidence prove these letters to be genuine and canonical Epistles of St. Paul, that there is nothing in the fragmentary hypothesis of recent writers or in the objections raised by critics to weaken the traditional view regarding the authenticity of these Epistles, and that we can safely affirm that they were written between the Apostle's liberation from his first Roman captivity and his death.

BIBLIOGRAPHY

Besides the commentaries on all the Epistles of St. Paul which have been referred to in the Bibliography for Ephesians, we give here only some of the others that are most useful.

The chief Patristic commentaries are those of St. Chrysostom, Theodore of Mopsuestia (edited by Swete, Cambridge, 1882), Theodoret, St. Jerome, and Ambrosiaster (see Migne, *P.G.* and *P.L.*).

Later Catholic commentators are: Bisping, *Erklärung der drei Past.* (Munich, 1866); Gmoulhic, *Les épîtres past.,* etc. (Paris, 1866); Padovani, *In Epist. ad Thess. et ad Tim.* (Paris, 1894); *In Epist. ad Titum,* etc. (Paris, 1896); Belser, *Die Briefe des Apost. Paulus an Tim. und an Tit.,* etc. (Freiburg, 1907); Sales, in *La Sacra Bibbia,* vol. II (Turin, 1914); Brown, in *The Westminster Series* (London, 1917).

Of the many modern non-Catholic commentators on the Pastoral Epistles we would give the following: Humphreys, *The Pastoral Epistles,* in *The Cambridge Bible for Schools and Colleges* (Cambridge, 1897); Bernard, *The Pastoral Epistles,* in *The Cambridge Greek Test.* (Cambridge, 1899); Lilley, *The Pastoral Epistles* (Edinburg, 1901); Weiss, *Tim. und Tit.* (Göttingen, 1902); Ramsay, *Historical Comm. on 1 and 2 Tim.* (*Expositor,* March and April, 1911); Vernon Bartlett, *The Historical Setting of the Pastoral Epistles* (*Expositor,* January–April, 1913); St. John Parry, *The Pastoral Epistles* (Cambridge, 1920); A. E. Burn and H. L. Goudge, in *A New Comm. on Holy Script.* (New York, 1928); W. J. Lowstuter, *The Pastoral Epistles,* in *The Abingdon Bible Comm.* (New York, 1929).

THE TWO EPISTLES
TO TIMOTHY

INTRODUCTION

I. Timothy. Of St. Paul's many faithful disciples Timothy seems to have been the one dearest to his heart and most according to his own mind. He wrote of him to the Philippians as follows: "I have no man so of the same mind, who with sincere affection is solicitous for you. For all seek the things that are their own, not the things that are Jesus Christ's" (Phil. ii. 20, 21). Timothy was born at Lystra in Lycaonia of a Greek father and a Jewish mother, named Unice (Acts xvi. 1; 2 Tim. i. 5). It seems that his father died young, and the child was reared and carefully trained in the Old Testament Scriptures by his devout mother and grandmother. It would appear also that these three embraced Christianity when St. Paul preached at Lystra on his first missionary journey (Acts xiv. 6 ff.). Timothy was about sixteen or seventeen years old at this time, and, when Paul revisited Lystra on his second journey, he chose the youthful and devoted convert as a special companion and helper in the work of the Gospel, having first circumcised him to facilitate his work among the Jews, and ordained him by the laying on of hands (Acts xvi. 1-3; 1 Tim. iv. 14; 2 Tim. i. 6, 7). Thereafter, from the frequent mention of his name in the Acts and in the Epistles, we see that he was almost constantly with the Apostle. Whether or not he was with his master during the latter's imprisonment at Cæsarea and on the voyage thence to Rome, we do not know; but it is certain that he was in the Eternal City while St. Paul was imprisoned there the first time, because his name appears in the opening verses of the Captivity Epistles—Philippians, Colossians and Philemon. He was also with the Apostle during the interval between the two Roman imprisonments; for it was at this time that St. Paul appointed him Bishop of Ephesus (Eusebius,

Hist. Eccl., III, iv, 6; *Apost. Constit.,* vii, 46), and left him in charge of that important see. When the Apostle was nearing his end during his second captivity in Rome, he wrote to Timothy to make haste to come to him before winter (2 Tim. i. 4, iv. 8, 21). After this we know no more about him, save from tradition, according to which he was martyred at Ephesus in his old age for interfering with the celebration of a licentious heathen feast. St. Jerome tells us that his body was brought to Constantinople and buried there. His feast, as that of a Martyred Bishop, is celebrated in the Latin Church on January 24. He has been declared a Saint also by the Greek, Armenian, Coptic, and Maronite Churches.

We may get an idea of St. Timothy's character from what is said of him in the Acts and especially in the Epistles, from the duties entrusted to him and the labors performed by him, and from the great love St. Paul bore him. He was intelligent, innocent, gentle, timid, and yet sufficiently strong, courageous, and fearless when virtue and religion were at stake. He could not so well brave the rough world and wicked opponents as did St. Paul, and yet by the grace of God, though trembling and naturally fearful, he could go when necessary into the thick of the battle. Paul could always depend upon him to do his best, in spite of his shrinking disposition and delicate health. He was ever the Apostle's "beloved son," tried and true, full of faith and hope and love. He had found the more excellent way, and by the grace of God he walked in it throughout his days. Cf. Heyes, *Paul and His Epistles,* pp. 465 ff.; Pope, *Student's "Aids" to the Study of the Bible,* vol. III, pp. 235 ff.

II. **Occasion, Time and Place of Writing.** (a) 1 TIMOTHY. In his discourse to the clergy of Ephesus at the close of his third missionary journey, St. Paul predicted that false teachers would arise among them, "speaking perverse things, to draw away disciples after them" (Acts xx. 29, 30). And later, when he was a prisoner in Rome, he doubtless heard that those disturbing spirits were already at their work. After his liberation, therefore, he and Timothy made it a point to go to Ephesus for the purpose of applying a remedy. But it happened that St. Paul soon had to go into Macedonia, and so he left Timothy behind, hoping before long to rejoin him at Ephesus. Counting on an early return, he had not given Timothy full instructions, and since he was delayed in Macedonia longer than had been expected, he wrote this first letter to assist his disciple in combating the false teachers, to give him rules regarding the careful choice of ministers of the Gospel, and to recall to his mind the principal duties of a faithful pastor of souls (1 Tim.. i. 2, 3, iii. 14, 15, iv. 7, 13 ff., vi. 4 ff.).

As regards the date of this letter and the place whence it was written, we may say with all those who admit its authenticity that it was composed about the year 65 A.D., while St. Paul was in Macedonia after leaving Timothy at Ephesus (1 Tim. i. 3, iii. 14, 15). If, as we suppose, the Apostle was liberated from his Roman imprisonment about the end of 63 A.D., and that he probably went immediately to Spain for a short visit and then proceeded with Timothy to Ephesus, it would be about 65 A.D. before we should find him in Macedonia writing this letter.

It is idle to try to maintain that the journey of St. Paul to Macedonia here spoken of was the same as that given by St. Luke in Acts xix. 21 ff.; for before this latter journey the Apostle had already dispatched Timothy and Erastus to Macedonia, and was himself remaining at Ephesus, though intending to follow them later into Macedonia on his way to Corinth. Furthermore, at the time mentioned by St. Luke the Ephesian Church was not sufficiently developed to receive such mature instructions regarding the clergy as were given by St. Paul to Timothy in this Epistle.

(b) 2 TIMOTHY. St. Paul was in prison in Rome for the second and last time when he wrote this pathetic but beautiful letter, telling of the hopelessness of his case and of his loneliness, with no one but Luke as his companion. He recalls the years of labor and the ties of affection that have bound him and Timothy together in a passionate love for the common cause of their Master, refers to a few of the false teachers and urges his beloved Timothy to come to him before winter to receive final instructions about his office and duties and the work which he will have to carry on henceforth without the aid of his spiritual father.

The letter is intensely personal and affectionate in tone, more so than any other of the Apostle's Epistles. The great preacher is about to lay down his life's labor, and he is solicitous only that it be faithfully carried on when he is gone. As for himself, he looks death in the face fearlessly, confident of the glorious issue. Labor for Christ has been the one grand passion of his life. He has fought a good fight, he has finished his course, he has kept the faith; and his crown is waiting for him (2 Tim. iv. 1 ff.).

We are justified, therefore, in holding that this Epistle was written shortly before the Apostle's death, probably in 67 A.D., which is the traditional year of his martyrdom.

III. **Division of Contents.** (a) 1 TIMOTHY. After an introduction (i. 1, 2) and a conclusion (vi. 20, 21), this letter may be divided into a number of instructions given by St. Paul to Timothy, as follows:

A. In this first instruction (1. 3-20) the Apostle begins by stressing the duty of combating the errors of the false teachers (3-11); and then to encourage Timothy he makes a personal digression, showing the saving power of the Gospel as manifested in his own conversion (12-17). Returning to the thought of verse 3, he reminds Timothy of the charge committed to him of guarding the interests of Christ as revealed in the Gospel (18-20).

B. In the second instruction (ii. 1-15) two thoughts come up for consideration, first, the Christian's duty of praying for all men, since Christ died for all (1-7); and, secondly, the proper ordering of public prayer, and the place and work of women in the saving ministry of the Church (8-15).

C. In the third instruction (iii. 1-16) St. Paul directs attention to the officials and other workers in the Church—bishops, priests, deacons, etc.—and tells Timothy first what sort of men ought to be chosen for the ranks of the clergy, especially as regards conduct and character (1-7); and secondly, what ought to be the qualifications of deacons and good women who are to assist the clergy (8-13). In his anxiety that all may go well with Timothy, St. Paul sends these instructions on ahead of the visit he hopes soon to make to the Church of Ephesus (14-16).

D. In the fourth instruction (iv. 1-16) Timothy is warned against heretics and their false teachings (1-5), and admonished to nourish his own soul by the solid doctrine that sustains and quickens faith, and to show by the example of his personal life the spiritual excellence of the Gospel (6-16).

E. The fifth instruction has to do with the administration of discipline in certain special cases (v. 1—vi. 2). Here the Apostle teaches Timothy how he is to deal with the old and the young of both sexes (v. 1, 2), with widows (v. 3-16), with the clergy (v. 17-25), and finally with slaves (vi. 1, 2).

F. The sixth and last instruction (vi. 3-19) returns to the subject of i. 3, again warns Timothy to be on his guard against the teachers of unsound doctrine (3-10), exhorts him to be faithful to his call and his trust as a true teacher (11-16), and adds a few words concerning riches and their proper use (17-19).

(b) 2 TIMOTHY. This Epistle consists of an introduction or greeting (i. 1, 2), an exhortation (i. 3—ii. 13), an instruction (ii. 14—iv. 18), and a conclusion containing greetings and a blessing (iv. 19-22).

A. In his introduction to this letter (i. 1, 2), St. Paul recalls the great privilege he has enjoyed in being elected by God to preach the Gospel, and greets Timothy, his beloved convert, who has so long been associated with him in this privileged work.

B. In the first main part of the Epistle (i. 3—ii. 13), the Apostle begins by thanking God for the graces that have been accorded Timothy, and exhorts him to stir up within him the grace he received at his ordination (i. 3-14). He then refers to those from Asia who have forsaken him, and prays for his faithful friend, Onesiphorus, who was probably dead at this time (i. 15-18). Finally, Timothy is exhorted to be diligent in the discharge of his duties, and to be ready to suffer for the Gospel (ii. 1-13).

C. In the second main part of this letter (ii. 14—iv. 18), St. Paul first instructs Timothy how he is to become the kind of workman that God would have him be. Holding fast to the great central truths of the Gospel, he is to avoid useless wranglings and contentious disputes, which are to no profit; he is to eschew the foolish desires of youth and to practise solid virtues, and by prudent, patient and tactful methods he is to lead the erring to repentance and to saving ways (ii. 14-26). But after insisting on these necessary qualifications of the workman of Christ—namely, undivided devotion to his Master, loyalty to Gospel teaching, willingness to suffer for the cause, and the practice of his own preaching on the part of Timothy—St. Paul now proceeds to warn his disciple that worse things are yet to come, and forthwith describes the character and the sins of evil men who will appear in the days ahead to shake the faith and pervert the multitudes (iii. 1-9). But Timothy will be equipped to meet these emergencies by holding to the doctrine he has received, by being ready to suffer for the faith as Paul has done, and by drawing help and strength from the Sacred Scriptures (iii. 10-17). The Apostle's work is finished, and he now issues a final charge to Timothy to be faithful to his duty of preaching the Gospel in the critical days ahead, and to be exact in the fulfillment of all his sacred trusts. As for himself, his end is at hand, his reward is waiting for him (iv. 1-8). He is alone with Luke: some have left him, others have been sent on duties elsewhere (iv. 9-12). A few final requests and observations close this part of the letter (iv. 13-18).

D. In the conclusion (iv. 19-22), St. Paul sends greetings to a number of persons at Ephesus, makes special mention of Erastus and Trophimus, urges Timothy to hasten his coming to him, includes the greetings of several of his friends in Rome, and terminates his last Epistle with a unique blessing, probably in his own handwriting.

The First Epistle to Timothy

CHAPTER I

1. Paul, an apostle of Jesus Christ, according to the commandment of God our Saviour, and of Christ Jesus our hope:

1-20. St. Paul left Timothy in charge of affairs in the Church of Ephesus as he himself made a journey into Macedonia. Timothy was young, delicate in health, and naturally timid; and there was reason for apprehension as to how he might get on with the false teachers at Ephesus, if St. Paul was long delayed in returning to him. The Apostle, therefore, decided to send a letter to him. In the opening section he first greets his beloved son (ver. 1-2); then repeats the warning against false teachers he had given before leaving him (ver. 3-11), citing his own conversion on the road to Damascus as an instance of the power of the Gospel to assist Timothy in his work and to correct the erring teachers (ver. 12-17); and terminates by reminding the youthful bishop of the charge that has been committed to him as a true teacher of the doctrines of Christ (ver. 18-20).

1. **Paul an apostle,** etc. St. Paul thus asserts his apostolic authority at the beginning of nine of his letters—in all, therefore, except Phil., Phlm., 1 and 2 Thess., and Heb. This he does in order to give greater weight and solemnity to his words, not only with the faithful and to those to whom he is writing, but also and especially with the false teachers or enemies whom, as in the present Epistle, he is combating.

The commandment, i.e., the divine command by which the apostolic office has been laid upon him.

God our Saviour. The title "Saviour," as attributed to God the Father, is peculiar to the Pastoral Epistles, where it occurs six

2. To Timothy, his true son in faith: Grace, mercy, and peace from God the Father, and from Christ Jesus our Lord.

3. As I desired thee to remain at Ephesus when I went into Macedonia, that thou mightest charge some not to teach otherwise,

times, reminding us that the Eternal Father is the ultimate source and fountain of salvation, and that Jesus Christ, to whom St. Paul usually attributes this title, is the divine medium through which the Father's salvation is conveyed to us.

Christ Jesus our hope, i.e., the object and foundation of our hope. It was not Moses or the Law of Moses, as the Judaizers taught, but Jesus Christ through whom we are to be saved.

2. **Timothy.** See *Introduction* to 1 Tim., No. I.

His true son in faith, seems to indicate that Timothy had been instructed in the faith and baptized by St. Paul; Timothy was St. Paul's spiritual child, and such he always remained to the venerable Apostle.

Grace, mercy, and peace. See on Eph. i. 2. The word "mercy" is here added to the salutation, as in 2 Tim. i. 2, perhaps because the aged Apostle now felt the greater need of this most attractive and conspicuous attribute of God, and also in order to draw attention to the source of "grace" and "peace."

The *dilecto* of the Vulgate ought to be *vero* or *sincero,* as in the Greek.

3. In verses 3-11 St. Paul reminds Timothy of the charge he had given him before leaving him at Ephesus, namely, that of combating the false teachers.

As I desired, etc. In characteristic fashion St. Paul leaves his sentence unfinished, as he seeks to pour out the stream of thoughts that flood his mind. We should naturally expect some termination like this: "So now I admonish you." No forger could have constructed such a Pauline sentence, without leaving a trace of his falsification. Some authorities think the apodosis of this sentence is in verse 18, "this precept I commit to thee, etc.," but the intervening passage is too long to make such a view likely.

It may be asked here whether this order given to Timothy "to remain at Ephesus" might not have occurred some time during the period covered by the Acts. The answer is in the negative; for the Acts mention only two occasions when St. Paul was at Ephesus

4. Not to give heed to fables and endless genealogies, which furnish questions rather than the edification of God, which is in faith.

5. Now the end of the commandment is charity, from a pure heart and a
good conscience and an unfeigned faith.

(Acts xviii. 19-22, and xix. 1 ff.). On the first of these visits the
Apostle was not going to Macedonia, but was on his way East, to
Cæsarea in Palestine. The second time he was indeed going to
Macedonia, whither he had already dispatched Timothy, instead of
leaving him behind at Ephesus.

That thou mightest charge some, etc. St. Paul does not name
these false teachers, but they were evidently Christians.

Not to teach otherwise. Better, "not to teach another doctrine,"
i.e., an irrelevant, an heretical doctrine. The Greek word for
"another doctrine" occurs only here and in vi. 3, below, in the
Greek Bible; and its meaning here is not so much *heretical* as irrelevant, as mischievous in practice, and therefore conducive to heresy.

4. **Fables** were most probably Jewish legends (Tit. i. 14), such
as are frequently found in the *Talmud*; and **genealogies** were
extravagant, legendary stories about the ancient patriarchs, such as
we find in the *Book of Jubilees.* Speculation on these useless subjects would lead away from the great truths of faith and the practical realities of Christian life; and thus vast harm would be done
to the Church and to souls.

The edification of God (i.e., the upbuilding of the Church of
God), **which is in faith** (i.e., which is based on the truths of faith).
The "edification of God" is according to the ordinary Greek, the
reading of the Latin Fathers, and a number of western versions,
and it gives a good sense; but the best Greek MSS. and the Greek
Fathers have "the dispensation of God," i.e., the divine plan of
salvation by means of faith, to which vain speculations about fables
and genealogies would be injurious. The sense is practically the
same in either reading.

5. In contrast with the irrelevant teaching just condemned, Timothy is now reminded that "the end of the commandment" (i.e.,
the scope or aim of the charge entrusted to him, which is the practical teaching of the Gospel) "is charity" (i.e., love for one's fellow-
man and his welfare), and this love comes (a) "from a pure heart,"
which, in Hebrew thought, was the spring of moral thought and

6. From which things some going astray, are turned aside unto vain babbling,

7. Desiring to be teachers of the law, understanding neither the things they say nor whereof they affirm.

8. But we know that the law is good, if a man use it lawfully,

9. Knowing this, that the law is not made for the just man, but for the lawless and disobedient, for the ungodly and for sinners, for the unholy and profane, for murderers of fathers, and murderers of mothers, for manslayers,

emotion; (b) from "a good conscience," or the practical judgment between right and wrong; (c) from "an unfeigned faith," i.e., a sincere and honest faith, which regulates man's relations with God and is the reason and basis of the love of the neighbor.

6. The false teachers have neglected "charity," "a pure heart, etc." (ver. 5), with the result that they have abandoned themselves to all sorts of vain and useless talk. The Greek verb which expresses "going astray" here is peculiar to the Pastorals, being found again only in 1 Tim. vi. 21, and in 2 Tim. ii. 18; and the Greek for "vain babbling" is found only in this place in the Greek Bible.

7. Those unpractical and misguided leaders posed as "teachers of the law," i.e., of the Law of Moses, the principles and meaning of which they did not understand themselves. This reference to the Law shows that the errors in question had their root in Judaism, and that the false teachers were therefore Christian Judaizers.

8. In verses 8-11 St. Paul digresses to explain the nature and purpose of the Mosaic Law, and of all law, for that matter, so as not to be understood as opposing that which was good.

But we (in contrast to the ignorant Judaizers) know that the law is good, provided it be used "lawfully," i.e., according to its nature and spirit, taking account of that in it which has only a temporal purpose and that which is of permanent value, and of that which is weighty and that which is trivial and irrelevant. The ceremonial part of the Mosaic Law was intended to prepare the way for and to lead to Christ, and now that Christ has come it has no place in the Christian life, but is rather an impediment and a hindrance. On the other hand, the moral precepts of the Law are permanent and good, and are not to be covered up and obscured by useless speculations and irrelevant discussions.

9. Knowing this. He now explains how the Law should be expounded by him who would "use it lawfully."

10. For fornicators, for them who defile themselves with mankind, for men-stealers, for liars, for perjured persons, and whatever else is contrary to sound doctrine.

11. This is according to the gospel of the glory of the blessed God, which hath been committed to my trust.

That the law is not made, etc., i.e., the Mosaic Law, as accompanied by threats and chastisements, was not framed or enacted for Christians who are justified from sin, for these fulfill the precepts of the Law, not out of fear of punishment, but out of love; and consequently the Law, as embodying threats and punishments, is of no use to those who have become Christ's.

But for the lawless, etc., i.e., for sinners, who are ruled by their passions, the Law with its threats of chastisement is necessary.

The Apostle now sketches a list of such sinners as he has in mind. Thus, the Law is for "the lawless," those who disregard all law; the "disobedient," those who are unwilling to submit to any rule; "the ungodly and sinners," those who have no fear of God; "the unholy and profane," those who act as if God did not exist. With this last class the Apostle begins a more definite description of the sinners he has in view, following the order of the Decalogue.

Murderers of fathers, etc. The meaning of the Greek is rather that of dishonoring parents and of hateful feelings against one's neighbor, and hence of violating the fourth and fifth commandments.

10. **Fornicators,** etc. Sexual and unnatural sins are now mentioned, that is, violations of the sixth commandment.

Men-stealers, i.e., slave-stealers, one of the worst crimes according to Roman Law, and punishable by death according to Mosaic Law (Exod. xxi. 16; Deut. xxiv. 7). This sin was a violation of the seventh commandment.

And whatever else is a general formula to include any other sins that have not been explicitly enumerated, as in Rom. xiii. 9; Phil. iv. 8.

Sound doctrine means wholesome teaching, the contrary of that of the false teachers. The word for "sound" here is peculiar to the Pastoral Epistles, and the Greek term for "doctrine" occurs fifteen times in these letters.

11. **This is according.** The Apostle explains what he means by the "sound doctrine" of which he has just spoken. It is in con-

12. I give him thanks who hath strengthened me, *even* to Christ Jesus our Lord, for that he hath counted me faithful, putting me in the ministry; 13. Who before was a blasphemer and a persecutor and contumelious. But I obtained mercy, because I acted ignorantly in unbelief:

formity with "the gospel of the glory of the blessed God," i.e., the Gospel which announces and manifests the glory, wisdom, goodness, mercy, etc. of God, who in Himself is infinitely happy, and who one day will make us partakers of His glory and blessedness, as He has promised in the Gospel (cf. Sales, *h. l.*). The word μακάριος here applied to God is found only in this passage and in vi. 15 below in the whole Bible. It means that God possesses in Himself the fullness of bliss or blessedness.

Which has been committed, etc. Better, as in the Westminster Version, "wherewith I have been entrusted," in contrast to the false teachers who have received no divine commission. This last phrase is characteristic of St. Paul (cf. Rom. iii. 2; 1 Cor. ix. 17; Gal. ii. 7; 1 Thess. ii. 4; Tit. i. 3).

12. The mention of the Gospel entrusted to him induces the Apostle to make a personal digression in verses 12-17, reflecting on his own life, and thanking God for the grace vouchsafed to him in spite of his unworthiness, while incidentally vindicating his authority against the Judaizers and proclaiming the saving mercy of Jesus Christ.

Who hath strengthened me, with His grace, not only at the time of my conversion, but throughout my ministry as an Apostle.

Christ Jesus. This is the order of these words everywhere in this Epistle. It is the *Anointed* of God (Christ) who is the *Saviour* (Jesus) of mankind.

Faithful, i.e., trustworthy, through the grace of Christ (1 Cor. vii. 25).

The ministry. The Greek word for "ministry" here in the time of St. Paul meant the apostolate, whereas in the second century it had come to designate the order of deaconship. Hence we have in the use of the word here an argument for the early date of this letter. St. Paul would hardly be speaking of himself as having been called to the deaconship.

13. Although he acted out of ignorance and misdirected zeal,

14. Now the grace of our Lord hath abounded exceedingly with faith and love which are in Christ Jesus.

15. Faithful is the saying, and worthy of all acceptation that Christ Jesus came into this world to save sinners, of whom I am the chief.

16. But for this cause have I obtained mercy: that in me as first Christ Jesus might shew forth all patience, for an example to them that shall believe in him unto life everlasting.

St. Paul can never forget or cease to regret that he opposed the cause of Christ, persecuted the Church, and outraged the rights of men (Acts vii. 58 ff., ix. 1 ff., xxvi. 9; 1 Cor. xv. 9; Phil. iii. 6). His sins were only material, but he will not excuse his blind conduct.

Contumelious means a wanton aggressor of men's rights (Acts xxii. 4).

The *Dei* of the Vulgate is not in the Greek.

14. **Abounded exceedingly.** The Greek for this expression is found only here in the Greek Bible. St. Paul means to say that the grace of God in him went beyond his conversion and made him an Apostle besides (Rom. v. 20). He mentions "faith," as opposed to his former infidelity, and "love," as opposed to his former hate and persecution of the Church of Christ.

15. **Faithful is the saying,** i.e., worthy of all belief. This is a formula peculiar to the Pastorals; it is found elsewhere in these letters in iii. 1 and iv. 9 below, in 2 Tim. ii. 11, and in Tit. iii. 8. It is used to introduce a truth of great importance.

And worthy of all acceptation, i.e., worthy to be accepted by everyone. The Greek for this expression is found again in the Bible only in iv. 9 below.

That Christ Jesus came, etc. This is the great truth the Apostle would teach, and it shows that the primary purpose of our Lord's coming to the earth in the Incarnation was to save sinners.

Of whom I am the chief, a characteristic expression of St. Paul (cf. 1 Cor. xv. 9; Eph. iii. 8), and not so much hyperbolical as expressive of a vivid appreciation of the degradation of sin, on the one hand, and the awful holiness of God and the preciousness of grace, on the other hand; and the Apostle is not speaking in the past but in the present tense. It is only the great Saints who can rightly apprehend sin and appreciate grace.

16. The Apostle explains why God has shown him so great mercy

17. Now to the King of the ages, immortal, invisible, the only God, be honor and glory for ever and ever. Amen.

18. This precept I commit to thee, son Timothy; according to the prophecies concerning thee, that thou war in them a good warfare,

in spite of his sins, namely, that he might be an example or illustration to others of the "patience," i.e., the longsuffering and gracious mercy of Christ in bearing with all poor sinners who "believe in Him," the consequence of whose faith in Christ Jesus will be "life everlasting."

In me as first, i.e., as chief of sinners (ver. 15).

An example. Literally, "an outline sketch." The Greek word is found only here and in 2 Tim. i. 13 in the whole Bible.

17. The Apostle now, after reflecting on the divine goodness and mercy, breaks out into a characteristic doxology, which is not a prayer or an aspiration, but a reverent and thankful statement of the divine glory (Bernard).

To the King of the ages, i.e., to the everlasting God. The same expression is found elsewhere in the Bible only in Tobias xiii. 6, 10, and Apoc. xv. 3.

18. In verses 18-20 St. Paul exhorts Timothy to fight the good fight for the faith, to be a good soldier of Jesus Christ, and not to allow himself to be led away by the example of the false teachers.

This precept most probably refers to the injunction of verses 3-4 against the false teachers.

The prophecies may refer to predictions made about Timothy at the time St. Paul chose him for the work of the Gospel at Lystra (Acts xvi. 3), or at the time of his ordination (1 Tim. iv. 14). These prophecies were certain revelations made by the Holy Ghost to St. Paul or to some of the faithful, as often happened in the Early Church, concerning the fitness of the person in question for the work of the ministry. Thus were St. Paul and Barnabas selected by a special revelation of the Holy Ghost to preach the Gospel to the Gentiles (Acts xiii. 1 ff.).

That thou war, etc. The purpose of recalling to Timothy the charge committed to him and the prophecies that were uttered concerning him is to encourage him to fight like a good soldier of Christ to maintain against the false teachers the purity and integrity of the faith.

19. Having faith and a good conscience, which some rejecting have made shipwreck concerning the faith.

20. Of whom are Hymenæus and Alexander, whom I have delivered up to Satan, that they may learn not to blaspheme.

19. The Apostle now explains what is required in order to fight the good fight, namely, "faith," i.e., the Christian faith, and a well-instructed conscience, accompanied by sanctity of life; Timothy must hold to sound doctrine and live in conformity with that doctrine. Some, failing to do this, have lost the faith.

20. Here are mentioned two of those who had lost the faith.

Hymenæus, who denied the resurrection of the dead, is spoken of as a heretic in 2 Tim. ii. 17.

Alexander, a Christian heretic, is not to be identified with Alexander the Jew mentioned in Acts xix. 33-34; but he may be the same person as the individual spoken of in 2 Tim. iv. 14 as a personal enemy of St. Paul's.

Delivered up to Satan, i.e., excommunicated from the Church (1 Cor. v. 5), thus leaving him exposed to the temptations and tortures of the Evil One, that he might be disciplined for his sins against our Lord.

CHAPTER II

GENERAL REGULATIONS FOR PUBLIC WORSHIP, 1-15

1. I desire therefore, first of all, that supplications, prayers, intercessions, and thanksgivings be made for all men:

1-15. St. Paul enjoins that prayers of various kinds be offered for all men, because it is the will of God that all men should be saved, as is evident from the fact that God is one, that there is only one supreme mediator between God and man, and that Christ gave Himself as a ransom for all. This is the Gospel which St. Paul is commissioned to preach (ver. 1-7). He next prescribes the manner in which these prayers should be offered, and lays down rules for the conduct of women in the public assembly (ver. 8-15).

1. **First of all.** This expression in Greek occurs only here in

2. For kings and for all that are in high stations, that we may lead a quiet and a peaceable life in all piety and chastity.

3. This is good and acceptable in the sight of God our Saviour,

4. Who will have all men to be saved, and to come to knowledge of the truth.

the New Testament, and it shows the primary importance of prayer as a means of avoiding evil and progressing in good (St. Thomas). There is question here of public, liturgical prayers, and it is not easy to distinguish between the first three mentioned. Perhaps if there is need of a distinction at all, we may regard "supplications" as made for oneself, "prayers" as acts of adoration, and "intercessions" as prayers offered for others.

2. **For kings**, etc., i.e., for all those who exercise lawful public authority. This attitude toward civil authority was especially necessary for the early Christians, lest they should be suspected of disloyalty and be subjected to persecution. Cf. Rom. xiii. 1 ff.

Piety. The Greek for this word occurs here for the first time in Paul's letters, and it is used frequently hereafter in the Pastorals.

Chastity would better be "gravity" or "reverence," to correspond with the Greek term here employed, which is also peculiar to the Pastorals.

3. The *enim* of the Vulgate here is not well supported in the Greek.

God our Saviour. See on i. 1, above.

4. The Apostle now explains why prayer for all men is pleasing and "acceptable in the sight of God" (ver. 3), namely, because God desires all to be saved. According to His primary intention and antecedent will, God wishes the salvation of all men without exception; but man, by the misuse of his free will, has the mysterious power of changing God's original plan for him, so to speak; and hence it happens that, when man freely chooses not to be saved, God has recourse, in our way of thinking and speaking, to a secondary intention and consequent will in man's regard, according to which He also wishes that man shall not be saved. This is our poor way of explaining, as best we can, a profound mystery. But when all is said and done, it is certain that no one is saved except

5. For there is one God, and one mediator of God and men, the man
Christ Jesus,
6. Who gave himself a redemption for all, a testimony in due times.

by the grace of God, and no one is lost except through his own
fault (see on Rom. ix. 12 ff.).   This text of St. Paul is a clear
refutation of the heretical opinions of Calvin and Jansenius, the
first of whom taught that, previously to all thought of demerit on
man's part, God predestined some men to hell; and the second of
whom said that Christ did not merit salvation for all men, having
died only for the predestined (see *Conc. Trid.*, sess. VI, *De justificatione*, can. 17).

And come to knowledge of the truth, which is the necessary
means of salvation, the way to life eternal.   The phrase "knowledge
of truth" is peculiar to these Pastoral Epistles (cf. Heb. xi. 26).

5. In verses 5-6 the Apostle proves that God wishes the salvation of all men, (a) because God is one, the first cause and final
end of all, and as such stands in the same ultimate relation to all;
(b) because there is only one supreme mediator between God and
man, namely, Christ Jesus, who in the same divine Person has
united the natures of God and man; (c) because Christ offered
Himself as the one supreme ransom for all men (Eph. i. 12, ii. 14;
Col. i. 20; Heb. viii. 6, ix. 14, xii. 14).

The man Christ Jesus.   St. Paul stresses the fact that our Lord
was man, for it was only as man that He was able to pay the price
of our deliverance; and had He not been God at the same time, He
could not have given to His death and sacrifice an infinite value,
which showed at once the perfection and completeness of His sacrifice for us and the extent of God's love for man.

It is unreasonable for Protestants, in view of this verse, to deny
all value to the invocation and intercession of the Saints, for it has
always been the teaching of the Church that the mediation of the
Saints is founded upon and derives all its value from the mediatorship of Christ.   Properly understood, this is a very reasonable
doctrine.   Cf. *Conc. Trid.*, sess. XXV, *De invocatione sanctorum.*

6. The Apostle now explains how Christ is our mediator, and
how He reconciled man to God.

Who gave himself.   It was not His death, but Himself that the

7. Whereunto I am appointed a preacher and an apostle (I say the truth, I lie not), a doctor of the Gentiles in faith and truth.

8. I will therefore that men pray in every place, lifting up pure hands, without anger and contention.

9. In like manner women also in decent apparel: adorning themselves with modesty and sobriety, not with plaited hair, or gold, or pearls, or costly attire,

Saviour gave as "a redemption" (or better, "a ransom") for all, i.e., a price that would be required to redeem a slave was paid for all without exception (Rom. iii. 24). The Greek for "redemption" here (ἀντιλύτρον) occurs nowhere else, though its meaning is contained in Matt. xx. 28, and Mark x. 45. The prefix ἀντί before λύτρον means "in place of," thus signifying the vicarious character of our Lord's sacrifice, who took our common human nature in order to suffer for us all, that is, in place of us all.

A testimony in due times. The meaning is that the incarnation of the Son and the redemption wrought by Him in the fullness of time completes the revelation begun in the Old Testament of God's eternal purpose regarding man's salvation, and is a witness of the friendly will of God that all should be saved.

7. With unexpected emphasis the Apostle here asserts his divine appointment to teach and preach the Gospel of universal salvation.

In faith and truth, i.e., in the Christian faith and the true teaching of the Gospel.

8. After having explained in verses 5-7 the reasons why we should pray for all men, the Apostle now in verses 8-12 gives instructions regarding the manner of making and of assisting at public prayers.

That men pray, instead of women (ver. 9), in the public assemblies.

Lifting up hands, referring to the posture of prayer among the Jews, and also among the early Christians, as we learn from the writings of Clement of Rome, Clement of Alexandria, and the representations in the Catacombs.

Without anger, etc., i.e., free from those internal dispositions that are alien to the spirit of prayer. The word "contention" refers to controversial disputations.

9. The reference is still to **public worship,** at which women are

10. But (as it becometh women professing godliness) with good works.

11. Let a woman learn in silence, with all subjection.

12. But I suffer not a woman to teach, nor to use authority over the man, but to be in silence.

13. For Adam was first formed, then Eve.

14. And Adam was not seduced; but the woman being seduced, was in transgression.

to appear with that decency and modesty of dress and demeanor that become their sex.

Sobriety. Better, "self-control," referring to woman's natural inclination to vanity in dress. It is indeed the duty of women to try to appear attractive, but always with modesty and decency, otherwise they defeat their very purpose in the eyes and judgment of every right-minded person (cf. 1 Peter iii. 3 ff.). St. Chrysostom used to ask the women of his congregation: "Have you come to assist at a ball?"

10. Here the Apostle says the kind of attire that most becomes a Christian lady is the garment of good works. Special stress is put on good works all through the Pastoral Epistles, doubtless because these were often obscured and lost sight of on account of the zeal displayed by the false teachers for controversy and useless doctrines. The Greek word for "godliness" occurs only here in the New Testament.

11-12. St. Paul is speaking of women's conduct in the public religious gatherings of the faithful, where to teach was an exercise of authority which belonged to men only. Women were not to teach in these public assemblies of the Christians, and this Apostolic ordinance was renewed in the Fourth Council of Carthage in 398 (cf. 1 Cor. xiv. 26 ff.). This prohibition, however, did not forbid women to teach the young privately, as we know from 2 Tim. iii. 14, and Tit. ii. 3 (cf. Acts xviii. 26; 1 Cor. ix. 5; Phil. iv. 3 ff.).

Nor to use authority over man, etc., i.e., in the public affairs of the Church.

13-14. The Apostle now gives two reasons why women are not to teach and exercise authority over men in the public assemblies of the faithful; the first of which is drawn from the order in which man and woman were created (Gen. ii. 7, 18-23), and the second

15. Yet she shall be saved through child-bearing; if she continue in faith and love and sanctification, with sobriety.

from the history of the Fall (Gen. iii. 11-13). Adam was created before Eve, and Eve was formed from Adam to be his helpmate. Again, at the time of the Fall, it was Eve who showed her weakness and unreliability in being seduced by the tempter, whereas Adam sinned with open eyes, fully conscious of what he was doing; the woman, therefore, is not a safe guide. Eve transgressed by putting faith in the serpent, and Adam by imitating the transgression of Eve.

15. Although woman is excluded from the office of public teaching and from the exercise of the sacred ministry, she will nevertheless be saved by the faithful discharge of the duties that belong to her sex, the chief of which is the bearing and rearing of children in God's fear and favor. But just as Adam, in punishment for his sin, must earn his bread by the sweat of his brow, so Eve, in consequence of her sin, will have to bring forth her children with pain and suffering (Gen. iii. 16-18). St. Paul, as is clear, is speaking of matrimony as the natural and normal state of woman; but he has by no means forgotten a superior state of virginity to which woman may be called, and of which he treated when writing to the Corinthians (1 Cor. vii. 7 ff.).

If she continue, etc. The Greek has, "if they continue, etc.," i.e., women in general, or perhaps the reference is to the husband and wife, living the life of "faith and love and sanctification, etc." Mere child-bearing, without the practice of the necessary Christian virtues of faith, love, etc., which make for woman's sanctification, will never save any woman; it is child-bearing accompanied by the practice of these virtues that will save her.

With sobriety. Better, "with self-control," as above in verse 9.

CHAPTER III

ST. PAUL EXPOUNDS THE QUALIFICATIONS REQUISITE FOR THE
OFFICIALS AND OTHER WORKERS IN THE CHURCH, 1-16

1. Faithful is the saying: If a man desire the office of a bishop, he desireth
a good work.

1-16. In this third section of his first letter to Timothy, the
Apostle, turning from a consideration of the general directions he
has just been giving for the whole Church, descends more to particulars and discusses the personal and moral requirements which
should be found in bishops (ver. 1-7), and in deacons and deaconesses (ver. 8-13). His imperative insistence on the high personal,
moral and ethical equipment of those who are to take a leading
part in the government and work of the Church springs from the
very nature and from the high and holy character of this organization to which God has committed His truth for the enlightenment
of the world and the salvation of mankind (ver. 14-16).

1. **Faithful is the saying.** See on 1 Tim. i. 15. This phrase here
more probably goes with what follows, "if a man desire, etc."

Desires, i.e., aspires to. The Greek equivalent is found elsewhere
in the Bible only in Heb. xi. 16, but it is common with profane
writers.

Bishop. Literally, "overseer," "superintendent." In Titus i. 5,
7 the term seems to be used convertibly with "presbyter," although
there the "bishop" of verse 7 can be understood as embracing the
"presbyter" of verse 5, since the bishops were doubtless chosen from
among the presbyters, and in later times elected by the latter. At
any rate, everywhere in the New Testament these terms are applied
only to those who, having received a special sacramental consecration, are placed in charge of churches with power to preach, celebrate the divine mysteries, etc. (cf. Acts xx. 28; Phil. i. 1; 1 Tim.
iii. 2; Tit. i. 5, 7). Hence, under the term "bishop" here St. Paul
probably includes also priests; and this would explain why he passes

in the next section (ver. 8-13) to speak of deacons, omitting all separate mention of priests as such.

There are some authorities who hold that during the lifetime of the Apostles they alone were the real bishops, and that those who are spoken of as "bishops" or "presbyters" were simple priests associated with the Apostles as missionary companions. Others think only bishops were consecrated, that is, that all priests received at their ordination the plenitude of Holy Orders, being at once elevated to the episcopate. See Sales, *h. l.*, and the other authors cited by him on this question. But both of these conclusions seem to disagree with the distinction which is made or can be made everywhere in the New Testament between the terms ἐπίσκοπος and πρεσβύτερος, and the distinction in persons and functions which the Apostolic Fathers made and took for granted between bishops, priests and deacons. The term πρεσβύτερος is common in the Old Testament and in the Gospels and Acts, and seems, therefore, to have been of Jewish origin; while ἐπίσκοπος, though frequent in the LXX, appears to have come from paganism where it was a common title of office in Greek societies and guilds. Of course, both these titles and offices were spiritualized in the Church in accordance with the elevated spiritual powers and functions which they implied and which were conferred in ordination.

Dean Bernard has a learned and convincing chapter on the distinction made in the New Testament and in the earliest Fathers and Apostolic writers between the terms ἐπισκοπος and πρεσβύτερος and their respective functions. He shows that there are only two passages in the New Testament (Acts xx. 28; Titus i. 7) "which even *suggest* the interchangeability of the terms ἐπίσκοπος and πρεσβύτερος," and that these "are susceptible of explanations which fall in with the supposition that the words represent distinct functions (which might on occasion be discharged by the same individual)." And thus he does "not regard these passages as inconsistent with the conclusions to which all the other evidence points." After a careful review of all the evidence the learned Dean comes to the following conclusions: "(1) the episcopate and presbyterate were distinct . . .; the difference in name points to a difference in duty, although no doubt many duties would be common to both, especially in primitive and half-organized communities; (2) the

2. It behoveth therefore a bishop to be blameless, the husband of one wife, sober, prudent, of good behavior, chaste, given to hospitality, a teacher,

bishops were originally selected by the presbyteral council, and probably from their own body; (3) there were often several bishops in one place, the number being a matter non-essential; (4) a conspicuous part of the bishop's duty was the administration of worship —the λειτουργία in the largest sense; he is above all things an *official*, the representative of his Church and the director of its discipline" (*Introd. to Pastoral Ep.*, Chap. V, in *Cambridge Greek Testament*).

Of course, the Council of Trent has settled for us the divine origin of the episcopate, the presbyterate, and the deaconate.

A good work, i.e., an excellent office, but one of labor and responsibility rather than of honor, as St. Augustine remarks (*De Civitate Dei,* xix. 19).

2. Since the office of bishop is so high and excellent, only those should be elevated to it who are worthy. St. Paul, therefore, now begins to enumerate some of the outstanding moral and ethical qualities which candidates for the episcopate should possess. Nearly the same qualifications are given in Titus i. 6-9.

Husband of one wife does not mean that a bishop had to be married, but that if he was married and his wife died he should not remarry. That such is the correct interpretation of this passage is made certain by the parallel clause in v. 9 below. All other explanations are decidedly unsatisfactory. Second marriages were looked upon as a sign of incontinence and self-indulgence, and so as unbecoming the high spiritual office of a bishop. General celibacy for the clergy was not practicable in the early years of the Church, when all the members were converts from Judaism or paganism and were usually already married; and hence the law of celibacy for the clergy was enacted later, though it was counselled in 1 Cor. vii.

Sober, i.e., temperate in demeanor rather than in appetite, for of this latter temperance there is question in the next verse, "not given to wine."

Given to hospitality, which was especially necessary in those times when the faithful were often despoiled of their possessions, persecuted, and driven from place to place.

A teacher. One of the principal duties of a bishop was to teach

3. Not given to wine, no striker, but modest, not quarrelsome, not covetous, but

4. One that ruleth well his own house, having his children in subjection with all chastity,—

5. (Indeed if a man know not how to rule his own house, how shall he take care of the church of God?) ;—

6. Not a recent convert, lest being puffed up with pride, he fall unto the judgment of the devil.

and preach, though in later times the functions of teaching and preaching seem to have devolved more upon the priests (presbyters).

3. No striker. Better, "not a brawler," i.e., not given to the use of hurtful and injurious words.

Not covetous. St. Jerome says: "Ignominia omnium sacerdotum est propriis studere divitiis" (*Ad Nepot.*, Ep. 52, no. 6).

4-5. In case the candidate for the office of bishop was married and had children, it was well first to see how he governed his own household, before allowing him to rule in "the church of God."

With all chastity. Better, "with all reverence," as in ii. 2. The phrase here is probably to be connected with "having," rather than with "children." Verse 5 is parenthetical and gives the reason for the direction contained in verse 4. A bad father of a family will make a bad ruler in the Church, and one of the chief functions of a bishop is to rule.

6. Not a recent convert, i.e., not recently converted to Christianity. The Greek for "recent convert" is found in the New Testament only here.

Puffed up, etc. Better, "beclouded, etc." The expression is common in Greek literature, but is found only here in the Bible.

Unto the judgment, etc., i.e., into the same condemnation as that passed on the devil for his pride (cf. Isa. xiv. 12-14; Ezech. xxviii. 11-17). Some authorities claim that in verses 6-7 here the context requires that we should take the phrase "of the devil" as a subjective, instead of an objective genitive, meaning the condemnation passed by the διάβολος, and not that pronounced on him; and that the word "devil" means here *slanderer* or *accuser* (as in iii. 11 below; 2 Tim. iii. 3; Tit. ii. 3). In this interpretation the *slanderer* or *accuser* would be "one of those people, to be found in every community, whose delight is to find fault with the demeanour and conduct of anyone professing a strict rule of life"

7. Moreover he must have a good testimony of them that are without, lest he fall into reproach and a snare of the devil.

8. Deacons in like manner chaste, not double-tongued, not given to much wine, not greedy of filthy lucre,

9. Holding the mystery of faith in a pure conscience.

(Bernard, *The Pastoral Epistles, h. l.,* in *Camb. Bible*) ; and so the candidate for the office of bishop must try to regulate his life in such a manner as not to fall under the "judgment" or condemnation of slanderers. Cf. Bernard, *op. cit., ad locum.*

7. The bishop, as the chief representative of the Church, must also have a good reputation with his heathen neighbors; otherwise he cannot hope to make converts to the faith, he is apt to lose prestige among the faithful themselves, and thus he becomes exposed to "reproach and a snare of the devil." For the interpretation of this last phrase, see above on the preceding verse.

8. In verses 8-13 St. Paul treats of the qualifications for deacons and deaconesses.

Deacons in like manner. The verb is to be supplied from verse 2, "it behooveth." The same construction occurs again in verse 11 below, speaking of the "women." It is noticeable that "deacons" is plural, whereas "bishop" above in verse 2 and in Titus i. 7 is singular. While both these classes belonged to the sacred ministry, it is clear that the bishop was a person of higher rank and authority, and that the deacons were only helpers and assistants to whom was entrusted the administration of temporal affairs in the Christian community. For the election and duties of deacons, see Acts vi. 1 ff.

Chaste, i.e., reverent, grave in their character and manner of acting.

Not double-tongued, i.e., not saying different things to different people (Pengel).

Not greedy of filthy lucre. The reference is to the illicit disposal of the funds of the Christian community, the administration of which was entrusted to the deacons.

9. **Holding,** rather than preaching, the truths of the Gospel, which constituted the object of faith.

The "mystery of faith" means the secret of salvation, long kept concealed from mankind, but now revealed to the world in Christ. Thus, Christ Himself is "the mystery of faith" (cf. Col. ii. 2).

10. And let these also first be proved; and so let them minister, having no crime.

11 The women in like manner chaste, not slanderers, but sober, faithful in all things.

12. Let deacons be the husbands of one wife, who rule well their children and their own houses.

13. For they that have ministered well shall secure for themselves a good degree, and much confidence in the faith which is in Christ Jesus.

In a pure conscience. There must be harmony between the faith professed and the conscience, and this applies not only to deacons but to all Christians.

10. **And let these also** (as well as the bishops, ver. 7) **be proved** (i.e., found worthy), in the estimation of the community.

Having no crime, i.e., being irreproachable in their lives.

11. **The women** were doubtless deaconesses, like Phœbe of Rom. xvi. 1. Women in general could not be meant, as that would be out of harmony with the context, which is speaking of persons connected with the sacred ministry. Nor could we understand the wives of the deacons, for if that were so we should expect in Greek the possessive pronoun *their*, relating them to the "deacons," their husbands. These deaconesses "in like manner" (i.e., as well as the deacons) are to possess the qualifications that will fit them for their duties as helpers in the work of the sacred ministry.

12. See on verse 2 above, where the same injunctions are laid down for bishops.

13. **For they that have ministered well,** etc., i.e., the deacons that have faithfully discharged their office shall merit thereby promotion to a higher degree of office in the hierarchy, namely, to the order of priesthood or of the episcopate.

Other authorities explain "a good degree" as a stepping stone to greater influence and repute among the faithful, rather than as a promotion to higher office, since we do not know that deacons were regularly, if at all, promoted to the priesthood in the Apostolic Church. Still others think there is question in this place of the deacons acquiring a higher degree of merit in this life or of greater glory hereafter. But this last opinion is excluded by the words that follow, "and much confidence, etc.," which evidently mean that deacons, by their promotion to higher office or their acquisition of greater influence in the community, will be able to preach with

14. These things I write to thee, hoping that I shall come to thee shortly:
15. But if I tarry long, that thou mayest know how thou oughtest to
behave thyself in the house of God, which is the church of the living God,
a pillar and ground of the truth.
16. And evidently great is the mystery of godliness: who was manifested
in the flesh, was justified in spirit, appeared unto angels, was preached
among the Gentiles, believed on in the world, taken up in glory.

greater zeal and courage the faith which has its roots "in Christ
Jesus."

14-15. These things, i.e., the instructions he has just given in
Chapters ii and iii about public worship and the officers of the
Church.

Shortly. Literally, "more speedily."

The church, i.e., the society of all the faithful under their legitimate pastors and superiors.

Of the living God, as opposed to the dead gods of the pagans
(1 Thess. i. 9).

A pillar and ground, etc., i.e., the Christian society which is
plainly visible, like a pillar in the air, and as unshakable in the
truth it teaches as the solid ground on which great material struc-
tures are erected. The words afford a clear proof of the visibility
of the Church and of its infallibility in guarding and teaching the
truth of the Gospel. St. Paul is speaking here about the Church
Universal, and not about any local community or congregation.

16. Having spoken of the truth confided to the Church, the
Apostle now sums it all up in a brief verse on the mystery of Christ
the Redeemer, which verse was probably taken from a Christian
hymn that was in use in the Early Church.

And evidently great, etc. Better, "and admittedly great is the
mystery of piety," which was spoken of in verse 9 above as "the
mystery of faith," and which is none other than Jesus Christ, who
is thus described because all true piety toward God and all real
religion are founded on faith in Jesus Christ, God and man. Christ
"was manifested in the flesh," i.e., was made man; He "was justified in spirit," i.e., by His words and works He was proved to be
what He claimed to be, namely, God and man; or He was proved
to be the true Son of God by His powerful resurrection from the
dead (Rom. i. 3-4); He "appeared unto angels," who adored Him
at His entrance into the world (Heb. i. 6), who ministered to Him

in His mortal life and were witnesses of His resurrection and
ascension, and who saw His work in the call and conversion of the
Gentiles (Eph. iii. 10; 1 Pet. i. 12) ; He "was preached among the
Gentiles," i.e., among the nations of the world; He was "believed
in the world," in spite of Satan and his agents to the contrary; He
was "taken up in glory," on the day of His ascension (Acts i. 9-10),
and sitteth at the right hand of the Father evermore.

CHAPTER IV

ST. PAUL ADVISES TIMOTHY REGARDING THE FALSE TEACHERS, 1-16

1. But the Spirit manifestly saith, that in future times some shall depart
from the faith, giving heed to spirits of error, and doctrines of devils,
2. Through the hypocrisy of those speaking lies, men seared in their own
conscience,

1-16. In this Fourth Chapter the Apostle warns against the false
teachers and their errors, and tells Timothy how he is to deal with
them, reminding him of his duty as regards his personal conduct.

1. **But.**   This adversative seems to go back to the thought of
verse 15 of the preceding Chapter, and to show that, although the
Church is the pillar and ground of truth, heresies will come from
some of her children.

The Spirit, i.e., the Holy Ghost, whether alluding to the prophe-
sies of our Lord (Matt. xxiv. 4 ff.), or to the words of some con-
temporary Christian prophet, or to a private revelation made to the
Apostle himself by the Holy Ghost.

Doctrines of devils, i.e., doctrines inspired by demons.

The *novissimis* of the Vulgate is a wrong rendering of the Greek,
which simply means "future" or "after," i.e., times future to the
speaker or writer.

2. **Through the hypocrisy of those speaking lies,** i.e., the demons
are to exercise their influence through lying human agents.   The
Greek for "speaking lies" is found only here in the Greek Bible;
likewise the term "seared," which in the phrase means that those
false teachers had the brand of sin in their own conscience, though
they pretended zeal and holiness on the outside before men.

3. Forbidding to marry, to abstain from foods, which God hath created to be received with thanksgiving by the faithful, and by them that have known the truth.

4. For every creature of God is good, and nothing to be rejected that is received with thanksgiving,

5. For it is sanctified by the word of God and prayer.

6. These things proposing to the brethren, thou shalt be a good minister of Christ Jesus, nourished up in the words of faith, and of the good doctrine which thou hast learned.

3. The exaggerated asceticism of the false teachers held that marriage was bad in itself and to be avoided, and also taught abstention from food on the ground that matter was bad, having been produced by an evil principle, as the Gnostics and Manicheans later taught quite openly; whereas, according to the true doctrine of Christianity, marriage is good (1 Cor. vii. 1 ff.), and all food, as coming from God, is good and is to be eaten with thanksgiving to the Giver of all good things (Gen. i. 31). It is only the abstention from marriage and food as the result of false principles that St. Paul is condemning; they are not bad in themselves, though celibacy is to be preferred to matrimony (1 Cor. vii. 7 ff.) and fasting from right motives is good.

To abstain from foods. We must understand before this elliptical phrase some word like *command*; so that the full reading would be, "commanding to abstain from foods."

The faithful, as contrasted with the unbelieving Jews.

By them that have known the truth, as contrasted with the false teachers and the weak, half-instructed Christians (Rom. xiv. 21).

4-5. The falsity of the erroneous teaching is now pointed out. Everything God has made is good in itself (Gen. i. 31), and also in its relation to man, despite the fall (Rom. viii. 20), provided it be received with thanksgiving.

For it is sanctified by the word, etc. This means that food was sanctified by the blessing said over it before eating, which blessing or prayer was made up of Scripture phrases taken from the Old Testament.

6. In verses 6-11 St. Paul tells Timothy what his attitude should be toward the false asceticism.

These things, i.e., what he has just been saying in verses 4-5. If Timothy will set these principles before the faithful committed

7. But avoid foolish and old wives' fables; and exercise thyself unto godliness.

8. For bodily exercise is profitable to little, but godliness is profitable to all things, having promise of the life that now is and of that which is to come.

9. Faithful is the saying and worthy of all acceptation;

10. For therefore we labor and are reviled, because we hope in the living God, who is the Saviour of all men, especially of the faithful.

to his care, he will "be a good minister, etc.," in the widest sense of the word "minister," as embracing all his duties as a real servant of Christ, nourished with the true faith and the sound doctrine he has learnt.

7. Timothy is to reject the false teachings of the heretics and discipline himself in piety.

Old wives. The Greek word is found only here in the Bible, but it occurs in profane writers; it means anile, like an old woman.

Fables, or myths. See on i. 4.

Exercise, i.e., discipline, alluding to the athletic games.

8. The Apostle now assigns the reason for the advice just given.

Bodily exercise, such as that of the arena or the race course, affords a limited and a passing benefit to the physical constitution and leads to a temporal reward (1 Cor. ix. 25); "but godliness" benefits the whole man, body and soul, "having the promise, etc.," i.e., causing or producing the present spiritual life, which is the foretaste of the enduring life to come hereafter (Matt. vi. 33, xix. 29; Mark x. 30).

9. See above, on i. 15. The reference is to what he has just said about godliness in verse 8, as the context shows.

10. A proof that "godliness" or piety is profitable for the present and the future life is in this, that it enables its possessors to toil and suffer in view of the rewards that "hope in the living God" holds out to them.

We labor, in the sense of toil or wearing fatigue, alluding to the contests in the arena.

Are reviled. A better reading has: "We struggle."

The living God. See on iii. 15.

The Saviour of all men, etc. See on ii. 3-4. It is only as regards "the faithful," i.e., in those that are really faithful, that God's will to save is fully realized; in them His grace is efficacious.

11. These things command and teach.

12. Let no man despise thy youth; but be thou an example of the faithful in word, in conversation, in charity, in faith, in chastity.

13. Till I come, attend unto reading, to exhortation, and to doctrine.

14. Neglect not the grace that is in thee, which was given thee by prophecy, with the imposition of the hands of the priesthood.

11. **These things**, i.e., what he has been saying in verses 7-10, Timothy is to insist on with authority.

12. In verses 12-16 St. Paul gives Timothy advice regarding his personal behavior. Timothy was not forty years of age at this time, and had been associated with St. Paul some fifteen years. He was young in comparison with the Apostle, who was then sixty or more. Moreover, in ancient times a man was considered young until after forty. St. Paul himself was spoken of as a young man at the martyrdom of St. Stephen (Acts vii. 57), when he must have been thirty years old at least.

Young people in authority are apt to be criticised and even despised by older persons, unless shining virtues supply in them for the lack of age. Hence, the aged Apostle tells the youthful bishop to be an example to the faithful in his outward actions and manner of life, and also in the internal virtues that grace the soul and ennoble the character. The classic Greek word for "chastity" is found only here and in v. 2 below in the New Testament. It means chastity of life and purity of motive.

13. St. Paul hopes to come to Ephesus soon, but meanwhile Timothy is to be faithful to the custom of reading and explaining the Scriptures in public, and to the exhortation or preaching that followed that reading, which should be grounded on solid doctrine or teaching. Although the injunction here is primarily to the public reading of the Sacred Scriptures to the faithful in their assemblies, it does not exclude but rather presupposes private reading and study.

14. Timothy is exhorted not to fail to exercise the spiritual gifts he received from God at the time of his ordination and consecration as bishop through the imposition of St. Paul's hands (2 Tim. i. 6). This verse and 2 Tim. i. 6 are the classic passages to prove that Holy Orders is a Sacrament (see on 1 Tim. i. 18). The reference in the present verse is to the episcopal consecration of Timothy in

15. Meditate upon these things, be wholly in these things, that thy profiting may be manifest to all.

16. Take heed to thyself and to doctrine: be earnest in them. For in doing this thou shalt both save thyself and them that hear thee.

the presence and with the approval of the Ephesian elders, according to the best authorities.

15. Timothy is to "meditate," i.e., ponder what St. Paul has been telling him regarding his office and personal duties, and thus make continual progress in the development of his own character and in the consequent better quality of his work.

16. Finally, St. Paul bids Timothy watch over himself and to be careful how he presents the doctrine he has received from the Apostles; and the result of this proper attention to self and to his duties towards others will be his own and their salvation.

CHAPTER V

HOW TIMOTHY IS TO DEAL WITH VARIOUS CLASSES IN THE CHURCH, 1-25

1. An elderly man rebuke not, but entreat him as a father; younger men, as brethren:

2. Elderly women, as mothers; young women, as sisters, in all chastity.

3. Honor widows that are widows indeed.

1-25. St. Paul now instructs his disciple how he is to act with the different classes of persons that make up the body of the Church, namely, (a) older and younger men and women (ver. 1-2); (b) widows, as to their maintenance (ver. 3-8), as an organized body of helpers in the Church (ver. 9-10), and as to those who are still young (ver. 11-16); (c) the clergy, their dignity and discipline (ver. 17-25).

1-2. **Rebuke not,** i.e., do not treat severely or harshly.

Young women, etc. St. Jerome says: "Either equally ignore, or equally love all girls and virgins of Christ."

3. **Honor** is here used not only in the sense of esteeming, but also in the sense of assisting, taking care of, as is evident from such passages as Matt. xv. 4-6; Acts vi. 1; 1 Tim. v. 17.

4. But if any widow have children, or grandchildren, let her learn first to govern her own house, and to make a return of duty to her parents; for this is acceptable before God.

5. But she that is a widow indeed, and desolate, let her trust in God, and continue in supplications and prayers night and day.

6. But she that liveth in pleasures is dead while she is living.

Widows that are widows indeed, i.e., women that have lost their husbands, that are destitute, and that have no relatives who can support them; such as these Timothy is told to assist out of the funds of the Church. Widows were a very destitute class among the Jews, and still more so in the Early Church.

4. Those widows are not to look to the Church for their support who have living relatives that can give them what they need.

Let her learn, etc. This is according to the reading of the Vulgate, and the meaning is that, if a destitute widow has children or grandchildren, she should give them her services, looking after their upbringing, training, education, etc., and through these offices receive her own support. But the Greek reads differently, as follows: "Let them first learn to practise piety, etc." This suits the context better, and the meaning is that living young relatives of destitute widows should assist them and take care of them as a matter of filial duty, remembering what their parents and relatives did for them when they were dependent and helpless in their infancy and early years. Respect to parents is the first duty of children, and the care of one's own household and relatives, when these latter are in need, is likewise a primary obligation binding those who have means sufficient to help (see ver. 8 below).

5. The characteristics of the true widow are now described.

A widow indeed, i.e., one who has no relatives to support her, who is alone without helpers, should put her hope in God and give herself to continual prayer. Instead of, "let her trust in God," the Greek reads, "has her hope in God," i.e., she has put all her hope in God as her sure refuge and strength. See the story of the widow Anna in Luke ii. 36 ff. It is a widow of this sort that deserves help from the Church, to which she makes return by her many prayers.

6. In contrast to the pious widow, who deserves help from the Church, "she that liveth in pleasures," i.e., she that lives wantonly,

7. And these things enjoin, that they may be blameless.

8. But if any man have not care of his own, and especially of those of his house, he hath denied the faith and is worse than an infidel.

9. Let a widow be chosen of no less than threescore years of age, who hath been the wife of one husband,

10. Having testimony for her good works, if she have brought up chil-

indulging in unlawful pleasures, is spiritually dead, and deserves no help from the Church.

The *nam* of the Vulgate should be replaced by an adversative conjunction, to agree with the Greek.

7. **And these things**, i.e., what he has just said in verses 5-6. The *et hoc* of the Vulgate should be *et hæc,* as in the Greek.

That they may be, etc., i.e., that the children and grandchildren, spoken of in verse 4 and alluded to in verse 8, may be blameless by giving help and support to their destitute relatives.

8. The Apostle now announces a general principle, which is illustrated by the duty spoken of in verse 4. If any one neglects to care for his needy and dependent relatives, and especially those of his own family, he has already denied the faith in practice; and he is worse than pagans, because even these unbelievers, in response to the dictates of the natural law, provide for their helpless relations.

9. There is most likely question in this verse of a special class of widows to whom special duties were entrusted, such as the care of the sick, orphans, and the like. For a possible allusion to this class of women in the Early Church, see Polycarp (*Phil.*, iv) and Ignatius (*Smyrn.*, 13). Their duties were analogous to those required of deacons, and the condition placed on them in regard to marriage was similar to that for bishops and deacons (see above on iii. 2, 11, 12). Yet, they were not the same as deaconesses, as we shall see.

Be chosen. Literally, "be enrolled," i.e., placed on the list.

Three score years of age. This condition seems to show that the widows in question constituted a special class; for, on the one hand, the Church would not deny help to all destitute widows until they were sixty years old, and, on the other hand, it would be unreasonable to require that deaconesses be so old before being admitted to active work.

10. Here are mentioned further qualifications required of those

dren, if she have received to harbor, if she have washed the saints' feet,
if she have ministered to them that suffer tribulation, if she have diligently
followed every good work.

11. But the younger widows reject. For when they have grown wanton
against Christ, they will marry,

12. Having damnation, because they have made void their first faith.

13. And withal being idle they learn to go about from house to house,
and are not only idle, but tattlers also, and busybodies, speaking things
which they ought not.

widows whose names were to be put on the church list. It was the
dispositions manifested by these works rather than their actual
performance that counted.

If she have brought up children, not necessarily her own.

If she have washed, etc. To wash the feet of guests was a
necessary complement of hospitality among the Orientals (Matt.
xxvi. 6; Luke vii. 44), and an act of extreme humility (John
xiii. 5 ff.).

11. In verses 11-15 St. Paul explains the reasons why certain
widows should not be put on the church list. It is supposed that
the women thus listed are enrolled for life in the service of the
Church; and if they are younger than sixty, they will want to
change and remarry "when they have grown wanton against Christ,"
i.e., when they have grown tired of the life to which they have
engaged themselves. The Greek word for "grown wanton" is found
only here, and the figure is that of a young animal that has tired
of its yoke and has become restive through fullness of vigor.

In the Vulgate, *in Christo* would better be *contra Christum*.

12. Those widows who had been enrolled on the church list had
consecrated themselves to a work for Christ which was incompatible with remarriage; and to break the pledge they had thus
freely made would bring upon them the guilt of being unfaithful
to their first troth, which was to the Heavenly Bridegroom.

Damnation here means the guilt of unfaithfulness. The punishment of eternal damnation is not at all necessarily involved or
implied in this instance; although, if there is unfaithfulness to
Christ in one direction, it can easily spread to every direction and
to all matters.

13. Another reason is now given why young widows should not
be listed for church work. Going about as their duties would require, they would turn the opportunity of doing good into one of

14. I will therefore that the younger should marry, bear children, be mistresses of families, give no occasion to the adversary to speak evil.

15. For some are already turned aside after Satan.

16. If any of the faithful have widows, let him minister to them, and let not the church be charged, that there may be sufficient for them that are widows indeed.

17. Let the priests that rule well be esteemed worthy of double honor, especially they who labor in the word and doctrine;

mischief and trouble-making in families and between neighbors, thus doing no end of harm and disgracing the Church. St. Paul was doubtless speaking from experience. The Greek word for "tattlers" is not found elsewhere in the New Testament, and that for "busybodies" occurs only here in St. Paul.

14. Therefore, i.e., in view of the reasons assigned in verses 11-13, the Apostle expresses the wish that those young widows, and all young women for that matter, who cannot live continently (1 Cor. vii. 9), should marry. His desire in this matter must be qualified by what he says in 1 Cor. vii. 8, 40, where he recommends virginity in preference to marriage, if the danger of incontinence be excluded. The context shows he is still speaking of widows in this verse.

Be mistresses of families is in Greek "rule their household."

Give no occasion to the adversary, i.e., to the Jews and pagans around, who would be only too ready to criticise Christians.

15. The Apostle's advice is based on experience; for "already" some of those young widows who had given themselves to Christ and His work, had turned to a life of dissipation, perhaps forsaking the faith.

16. If any of the faithful. The best reading of this phrase is "if any believing woman" (*si quæ fidelis*, in Latin), though there is good evidence in the MSS., versions, and Fathers for "if any believing man or woman." The context seems to show that the reference is to those destitute young widows who do not remarry and whose age prevents them from being enrolled on the list of the Church. These should be cared for by their relatives, when possible, so that the church funds may be used to help those who are widows indeed, that is, who have no one else to relieve them in their need.

17. In verses 17-25 St. Paul tells Timothy how he is to treat the clergy.

18. For the scripture saith: *Thou shalt not muzzle the ox that treadeth out the corn;* and, *the laborer is worthy of his reward.*

19. Against a priest receive not an accusation but under two or three witnesses.

20. Them that sin reprove before all, that the rest also may have fear.

Priests, literally, "elders" (presbyters). See on iii. 1. There is not question here, as in verse 1 above, of elderly men, but of officials of the Church, whether priests or bishops.

Double honor is a Hebraism meaning here more ample material reward or provision. Those of the clergy who fulfill their duties faithfully should be well taken care of by the Church, and especially those who preach the Divine Word and teach the doctrines of faith to others. This verse seems to distinguish between those who were engaged in preaching and those who were occupied in ministerial work, and to show that some of the presbyters of the Pastoral Epistles did not teach. See St. Cyprian (*Epist.,* xxix) on the *presbyteri doctores.*

18. The first quotation of this verse is from Deut. xxv. 4, and is found also in 1 Cor. ix. 9. The second quotation is not in the Old Testament, but occurs in Luke x. 7 (cf. Matt. x. 10). Could St. Paul at so early a date be quoting St. Luke as Scripture on a level with the Old Testament? Hardly so; and yet possibly so. The best explanation seems to be that this second quotation was a familiar proverb to which both St. Paul and our Lord appealed to enforce a moral principle. "The Scripture saith" then would apply only to the first quotation.

19. In verses 19-21 St. Paul explains to Timothy how he is to deal with priests who have been guilty, or suspected of some fault.

Receive not an accusation, etc. This rule was laid down in Deut. xix. 15 as a norm for all, and it is especially necessary for the clergy, both on account of their dignity and the danger of accusation to which their high and responsible offices expose them. For an appeal to this same general principle see 2 Cor. xiii. 1; Matt. xviii. 16; John viii. 17 (cf. Deut. xvii. 6).

20. **Them that sin,** etc. There is question here of public sins on the part of the clergy, as the context shows. These offenders are to be reproved by Timothy in the presence of all the presbyters, that all may take warning for their own conduct. The case mentioned in Matt. xviii. 15 has to do with private sins between private individuals.

21. I charge thee before God, and Christ Jesus, and the elect angels, that thou observe these things without prejudice, doing nothing by declining to either side.

22. Impose not hands lightly upon any man, neither be partaker of other men's sins. Keep thyself pure.

23. Do not still drink water, but use a little wine for thy stomach's sake, and thy frequent infirmities.

24. Some men's sins are manifest, going before to judgment; and some men they follow after.

25. In like manner also good deeds are manifest; and they that are otherwise, cannot be hid.

21. **I charge thee,** etc. Better, "I solemnly charge thee, etc." The same solemn formula occurs again in 2 Tim. ii. 14, iv. 1.

The elect angels, i.e., the heavenly messengers whom God has chosen to do His special bidding and to look with care after the affairs of men (cf. 1 Tim. iii. 16; 1 Cor. iv. 9).

These things, i.e., the precepts of verses 19-20.

22. **Impose not hands,** etc. The majority of the best commentators see in these words a warning against ordaining unworthy candidates to the sacred ministry. The general context also favors this view. *Imposition of hands* is the regular New Testament phrase to signify ordination (1 Tim. iv. 14; 2 Tim. i. 6; Acts vi. 6, xiii. 3).

Neither be partaker, etc., by carelessly ordaining unworthy persons.

Keep thyself pure, i.e., free from responsibility for others' sins and guiltless in your personal and private life. That the foregoing words, "impose not hands, etc.," have reference to the reconciling of public penitents is very improbable.

23. **Do not still drink water.** More literally, "be no longer a water-drinker," in the sense of a total abstainer. St. Paul is cautioning Timothy against too much mortification, to which he seems to have been inclined, because of his naturally delicate health. This verse, like 2 Tim. iv. 13, "is a little touch of humanity which is a powerful argument for the genuineness of the Epistle in which it is found" (Bernard, *op. cit., h. l.*).

24-25. Timothy is given two final maxims by which he is to be guided in judging the character of his candidates for the ministry. First, Paul says the sins of some men are evident before investigation, while the sins of others are brought out by investigation;

secondly, in like manner, some good works are conspicuous, and those that are not cannot be kept hidden if full investigation be made. Timothy, therefore, is to proceed cautiously in his choice of persons for the sacred ministry.

CHAPTER VI

THE DUTIES OF SLAVES TO THEIR MASTERS, WHETHER HEATHEN OR CHRISTIAN, 1-2

1. Whosoever are servants under the yoke, let them count their masters worthy of all honor; lest the name of God and *his* doctrine be blasphemed.
2. But they that have believing masters, let them not despise them, because they are brethren; but serve them the rather, because they are faithful and beloved, who are partakers of the benefit. These things teach and exhort.

1-2. In Eph. vi. 5-9 and Col. iii. 22—iv. 1, St. Paul had already treated at length of the mutual duties and relations of slaves and masters. Here, however, he speaks only of slaves, doubtless because there was somehow more cause for treating only of the one class. He was not in any way approving of slavery, for it was his repeated teaching that in Christ there was "neither bond nor free" (Gal. iii. 28); like the other Apostles, he was simply taking the existing conditions of society as he found them, and adapting himself to them as the circumstances required. See on Eph. vi. 5-9; see also *Introduction* to Philemon, No. V.

The slaves addressed in both of the present verses were Christians; and St. Paul tells Timothy to instruct those slaves to conduct themselves with all respect and obedience toward their heathen masters, so as to reflect credit on their profession as believers in God and followers of Christ; any failure in their duties as slaves would only cast discredit on their religion.

The *Domini* of the Vulgate should be *Dei,* as in the Greek.

In the second verse the masters also are Christians, and this fact calls for even better service on the part of their slaves.

Because they are faithful and beloved, i.e., because those masters are Christians, and consequently beloved by God. This is the reason why their Christian slaves should render them special service.

Who are partakers of the benefit. This does not mean the

3. If any man teach otherwise, and consent not to the sound words of our Lord Jesus Christ, and to that doctrine which is according to godliness,

4. He is proud, knowing nothing, but sick about questions and strifes of words; from which arise envies, contentions, blasphemies, evil suspicions,

5. Conflicts of men corrupted in mind, and who are destitute of the truth, supposing godliness to be gain.

benefit of redemption which the masters enjoy by being Christians, nor the benefits which the masters confer on their slaves, but the improved and special service which those masters receive from the fidelity and obedience of their slaves. Therefore, translate the second part of the verse with the Westminster Version as follows: "But serve them all the more, for that they who claim their good service are believing and beloved."

These things, i.e., the directions just given about slaves, or perhaps all the instructions so far given in this letter, Timothy is to "teach and exhort."

CLOSING INSTRUCTIONS TO TIMOTHY, 3-21

3-21. In the closing section of his letter (ver. 3-21) St. Paul utters renewed warnings against the false teachers (ver. 3-5), speaks of the vanity and perils of wealth (ver. 6-10), personally exhorts Timothy to the practice of virtue and the preservation of the teachings he has received (ver. 11-16), issues a charge to the rich of Ephesus (ver. 17-19), and terminates by recalling to Timothy the principal thought of the Epistle and imparting his blessing (ver. 20-21).

3-5. Teach otherwise, i.e., teach a different doctrine from that taught by St. Paul (see on i. 3).

And consent not to the sound words, etc., i.e., to the true teaching contained in our Lord's words.

And to that doctrine which is according to godliness, i.e., which teaches the true way in which God is to be worshipped. The false teaching the Apostle has in mind, therefore, is out of harmony with that which Timothy is to "teach and exhort" (ver. 2). The false teacher himself and the practical results of his teaching are next described (ver. 4-5).

He is proud, knowing nothing, about that which he ought to know, and which constitutes the true doctrine; he is "sick" from feeding his mind on unwholesome speculations and disputes which

6. But godliness with contentment is great gain.

7. For we brought nothing into this world, and certainly we can carry nothing out.

8. But having food and wherewith to be covered, with these we are content.

9. For they that will become rich, fall into temptation, and into a snare, and into many unprofitable and hurtful desires, which drown men into destruction and perdition.

10. For the desire of money is the root of all evils; which some coveting have erred from the faith, and have entangled themselves in many sorrows.

consist only in words, and which result in envy of rivals, quarrels with opponents, suspicions of unworthy motives, and the like. Such men, "corrupted in mind," pervert the Gospel and subordinate piety and the worship of God to material gains.

In the Vulgate of verse 5, *quæstum esse pietatem* should be reversed, *pietatem esse quæstum*, as the position of the article and the order of the words in the Greek indicate.

6. While "godliness" or piety is not to be prostituted to material gain, there is, nevertheless, great gain in its possession, for it teaches one to be content with what one has, not desiring to have more (Phil. iv. 11-13).

7. He now explains why man ought to be content with little in this world. Material goods serve only for the present life; we come into the world without them, and we must leave them behind when we die. It is only what a man is in himself—his spiritual attainments, his character, his good or bad habits—that he takes with him into the next world; all else he leaves behind at death.

8. Food and raiment are the chief necessities of our material existence, but we must remember that we are far more than these, and that we are not to be over-anxious about them (Matt. vi. 25 ff.).

9. It is the desire for wealth and an inordinate attachment to material things that St. Paul is here condemning, the disastrous consequences of which are clearly attested to by history and experience. Those whose minds are set on wealth are exposed and expose themselves to many perils.

Destruction, etc. See on Phil. i. 28, iii. 19; 2 Thess. i. 9.

The *diaboli* of the Vulgate is not in the best Greek.

10. In rhetorical language the Apostle stresses the peril of a love of material wealth. It is "the root," or, as in the Greek, "a root of all evils," i.e., of all moral evils, inasmuch as it will induce a

11. But thou, O man of God, fly these things: and pursue justice, godliness, faith, charity, patience, mildness.

12. Fight the good fight of faith; lay hold on eternal life, whereunto thou art called, and didst make the good confession before many witnesses.

13. I charge thee before God, who quickeneth all things, and before Christ Jesus, who gave testimony under Pontius Pilate, a good confession:

14. That thou keep the commandment without spot, blameless, unto the coming of our Lord Jesus Christ,

person to commit any evil or sin to attain it, when the passion becomes all-absorbing. At all times the love of money is fraught with very dangerous consequences, and if it does not go so far as to lead one away from the faith, it nevertheless chills the spirit of religion, and deadens a person to the appeal of the higher things of the mind and soul.

11. St. Paul now exhorts Timothy to flee the love of money and its attendant evils, and to pursue virtue.

Man of God is the regular Old Testament expression for a prophet or ruler of God's people (1 Kings ix. 6; 3 Kings xii. 22, xiii. 1 ff.).

12. **Fight the good fight.** The metaphor is taken from the athletic games, and is frequently employed by St. Paul (1 Cor. ix. 24; Phil. iii. 12, 14; 2 Tim. iv. 7). "Fight" is in the present tense in Greek, showing the constant struggle; while "lay hold" is aorist, to indicate the single act.

Whereunto thou art called, etc., doubtless refers to Timothy's baptism, and to the confession then made of the Divinity of Jesus Christ. Some think the confession referred to was at the time of Timothy's ordination or consecration as bishop.

13-14. St. Paul now charges Timothy before God, the Creator, "who quickeneth all things" (better, "who preserveth all things in life") and before His Son Jesus Christ, "who gave testimony, etc." (i.e., who made the good confession of His divine Kingship and Sonship in the presence or at the time of Pontius Pilate, Matt. xxvii. 11; Mark xv. 2; Luke xxiii. 3; John xviii. 33 ff.), to practise, profess, and defend the faith; it is this divine example of our Lord that will enable Timothy to "keep the commandment without spot," i.e., the commands and precepts, implied or expressed, which were laid on him at the time of his baptism or ordination (ver. 12).

Unto the coming, etc., i.e., till the Second Coming of the Lord in glory. The Greek word for "coming" here is found again in the

15. Which in his times he shall shew who is the Blessed and only Mighty, the King of kings, and Lord of lords;

16. Who only hath immortality, and inhabiteth light inaccessible, whom no man hath seen, nor can see; to whom be honor and empire everlasting. Amen.

17. Charge the rich of this world not to be high-minded, nor to trust in the uncertainty of riches, but in God, who giveth us abundantly all things to enjoy,

18. To do good, to be rich in good works, to give easily, to communicate to others,

19. To lay up in store for themselves a good foundation against the time to come, that they may lay hold on the true life.

New Testament only in 2 Thess. ii. 8; but it occurs often in the LXX. On the other hand, St. Paul uses a great variety of expressions to describe the Second Advent (cf. 1 Thess. ii. 2; 1 Cor. i. 8, v. 5; Phil. i. 10; 2 Tim. i. 12, etc.).

15-16. The Second Coming or final manifestation of Jesus Christ will occur "in his times," i.e., in the season known only to him.

Who is the Blessed and only Mighty, etc. It is probable that these words and those of verse 16, which constitute a magnificent doxology, belonged to a primitive hymn. The phrase "King of kings and Lord of lords" is found also in Dan. iv. 34 (cf. Deut. x. 17; Ps. cxxxv. 3). God alone has essential and underived immortality; He dwells in light because He is light; and He cannot be seen as He is in Himself by mortal man in this life, nor in the life to come save as the human soul is elevated and strengthened by the light of glory.

17. In verses 17-19 St. Paul returns to the thought of verses 9-10, directing his words, no doubt, to the well-to-do of Ephesus, whose pursuit of wealth he had interfered with years before (Acts xix. 25 ff.

The rich of this world. Better, "those who are rich in the present world," as contrasted with those who lay up treasure for the world to come (ver. 19 below). They must not put their trust in riches, which are uncertain, but in God, who has given them all they have, to be enjoyed indeed but also to be used for the other good purposes which he proceeds to mention in the following verses.

The *vivo* of the Vulgate is not in the best MSS., and the brackets are unnecessary.

18-19. Wealth is not only for the pleasure of its possessor, but

20. Timothy, keep that which is committed to thy trust, avoiding the profane novelties of words, and oppositions of knowledge falsely so called,
21. Which some professing, have erred concerning the faith.   Grace be
with you. Amen.

it is also to be used for the benefit of others, and thus to enable
its owner to become spiritually rich.

To give easily . . . to communicate. The two equivalent Greek
expressions do not occur elsewhere in the Greek Bible, and they
signify a ready hand and a ready heart in giving. Thus, to use
wealth for the benefit of others is to lay up treasure for the life
to come (Matt. vi. 20), the only true life.

20-21. In conclusion, St. Paul addresses solemn words to Timothy, admonishing him diligently to guard the faith he has received
and to pass it on unsullied. This he will be able to do by avoiding
in his own teaching, and rebuking in others, vain and useless speculations and subtleties of knowledge, falsely so called, which the
false teachers professed to have, and so have erred from the faith.

Keep that which is committed to thy trust. Better, "guard
the deposit," i.e., the deposit of faith.

Profane novelties of words. Better, "profane babblings," i.e.,
empty, useless talk; the Greek word for "babblings" occurs only
here and in 2 Tim. ii. 16. The words for "oppositions" and "falsely
so called" are not found elsewhere in the Bible, but are common
in profane Greek.

Which some professing, etc., i.e., which empty babblings and
subtleties the false teachers have professed to their own spiritual
destruction. The Greek for "have erred" is aorist, indicating a
definite and final loss.

The Apostle terminates his letter with a brief blessing. The
tecum of the Vulgate is *vobiscum* in the best Greek MSS.

The Second Epistle to Timothy

CHAPTER I

INTRODUCTION AND GREETING, 1-2

1. Paul, an apostle of Christ Jesus, by the will of God, according to the promise of the life, which is in Christ Jesus.
2. To Timothy my beloved son: grace, mercy, *and* peace, from God the Father, and from Christ Jesus our Lord.

1-2. Again, as in the first letter, asserting his Apostolic authority and divine election to preach the Gospel, St. Paul salutes Timothy, his beloved child, whom he has begotten in Christ Jesus.

1. See on 1 Tim. i. 1.

By the will of God, as in 1 Cor. i. 1; Eph. i. 1; Col. i. 1. St. Paul was not a self-appointed Apostle, but a vessel of divine election.

According to the promise, etc., means that the aim and purpose of St. Paul's election and call to the Apostleship was to proclaim the fulfillment in Christ of the promises of eternal life which were given in the Old Testament.

2. See on 1 Tim. i. 2.

THE APOSTLE THANKS GOD FOR TIMOTHY'S FAITH, AND EXHORTS THE YOUNG BISHOP TO BE READY TO SUFFER, 3-14

3-14. St. Paul first thanks the God of his forefathers for Timothy's faith, asserting his remembrance of him in his prayers and his desire to see his devoted son (ver. 3-5). He then exhorts him to rekindle the grace of his ordination and to be courageous in laboring and suffering for the Gospel, relying on that divine power whereof God has already given us a manifestation in the gratuitous salvation imparted to the world through Christ (ver. 6-10). For his election to preach the Gospel and his faithful discharge of his duty Paul now languishes in prison and faces death, but his

3. I give thanks to God, whom I serve from my forefathers with a pure conscience, as without ceasing I have a remembrance of thee in my prayers, night and day,

4. Desiring to see thee, being mindful of thy tears, that I may be filled with joy,

5. Calling to mind that faith which is in thee unfeigned, which also dwelt first in thy grandmother Lois, and in thy mother Eunice, and I am certain that in thee also.

6. For which reason I admonish thee, that thou stir up the grace of God which is in thee, by the imposition of my hands.

faith is undaunted. Let Timothy likewise hold fast to the faith taught him, and be true to his trust (ver. 11-14).

3-4. St. Paul thanks God for Timothy's faith (ver. 5), as he remembers him in his prayers every day and every night; and he is longing to see him, recalling the tears that were shed at their parting.

Whom I serve, etc. The Apostle's Jewish opponents had accused him of betraying the religion of his ancestors, but he here asserts that the God whom he serves is the same God that his forefathers adored, and that his service of Him is pure and free from self-interest, unlike their service of that same God of whom they boast.

5. It was the recollection of the readiness and generosity with which Timothy received the faith from his mother and grandmother that moved St. Paul to give thanks to God (ver. 3).

Unfeigned, i.e., unmixed with error or hypocrisy.

Which also dwelt first, etc., i.e., Lois (most likely the mother of Unice) and Unice embraced the faith first, when Paul preached at Lystra (Acts xiv. 6, xvi. 1), and under their instruction Timothy readily followed their example. It would seem that Unice was a widow at the time of Timothy's circumcision, and this is probably the reason why St. Paul does not make any mention of her husband in his Epistles.

6. **For which reason,** etc. Having reminded Timothy of the alacrity with which he had received the faith, the aged Apostle now exhorts him to "stir up"—more literally, "kindle to fresh flame" (the word occurs only here in the New Testament)—the sacramental "grace of God" which he received when Paul ordained him, and which remains with him still (cf. 1 Tim. iv. 14). Timothy was naturally timid and may have been somewhat remiss in the

7. For God hath not given us the spirit of fear; but of power, and of love and of sobriety.

8. Be not thou therefore ashamed of the testimony of our Lord, nor of me his prisoner; but endure your share of suffering for the gospel, according to the power of God;

9. Who hath saved us and called us by his holy calling, not according to our works, but according to his own purpose and grace which was given us in Christ Jesus before the times of the world,

exercise of his sacred powers. But perhaps St. Paul is only anxious that his young disciple will ever be courageous and faithful in spite of difficulties. The Council of Trent (sess. XXIII, cap. 3) cites this verse to prove that Holy Orders is a true Sacrament.

7. In this verse the Apostle gives the reason why Timothy should rekindle in himself the grace of his ordination; for God has given his chosen Apostles the graces and powers necessary for a faithful and rigorous fulfillment of all their duties, however great the obstacles they may encounter.

Us refers to Paul and Timothy both. St. Paul includes himself so as to soften his words. In giving His Apostles the Holy Ghost, God has endowed them with the spirit (a) of "power," to discharge all their offices and to encounter all difficulties, (b) of "love," to endure all things patiently for Christ's sake, (c) of "sobriety" (better, "wisdom" or "prudence") in dealing with others, and therefore in the exercise of discipline.

8. Timothy must not be ashamed to bear witness to Christ in preaching the Gospel; nor should he be ashamed of his master who is in prison for preaching the Gospel. On the contrary, he must be willing to endure his share of suffering, along with Paul, for the sake of the Gospel, not trusting in his own strength, but in the "power of God," which will never fail him.

The *collabora* of the Vulgate does not express the sense of the Greek, which means "suffer with," i.e., to take one's share in suffering for the Gospel. The word is found only here and in ii. 3 below in the Greek Bible.

9. A proof that God will never fail His faithful followers is to be seen in the fact that it is He who has already freely saved us from our sins and called us to holiness of life. All this He has done, not in virtue of any works or merits of ours, but in virtue of His own eternal plan and purpose and by the help of His saving grace, which from eternity He determined to carry out and bestow

10. But is now made manifest by the illumination of our Saviour Jesus Christ, who hath destroyed death, and hath brought to light life and incorruption by the gospel:

11. Whereunto I am appointed a preacher and an apostle and teacher of the Gentiles.

12. For which reason I also suffer these things; but I am not ashamed. For I know whom I have believed, and I am certain that he is able to keep my deposit unto that day.

on us in Christ. The Apostle here indicates the two causes of our salvation, namely, the eternal cause, which was divine predestination, or God's eternal purpose to show us mercy; and the temporal cause, which is sanctifying grace (St. Thomas).

Not according to our works. This phrase at once tempers the stress put on good works in the Pastoral Letters and shows against the Pelagians the existence and the gratuitousness of the grace by which we are led to faith and salvation.

But according to his own purpose, etc. From all eternity God predestined our salvation and the means to that end, which means were the merits and grace of Christ. Hence it was that the Incarnation of Christ was predestined from all eternity, and that in Christ from all eternity God prepared for us the grace which is at length conferred, and by which we are sanctified and saved in time. See on Eph. i. 3-6; Tit. iii. 5; Rom. viii. 30, ix. 12.

The *liberavit* of the Vulgate ought to be *salvavit,* as in the Greek.

10. God's eternal purpose and the grace He prepared for us from eternity have now been made manifest to us "by the illumination, etc.," better, "by the appearing of our Saviour Jesus Christ," i.e., through the Incarnation of our Lord in time, who by His passion and death for us on the cross has satisfied God for our sins, and has destroyed sin and death, the effect of sin (Rom. vi. 23), thus making known to us through the revelation of the Gospel the spiritual life of the soul and the future resurrection of the body.

11. Having spoken of the Gospel, St. Paul now encourages Timothy (ver. 11-12) by citing his own experience and example. It was for preaching this very Gospel to the world that he is now a prisoner.

The Vulgate *in quo* should be *ad quod,* i.e., for which Gospel, etc.

12. **For which reason,** etc., i.e., for preaching which Gospel the Apostle is now a prisoner in chains.

Have believed. The perfect tense shows the continued unshaken faith and confidence in his Saviour.

13. Hold the form of sound words which thou hast heard from me, in faith and in the love which is in Christ Jesus.

14. Keep the good deposit through the Holy Ghost, who dwelleth in us.

My deposit. The Greek word for "deposit" here is found in the New Testament only in the Pastoral Letters. It occurs again in verse 14 below and in 1 Tim. vi. 20; and from these parallel passages we can safely conclude that its meaning here is the Gospel teaching which Paul has been commissioned by God to preach, and which in turn he has entrusted to Timothy to keep and to teach. The Apostle's stay in this world is now very short, but he is certain the Gospel will not suffer with his passing; for the Almighty God who gave it to him to preach is able to preserve it inviolate and uncorrupted till the end of time, till the day of the General Judgment.

Others understand "deposit" to mean Paul's faith, which he is sure God will preserve unshaken till the end. Still others think the expression refers to the Apostle's labors, sufferings and fatigues, which the Lord will change to a crown of glory in the Day of Judgment.

13-14. Timothy is earnestly exhorted to guard faithfully the Gospel teaching which he has been taught by St. Paul; and the means by which he will be able to do this are faith and love, assisted by the grace of Christ. The word for "form" is found only here and in 1 Tim. i. 16 in the New Testament, and it means "model," "pattern," "norm."

Which thou hast heard. These words show that the doctrines of faith are contained not only in what is written, but also in the unwritten words of Apostolic tradition.

In faith, etc. Here we have indicated the means by which the sound doctrine can be preserved; it can be done only through the grace of Christ and His Holy Spirit.

In the Vulgate there should be a comma after *audisti,* instead of after *fide.*

ST. PAUL COMMENDS A FAITHFUL FRIEND, 15-18

15-18. The Apostle reminds Timothy that certain former followers turned away from him when he needed their help, mentioning two in particular, who were probably now back in Ephesus, their own city. Unlike these deserters, his true friend, Onesiphorus,

15. Thou knowest this, that all they who are in Asia, turned away from me: of whom are Phigellus and Hermogenes.

16. The Lord give mercy to the house of Onesiphorus, because he hath often refreshed me, and hath not been ashamed of my chain;

17. But when he was come to Rome, he carefully sought me, and found me.

18. The Lord grant unto him to find mercy of the Lord in that day; and in how many things he ministered unto me at Ephesus, thou very well knowest.

who had been kind to him in Ephesus, also stood by him in his need in Rome. He seems now to be dead, and the Apostle commends him and his household to the mercy of God.

15. All who are in Asia. This does not mean all the Christians of Asia Minor, but certain ones who were at this writing in Asia, and who had been with St. Paul and had abandoned him at a critical time, whether before his arrest in Troas or as the time of his trial in Rome was drawing nearer. Of the two here mentioned we know nothing further, except that Hermogenes is spoken of in the beginning of the apocryphal *Acts of Paul and Thecla* as "full of hypocrisy." Timothy must be on his guard against such as these.

16-17. St. Paul prays for the household of Onesiphorus, which was at Ephesus (iv. 19).

Give mercy, a phrase occurring only here in the New Testament.

Refreshed. This word also is found only here in the New Testament, but the corresponding substantive is used in the LXX of Psalm lv. 12, where it means a place of refreshment.

He carefully sought me. It was not easy to find St. Paul at this time in Rome, where many prisoners were held for trial, and when he was not allowed to enjoy a private lodging as during his first captivity (Acts xxviii. 16).

18. In verse 16 St. Paul prayed for the household of Onesiphorus, and now he utters a prayer to our Lord for the man himself, that God the Father may show him mercy on the Day of Judgment. The obvious implication here seems to be that Onesiphorus was dead. The Jewish practice of praying for the dead is thoroughly established by 2 Mach. xii. 43-45; and that this practice was taken over from the Jews by the early Christian Church, as in the light of Christ's revelation it realized the full implication of the consoling underlying doctrine, is clear from many sepulchral inscriptions in the Catacombs and elsewhere.

CHAPTER II

TIMOTHY IS EXHORTED TO FAITHFULNESS AND PATIENCE, 1-13

1. Thou therefore, my son, be strengthened in the grace which is in Christ Jesus:
2. And the things which thou didst hear of me by many witnesses, the same commend to faithful men, who shall be fit to teach others also.

1-13. The Apostle's end is near. He exhorts Timothy to be strengthened in grace and to pass on to other faithful workers the truths he has learned from his master. Timothy's fidelity and devotion must be like that of a good soldier who wishes to please his leader; he must be like the athlete who adheres to the rules of his game in order to win the prize, like the husbandman who toils faithfully that he may reap a good harvest (ver. 1-6). The Lord will help him to understand his heavy responsibility; and his duties will become ever more clear if he keeps in mind the Resurrection of Christ, which is according to the Gospel for which Paul suffers. The word of God cannot be stopped; and hence St. Paul endures all things for the sake of the salvation of the elect. We have God's word for it that we shall not suffer for Him in vain (ver. 7-13).

1. **Therefore** refers back to the unfaithfulness spoken of in verse 15 of the preceding Chapter, and aims to impress on Timothy the need of the grace of Christ for a faithful fulfillment of his duties.

2. **Didst hear.** The aorist refers to something definitely past, for which see verse 13 of the preceding Chapter.

By many witnesses, or "through many witnesses," or "in the presence of many witnesses" (St. Chrysostom). The Apostle is alluding to the instruction he had given Timothy in the presence of others, perhaps at the time of the latter's ordination (1 Tim. iv. 14, vi. 12; 2 Tim. i, 6), and also to his own preaching of which Timothy and many more had been frequent hearers, and of which Timothy had heard indirectly from others. All this teaching of the Apostle, which Timothy has heard and learned, he is to transmit to other faithful custodians, who in turn are to teach it to the

3. Endure your share of suffering as a good soldier of Christ Jesus.

4. No man being a soldier to God, entangleth himself with secular businesses, that he may please him to whom he hath engaged himself.

5. For he also that striveth for the mastery is not crowned, except he
strive lawfully.

6. The husbandman that laboreth must first partake of the fruits.

7. Understand what I say, for the Lord will give thee in all things understanding.

faithful in general. Here again we have a strong argument for
the authority of unwritten Apostolic tradition.

3. In verses 3-6 St. Paul endeavors to stimulate the zeal of
Timothy by citing the example of a soldier, of an athlete, and of
a husbandman, whose devotion and efforts for temporal success the
young bishop is to emulate for success in spiritual things.

Endure your share, etc. See above on i. 8.

A good soldier, etc. See on Eph. vi. 14 ff. As Jesus Christ,
our divine Captain, suffered and died for the Gospel, so all His
faithful followers, and especially His ministers, must be ready to
suffer and die for the Gospel.

4. The singleness of devotion needed for success as a soldier of
Christ requires as a consequence that one keep oneself free from
entanglements in temporal affairs.

Secular businesses is in Greek "the affairs of life," i.e., of this
present temporal life (τοῦ βίου); we cannot serve God and mammon.

That he may please him, etc. The Greek is "that he may please
him who enrolled him as a soldier." The verb here, meaning "to
enroll as a soldier," is not found again in the Greek Bible.

5. The Greek of this verse is as follows: "Again, if any man
strive as an athlete, he will not be crowned unless he strive according to the rules." St. Paul was fond of appealing to the Olympic
games to illustrate the spiritual contest (see below iv. 7; 1 Tim. vi.
12 ff.; 1 Cor. ix. 25 ff.). See on 1 Cor. ix. 25 ff.

6. The thought in this and the two preceding verses is that discipline, labor and toil are the necessary conditions of success in
temporal enterprises, and therefore in spiritual undertakings also.

First, i.e., he that labors strenuously will have his reward ahead
of him that does not labor so well; or, according to others, the
meaning is that he who would be successful must first put forth
the required efforts. See on 1 Tim. v. 17. The verb for "partake"
here does not occur elsewhere in St. Paul's writings.

7. Without making application of the three illustrations just

8. Be mindful that Jesus Christ is risen again from the dead, of the seed of David, according to my gospel.

9. Wherein I suffer evils, even unto bonds, as an evildoer; but the word of God is not bound.

10. Therefore I endure all things for the sake of the elect, that they also may obtain the salvation, which is in Christ Jesus, with heavenly glory.

11. Faithful is the saying: For if we be dead with him, we shall live also with him:

12. If we suffer, we shall also reign with him: if we deny him, he will also deny us:

given, St. Paul tells Timothy to reflect on them attentively and the Lord will make him understand their pertinence to himself.

All things, that are necessary for a faithful discharge of Timothy's duties.

8. Timothy will be encouraged and sustained in his labors and trials by keeping ever in mind his Risen Saviour, who is at once the pledge and the exemplar of our own glorious future state.

Of the seed of David, i.e., the Risen Saviour, who is the centre and source of the New Dispensation, took His humanity from the stock of David, according to the hopes and promises of the Old Dispensation. See on Rom. i. 3.

According to my gospel, i.e., the teaching just enunciated is according to the doctrine Paul has been commissioned to preach.

The *Dominum* of the Vulgate is not in the Greek.

9. To help Timothy to bear his trials for the Gospel, the Apostle now cites his own sufferings for the same cause; but he observes that, while he may be impeded from working, the Gospel preaching cannot be restrained: it is being done by other workers and is spreading over the world.

The *laboro* of the Vulgate does not express the Greek, which means "I suffer evils," or "am ill-treated."

10. **Therefore,** i.e., since the Gospel is going forward, the Apostle gladly endures all his sufferings, that all of God's chosen ones may have a share in the saving graces of the Gospel, which Christ has provided, and whose ultimate issue is eternal glory. The "elect" here are all those whom God would have come to a knowledge of the truth and whom He would save unto life eternal.

11-12. **Faithful is the saying.** See on 1 Tim. i. 15, iii. 1, iv. 9. This formula in the present passage without doubt refers to the words that follow here and in verse 13, which seem to be a portion of an ancient hymn on the glories of martyrdom, and which at the

13. If we believe not, he continueth faithful, he cannot deny himself.

14. Of these things put them in mind, charging them before God to contend not in words, for it is to no profit, but to the subverting of the hearers.

end of verse 12 become a quotation of our Lord's words in Matt. x. 33, and Luke xii. 9. These quotations are given as an incentive to courage and patience in suffering in union with Christ in view of the glories to come in heaven. See on 1 Tim. iii. 16; Rom. vi. 3, viii. 17 ff.; 1 Cor. xii. 26; Eph. i. 23, etc.

13. **If we believe not.** Better, "if we are unfaithful," in refusing to accept the doctrines God has revealed to us, "he continueth faithful," i.e., true to His promises to reward the good and punish the wicked; for "he cannot deny himself," by going counter to His nature and the laws He has established.

THE APOSTLE COUNSELS TIMOTHY FURTHER, 14-26

14-26. Timothy is admonished to avoid irrelevant controversies, which only distract from the main truths of revelation and do much harm to the faith. He is to preach the sound doctrine by word and example, remembering the fatal mistakes of Hymenæus and Philetus who, in their wranglings about the resurrection, fell into error themselves and upset the faith of others. In spite of such false teachers, the relations God has established with man remain unshaken: He knows who are His, whom He has predestined for salvation; and all those who have been thus chosen must manifest it in their lives by a free and complete rejection of sin and all unrighteousness (ver. 14-19). As in a large house there are many vessels, some for honorable and some for dishonorable purposes, so it is with the Church and its members. Timothy must see that he is a vessel of the former class by fleeing degrading sins, practising Christian virtues, and keeping company with the good. He must be peaceful, gentle, patient, and thus by meek methods lead the erring to better ways (ver. 20-26).

14. **Of these things,** etc. Timothy should remind men of the need and the reward of courage and patient endurance spoken of in the preceding verses, charging them before God to avoid controversy, which only leads to the ruin of the faith of the hearers. The

15. Carefully study to present thyself approved unto God, a workman that needeth not to be ashamed, rightly handling the word of truth.

16. But shun the profane babblings; for they will grow much towards ungodliness,

17. And their speech will spread like a cancer: of whom are Hymenæus and Philetus,

18. Who have erred from the truth, saying that the resurrection is past already, and they subvert the faith of some.

word for "subverting" occurs only here in the New Testament, but it is found in the LXX.

We have corrected the translation of this verse so as to agree with the best Greek, and the Vulgate should be corrected likewise.

15. Timothy by his example will best show others how God is to be served, and to this end he must see that his work be of such quality as to merit the approval of his Master. The word here rendered "rightly handling" does not occur again in the New Testament; but it is found twice in the LXX (Prov. iii. 6, xi. 5), where it conveys the idea of making a straight road, or more literally, of "cutting stones square to fit," as for a road or building. The translation given in our version seems to express the meaning here, where Timothy is told to deliver the teachings of the Gospel properly and correctly without yielding to error of any kind.

16. **The profane babblings,** i.e., of the false teachers.

They will grow, etc. The subject of the verb here is the false teachers, as is evident from the following verse; they will go from bad to worse.

We have revised the English of this verse so as to conform to the Greek, and the Vulgate needs a similar revision.

17. The Apostle here describes the baneful progress of the demoralizing talk of the false teachers, which "will spread" (literally, "will have pasture") like a cancer. The word for "cancer" is found only here in the Bible. Hymenæus is mentioned in 1 Tim. i. 20. Of him or Philetus we know nothing further.

Serpit of the Vulgate should be future, as in the Greek.

18. It appears that the two heretics just mentioned, like the Gnostics after them and some so-called preachers of the Gospel today, gave a mystical explanation of the doctrine of the resurrection, denying its physical reality and holding that it consisted in the soul's transition from error to truth, from a state of sin to a state

19. Howbeit the firm foundation of God standeth, having this seal: the Lord knoweth who are his; and let every one depart from iniquity who nameth the name of the Lord.

20. But in a great house there are not only vessels of gold and silver, but also of wood and of earth; and some indeed unto honor, but some unto dishonor.

of grace. Their false conclusion was probably drawn from such passages as Rom. vi. 1 ff., Col. ii. 12, and the like.

In the Vulgate *subverterunt* should be present tense.

19. Despite the errors and aberrations of some members of the Christian society, the Church itself remains firm and unshaken, for it is the pillar and ground of truth (1 Tim. iii. 14-16); and this solid and immovable character of the Church is distinguished by two seals or fundamental truths, namely, the predestination by God of the salvation of the elect and the free acceptance of grace and the rejection of sin on the part of the faithful. The first of these truths is announced in the words of Num. xvi. 5; the second, more freely, in Num. xvi. 26, Isa. xxvi. 13, lii. 11, and other passages. God knows who are to be with Him in glory; and those who would belong to Christ here and hereafter, must keep themselves free from the corruption of error and false teachers.

Who nameth the name, etc., i.e., he that professes to belong to Christ must see to it that his life corresponds with his profession.

20. The metaphor now changes. In the preceding verse the Apostle spoke of the faithful as the stones with which the Church is built (1 Cor. iii. 10-15), but here he regards them as utensils which go to make up the furnishings of the same great house (Rom. ix. 19-24). St. Paul is probably forestalling now a misunderstanding of what he said in the preceding verse, from which it might be wrongly concluded that only good members would be found in the Church; hence the adversative conjunction with which this verse is introduced. We are admonished here, as in Matt. xiii. 24 ff., that we must expect to find in the Church both good and bad members and varying degrees of goodness and badness in those members; and that some will be saved, while others will be lost if they do not repent of their sins. The grace of God makes it possible for all to be saved, but the abuse of free will makes it possible for some to be lost; none will be saved without the grace of God, and no one will be lost without his own fault.

21. If any man therefore cleanse himself from these, he shall be a vessel unto honor, sanctified and profitable to the Lord, prepared unto every good work.

22. But flee thou youthful desires, and pursue justice, faith, charity, and peace, with them that call on the Lord out of a pure heart.

23. And avoid foolish and unlearned questions, knowing that they beget strifes.

24. But the servant of the Lord must not wrangle: but be mild towards all men, apt to teach, patient,

25. With meekness admonishing them that resist, if peradventure God may give them repentance to know the truth,

26. And they may recover themselves from the snares of the devil, by whom they are held captive at his will.

21. **Cleanse himself from these.** It is uncertain whether "these" refers to the false teachers or to their erroneous teachings. The sense would be the same in either case. The servant of God must keep himself fit for the work of His Master; a higher motive for holiness he can hardly have.

22. Speaking now more directly to Timothy, St. Paul admonishes him to guard against the passions and desires (ἐπιθυμίας) which are apt to allure a young man, and to pursue those virtues which make for the finest Christian character. The word for "youthful" is found only here in the New Testament.

23. See on 1 Tim. i. 4; 2 Tim. ii. 16-18. The term "unlearned" occurs only here in the New Testament, and means "uneducated," "untaught," and so "ignorant."

24-25. Special qualities of every servant of the Lord, and in particular of the Christian minister, are here stressed. First, he must be apt to teach, then patient with those who are difficult, and finally meek with those who resist; and all this with the consistent purpose of fitting his hearers and subjects for the acceptable time of God's grace. The word here translated "patient" does not occur elsewhere in the Greek Bible, and the term "peradventure" is found only here in St. Paul.

Veritati in the Vulgate of verse 25 is not represented in the Greek.

26. **May recover themselves,** better "may return to soberness." The phrase is expressed by one verb in Greek, which does not occur elsewhere in the Greek Bible.

From the snares of the devil, etc. The rest of this verse causes a difficulty because of the use of two different pronouns in Greek (αὐτοῦ and ἐκείνου), both of which are referred to the devil by some scholars, as in our version and in the Westminster Version. The Revisers refer the first pronoun to "the servant of the Lord" of verse 24, and the second to "God" of verse 25. Still others refer αὐτοῦ to the devil and ἐκείνου to God, thus making the whole verse read quite literally from the Greek: "And may return to soberness out of the snare of the devil, having been caught alive by him (the devil) unto his (God's) will," i.e., to do God's will. The verb "to catch alive" is found only here and in Luke v. 10 in the New Testament.

CHAPTER III

EVIL DAYS AHEAD, 1-9.

1. Know also this, that in the last days shall come dangerous times.
2. Men shall be lovers of themselves, covetous, haughty, proud, blasphemers, disobedient to parents, ungrateful, wicked,

1-9. In order to impress more forcefully on Timothy the need of cultivating undivided devotion to Christ, loyalty to the teachings of the Gospel, readiness and courage to suffer, and a Christian character that would exemplify his faith and be an inspiration to all with whom he might come in contact, the Apostle now warns him of frightful evils to come, when all manner of revolting sins will be rampant, committed by men who pretend to be godly but who will never be able to come to a knowledge of the truth, being depraved in mind and reprobate as regards faith, like Jannes and Jambres of old. Against these, who are already appearing, Timothy must be on his guard and fight, though their wickedness will be cut short as soon as their true character becomes known.

1. **The last days** are not to be limited to the times just before the Second Coming of the Lord; for the evils that will darken those days are already present to some extent (ver. 5), though their number and extremity will increase as the end of the world draws near.

2-4. For a somewhat similar list of vices see Rom. i. 29-31.

Lovers of themselves. The Greek expression here does not occur elsewhere in the Greek Bible. Inordinate self-love is the root

3. Without affection, without peace, slanderers, incontinent, unmerciful, without kindness,

4. Traitors, stubborn, puffed up, and lovers of pleasures more than of God;

5. Having an appearance indeed of godliness, but denying the power thereof. Now these avoid.

6. For of these are they who creep into houses and lead captive silly women laden with sins, who are led away with divers desires,

7. Ever learning, and never attaining to the knowledge of the truth.

of all vices, and is rightly placed at the beginning of the catalogue that follows.

Blasphemers should rather be "railers," meaning evil-speakers against men rather than against God.

Without peace. Better, "implacable." The word is found only here in the Bible.

Without kindness. Better, "without love for the good." The word occurs only here.

Lovers of pleasure more than of God. Literally, "lovers of pleasure more than lovers of God." There is a play on the words in Greek, and the two substantives do not occur elsewhere in the New Testament.

5. From this and the following verses we see that the corruptions in question were already a present danger, which Timothy was to avoid. The most dangerous characteristic of these evil men is their semblance of piety, which makes their influence the more seductive, while internally they are devoid of all religion; they are wolves in sheep's clothing (Matt. vii. 15).

6-7. These false Christians appeal to the weaknesses and suscep- tibilities of silly and unstable women as proselytes and propagators of their errors, knowing that these weaker creatures, being them- selves sin-laden, will welcome any teaching that gives promise of easing their consciences, and that they will be the most effective mediums through which to spread false teachings.

Divers desires. The reference is not only to fleshly lusts, but to those of the spirit also, such as curiosity, love of novelty, and the like, which cause these flighty women to run after false rather than true teachers of religion. These people are endlessly seeking and discussing religious matters, but they never attain to a knowl- edge of the truth, because their seeking is neither with a sincere and pure heart nor in the right direction.

8. Now, as Jannes and Mambres resisted Moses, so these also resist the truth, men corrupted in mind, reprobate concerning the faith.

9. But they shall proceed no farther; for their folly shall be manifest to all men, as theirs also was.

10. But thou hast fully known my doctrine, manner of life, purpose, faith, longsuffering, love, patience,

8. The Apostle now cites an incident of Jewish history illustrative of that which was taking place in Ephesus at this time.

Jannes and Mambres (or Jambres) are the traditional names of two of King Pharaoh's principal magicians who opposed Moses and tried to duplicate his prodigies, thus hardening Pharaoh's heart against the demands of the people of Israel (Exod. vii. 11 ff., viii. 7). These two names are not mentioned in Scripture, but they have come down variously transcribed from tradition. They are mentioned in the Targum of Jonathan on Exod. vii. 11, in the Talmud (Buxtorf, *Lex Chald. talm. rabb.*, pp. 945 ff.), in Pliny (*Hist. nat.*, xxx. 1), in Apuleius of the second century (*Apol.*, p. 544), in Eusebius (*Præp. evang.*, ix. 8), and in Origen (*In Matt.*, xxvii. 9). As these two resisted Moses, so do the false teachers at Ephesus resist the Gospel, being "corrupted in mind" (i.e., perverted in their judgment of the truth) and "reprobate concerning the faith" (i.e., heretics, who have lost the faith).

9. While these wicked men always grow worse in their evil ways (ii. 16 above and ver. 13 below), nevertheless their wickedness will not prevail against the truth any more than did the efforts of the Egyptian magicians prevail against Moses (Exod. viii. 18-19). No intellectual victory can ever be won against faith rightly understood; for God is the author of both the truths of faith and the intellectual faculties of man, and truth is not contradictory.

TIMOTHY IS ABLE TO MEET THE SITUATION, 10-17

10-17. Timothy is equipped to encounter and deal with the difficulties that now confront him, and with worse ones that may arise in the future; for he has before him Paul's example and that of all those who desire to live piously in Christ Jesus, he has been instructed by Paul himself, and the Sacred Scriptures are always at his disposal for his guidance and comfort.

10-11. St. Paul is near to death and is writing a private letter to his dear son in the faith; and to encourage him to suffer and endure,

11. Persecutions, afflictions: such as came upon me at Antioch, at Iconium, and at Lystra: what persecutions I endured, and out of them all the Lord delivered me.

12. And all that will live godly in Christ Jesus, shall suffer persecution.

13. But evil men and seducers shall grow worse and worse, erring and driving into error.

14. But continue thou in those things which thou hast learned and hast been assured of, knowing from whom thou hast learned *them;*

he speaks openly and familiarly about his own teaching, manner of life, and sufferings. He mentions in particular what he endured in the cities of Southern Asia Minor, because Timothy himself was from Lystra and was more familiar with these persecutions of his master than with the more severe ones later endured at Philippi and elsewhere.

But thou, in contrast with the false teachers.

Purpose, i.e., the aim he had in all his actions.

Antioch, Iconium, Lystra. See Acts xiii. 50, xiv. 2 ff., xiv. 18 ff.

The Lord delivered me. This fact is mentioned so that Timothy will not lose courage in his sufferings and trials.

12. Timothy will be further encouraged to suffer willingly and gladly for the Gospel by reflecting that such is the lot of all whose habitual desire and effort it is to live that life which is in Christ Jesus: "And you shall be hated by all men for my name's sake, etc." (Matt. x. 22); "Blessed are they that suffer persecution for justice' sake, etc." (Matt. v. 10).

13. See above on verse 9.

But evil men, etc. In contrast with the godly of the preceding verse, the wicked and impostors will go from bad to worse, because they have no persecution to suffer. This may be the meaning here, though some expositors think this verse gives the reason of the preceding: the good are persecuted because of the progress of the wicked in evil.

Seducers. More literally, "imposters," "wizards." The word occurs only here in the Greek Bible. Probably these deceivers practised màgical arts at Ephesus (Acts xix. 19).

14. In contrast with the impostors, Timothy must continue firm in the faith which he has received, being mindful of those by whom he was taught it.

15. And that from thy infancy thou hast known the holy scriptures, which can instruct thee to salvation through the faith which is in Christ Jesus.

16. All scripture is inspired of God and profitable to teach, to reprove, to correct, to instruct in justice;

And hast been assured of. This is the meaning of the Greek here, which the Vulgate has missed.

Knowing from whom, etc. The best Greek reading makes "whom" plural in this phrase, and hence the reference is to St. Paul and Timothy's mother and grandmother (see above, on i. 5).

The Vulgate *a quo* should be *a quibus.*

15. The Jews were obliged to teach the Scriptures to their children (Exod. x. 2, xii. 26; Deut. iv. 9, etc.), and the Rabbins enjoined that this instruction should begin when they were five years old. Thus, Timothy's Jewish mother had taught him the Old Testament from his infancy.

The holy scriptures. The best Greek reading here retains the article. This is the only passage in the New Testament where the adjective ἱερός is applied to the Scriptures, meaning *sacred* as opposed to *profane* writings. But τὰ ἱερὰ γράμματα was a quasi-technical expression signifying the Old Testament Scriptures, as we learn from Philo (*Vita Mos.,* III, 39, and *Frag. in Exod.,* Mangey's ed., II, 657, and cap. *de Vit.,* cont. 3) and from Josephus (*Ant. Proem.* 3 and X, 10, 4). Clement of Alexandria was the first Christian writer to apply this phrase to the New Testament (*Strom.,* I, 20, § 98). Cf. Bernard, *op. cit., h. l.*

Which can instruct thee, etc. Better, "which can make thee wise unto salvation." Other books impart knowledge, but the Divine Scriptures give also wisdom—a wisdom that is not of this world; but for their true and full meaning they must be studied in the light of the faith of Jesus Christ, because they are all directly or indirectly ordained to Christ, and speak directly or indirectly of His Person, ministry, life, work, Church, etc.

16. We must understand this verse in the light of the preceding one, and hence "scripture" here must mean the Old Testament. Moreover, the word γραφή, *scripture,* occurs some fifty times in the New Testament, and everywhere it means the Old Testament.

All scripture. It is better to translate "every scripture," meaning each and every part of the Old Testament.

17. That the man of God may be perfect, furnished unto every good work.

Inspired of God, etc.   We may translate as in the Douai version, since the verb is not expressed in Greek; but it is perhaps better to render, "is inspired by God and profitable for teaching, etc." St. Paul seems to be impressing on Timothy the usefulness of the Holy Scriptures, *as inspired by God,* for wisdom unto salvation (ver. 15) and for teaching, reproving, correcting, etc. (ver. 16).   If we adopt the first rendering, it will mean that St. Paul is taking the inspiration of Scripture for granted by Timothy, and is insisting here on its profitableness for teaching, reproving, etc.   In either case the inspiration of the Old Testament and all its parts is certain to the mind of St. Paul.   The word here translated "inspired" does not occur elsewhere in the Greek Bible, but is common in Greek literature.   It was first applied to the New Testament by Clement of Alexandria (*Strom.,* VII, 16, § 101).

Four uses of Scripture are here stressed: (a) "to teach," the truths of faith; (b) "to reprove," or refute the errors against faith; (c) "to correct," vices and sins; (d) "to instruct in justice," by giving practical norms for the practice of virtue and the attainment of sanctity.

17. The final result for Timothy of a study of the Divine Scriptures will be to fit him for a perfect discharge of his ministry.

Man of God.   See on 1 Tim. vi. 11.   Here the expression means the minister of Christ, as the context shows.

Perfect.   The Greek word is a common one, but it is found only here in the Bible.

Unto every good work, pertinent to his ministry.

CHAPTER IV

A LAST APPEAL TO TIMOTHY, 1-8

1-8. Now that the end is drawing near, the aged Apostle, feeling his days are numbered and his work is done, adjures Timothy incessantly to continue the labors of the ministry and to bear up under its trials, being prepared for the onslaughts of future false teachers.   As for Paul himself, he is about to pour out his blood

1. I charge thee, before God and Christ Jesus, who shall judge the living and the dead, by his coming and his kingdom:
2. Preach the word: be instant in season and out of season: reprove, entreat, rebuke in all patience and doctrine.
3. For there shall be a time when they will not endure sound doctrine; but according to their own lusts they will heap to themselves teachers, having itching ears:
4. And will indeed turn away their hearing from the truth, but will be turned unto fables.

as a sacrifice for the cause; but he is ready and his reward is waiting for him. The just Judge will never fail him, nor anyone else who has lived and labored for the cause.

1. St. Paul in verses 1-4 solemnly charges Timothy so much the more to preach the word of God as the wicked stray farther from the truth.

I charge thee, etc. See on 1 Tim. v. 21.

The living and the dead. See on 1 Thess. iv. 16-17.

His coming, in General Judgment to render to each one according to his works.

His kingdom, which the good will be invited to share. The word "coming" and "kingdom" are accusatives of adjuration in Greek and form part of the Apostle's oath.

2. **The word,** i.e., the Gospel message (Gal. vi. 6; Col. iv. 3). This Timothy is to proclaim incessantly, in order that all may hear it and have the opportunity to embrace its teachings.

In doctrine. Preaching without doctrine is of little value, since it lacks substance and leaves rebuke and exhortation without a reason and basis.

3. The reason is now given why Timothy must redouble his zeal; for during his own lifetime there will be persons who, following their own lusts and craving for novelties, will reject sound doctrine; they will repudiate and turn away from the dogmas of the Church, and instead will seek out teachers whose doctrines appeal to the passions and lower appetites. In our own time this is precisely what is taking place. Multitudes are now ridiculing the very notion of dogma as old-fashioned and out of date, and are running after those preachers who justify artificial birth-control, trial marriages, divorces, and similar disorders.

Having itching ears, i.e., they will be eager for all kinds of novelties.

4. **Fables.** See on 1 Tim. i. 4, iv. 7.

5. But be thou sober, labor in all things, suffer hardship, do the work of an evangelist, fulfill thy ministry.

6. For I am even now ready to be sacrificed: and the time of my departure is at hand.

7. I have fought the good fight, I have finished my course, I have kept the faith.

8. As to the rest, there is laid up for me a crown of justice, which the Lord the just judge will render to me in that day; and not only to me, but to them also that love his coming.

5. The Vulgate of this verse should be made to read as we have corrected the English, following the Greek. In the face of the difficulties just described, Timothy is to be prudent and well poised in all things, to endure hardship, to preach the Gospel, and faithfully to fulfill all his duties as a minister of Christ, entrusted with his master's business.

Evangelist. See Acts xxi. 8; Eph. iv. 11.

Ministry. See on 1 Tim. i. 12.

6. The secret of the Apostle's anxiety about Timothy's preparedness, zeal, readiness to suffer, etc., is now revealed; the old champion of the Gospel is going to leave him very soon, he is looking into his open grave.

Ready to be sacrificed. Better, "being poured out in sacrifice," i.e., he was about to shed his blood as a sacrifice to God, as the drink-offering of wine used to be poured out as a libation to God in certain of the old Jewish sacrifices (Num. xv. 1-10); the Apostle's death is at hand.

My departure. Another image to signify the imminence of his death.

The Vulgate *resolutionis* does not express the Greek, which means "departure," as in 2 Mach. ix. 1; Luke xii. 36.

7-8. The metaphors are here drawn from the arena and the race-course. Like a strong athlete, the Apostle has fought the good fight in defence of the faith (1 Tim. vi. 12); like a faithful runner in the race, he has completed the course; he has fulfilled all his duties and preserved the deposit of faith entrusted to him. Now he is ready for the crown, the reward with which the Lord, his just Judge, will recompense him.

This reward is called "a crown of justice," because it has been merited; it is something due the Apostle in justice. Here we have an explicit proof that the just, by means of good works performed in the state of grace, can merit eternal life *de condigno.* And yet

9. Make effort to come to me quickly. For Demas hath left me, loving this world, and is gone to Thessalonica;

10. Crescens into Galatia, Titus into Dalmatia.

it remains true that the joys of heaven are a gratuitous gift; for God from eternity has gratuitously predestined the just to life eternal, and in time He gratuitously confers on them the grace by which they work out their salvation and merit eternal rewards. Cf. *Conc. Trid.*, sess. VI, can. 32.

In that day, i.e., on the day of the Last Judgment. Immediately after death the Apostle, as is the case with all the just, received his crown, but the crown of life will not shine in all its splendor till the final judgment is over, when the body will have its reward along with the soul.

SOME PERSONAL MESSAGES, 9-18

9-18. St. Paul bids Timothy to make haste to join him in Rome; for Demas has deserted him, and all his other companions, save Luke, have been dispatched to other places. He requests Timothy to bring with him Mark and certain effects that had been left behind at Troas, and warns him against Alexander the coppersmith (ver. 9-15). At his first hearing all deserted him, but the Lord stood by him and strengthened him that he might have time to complete his work (ver. 16-18).

9. Timothy was to come to St. Paul by way of Troas and the great Via Egnatia from Philippi to Dyrrachium, and thence to Brundisium. This would require some time, but it seems the Apostle thought his life would be spared long enough for Timothy to make the journey.

Demas, who was a Gentile convert, was with St. Paul during the first Roman captivity (Phlm. 24). He is also mentioned in Col. iv. 14. For fear of being associated with Paul at this critical time and most likely for business purposes also, he forsook him and returned to Thessalonica, probably his native town. His name is an abbreviation of Demetrius, which Lightfoot tells us occurs twice in the list of politarchs of Thessalonica.

10. **Crescens**, of whom we know nothing further from St. Paul. Tradition says he became a Bishop of Gaul.

Galatia, most probably the Asiatic province by that name, though

11. Only Luke is with me. Take Mark and bring him with thee, for he is profitable to me for the ministry.

12. But Tychicus I have sent to Ephesus.

13. The cloak that I left at Troas with Carpus, when thou comest, bring with thee, and the books, especially the parchments.

Gaul was sometimes called Galatia, and some few MSS. read Gaul here.

Titus, the Bishop of Crete, to whom St. Paul had already addressed a letter.

Dalmatia, a part of the Roman province of Illyria on the eastern coast of the Adriatic.

11. **Luke,** who was with St. Paul also during the first captivity (Col. iv. 14), and who wrote the Third Gospel and the Book of Acts. All the other companions and disciples of the Apostle had left him.

Mark, the author of the Second Gospel, who was also with St. Paul during the first Roman imprisonment (Col. iv. 10), but who at this time must have been some place along the route Timothy would take going to Rome from Ephesus.

For the ministry, i.e., for the work of the Gospel, or probably for personal service in place of Tychicus (Eph. vi. 21; Col. iv. 7; Acts xx. 4).

12. **Tychicus,** who had been the bearer of the letters to the Ephesians and Colossians (Eph. vi. 21; Col. iv. 7), very probably was taking this present Epistle to Timothy in Ephesus and was to remain in that city to look after the affairs of the Church there during Timothy's absence. Tychicus is also mentioned in Acts xx. 4; Titus iii. 12.

I have sent is very likely an epistolary aorist.

13. **The cloak,** probably a heavy outer garment for winter wear. Some translate the word "wrapper," meaning a satchel for carrying or protecting books.

Carpus, an otherwise unknown Christian of Troas.

The books, i.e., rolls of papyrus, a kind of writing material generally used in the first century for writing letters of ordinary importance. Paul wrote on papyrus but his Epistles were later copied on vellum rolls.

Parchments, i.e., rolls of vellum, a much more valuable and durable writing material made from the skins of animals. Probably the parchments contained the Old Testament Scriptures, and

14. Alexander the coppersmith hath done me much evil: the Lord will reward him according to his works:

15. Whom do thou also avoid, for he greatly withstood our words.

16. At my first defence no man stood with me, but all forsook me: may it not be laid to their charge.

17. But the Lord stood by me, and strengthened me, that by me the preaching may be completed, and that all the Gentiles may hear; and I was delivered out of the mouth of the lion.

the papyrus was used by the Apostle for his letters. This would explain the early disappearance of the original copies of the latter, because papyrus was not a very durable material like parchment.

From the way St. Paul speaks in this verse and in verse 20 below it is sufficiently evident that he is referring to a recent visit to Asia Minor, doubtless between the two Roman Captivities, and not to his sojourn there years before, of which there is question in Acts xx. 6.

14. **Alexander.** See on 1 Tim. i. 20. Perhaps this enemy of St. Paul's lived at Ephesus or was there at this time, but had been in Rome testifying against the Apostle.

The Lord will reward, etc. These words are from Psalm lxi. 12, but the reading which makes them an imprecation here is less probable.

15. **He greatly withstood,** etc. The aorist points to a definite occasion, very probably during St. Paul's trial in Rome when the Apostle was defending his cause and the preaching of the Gospel.

16. **At my first defence.** It is remarkable that St. Chrysostom, St. Thomas, and many modern commentators take these words to refer to the Apostle's first Roman captivity, and verse 17 to his preaching between the two Roman captivities. It seems more consistent with the context to refer them to his first hearing or the first stage in his trial before his judges (called in Roman law the *prima actio*) during the second and last imprisonment in Rome. At this crisis no one came to his defence, doubtless out of fear and human weakness, as the words that follow would indicate.

17. By the grace and help of God St. Paul was not condemned at his first hearing, but was given another chance of explaining himself and his cause, and thus of completing the preaching of the Gospel there in Rome, the official centre of the empire and of the world.

Out of the mouth of the lion expresses the extreme peril from which he was delivered, though many of the Fathers understood

18. The Lord shall deliver me from every evil work, and will preserve me unto his heavenly kingdom, to whom be glory for ever and ever. Amen.
19. Salute Prisca and Aquila, and the household of Onesiphorus.
20. Erastus remained at Corinth, and Trophimus I left sick at Miletus.
21. Make haste to come before winter. Eubulus and Pudens, and Linus and Claudia, and all the brethren, salute thee.
22. The Lord be with thy spirit. Grace be with you. Amen.

the reference to be to Nero. This same phrase is found in Psalm xxi. 21; Dan. vi. 20.

18. The Apostle is confident of his final liberation from all evil and his reception into Christ's heavenly kingdom, though the gateway will be martyrdom.

The tense of *liberavit* of the Vulgate, instead of the future, has little support in the MSS., and so should be changed.

FINAL FAREWELL, 19-22

19. **Prisca and Aquila** are first mentioned in Acts xviii. 2 ff., then in xvi. 3, and 1 Cor. xvi. 19. They were probably among the first Christians in the Roman Church. Prisca is the same as Priscilla.

The household of Onesiphorus. See above, on i. 16.

20. **Erastus** was probably the same person spoken of in Acts xix. 22, who accompanied Timothy from Ephesus to Macedonia; he is hardly to be identified with the Erastus of Rom. xvi. 23.

Trophimus is mentioned in Acts xx. 4, xxi. 29. He was a Gentile Christian of Ephesus. St. Paul left him at Miletus some time between the first and second Roman imprisonments.

21. St. Paul urges Timothy to come to him before winter, either because the traveling would be harder in winter, or because he felt that winter would bring the end of his life. The Apostle sends the greetings of a number of persons whose acquaintance Timothy had apparently made during his stay in Rome when St. Paul was a prisoner there the first time. Of the four names here given we know nothing for certain, except that Linus was the first successor of St. Peter as Bishop of Rome (Irenæus, *Adv. Hær.*, iii. 3; Eusebius, *Hist. Eccl.*, iii. 2).

22. The blessing is to Timothy and the whole Church at Ephesus; it is not like any other blessing at the end of the Apostle's Epistles. The *Jesus Christus* and the *Amen* of the Vulgate are not in the best Greek.

THE EPISTLE TO TITUS

INTRODUCTION

I. Titus. After Timothy, Titus was one of the most favored disciples of St. Paul. Strange to say, his name does not appear in the Book of Acts; but from this Epistle, as well as from Galatians and Second Corinthians, we learn the part he played in the early history of the Church, what important offices were entrusted to him, and how capable a man he was. He was a Greek by birth (Gal. ii. 3), and probably a native of Antioch. St. Paul addresses him as his "beloved son" (Tit. i. 4), from which it is argued that the Apostle very likely had converted and baptized him. He accompanied the Apostle and Barnabas to the Council of Jerusalem (Acts xv. 1 ff.; Gal. ii. 1), where the question of the Mosaic observances was discussed and it was decided that Titus and other Gentile converts need not submit to circumcision and the Jewish ceremonial law. Whether or not he joined St. Paul on the latter's second missionary journey, we are not told; but later, on the third journey, he was with the Apostle at Ephesus, and was thence dispatched to Corinth about a year before the writing of 2 Corinthians to arrange for the collection of alms for the poor in Jerusalem, perhaps conveying to Corinth at the same time our 1 Corinthians (2 Cor. viii. 6, 10, xii. 18). A little later, when serious troubles arose in the Church at Corinth, Titus was again St. Paul's envoy to investigate matters and report to him (2 Cor. ii. 12, 13, vii. 6, 7). The two met in Macedonia, and as a result of the report given by Titus St. Paul there wrote 2 Corinthians and sent Titus back to Corinth with it, asking him to make final arrangements for the collection to be sent to the faithful in Jerusalem (2 Cor. viii. 6, 16, 17).

Thus it appears that Titus was charged with three important visits to the Church of Corinth; and from this Epistle we know that to him was entrusted by St. Paul the organization of the Church of Crete, of which he was made the bishop (Tit. i. 5), that he was afterwards summoned to Nicopolis in Epirus where the Apostle had determined to spend the winter (Tit. iii. 12), and that finally, during the last Roman captivity, he was sent on a mission to Dalmatia (2 Tim. iv. 10). According to tradition, he returned again to his bishopric in Crete, where he continued to exercise his episcopal office till his death at the age of ninety-four. He was buried at Gortyna, but some centuries later the Venetians carried away his head to Venice, and there it is now preserved as a relic in St. Mark's Cathedral.

From the more impersonal and business-like tone of this letter, as compared with the letters to Timothy, it is concluded that Titus was older than Timothy, and also a stronger personality and a more capable worker than the "beloved son." He had a hard mission in Crete, for the Cretans were a wayward and perverse people, given to lying, gluttony, indolence and sensuality; but Titus was able to handle them. He was a vigorous and efficient administrator, and yet tactful and prudent in the exercise of his strength and authority. The few personal notes that appear in this letter show the high regard in which he was held by St. Paul, and the unreserved confidence which the Apostle was able to place in him. Titus had less need for personal guidance and instruction than the more timid and youthful Timothy, and still the counsels and directions given him in this Epistle are very similar to those in the Epistles to Timothy. Of course, his task was doubtless more difficult than Timothy's, but he was equal to it.

It is hard to understand how so great a disciple of St. Paul's should not have been mentioned by St. Luke in the Book of Acts. Fr. Pope has very plausibly explained this remarkable omission by suggesting that Titus was St. Luke's brother, and that, just as St. John in the Fourth Gospel is silent about his relatives, so Luke makes no mention of his relatives in the Acts. For the development of this argument, see Pope, Student's "Aids" to the Bible, vol. III, pp. 241 ff.

II. **Occasion, Date and Place of Composition.** The reasons which prompted the writing of this letter were much the same as those that occasioned the First Epistle to Timothy. Paul had left Titus in Crete as bishop of that see (Tit. i. 5), and the charge was a difficult one, owing partly to the character of the population (who were a mixture of Asiatics and Greeks, lazy, superstitious, and unreliable), and partly to the presence of false teachers, and partly to the mischief of Judaizers—all of whom were causing trouble (Tit. i. 10-16, iii. 10, 11). Apparently Titus, feeling the need of advice in his difficult circumstances, wrote to Paul, and this letter is the Apostle's reply. It "might be summed up in the word 'discipline.' Titus is to teach sound 'doctrine,' he is to organize the Church in the island, to ordain fit men, to avoid idle disputations, and to be firm" (Pope *op. cit.*, p. 243).

We cannot say for certain just when this Epistle was written, but in all probability it was composed some time between the two Roman captivities—perhaps shortly after the writing of 1 Timothy, in the year 65 A.D. It must have been at this period that St. Paul visited Crete with Titus, and left the latter there as bishop to organize the Church and reform the discipline. It seems certain, however, that this visit by Paul and his disciple was not the first evangelization of the Island of Crete, since this letter presupposes the spread of the Christian community there and the existence of heresies and other disorders, which Titus was to correct (Tit. i. 6-11, 14, ii. 1-10, iii. 9). Perhaps the faith was first carried to the island by some of those Cretans who were present at the first Christian Pentecost (Acts ii. 11). It is also apparent that St. Paul did not tarry long in Crete at this time. Having surveyed the situation and the conditions, he left Titus there with general instructions, then proceeded to visit the Churches in Asia Minor, Greece, and Macedonia, and wrote this Epistle on his way to Nicopolis (Tit. iii. 12). St. Jerome says explicitly that the letter was written from Nicopolis itself.

III. **Analysis of Contents.** Besides an introduction (i. 1-4) and a conclusion (iii. 12-15), this letter has three parts which constitute its body (i. 5—iii. 11).

A. INTRODUCTION (i. 1-4). Here St. Paul, first asserting his apostolic authority, addresses Titus as his beloved son, who shares with him the peace and grace of God that are bestowed in Jesus Christ.

B. FIRST PART (i. 5-16). After referring to the reason why he left Titus in Crete, the Apostle gives instructions relative to the requirements for Sacred Orders in those who are to become priests and bishops (5-9), insisting especially on the necessity of soundness of doctrine because of the presence of false teachers and the character of the Cretans (10-16).

C. Second Part (ii. 1-15). St. Paul now recalls to Titus what he is to teach the faithful, young and old, of both sexes (1-10), all of whom are to fulfill their respective duties from supernatural motives, because of the grace of God that has been given us and the glory that awaits us in the coming of our Saviour Jesus Christ (11-15).

D. Third Part (iii. 1-11). In this last part the Apostle explains to his disciple what in particular he should teach the Cretans, namely, obedience to authority (1), love of one's neighbor (2-7), and the practice of good works (8-11).

E. Conclusion (iii. 12-15). St. Paul makes plans to facilitate Titus' joining him at Nicopolis, asks him to provide for Zenas and Apollo, adds a final exhortation to good works, and bestows his blessing.

The Epistle to Titus

CHAPTER I

INSCRIPTION AND GREETING, 1-4

1. Paul, a servant of God, and an apostle of Jesus Christ, according to the faith of the elect of God and the acknowledging of the truth which is according to godliness

1-4. The introduction to this letter is somewhat longer than usual. St. Paul asserts his divine authority to preach the faith to God's chosen ones, that they may sanctify themselves and thus become worthy of the promise of eternal life which was given long ago and has now been revealed through the Gospel. Paul is the preacher of this heavenly message according to the command of God, and he writes to Titus as a son in Christ, since they both share that common faith and the resultant peace and grace which God bestows in Christ Jesus.

1. **Servant of God,** a phrase found only here in St. Paul's letters, and therefore a mark of the genuineness of the Epistle since no forger would be likely to use a strange expression in the very first line of his letter.

An apostle, i.e., a commissioned agent. The Apostle proclaims his authority and commission on account of the false teachers in Crete.

According to the faith. This points out the purpose of the Apostle's commission, which was to preach the faith "of the elect of God," i.e., the faith common to all Christians, which all mankind are called to share, so that all may come to a knowledge of the truth "of the Gospel," which truth "is according to godliness," i.e., it teaches us how to worship God as we should and live according to His will.

2. Unto the hope of life everlasting, which God, who lieth not, promised before the times of the world,

3. But hath in due times manifested his word in preaching, which is committed to me according to the commandment of God our Saviour:

4. To Titus my beloved son, according to the common faith, grace and peace from God the Father, and from Christ Jesus our Saviour.

2. Unto the hope, etc. The purpose of the Apostle's preaching and of the Gospel truth which he proclaims is to stimulate the hope of life eternal which the ever-truthful God "promised before the times of the world," i.e., from all eternity (see 2 Tim. i. 9). This last phrase is understood by some expositors to refer to the promise made in Old Testament times to the Patriarchs and Prophets, but the first explanation is thought to be more probable.

3. The construction here is difficult, but the meaning is clear enough. The promise to give eternal life to the elect, which God had decreed from eternity, was made manifest in due time in the preaching of the Gospel message, which Paul had been commissioned to preach by God Himself.

God our Saviour. See on 1 Tim. i. 1.

4. **Titus.** See *Introduction* to this Epistle, No. I.

The common faith, which was the bond of their spiritual relationship.

Christ Jesus our Saviour. In the preceding verse we had "God our Saviour," which shows that our Lord is true God.

DUTIES DEVOLVING UPON TITUS, 5-16

5-16. St. Paul has left Titus in Crete to set things in order, and to this end one of the first things that should engage the attention of the young bishop will be the appointment of proper church officials, priests and bishops of high moral and spiritual character, whose doctrine is above question and whose manner of living is a perfect reflection of that doctrine (ver. 5-9). This is at all times necessary, but especially so in conditions such as confront Titus in Crete, where there are abroad certain false teachers, the worst of them Jewish, who for the sake of money are circulating ideas and discussing questions that are unsettling the faith and demoralizing the lives of Christians. The Cretans are only too much disposed to vice and disorder, and hence Titus must sharply rebuke those false

5. For this cause I left thee in Crete, that thou shouldest set in order the things that are wanting, and shouldest ordain priests in every city, as I also appointed thee:

6. If any be without crime, the husband of one wife, having faithful children, not accused of riot, or unruly.

7. For a bishop must be without crime, as the steward of God: not arrogant, not subject to anger, not given to wine, no striker, not greedy of filthy lucre:

8. But given to hospitality, a lover of good, sober, just, holy, continent;

9. Embracing that faithful word which is according to doctrine, that he may be able to exhort in sound doctrine and to convince the gainsayers.

and misleading guides, and recall the faithful to soundness of doctrine and rightness of conduct. Those false teachers are defiled from within, and they deny by their lives the God whom they profess with their lips (ver. 10-16).

5. For this cause, etc. St. Paul refers to a time when he and Titus visited the Island of Crete together, which must have been between the first and second Roman imprisonments. We cannot identify this visit with the passing glimpse of Crete which is related in Acts xxvii. 7-13, when Paul as a prisoner was on his way to Rome from Cæsarea; for at that time it seems the Apostle did not land at all.

The things that are wanting, i.e., the reforms that St. Paul was unable to complete before he was called away.

Priests. See on 1 Tim. iii. 1.

As I also appointed thee, i.e., as St. Paul had instructed him to do when leaving him there.

6-9. These verses are nearly identical with those of 1 Tim. iii. 1-7, on which see notes.

Faithful children, i.e., children who are Christians.

Not accused of riot, i.e., of riotous and profligate living.

A lover of good, i.e., of everything good. The word occurs only here.

Just, holy. These qualities, though understood, are not mentioned in 1 Tim. iii. 1-7.

Embracing that faithful word, etc., i.e., that teaching which was taught by our Lord and the Apostles. Throughout these letters St. Paul is insisting on the need of sound doctrine, sound teaching, sound faith (cf. 1 Tim. i. 10, vi. 3, 20; 2 Tim. i. 13, iv. 3; Titus i. 9, 13, etc.).

And to convince, etc. If a bishop or priest is not a master of

10. For there are many disobedient, vain talkers, and seducers: especially they who are of the circumcision:

11. Who must be reproved, who subvert whole houses, teaching things which they ought not, for the sake of base gain.

12. One of them, a prophet of their own, said: *The Cretans are always liars, evil beasts, slothful bellies.*

13. This testimony is true. Wherefore rebuke them sharply, that they may be sound in the faith;

sound doctrine himself, how can he convince unbelievers and refute heretics? He must first know and be persuaded himself before he can teach and persuade others.

10. In verses 10-16 St. Paul gives two more reasons why he requires in the clergy of Crete the qualifications just enumerated, namely, because of the presence in the island of many false teachers, and because of the perverse character of the Cretans.

Disobedient. Better, "insubordinate," to the teachings of the Gospel and their lawful superiors.

Vain talkers is one word in Greek, and it occurs only here in the Bible.

Of the circumcision, i.e., Christian converts from Judaism; these were causing most of the trouble. See on 2 Tim. ii. 16-18.

Etiam of the Vulgate is not in the best Greek.

11. **Who must be reproved.** The Greek reads: "Whose mouth must be stopped."

Who subvert, etc. These false teachers carry their pernicious doctrines into families and upset whole households, putting one against another; and all this is done for the sake of the money they thereby get, which is therefore rightly called "base gain."

12. **One of them,** i.e., one of the Cretans.

Prophet. This title the Greeks were accustomed to give to their poets, who were thought to be inspired by the gods. The Cretan poet here alluded to was Epimenides, who lived about 600 B.C., and the verse quoted is from his *Minos.* The first part of this verse was later quoted by the Alexandrian poet Callimachus (300-240 B.C.) in a hymn to Zeus, and applied to the false Cretan story that Zeus (the Greek Jupiter) was killed and that his tomb was in the Island of Crete. The verse seems to have been well known as an accurate description of the character and conduct of the Cretans.

13. Without qualification the Apostle accepts the testimony of Epimenides regarding his fellow-Cretans; but of course this is to

14. Not giving heed to Jewish fables and commandments of men who turn themselves away from the truth.

15. All things are clean to the clean; but to them that are defiled, and to unbelievers, nothing is clean; but both their mind and their conscience are defiled.

16. They profess that they know God, but in their works they deny *him;* being abominable, and incredulous, and to every good work reprobate.

be understood of the people generally, and in particular of the false teachers, who are to be "rebuked sharply" for the sake of the faith which they are imperilling.

14. **Jewish fables.** See on 1 Tim. i. 4.

Commandments of men. See on 1 Tim. iv. 6; Col. ii. 21; Matt. xv. 2 ff.

Who turn away, etc. The Greek reads: "Who turn their backs upon the truth."

15. Soundness in faith and soundness in morals are linked together in the Pastoral Letters; and of course the contrary is equally true: bad teaching leads to bad living. The Cretan Judaizers were drawing distinctions between clean and unclean foods according to Old Testament prescriptions; but St. Paul would have them understand that all foods in themselves, as created by God, are good and pure, and that it is only the wrong intention and the wrong mind which make them bad or unclean.

16. These Judaizers of Crete, like all the Jews, were proud of their knowledge of the true God, in contrast with the Gentiles who worshipped idols, but by their false teachings and false practices they really denied God and became abominable in His sight, useless for every good work.

CHAPTER II

TITUS' TEACHING OF VARIOUS CLASSES OF PERSONS, 1-15

1-15. Here St. Paul tells Titus that the best way to correct the unwholesome teachings of the false guides in Crete will be to set before the people the simple positive doctrines of the Gospel as regards all classes, old and young of both sexes; and in doing all this Titus must show himself an example in doctrine and practice, so as to disarm adversaries. Even slaves and servants, by their

1. But speak thou the things that become sound doctrine:

2. That the aged men be sober, chaste, prudent, sound in faith, in love, in patience.

3. The aged women, in like manner, in holy attire, not false accusers, not given to much wine, teaching well:

4. That they may teach the young women to be wise, to love their husbands, to love their children,

obedience, honesty, and fidelity, may be an ornament in all respects to the doctrine of their God and Saviour (ver. 1-10). These teachings of the Gospel are entirely within the power of all to practise; for we have as helps the grace of God which has been manifested for the salvation of all mankind, and the glorious prospect of seeing hereafter the Saviour who gave Himself for us that He might free us from all sins and perfect us in every good work. Let Titus preach these things with all authority (ver. 11-15).

1. In contrast with the false teachers who were unsettling whole households by their fables and the commandments of men (i. 11, 14), Titus is to instruct the faithful in the sound doctrine of the Gospel which has come from God.

2. The Apostle now begins to indicate in the concrete what he means by the "sound doctrine" that Titus is to teach. And first, as regards older men, they should practise those virtues which in a special manner become their years and which age sometimes makes hard.

Aged men. Though the Greek word here used is different from that employed in 1 Tim. v. 1, the meaning is the same. See note there.

3. **Aged women,** a Greek word found only here in the Canonical Scriptures, but the same in meaning as the similar word in 1 Tim. v. 2.

In holy attire. Better, "devout in demeanor," referring to habits of mind and heart, as well as outward actions and appearance.

False accusers, i.e., slanderers.

Not given to much wine, as was too often the case among pagan women.

Teaching well, i.e., privately in families. See on 1 Tim. ii. 10-12.

4. The Apostle now points out the object and motive of the good

5. To be discreet, chaste, sober, having a care of the house, gentle, obedient to their husbands, that the word of God be not blasphemed.

6. Younger men, in like manner, exhort that they be sober.

7. In all things shew myself an example of good works, in teaching, in integrity, in gravity,

8. The sound word that can not be blamed, that he who is in opposition may be afraid, having no evil to say of us.

teaching on the part of older women spoken of at the end of the preceding verse; they are to exercise this good office on younger women, especially young married women, so as to instruct them in the duties peculiar to their state.

To love their husbands, etc. Quite literally, "to be husband-lovers, children-lovers." The first Greek substantive is found only here in the Greek Bible, and the second only here in the New Testament. Love is the domestic source of strength and influence for married women; it is like a central heating plant which warms and cheers the whole person and extends its radiation to all around.

5. **Having a care of the house.** It is disputed whether we should read here, quite literally, "keepers at home" or "workers at home." The former is descriptive of the ideal wife among the Greeks, and hence very probable; but the latter has the support of the best MSS., and so it is to be preferred.

That the word of God, etc. The conduct and example of Christian wives would have great influence on pagan outsiders; hence they should give no occasion for adverse criticism.

6. **Sober,** i.e., sober in mind and conduct. The Greek word here literally means "wise"; it may also be translated "self-control."

7. **In all things.** St. Jerome and some other authorities join these words to the end of the preceding verse. Titus, like every bishop, is to be an example to all (1 Tim. iv. 12; 1 Peter v. 3)— but especially to younger men—in blameless conduct and sound teaching.

8. **The sound word,** etc. Titus' discourse or preaching must reflect the soundness of his doctrine.

That cannot be blamed is one word in Greek, and means "irreprehensible"; it is found elsewhere in the Bible only in 2 Mach. iv. 47.

That he, etc., i.e., that the adversary may be silenced. A simple presentation of the true doctrine will shame the enemy.

9. *Exhort* servants to be obedient to their masters, in all things pleasing, not gainsaying,

10. Not defrauding, but in all things shewing good fidelity, that they may adorn the doctrine of God our Saviour in all things.

11. For the grace of God appeared bringing salvation to all men;

12. Instructing us that denying ungodliness and worldly desires, we should live soberly, and justly, and godly in this world,

13. Looking for the blessed hope and coming of the glory of the great God and our Saviour Christ Jesus,

9-10. See on Eph. vi. 5-9; 1 Tim. vi. 1-2.

11. The Apostle now (ver. 11-14) gives reasons why Christians should observe the precepts he has been enjoining, namely, first, because the grace of God has appeared in the Incarnation of God's only Son, "bringing salvation to all men" (ver. 11-12), and secondly, because by observing those precepts and living holy lives we prepare ourselves for the glorious coming of our Saviour (ver. 13-14).

The aorist "appeared" indicates the definite appearance of the Saviour at the time of His Incarnation. The adjective here translated "salvation" does not occur elsewhere, and it is to be connected with "all men."

12. The purpose of the Incarnation was to save us from our sins and to teach us the way to heaven.

That denying, etc. This phrase expresses the negative duties of the Christian life, while the following words, "we should live, etc.," express the positive requirements of the same life. The words "soberly, justly, godly" embrace all our Christian obligations —to ourselves, to our neighbor, and to God.

13. The practice of the holy life taught us by our Saviour carries with it the right and privilege on our part of looking forward one day to a glorious realization of our hope, that is, of seeing the blessed object of our hope, our Lord and Saviour Jesus Christ.

Coming would be better translated "appearing," and the absence of the article before it shows its close connection with "hope"; its Greek equivalent is found only in the Pastoral Letters and in 2 Thess. ii. 8, and it refers to our Lord's Second Coming everywhere, except in 2 Tim. i. 10, where it means His First Advent. Since, therefore, the word "appearing," here as everywhere, is applied to our Lord and never to God the Father, and since there is only one

14. Who gave himself for us, that he might redeem us from all iniquity, and might cleanse to himself a chosen people, zealous for good works.

15. These things speak, and exhort and rebuke with all authority. Let no man despise thee.

preposition governing "great God" and "Saviour Jesus Christ," it is next to certain that the Apostle in this verse is speaking only of our Lord, and not of God the Father and our Lord. That he should speak of our Lord as "the great God" is only to emphasize the glory of His coming. We have, therefore, in this verse an implied but solemn proof of the divinity of our Lord.

14. **Who gave himself,** etc. See on Eph. v. 2; 1 Tim. ii. 6.

Redeem, cleanse. These words express respectively the negative and positive aspects of the one process of sanctification.

From all iniquity. Literally, "from all lawlessness."

A chosen people, i.e., a people who would be His own property or possession. This is the meaning of the Greek. The language here is from Psalm cxxx. 8, Exod. xix. 5, Deut. vi. 6, xiv. 2, etc., where God's choice and formation of Israel as His own people are in question.

15. The foregoing exhortations and precepts Titus must preach and announce with full power and authority, and he must not hesitate to rebuke the wayward and disobedient, for he speaks not as a private person but as God's minister and in God's name. See on 1 Tim. iv. 11-12.

CHAPTER III

WHAT THE CRETANS ARE TO DO, WHAT THEY ARE TO AVOID, 1-11

1-11. In this last section of his letter St. Paul gives Titus certain counsels which he is to set before all the faithful of Crete. They are to be obedient to authority, helpful to others, and considerate of outsiders, remembering their former sinful state out of which God's pure mercy and grace delivered them, thus making them heirs of eternal life (ver. 1-7). Titus must insist that being a Christian carries with it the obligation of producing fruit in good works. Useless discussions are to be avoided, and those who persist in them are to be shunned (ver. 8-11).

1. Admonish them to be subject to princes and powers, to obey, to be ready for every good work.

2. To speak evil of no man, not to be litigious but gentle, shewing all mildness towards all men.

3. For we ourselves also were some time unwise, incredulous, erring, slaves to divers desires and pleasures, living in malice and envy, hateful, and hating one another.

4. But when the kindness and love for men of God our Saviour appeared,

5. Not by the works of justice, which we have done, but according to his mercy, he saved us by the laver of regeneration and renovation of the Holy Ghost;

1. **Admonish them,** i.e., the Christians of Crete.

Princes, powers, i.e., both the supreme and subordinate authorities. The Cretans were notorious for sedition.

Dicto of the Vulgate is not in the Greek.

2. The graces of Christianity are to be shown to outsiders, as well as to fellow-Christians. Gentleness "is the indulgent consideration of human infirmities" (Aristotle, quoted by Lock).

3. In verses 3-7 the Apostle reminds the Christians of Crete of the reasons why they should be charitable and kind towards all men, even sinners. They themselves were once in a pitiable condition (Rom. i. 30 ff.), and it is only through the goodness and mercy of God that they have been saved.

Some time, i.e., before we were Christians.

Unwise, incredulous, etc. Let the Christians of Crete, whether of Jewish or Gentile origin, reflect on their own past non-Christian lives, and they will find no reason for boasting, but rather every reason to feel humble and to be kind to their pagan neighbors. The common Greek word for "pleasures" occurs only here in St. Paul, and the term for "hateful" is not found elsewhere in the Bible.

4. Over against the malice and hatefulness of men St. Paul sets the kindness and love of God. We have revised the wording of the verse in accordance with the Greek, and the Vulgate should be likewise changed.

God our Saviour is here applied to God the Father, as in 1 Tim. i. 1. The goodness and love of the Eternal Father towards us have been manifested in the Incarnation of our Lord and in our justification.

5. Before describing the works of God's love in our behalf the Apostle affirms their absolute gratuitousness, stating that our justifi-

6. Whom he hath poured forth upon us abundantly, through Jesus Christ our Saviour,

7. That, being justified by his grace, we might be heirs according to hope of life everlasting.

8. Faithful is the saying: and these things I will have thee affirm constantly: that they who believe in God may be careful to excel in good works. These things are good and profitable unto men.

cation and salvation are not due to any meritorious works done by us, whether in the state of nature or under the Mosaic Law, but only and entirely to the pure mercy of God (cf. Rom. iii. 20 ff.; 2 Tim. i. 9; Eph. ii. 8-10); and the medium or instrumental cause employed by Almighty God to confer on us the graces of justification and salvation is "the laver of regeneration and renovation," i.e., the Sacrament of Baptism.

Of the Holy Ghost, to whom is attributed the work of our spiritual regeneration and renovation, as being a work of love. See on 2 Tim. i. 9.

6. Since the Holy Ghost proceeds from the Father and the Son by way of love, we attribute to Him works of love; but that our justification and salvation are in reality the work of the whole Divine Trinity is evident from this verse.

Whom means the Holy Ghost, of whom there has just been question; and "he" means God the Father, who is the subject of the whole sentence. God the Father in Baptism has abundantly poured into our souls the Holy Ghost, i.e., sanctifying grace and the other gifts of the Divine Spirit, which Jesus Christ by His sufferings and death has merited for us.

7. **That** indicates the final purpose of the justification we have received through the rich outpouring of the Holy Ghost upon our souls in Baptism, which is to make us "heirs of life everlasting." This final and glorious issue of our spiritual lives we now possess in hope.

8. The Apostle concludes the exhortation of verses 3-7 by inculcating the performance of good works, on which he is ever insisting throughout the Pastoral Epistles.

Faithful is the saying, i.e., worthy of all belief, referring to what he has been saying in the verses just preceding; these truths St. Paul wishes Titus to preach constantly, so that the faith of his hearers may be living and fruitful in good works.

9. But avoid foolish questions and genealogies and contentions and strivings about the law. For they are unprofitable and vain.

10. A man that is a heretic, after the first and second admonition, avoid,

11. Knowing that he that is such an one, is perverted and sinneth, being condemned by his own judgment.

12. When I shall send to thee Artemas or Tychicus, make haste to come unto me to Nicopolis. For there I have determined to winter.

These things, etc., i.e., the truths he has been stressing.

9. In verses 9-11 St. Paul tells Titus to avoid the foolish questions and quarrels of the heretics and the heretics themselves. See on 1 Tim. i. 4, vi. 4, and 2 Tim. ii. 23, where the same advice is given.

10. **Heretic.** According to its primary meaning this word means one who makes divisions, factions—therefore, a factious person. But since there is question now of doctrine and of adhering stubbornly to error, it seems the term must here be given the strict meaning it came to have in later times. The adjective does not occur again in the New Testament, but the corresponding substantive is found in a number of places in St. Paul and the Acts.

11. He now explains the reason why the pertinacious heretic is to be avoided. Such a one "is perverted," i.e., beyond hope of repair, because he has separated himself from the foundation which is faith; he is "condemned by his own judgment," because it is his persistence in error that has put him out of the Church.

CONCLUSION, 12-15

12-15. St. Paul provides helpers to take Titus' place during the latter's temporary absence from Crete, and he asks Titus to look after the wants of Zenas and Apollo. He warns the Cretans against their chronic habit of idleness, sends greetings and good wishes, and imparts his blessing.

12. **Artemas,** of whom we know nothing further for certain. According to tradition he became Bishop of Lystra.

Tychicus. See on 2 Tim. iv. 12; Eph. vi. 21; Col. iv. 7; Acts xx. 4.

Nicopolis, most probably the city of that name in Epirus, which at this time was an important place built by Augustus after the battle of Actium, deriving its name from that victory. There was

13. Send forward Zenas, the lawyer, and Apollo, with care, that nothing be wanting to them.

14. And let our men also learn to excel in good works for necessary uses, that they be not unfruitful.

15. All that are with me salute thee: salute them that love us in the faith. Grace be with you all. Amen.

also a Nicopolis in Cilicia and in Thrace; but neither of these would agree so well with 2 Tim. iv. 10, where it is said that Titus had gone to Dalmatia. It is clear from the closing words of this verse that St. Paul was entirely at liberty at this time. Ramsay thinks he meant to make Nicopolis a centre for preaching in Epirus and that he was arrested there. The opinion seems probable.

13. Zenas, mentioned only here. He apparently was skilled in Jewish or Roman law. Tradition says he became Bishop of Diospolis and was the author of an apocryphal work known as "The Acts of Titus."

Apollo, the eloquent Alexandrian preacher, of whom there is question in Acts xviii. 24, xix. 1; 1 Cor. i. 12, iii. 4, etc.

14. As a last word St. Paul emphasizes the need of industry and the performance of good works on the part of the Christians of Crete.

15. All that are with me, etc., i.e., his traveling companions and co-laborers.

Salute them, etc., i.e., the Christians of Crete, who were united to the Apostle and his companions by the same "faith," i.e., loyalty to Christ and His teachings. The blessing is to Titus and the whole Church of Crete.

Dei and *Amen* of the Vulgate are not represented in the Greek.

THE EPISTLE TO THE HEBREWS

INTRODUCTION

I. Authorship and Canonicity. From the beginning the question of the authorship of this Epistle has been a very vexing one. In the East, however, until the appearance of Arius in the fourth century, the letter seems to have been regarded everywhere as St. Paul's, though the form in which it is expressed was by some thought to be due to one of the Apostle's disciples. In the West it was known very early, for it is frequently quoted and referred to by Clement of Rome in his letter to the Corinthians written about 95 A.D., and *The Pastor of Hermas* also seems to have been acquainted with it (*Vis.*, II, iii., 2; *Sim.*, I, i. ff.). But until after the middle of the fourth century the Latin Fathers were disinclined to accept it as an authentic Epistle of St. Paul's.

The main reasons for these doubts about the authorship of Hebrews were: (a) the absence of Paul's name and the customary greeting at the beginning; (b) remarkable differences in the language and style of this letter as compared with the other letters of St. Paul; (c) the fact that the writer in several places (ii. 3; xiii. 7) seems to speak as if he were not an Apostle, but rather belonged to the second generation of Christians; (d) a subject-matter different in many respects from the subjects commonly treated in the other Pauline Epistles.

Observing these differences Origen said the thoughts and ideas of the letter were St. Paul's, but that the form in which they were expressed was furnished by someone else. "Who really wrote the Epistle," he says, "God knows. The statement of some of our predecessors is that Clement, Bishop of the Romans, wrote the Epistle; others say that Luke, the author of the Gospel and the Acts, wrote it" (Eusebius, *Hist. Eccl.*, VI, xxv, 11-14). Clement of Alexandria said the letter was St. Paul's; that the Apostle wrote it in Hebrew and St. Luke translated it into Greek; that the style was similar to the style of Acts; and that St. Paul's name was probably omitted from the address so as not to antagonize the Jews who were prejudiced against the Apostle (Eusebius, *Hist. Eccl.*, VI, xiv, 2-4; *Strom.*, vi, 8). The authority of the presbyter Pantænus is cited to the same effect (Eusebius, *Hist. Eccl.*, VI, xiv). Likewise Denis of Alexandria, Alexander of Alexandria, St. Athanasius, and all the other Fathers and ecclesiastical writers of the Churches of Alexandria, Antioch, Palestine, and Cappadocia, affirm that St. Paul was the author of this Epistle. See Westcott, *The Epistle to the Hebrews*, London, 1906, pp. lxii-lxxii.

In the West the case was different. As we have said above, this Epistle was known at an early date to St. Clement of Rome, and perhaps also to *The Pastor of Hermas*, both of whom seem to have accepted its authenticity. But later it was regarded with suspicion until the fourth century. St. Philastrius (*Hær.*, LXXXIX) gives us the reason for this change of attitude, namely, because some of its doctrines were not understood, because of its rhetorical style, and because the Novatians abused its teaching on penance. Thus it appears that Hippolytus, Irenæus, and the Roman presbyter Caius did not look on the Epistle as the work of St. Paul (Eusebius, *Hist. Eccl.*, VI, xx). Nor is it found in the Muratorian Canon. St. Cyprian says St. Paul wrote only to seven Churches, and so seems to exclude the Epistle to the Hebrews (*De exhort. mart.*, XI). Tertullian calls it the work of Barnabas (*De pudic.*, 20), as does also the Codex Claromontanus.

In the fourth century, however, the Epistle to the Hebrews began to be regarded as St. Paul's, even in the West; and by the end of that century it was pretty generally accepted as one of the authentic letters of the great Apostle. Thus, while St. Jerome and St. Augustine admitted it with some hesitation and the Council of Carthage (397 A.D.) spoke of "the thirteen Epistles of St. Paul, and one by the same to the Hebrews," nevertheless it was cited as St. Paul's by St. Hilary, St. Ambrose, Rufinus, Innocent I in his Catalogue of the Canonical Scriptures (401 A.D.), the Fifth Council of Carthage, etc. (cf. Sales, *La Sacra Bibbia*, vol. II, p. 437; Pope, *Student's "Aids" to the Study of the Bible*, vol. III, pp. 256 ff.).

In brief, we can say that from the end of the fourth century until the rise of Protestantism this Epistle was accepted as a genuine work of St. Paul's by all Churches and ecclesiastical writers both in the East and in the West. Even the Reformers, while subjecting the Epistle to a fresh examination, did not generally reject it until the nineteenth century. Today, however, on account of the reasons given above, its authenticity is denied by all non-Catholics, some assigning as the real author Barnabas, others Luke, others Clement of Rome, others Apollo, others Priscilla assisted by her husband Aquila, etc.

For Catholics the question is a closed one, inasmuch as we must hold that Hebrews is not only divinely inspired, but that it is Pauline in origin, as containing the doctrine and teaching of St. Paul. We are not obliged to believe that St. Paul actually supplied the exact language and style in which the doctrines are expressed; although on this latter point we must be prepared to accept further possible pronouncement by the Church (cf. Decrees of the Biblical Commission, June 24, 1914).

Of course, the divine inspiration or canonicity of a letter or passage of Scripture does not require that it should have been actually written by an Apostle, as we see in the cases of the Gospels of St. Luke and of St. Mark. Hence, whatever the doubts about the composition and the writer of the Epistle to the Hebrews, its canonicity and divine inspiration remain unquestioned and have always been admitted, although in the West it was for a time not used in public nor included in certain lists of the Pauline Epistles, for the reasons given above from St. Philastrius. And while St. Jerome was aware of the doubts entertained by some of the Latins regarding the canonicity of Hebrews, he himself accepted it without question since, as he observes, older writers had no hesitation in admitting it (*Comm. in Matt.*, xxvi. 8, *in Isa.*, vi. 2, 9; *Ep.* cxxix., 3, etc.). Likewise, St. Augustine was moved to admit the Epistle as divine because of the unanimous acceptance of it by the Eastern Church (*De peccat. merit. et remiss.*, i. 27). Hence we may say that from the time of the Council of Hippo in 393 and the Council of Carthage in 397 the whole Church received this Epistle both as canonical and authentic. Even Protestant scholars, all of whom now reject the Pauline authorship of this letter, admit its divine inspiration and canonicity. Speaking of the different views entertained regarding it by the East and the West in the early centuries, Dr. Westcott says: "Experience has shown us how to unite the conclusions on both sides. We have been able to acknowledge that the apostolic authority of the Epistle is independent of the Pauline authorship. The spiritual insight of the East can be joined with the historic witness of the West."

At first sight the position of the Catholic Church regarding the authenticity of the Epistle to the Hebrews may seem somewhat astonishing in the face of all non-Catholic scholarship, which today, as just said, rejects the Pauline authorship of this letter altogether. But if we keep in mind the external arguments so far adduced in favor of that authorship, and consider further some of the internal facts which point in the same direction, we shall be able to see the entire reasonableness of the position the Church has taken in this matter. For here, in spite of differences of style and language, we shall see much of the teaching of St. Paul everywhere.

Thus, in the first place, there is the same doctrine about Christ, whom the writer represents as the brightness of the glory and the image of the Eternal Father through whom God has created and sustains all things (Heb. i. 3; Col. i. 15; Phil. ii. 7; Rom. viii. 34). This Jesus is seated at the right hand of God (Heb. i. 3; Col. i. 17); He is superior to all the angels (Heb. i. 5, 6; Eph. i. 21); and has received a name that is above all names (Heb. i. 4; Phil. ii. 9). Moreover, He humbled Himself in order to redeem us (Heb. ii. 14, 15; Phil. ii. 8); He shed His blood for our sakes (Heb. ix. 14, 18; Rom. v. 9); He regards us as brethren (Heb. ii. 11; Rom. viii. 17); He is the source of all the graces we have received (Heb. iv. 16; Rom. i. 5 ff.); etc.

Secondly, there is the same teaching about the Old Law, which was given through angels (Heb. ii. 2; Gal. iii. 19), which was a law of fear and bondage (Heb. ii. 15, xii. 18-21; Gal. v. 1; Rom. viii. 15), which was only a figure and a shadow of things to come, and was therefore impotent to justify men (Heb. viii. 5, ix. 1 ff.; Col. ii. 17; Rom. iii. 21, viii. 2-4). Justification is only through faith in Christ Jesus (Heb. x. 38, xi. 6, xii. 2; Rom. i. 17, iii. 28), etc.

Thirdly, we find here so much of the same teaching in practical

matters. For example, the author exhorts his readers to live in
peace with all men (Heb. xii. 14; Rom. xii. 8) ; they must practise
hospitality (Heb. xiii. 2; Rom. xii. 13), exercise patience (Heb. vi.
12, x. 36; Rom. v. 3, 4), and give themselves to prayer (Heb. iv.
16; Eph. vi. 18), etc.

Finally, even in the matter of language and style there is a striking similarity in many places between this letter and other letters
of St. Paul. First of all, we have here, as in those other Epistles,
many digressions from the main arguments. Thus, for example,
after showing in Chapter i the superiority of Christ to the angels,
the writer digresses in Chapter ii to call attention to the necessity
of observing the New Law to whose Author God has subjected all
things, and to discuss the significance of the sufferings of Christ.
Again, in Chapter iii the author shows in the first six verses the
superiority of Christ to Moses, and then enters upon a long digression (iii. 7—iv. 16) in which he discusses the necessity of seeking
the rest of Christ and the means to obtain it. From v. 11 to vi.
20 there is another extended digression warning against relapse and
describing the perils involved in forsaking the faith of Christ. In
x. 19-39 we have a further strong appeal for faith, hope and charity,
followed by a solemn warning of the dreadful fate of those who
give up their Christian profession.

It is true that some expositors do not consider these passages as
real digressions, since they belong to the main object which the
writer has in mind, namely, to check the tendency to relapse from
the Gospel back into Judaism; but whether we call them digressions
or mere applications of his teaching, they do deviate from the line
of argument, and to that extent they are digressions.

And not only in the digressions, but also in the texts of Scripture
cited and in the manner in which they are used, do we find many
and striking resemblances between this and other Epistles of St.
Paul. Compare, for instance, Heb. i. 3, 13 ff. with Rom. viii. 34
ff.; Heb. ii. 6-8 with 1 Cor. xv. 27 ff.; Heb. x. 38 with Rom. i. 17
and Gal. iii. 11; Heb. x. 30 with Rom. xii. 19; Heb. xii. 14 with
Rom. ix. 7 ff. We have the same examples of the faith of Abraham
(Heb. xi. 19; Rom. iv. 17), and of the incredulity of the Israelites
in the desert (Heb. iii. 8, 9; 1 Cor. v. 9, 10). The word of God
is a two-edged sword (Heb. iv. 12; Eph. vi. 17). The Church is

the house or temple of God (Heb. iii. 2-6; 1 Cor. iii. 9 ff.). The Christian life is a warfare (Heb. x. 32, xii. 1; 1 Cor. ix. 24, 27 and Gal. v. 7). The faithful are divided into two classes, one of beginners who need milk and the other of adults who can take strong food (Heb. v. 13, 14; 1 Cor. iii. 1, 2, xiv. 20 ff.).

Many other resemblances between this and the rest of the Pauline letters might be cited; but these are enough to show why the Church, basing its conclusion on both internal and external evidence, insists that St. Paul was the author of the Epistle to the Hebrews. The distinctive features of the letter can all be explained quite satisfactorily without denying the Pauline authorship. Thus, it is reasonable to say that Paul's name was omitted from the introduction in order not to antagonize his enemies among the Jews. The differences of style and language are accounted for by the disciple whom Paul employed to express his thoughts and ideas in literary form. If at times the author associates himself with his readers and speaks to them of their predecessors in the faith, this does not prove that he belonged to the second generation of Christians, but shows only that he was using a more familiar and forceful method of writing, as he did also in Rom. xiii. 11 ff., or (if we assume that the Epistle was addressed to the Christians of Jerusalem) that he was deferring to those who had known the Lord in the flesh.

As regards the doctrines treated in this Epistle, we can see from what has been said above that much of the teaching of the admittedly Pauline letters is here repeated under another form, while the rest is naturally explained by the different purpose which prompted this letter and the readers to whom it was directed. The doctrine, or rather the aspects of doctrine, which St. Paul gives in each of his Epistles is always determined, as we should expect, by the people addressed and by the conditions and circumstances in which those people lived at the time he wrote. Hence it would be absurd to expect him to give the same identical doctrine to all the Churches to which he wrote. But this is very far from saying that there is a contradiction between the teaching of this Epistle and the other Epistles of St. Paul. There is no such contradiction, either on the surface or underlying the surface of this letter. It cannot be shown that there is anything taught in Hebrews which is out of harmony with the Apostle's teaching elsewhere. On the contrary, as we saw above, this letter has much in common with the admitted teaching of St. Paul as found in his other Epistles. So much so, indeed, that those who here postulate another author must at least admit that he was saturated with the Apostle's doctrines.

As a final argument in favor of the Pauline authorship of Hebrews, we may observe that the letter closes with the Apostle's usual salutations and good wishes, and that the author speaks intimately of his beloved disciple Timothy, who has recently been given his liberty (cf. Sales, *op. cit.*, vol. II, pp. 438 ff.).

II. **Time and Place of Composition.** The best and most recent non-Catholic scholars date this Epistle between the years 60 and 96 A.D. This allows a wide margin, and one which can be easily trimmed down to a considerable extent from the *terminus a quo*. Thus, the letter was certainly written by or before 95 A.D., because it was freely quoted about that time by Clement of Rome in his Epistle to the Corinthians. More than this, it must have been written before the year 70 A.D., for it clearly assumes that the Temple was still standing and that the priests were still carrying out the Jewish sacrificial ritual in all its completeness and splendor (viii. 4, ix. 6-9, 13, x. 1 ff., xiii. 10). The writer is fearful lest his readers be seduced by the attractiveness of the ancient services to abandon their new faith; whereas, "had the temple been destroyed, and the old worship brought to an end with no hope of revival, he would have had to hand so obvious and complete a vindication of his root principle that the old covenant was doomed to disappear and be merged in the new order, that it is inconceivable he should not have made use of it in the epistle, still less that he should have talked as if the Jewish cultus were still in operation" (S. C. Gayford, in *A New Commentary on Holy Scripture*, II, p. 597).

Again, this Epistle must have antedated the outbreak of the Jewish War in 67 A.D., since it contains no mention of so great an event; while, on the other hand, it gives clear indication of having followed not long after some special persecution of the faithful. If it was written to the Jewish Christians of Palestine, as seems very probable, the persecution which included the death of James the Less, the Bishop of Jerusalem, in 62 A.D., would explain very well the sufferings and trials of the faithful which occasioned the Epistle, and would give us a date around 63 A.D. This was the time when St. Paul was expecting an early release from his first Roman captivity, and it would fit in nicely with Heb. xiii. 23, where the writer expresses the hope of seeing his readers soon in company with Timothy. From this passage it also appears that Timothy was at the time absent on some mission and the writer was waiting for him to return shortly; and we know from Phil. ii. 19 that St. Paul was going to send Timothy on a mission to the Philippian Church, and that Timothy was to return to him with a report of conditions in Philippi. All this makes it very probable that Hebrews was written shortly before or shortly after St. Paul's release from his first Roman captivity around the end of 63 A.D.

But if we hold, with many modern writers, that Hebrews was addressed to Jewish converts in Rome, we shall have to assign the Neronian persecution or the persecution under Domitian as the one from which the faithful were suffering. In the first supposition the Epistle could be dated between 64 and 67 A.D., but it is objected that Heb. x. 32-34 is too mild a passage to be descriptive of the horrors endured by the Christians under Nero, and hence cannot refer to that persecution. The same objection may be made to the second supposition, which would put the date of the Epistle between 80 and 90 A.D. This latter date would also destroy the Pauline authorship of the letter, unless it were maintained that Paul wrote or dictated its entire substance before his death and charged some one of his disciples (say, Barnabas) to put it in form and publish it, or have it published, years after the Apostle's death—a supposition which it would be difficult to establish with any degree of probability. As regards the passage in x. 32-34, it should be noted that those verses seem to refer to sufferings long past as an incentive to the readers of the letter to bear with patience and courage their present trials, and that consequently those verses are not a descripion but rather an illustration of the persecution which the faithful were enduring when this Epistle was written.

As to the place of composition, we may assign Rome or some other city of Italy, relying on the words of xiii. 24, "the brethren from Italy salute you." Rome is the traditional place of origin. The inscription at the end of the Codex Alexandrinus reads "from Rome." The Syriac or Peshitto version gives Italy as the place of writing.

III. Occasion and Readers of This Letter. From the contents of this letter it is clear that it was written to Christian converts from Judaism who were suffering much because of their new faith, and who consequently were sorely tempted to fall back into Judaism, thus committing the awful sin of apostasy. The writer's purpose, therefore, is to hearten and console his readers, and to warn them against lapsing into the Mosaic worship. The Christian faith, he says, is not only the fulfillment of all the Old Dispensation promised in figure and shadow, but it is God's perfect and final revelation to man, guaranteed by the Son of God Himself (i. 2, 3, 8-10). And as for suffering, that same Incarnate Son has provided an example, winning victory over death by suffering and humiliation (xii. 2 ff.). We must, therefore, be ready to endure anything and to forego everything rather than abandon this New Covenant to which we have been admitted and the blessings of which we have been privileged to taste.

According to the title given this Epistle in all the ancient MSS., it was addressed "to the Hebrews," that is, to Christian converts from Judaism. This does not mean, however, Jewish Christians in general, wherever they might be in the world, but a particular group of converts. The writer speaks to them in a particular manner, regretting the slowness of their Christian development (v. 11, 12), yet praising their charitable services to the saints (vi. 10, 11); they have had their peculiar history and experiences, their present conditions are particular and individual, and the writer hopes to visit them soon (xii. 4 ff., xiii. 19, 23). The author, therefore, is addressing a particular group of Jewish Christians, and not Hebrew converts in general.

But where this community lived is another question, upon which scholars are not agreed. Some have thought the Jewish Christians of Alexandria were the first recipients of this Epistle. The main reason for this opinion is that the Muratorian Canon mentions a letter of Paul's to the Alexandrians—a poor argument indeed. Modern non-Catholic opinion favors Rome. The chief arguments in support of this view are: (a) Clement of Rome quoted this letter about the year 95 in his own letter to the Corinthians, and he is both the oldest Christian writer outside the New Testament and the first one to quote this Epistle, as far as we know; (b) the pas-

sage in xiii. 24, "The brethren from Italy salute you," is understood to refer to Italian friends of the Roman community who were
in contact with the author of this letter when he was writing from
some other part of Italy, or from some other country where Italians
were living.

But here again the contents of the Epistle will be our best guide.
We see that the writer is addressing a Church that is well organized, and that is made up entirely of Jewish converts (iii. 12, vi.
4-8, x. 24, 25, 29, xii. 25, xiii. 7, 24) ; there is no question of har-
monizing divergent elements, or of warning the readers against the
idolatry and vices of paganism, but only of the danger of abandon-
ing the humble cult of Christianity for the elaborate Jewish ritual
which was then being carried out in all its splendor. Furthermore,
the author assumes that his readers are perfectly familiar with his
detailed description of the Tabernacle and the Levitical ceremonies
and worship, and that they understand without explanation his
words: "Jesus also, that he might sanctify the people by his own
blood, suffered without the gate" (xiii. 12). Again, the recipients
of this Epistle have been Christians for a long time (v. 12) ; the
Gospel was preached to them by the Apostles (ii. 3) ; they have
suffered persecution for their faith, but have not yet poured out
their blood as some of their leaders have done (x. 32, xii. 4, xiii. 7).

Now, what locality and community of Christians could so perfectly correspond to the foregoing facts and implications as the
City of Jerusalem and the Jewish converts of Palestine? The
Church in Jerusalem was founded on the first Pentecost Sunday.
There persecution soon spread, claiming in due time such leaders in
the faith as St. Stephen, St. James the Greater, James the Less, the
first bishop of that see, etc. "There alone the Levitical worship
was known to all by the daily offering of sacrifices and the great
celebrations of the Day of Atonement and of the other feast-days.
There alone this worship was continuously maintained according to
the ordinances of the Law until the destruction of the city in the
year 70" (Fonk, in *Catholic Encyclopedia*, vol. VII, p. 182). It
seems to us, therefore, far more probable than otherwise that Jewish
converts of Palestine, and especially of Jerusalem, were the immediate recipients of this letter to the Hebrews. Cf. Sales, *op. cit.*,
pp. 440 ff.

Against this opinion it is objected that the Epistle was written in Greek, whereas a letter to Christians in Palestine would more likely have been composed in Aramaic. The objection has little weight, since Greek was freely spoken in the Holy Land, along with Aramaic, long before this letter was written; and also since St. Paul was accustomed to write his letters in Greek. Most likely the disciple to whom the Apostle entrusted the composition of the Epistle was far more ready in Greek than in Aramaic, for the writer seems to be using his native tongue.

It is also objected that the author of this Epistle is speaking of an ideal Judaism, Temple, and Levitical ritual. But, in the first place, it may be asked why his fears are so real if there is question only of something ideal. Why is he so fearful that his readers may lapse into Judaism, if there is not a real one that attracts them? If his description is ideal and not real, then he is painting a picture so vivid and attractive that he would seem to be inciting his readers to do the very thing he is warning them against. In the second place, we may observe that, whether ideal or real, his description presupposes the same degree of accurate knowledge as regards Judaism and its ritual, and that this could not be so easily and naturally explained in any opinion which does not make Jerusalem and Christian converts of Palestine respectively the destination and the readers of this Epistle.

IV. **Language and Style.** It was the opinion of Clement of Alexandria that St. Paul wrote this letter in Hebrew and that one of his disciples translated it into Greek, but all critics are now agreed that it was composed in Greek. Antiquity knows nothing of any Hebrew copy of the Epistle, and all the oldest versions that we know of were made from the Greek. Furthermore, all citations of the Old Testament are from the Septuagint. There are also peculiar turns of expression, idiomatic uses, plays on words, etc., which it would be impossible to explain if the letter had not originated in Greek.

The use of words here is also peculiarly rich and varied. The Epistle contains 168 terms which occur nowhere else in the New Testament, 40 words which are not in the Septuagint, and 10 words which are found in neither classical nor Biblical Greek. The writer is also fond of compound words.

The style of the letter is the best in the New Testament. All authorities have noticed and acknowledged its purity and elegance. It would seem, therefore, that Origen voiced the judgment of the best critics when he said that the thoughts and ideas of Hebrews are those of St. Paul, but that the language and style were supplied by someone else.

V. **Analysis of Contents.** The Epistle to the Hebrews is both speculative or intellectual and practical or moral, but these different elements are so closely intermingled as to make impossible a very clear-cut and connected division of either. The main arguments are followed by digressions consisting of moral applications, exhortations, and the like. The Epistle also begins without the customary address, though it has an introduction. We may divide it as follows: Introduction (i. 1-3); Doctrinal Part (i. 4—x. 18); Moral Part (x. 19—xiii. 17); Conclusion (xiii. 18-25).

A. The Introduction (i. 1-3) contains the theme of the Epistle, namely, the superiority of the New Covenant revelation, made through Christ, to the Old Covenant revelation, made to the Patriarchs through the Prophets.

B. In the Doctrinal Part (i. 4—x. 18) the author essays to prove his thesis, namely, that the New Dispensation is superior to the Old. This he does by showing: (a) that Christ, the author and mediator of the New Covenant, is far superior to the Angels through whose ministry the Old Law was given (i. 4—ii. 18); (b) that He is superior to Moses, the mediator of the Old Covenant (iii. 1—iv. 13); (c) that the Priesthood of Christ is superior to the Levitical priesthood (iv. 14—x. 18). This last point is thus proved: (a) from the dignity of the Person who is the High Priest of the Christian Dispensation, namely, Christ (iv. 14—vii. 28); (b) from the place in which the functions of this Priesthood are exercised, namely, the heavenly Sanctuary (viii. 1-5); (c) from the greater excellence of the Covenant of which this Priesthood is a part, namely, the Gospel (viii. 6-13); and (d) from the superior dignity of the Victim that is offered in sacrifice by the High Priest of the New Law, namely, Christ Himself (ix. 1—x. 18).

C. In the Moral Part (x. 19—xiii. 17) we have the practical consequences of the foregoing doctrines and the moral lessons that are to be deduced from the Epistle, consisting of exhortations to perseverance in faith (x. 19—xii. 29) and to the practice of various virtues (xiii. 1-17). Here the Apostle first exhorts his readers in a general way to the practice of faith, hope, and charity, warning them again of the dreadful consequences of apostasy (x. 19-31), and reminding them of the beautiful constancy in faith, in spite of persecution, which they exhibited in the early part of their Christian lives (x. 32-39). Since faith is so important, he then proceeds to describe it, and to show its fruits and efficacy by an appeal to the glorious faith of the ancient Patriarchs, Abel, Henoch, Noe, Abraham, etc. (xi. 1-40). From this he draws the conclusion that his readers must imitate the faith of these heroes of the past and bear their sufferings bravely (xii. 1-13) ; they must seek after peace with all men, and pursue holiness and practise vigilance (xii. 14-29) ; they must exercise themselves in the virtues of charity and chastity, and fly covetousness (xiii. 1-6) ; finally, they must remember the teaching they have received and be obedient to their prelates, who have to render an account of their souls (xiii. 7-17).

D. In the Conclusion (xiii. 18-25) the Apostle begs the prayers of his readers and prays for them (xiii. 18-21) ; he asks them to accept his "word of consolation," tells them that Timothy is set free, expresses his hope of coming to them soon, and terminates with the salutations of "the brethren from Italy" and his Apostolic blessing (xiii. 22-25).

BIBLIOGRAPHY

For a fairly complete bibliography on this Epistle, extending from the Patristic age to recent times inclusively, see that by E. Jacquier in Vigouroux's *Dict. de la Bible,* vol. III, coll. 551–552. In particular we would draw attention to the commentaries by St. Chrysostom, St. Thomas and Cardinal Cajetan, among the older Catholic works; and to the following by more recent Catholic writers: Ribera, *Comm. in Epist. ad Hebræos* (Salamanca, 1598); Tena, *Comm. et disputatio in Epist. ad Hebr.* (Toledo, 1611); Klee, *Auslegung des Briefe an die Hebr.* (Mainz, 1833); Maier, *Komm. über den Briefe an die Hebr.* (Freiburg, 1861); Zill, *Der Brief an die Hebr., etc.* (Mainz, 1879); Paneck, *Comm. Beati Pauli Apost. in Epist. ad Hebr.* (Innsbrück, 1882); Schäfer, *Erklärung des Hebr.* (Münster, 1893); Padovani, *Comm. in Epist. ad Hebr.* (Paris, 1897); Huyghe, *Comm. in Epist. ad Hebr.* (Ghent, 1901); Heigl, *Verfasser des Briefes an die Hebr.* (Freiburg, 1905); Seisenberger, *Erlärung des Briefes an die Hebr.* (Ratisbon, 1909); Sales, in *La Sacra Bibbia,* vol. II (Turin, 1914); Boylan, in *The Westminster Series* (London, 1924).

Of the many recent non-Catholic commentators on this Epistle we would mention the following: M'Call (London, 1871); Moulton (London, 1878); Farrar, in *Cambridge Greek Test.* (Cambridge, 1893); Meyer-Weiss (6th ed., Göttingen, 1897); Westcott (3rd ed., London, 1906); S. C. Gayford, in *A New Comm. on Holy Script.* (New York, 1928); H. T. Andrews, in *Abingdon Bible Comm.* (New York, 1929).

The Epistle to The Hebrews

CHAPTER I

1. God who, at sundry times, and in divers manners, spoke in times past to the fathers by the prophets, last of all,

1-3. With no personal references or salutations, as was customary in ordinary letters, the author here plunges at once into the theme of his book, stating immediately the thesis he intends to prove, namely, that the New Covenant is more excellent than the Old Covenant. The writer here replies to the twofold question: What is the relation between the Old Testament and the New, between Christ and God? The revelation of the Old Testament was fragmentary and piecemeal, having been given at widely separated times, through a great variety of means and agents, and at most it was incomplete; whereas the revelation of the New Testament is complete and final, having been given to the world through God's own Son, whom the Father made the heir of all things, through whom the world was created, who is of the very essence of Divinity and conserves and sustains all creation, and who, having redeemed mankind, is now seated as man in the place of honor and majesty at the Everlasting Father's right hand.

1. **God.** By the use of this term the author, from the very outset of his letter, professes his belief in and assures his readers of the divine origin of the Old Testament Dispensation; the same God who spoke of old through the Prophets has spoken of late through His Son.

At sundry times, etc. The meaning is, fragmentarily, by many partial revelations; and by a great variety of methods and means of communication. God revealed Himself and His will gradually, part by part, according to the increasing capacity and fitness of the human race to receive His unveiling. Under the pre-Gospel dis-

2. In these days hath spoken to us by his Son, whom he hath appointed heir of all things, by whom also he made the world.

pensations He spoke first to Adam, then to Noe, then to a great array of succeeding messengers, like Abraham, Isaac, Jacob, Moses, David, and the long line of Prophets strictly so called; and His message to these patriarchs, legislators, historians, and seers was delivered in many ways—by words, by dreams, by visions, by symbolic actions, and the like.

In times past, i.e., under the old dispensations; the writer has especially in mind the Old Testament Dispensation, from Abraham, the Father of the Hebrew people, to Malachy, the last of the Old Law Prophets.

The fathers, i.e., the ancestors of the writer and the readers of this Epistle.

Prophets. The term is here used in a wide sense, embracing all those who, before the Gospel era, received revelations from God to be communicated to mankind.

2. In contrast with the many mediums and methods employed for communicating divine messages to man under the Old Testament Dispensation, the Gospel revelation has been made through one person and in one way only, namely, through Christ, the Incarate Son of God. The superiority and finality of the new revelation are here set over against the fragmentariness and incompleteness of the previous revelations.

In these days, i.e., in the period which has succeeded to the era of the Prophets and inaugurated the Messianic age. This period is also called "the fullness of time" (1 Cor. x. 11; Gal. iv. 4; 2 Tim. iii. 1), because in it God has given His complete and final revelation, a revelation to which nothing shall be added in this world, though it will be more and more unfolded and explained by the teaching of the Church as time goes on and as necessity requires.

By his Son. Literally, "in a Son," i.e., in one who, unlike the Prophets, had the very nature of God Himself, and who consequently is the natural "heir of all things." But the Son whom the Father "hath appointed heir of all things," i.e., the Lord Jesus Christ, has two natures, divine and human; and according to His divine nature He needed not to be made an heir, but was from eternity the natural heir of the Father, whose common essence,

3. Who being the brightness of his glory, and the very image of his substance, and upholding all things by the word of his power, having made a
purgation of sins, sitteth on the right hand of the majesty on high,

power, dominion, etc. He shared.   It was, therefore, according to
His human nature that the Son was "appointed heir of all things"
by the Eternal Father, received from the Father "all power in heaven
and on earth" (Matt. xi. 27, xxviii. 18; John xiii. 3, xvii. 2), and
had all things put under His feet, as had been promised far back
in Old Testament days (Psalm viii. 8), and as St. Paul has repeatedly taught in his other letters (1 Cor. xv. 26; Eph. i. 22; Phil. ii.
9).   Of course, this supreme and universal dominion over all things
will not be exercised to its full extent by our Lord until His Second
Coming at the end of time (ii. 8 below; 1 Cor. xv. 24 ff.).

By whom also he made the world.   The Son is considered here
according to His divine nature, in which He is equal to the Father,
having the same power and operation.   Creation, like all the works
of God *ad extra,* is common to all the three Divine Persons; and
hence the Son or the Holy Ghost is just as much the efficient cause
of creation as the Father is.   See on Col. i. 16.

The world.   Literally, "the ages," which means all the things
of time.   The *cosmos* is the material world considered in its order,
beauty and harmony.

3. Having spoken in the preceding verse of what the Father has
done for and through the Son, the author in this verse goes on to
describe the Son in Himself, in His relation to the Father, and in
His work and triumph as man.   Two figures are employed to
describe the Son as God; first, He is "the brightness of his glory,"
or better, "the effulgence of his glory," i.e., the shining-forth of the
light and majesty of the Father, somewhat as the light streams from
the sun, though substantially and infinitely more perfectly.   He is
Light of light and God of God, as we say in the Creed.   The same
figure is used in the Book of Wisdom to describe Uncreated Wisdom (Wis. vii. 26).   In this phrase we are taught the following
doctrines: (a) that the Son is consubstantial and co-eternal with
the Father, and yet distinct from Him; (b) that the Son proceeds
from the Father by nature, and not through the Father's free will;
(c) that the Father in generating the Son does not suffer any change
or imperfection.   Cf. St. Thomas and Theophylact, *h. l.*

The very image of his substance.   This second figure used to

describe the Son is different. "Image" here means the impress made
on a seal by a stamp cut by a die, which therefore exactly repro-
duces the original in all its perfection; and the application of the
figure would be that the Son has the same identical nature, substance, perfections, and all else that the Father has, except of
course the relationship of paternity by which He is distinguished
from the Father. Thus, our Lord said to Philip: "He that seeth
me seeth the Father also" (John xiv. 9).

Substance means God's being, nature, essence.

Upholding all things. The writer now begins to describe the
work of the Son, first, as regards all creation, of which He is the
sustainer and conserver (see on Col. i. 17), and then as the Redeemer of man. The Son is not only the creator of the universe,
He is also its conserver, in whom "all things consist" (Col. i. 17).

The word of his power means the command of His power, or
His powerful command, by which He sustains all things.

Having made a purgation of sins means when He had cleansed
mankind from their sins, alluding to the Jewish sacrifices or sin
offerings on the Day of Atonement, when the priest made a purification of sins by sprinkling some of the blood of the victims upon
the mercy-seat.

Sitteth on the right hand. More literally, "sat down," or "took
his seat on the right hand." The metaphor describes our Lord's
entry as man into peaceful and triumphant possession of His kingdom and His session in the highest place of honor next to the
Divinity (see on Eph. i. 20; Col. iii. 1). By His sufferings and
death our Lord not only satisfied for our sins, but also merited for
Himself as man the highest exaltation (see on Phil. ii. 8 ff.; Luke
xxiv. 26).

In these opening verses are indicated the three Messianic offices
of our Saviour: Prophet (ver. 1-2), Priest and King (ver. 3).

CHRIST IS SUPERIOR TO THE ANGELS, 4-14

4-14. With verse 4 begins the Dogmatic Part of the Epistle (i.
4—x. 18), on which see *Introduction*, No. V, B. In these verses
and in Chapter ii the writer shows the superiority of Christ to the
angels, which is his first great argument in proof of his thesis,
namely, the superiority of the New Covenant to the Old. In this

4. Being made so much better than the angels, as he hath inherited a more excellent name than they.

present section he first states his proposition, that Christ is superior to the angels (ver. 4), and then proves it by showing (a) that Christ is the natural Son of God (ver. 5-6), and (b) that the angels are only ministering spirits, whereas Christ is the King, Creator, and triumphant Lord of all things (ver. 7-14).

To appreciate the force of the argument developed in the rest of this and in the following Chapter, we must bear in mind that according to Jewish tradition and belief the old revelation, known as the Old Law, was given by God to Moses on Sinai through the hands of angels (Deut. xxxiii. 2; Acts vii. 53; Gal. iii. 19) and to the people of Israel through Moses, and that, consequently, the angels and Moses were the intermediaries of the Old Law; whereas the new revelation has been given to the world through Christ, who is the Son of God and the Creator of the angels and of all things, and that therefore the New Law must be far superior to the Old Law: the superiority of the medium or mediator proves the superiority of the revelation.

4. **Being made.** Better, "having become," i.e., the Son having become in His human nature, from the first moment of the Incarnation, as much superior to the angels as His name is greater than theirs. According to St. Chrysostom and other Greek Fathers, "having become" here means "having been shown to be." The expression would thus refer to the glorification which our Lord merited by His passion and death (John xv. 8; Rom. i, 4; Phil. ii. 9), by which He was shown to be the true Son of God.

So much, a classic expression in Greek and characteristic of this letter; it is not found in the other Epistles of St. Paul.

Better means a superiority of perfection and excellence. The word occurs thirteen times in this Epistle but only three times in the other Pauline letters, and then somewhat differently.

Hath inherited, as man. See on Phil. ii. 9.

A more excellent name, which was that of Son of God, and which our Lord received according to His human nature from the first moment of the Incarnation, but which according to His divine nature He possessed from eternity. The author says that our Lord "inherited" this name, to show that it was due Him by reason of

5. For to which of the angels hath he said at any time: *Thou art my Son, this day I have begotten thee?* And again: *I will be to him a Father and he shall be to me a Son?*
6. And again, when he brringeth in the first-begotten into the world, he saith: *And let all the angels of God adore him.*

His origin, and not by grace (St. Thomas). The name "angel" means *messenger, legate;* but Jesus Christ has the name of *Son of God*; therefore, His name is far superior to that of the angels.

5. In verses 5-14 the Apostle cites seven texts of the Old Testament, of which the first three prove that our Lord was the true Son of God (ver. 5-6), the next three that He was King and Creator (ver. 7-12), and the last that He is seated on the right hand of the Father (ver. 13-14). These texts constitute five arguments showing the superiority of Christ to the angels.

It may be said here once for all that the author of this Epistle invariably quotes the Old Testament according to the Septuagint version, and never according to the Hebrew original; his Bible was the LXX. And this was the usual practice of St. Paul.

The two texts cited in the present verse are respectively from Psalm ii. 7 and 2 Kings vii. 14. Psalm ii is understood as Messianic in its literal sense throughout the New Testament (Acts iv. 25, 28, xiii. 33; Apoc. ii. 27 ff., xii. 5, xix. 15), and hence in the words, "Thou art my Son, etc.," the Eternal Father is addressing His Son, whom He has begotten from eternity. The expression "this day" signifies the abiding present of eternity, where there is no past or future; the opinion which understands it of the time of our Lord's Resurrection or Ascension has little support.

In the second quotation the Prophet Nathan, speaking in the name of God, is announcing to King David that the honor of building a Temple to God will be reserved to one of his successors, whose throne will be eternal and to whom God will be "a Father, etc." In their literal sense the Prophet's words refer to King Solomon, but in their spiritual sense, which is that intended by the Holy Ghost, they refer to the Messiah, of whom Solomon was a figure and in whom alone they can be understood in their full significance. The argument from these two texts is that, while the angels may be spoken of in Scripture as sons of God in a wide sense, as adopted sons, they are never so addressed in the strict and natural sense of the term in which it is here applied to Christ.

6. **And again.** According to some, these words are used to intro-

7. And to the angels he saith: *Who maketh his angels winds and his minis-ters a flame of fire.*

duce another Scripture quotation, and the words that follow refer to our Lord's First Coming at the time of the Incarnation, which was announced by an angel (Luke ii. 10 ff.); but the majority of interpreters understand the reference to be to our Lord's Second Coming in judgment at the end of the world, and make the verse read: "And when he again bringeth the first-born, etc." The Scripture references are to Psalm xcvi. 7, and the LXX of Deut. xxxii. 43, which describe the Coming of the Lord in judgment. The argument is that God commands the angels to worship Christ, which shows how far they are inferior to Him, who deserves the worship of *latria*. As God, our Lord is the "only-begotten of the Father" (John i. 14), but as man He is "the first-born amongst many brethren," i.e., adopted brethren (Rom. viii. 29).

Into the world, which belongs to the Son by inheritance.

He saith, i.e., God the Father said.

And let all the angels, etc. The "and" is not in Psalm xcvi. 7, but it is in the LXX of Deut. xxxii. 43. The Psalmist, describing Jehovah who comes to judge the world, invites all the angels to adore Him. St. Paul here shows the words have a Messianic sense, and so applies them under divine inspiration to our Lord, true God and true man, the Supreme Judge of the living and the dead.

7. The third argument shows (ver. 7-9) the pre-eminence of the Son over the angels from the fact that they are but servants and ministers of God, essentially changeable in their nature; whereas the Son is an eternal ruler, an anointed king, who Himself is called God.

The reference in this verse is to Psalm ciii. 4, which in the Hebrew does not seem to speak of angels, but of the forces of nature which God uses as His agents. The LXX translators, however, who knew the meaning of the original, and who may have had a different Hebrew MS. before them, interpreted the "messengers" of the Hebrew as "angels"; and St. Paul by his adoption of the LXX rendering shows that such can be the meaning of the original.

And to the angels, etc. The meaning is: "And with reference to the angels he saith."

8. But to the Son: *Thy throne, O God, is for ever and ever: a sceptre of justice is the sceptre of thy kingdom.*

9. *Thou hast loved justice, and hated iniquity: therefore God, thy God, hath anointed thee with the oil of gladness above thy fellows.*

Who maketh his angels, etc., i.e., who makes use of His angels and His ministers as He does of the winds and flaming fire; the angels, like the inanimate things of nature, are but instruments in the hands of God to do the bidding of His will.

8-9. **But to the Son,** etc. The meaning is: "But with reference to the Son," our Lord Jesus Christ, how differently do the Scriptures speak! For the Psalmist, in the Messianic Psalm xliv. 6-7, addresses the Son as God, seated on an eternal throne and holding in His hand a sceptre, the symbol of His regal power which He exercises with justice. This Messiah King, the Psalmist says, has "loved justice," and has come into the world to make men just and to teach them how to live justly by doing the will of God in all things; He has "hated iniquity," and in order to satisfy for man's sins has died on the cross.

Therefore, i.e., for all this justice and faithfulness on the part of the Messiah, God the Eternal Father has "anointed" Him with the oil of coronation and perfect triumph above all the angels. The Psalmist uses the metaphor of anointing here to show that our Lord, the Messiah, was a king and a priest; because it was customary in the Old Testament to anoint kings and priests for their office. As man, our Lord was anointed by the Eternal Father from the first moment of His Incarnation, inasmuch as He then received the plenitude of the graces and gifts of the Holy Ghost; but the crowning here in question probably alludes to the glorification which took place at the Ascension, but which will not be realized in all its fullness till the end of time (1 Cor. xv. 24 ff.; Phil. ii. 8 ff.).

Oil of gladness refers to the perfumed oil which at times in Old Testament days was poured over the head of those who deserved special honor (Ps. ciii. 15; Isa. lxi. 3). Here it signifies the supreme glory and exaltation which our Lord enjoyed after His triumph over suffering and death.

Above thy fellows. The meaning is that the anointing which the Messiah received from the Eternal Father was far superior to that conferred on any kings of earth or angels of heaven or faithful members of His kingdom. The "O God" of verse 8 and the

10. And: *Thou in the beginning, O Lord, didst found the earth; and the works of thy hands are the heavens.*

11. *They shall perish, but thou shalt continue; and they shall all grow old as a garment,*

12. *And as a vesture shalt thou change them, and they shall be changed; but thou art the self-same, and thy years shall not fail.*

13. But to which of the angels said he at any time: *Sit on my right hand, until I make thy enemies thy footstool?*

14. Are they not all ministering spirits, sent to minister for them who shall receive the inheritance of salvation?

"God" of verse 9 both refer to the Messiah. To translate in verse 8, "thy throne is God," would be possible, but the sense would not be so good.

10-12. The fourth argument is drawn from Psalm ci. 25-28, where the Psalmist is describing Jehovah as the omnipotent and immutable creator of all things, including the angels, and which St. Paul here applies to Christ, showing that Christ is God.

And. After this word we must understand and supply something like the following: "The Scripture says, etc." The heavens and all creatures that God has made will grow old and pass away, but God, the creator of all, remains ever the same.

Shalt thou change them. Literally, "shalt thou roll them up."

13-14. The final argument is taken from the Messianic Psalm cix. 1, which describes the Messiah as a triumphant king seated at the right hand of God in heaven after having subdued all opposition. No such words as those of the Psalmist could ever be addressed to angels. Christ is the author of human salvation; the angels are but ministering spirits sent forth to do God's errands in rendering service to men.

Sent is a present participle in the original, showing the continual ministry of the angels. All the angels are alike in this, that they are ministering spirits, and all their ministries are ordained to the salvation of the elect.

CHAPTER II

APPLICATION OF THE PRECEDING ARGUMENT, 1-4

1. Therefore ought we more diligently to observe the things which we have heard, lest perhaps we should let them slip.
2. For if the word spoken by angels became steadfast, and every transgression and disobedience received a just recompense of reward,
3. How shall we escape if we neglect so great salvation? which having begun to be declared by the Lord, was confirmed unto us by them that heard *him*,

1-4. The Apostle interrupts the line of his argumentation to make a practical application in these verses of the dogmatic teaching he has just given. Since Christ is far superior to the angels, it follows that we ought to give much greater heed to His doctrines than to those of the Old Law, which was revealed through the medium of angels. If transgression and neglect of the former Dispensation were so severely punished, what will be the chastisement for disregard of this new means of salvation, which was first proclaimed by the Lord Himself, then passed on to others, and all along has been confirmed by miracles and the outpouring of the Holy Spirit?

1. **Therefore,** i.e., because of the more excellent character of the New Law.

Which we, etc., i.e., which we Christians have received through the Gospel.

Lest perhaps, etc. Better, "lest we drift away," under the stress of persecution.

2-3. **The word spoken by angels,** etc. According to Jewish belief and teaching the Old Law was delivered through the instrumentality of angels (Deut. xxxiii. 2; Ps. lxvii. 17; Acts vii. 53; Gal. iii. 19).

Became steadfast, etc., i.e., had such a sanction that all its transgressions were severely punished. If such was the binding force of the Old Law, how shall we Christians escape severe punishment if we neglect so great a means of salvation as that provided in the

4. God also bearing them witness by signs, and wonders, and divers miracles, and distributions of the Holy Ghost, according to his own will.

5. For he hath not subjected unto angels the world to come, whereof we speak.

Gospel of Christ? This Gospel was first promulgated by the Lord Himself, and was afterwards "confirmed unto us, etc.," i.e., was made certain to us Christians by the Apostles of that same Lord.

All non-Catholic scholars take this last statement of verse 3 as a certain proof that this Epistle was not written by St. Paul, who always insisted on the primary, direct, and independent character of the Gospel he preached (Acts xxii. 10, xxvi. 16; Gal. i. 1, 12; 1 Cor. xi, 23, xv. 3, etc.). On the assumption, however, that the Epistle was addressed to the Christians of Jerusalem, the statement is a natural deference to the testimony of those who had heard and associated with our Lord in the flesh.

4. The preaching of the Gospel by the Apostles was accompanied by divine interventions manifested through miracles (Acts ii. 22; Mark xvi. 29; Rom. xv. 19; 2 Cor. xii. 12; 2 Thess. ii. 9) and the outpouring of the gifts of the Holy Ghost (1 Cor. vii. 17, xii. 8 ff.; Rom. xii. 3).

Divers miracles. More literally, "manifold deeds of power."

ANOTHER PROOF OF CHRIST'S SUPERIORITY TO THE ANGELS, 5-9

5-9. The Apostle here returns to the argument broken off at i. 14, and gives an additional proof to show that Christ is superior to the angels, namely, because He is to be Lord of the world to come, that is, of the Messianic Kingdom, as is clear from the spiritual sense of Psalm viii. For a brief space of time Christ humbled Himself in His sufferings even below the angels, but this was only that He might triumph in the end as Lord of all.

5. **For.** The thought now goes back to i. 14, though we may establish a very good connection between this verse and what immediately precedes as follows: those who offend against the Gospel Dispensation will be more severely punished than were those who sinned against the Old Law, because Christ is the head of the Messianic Kingdom, and it is clearly worse to sin against the Head and Master than against the servants of the Master (cf. St. Thomas, *h. l.*).

6. But one somewhere hath testified, saying: *What is man, that thou art mindful of him: or the son of man, that thou visitest him?*

He hath not subjected, etc., i.e., God the Father has not made subject to angels but to Christ the Messianic Kingdom, which begins with the Church Militant in this world and is perfected in the Church Triumphant in the next world.

The world to come was a common phrase among the Jews to signify the Messianic Kingdom, as when Isaias foretold that the Messiah was to be "father of the world to come" (Isa. ix. 5).

6-8. In these verses the Apostle cites Psalm viii. 5-7, which in its spiritual sense proves that the Messianic world is to be subject to Christ and not the angels. Literally, the Psalmist is speaking of mere man and the natural world, and he is saying that as compared with God, and materially as compared with the physical universe around him, man is indeed insignificant; but when considered as made in the image and likeness of God, as the recipient of God's supernatural gifts and as possessing a spiritual and immortal soul, he is only a little less than the angels and is superior to all material creation. And even though man, in his present fallen condition, has lost control of material things and has to some extent become enslaved by them, he will regain in his glorified state the dominion over the material world which at first was his in the state of innocence.

In the spiritual sense of these verses of Psalm viii, which the Apostle is here applying, the Psalmist is speaking of the ideal man, Christ Jesus, and of the Messianic world; and he means to say that as man, as to His human nature, Jesus was inferior to God, and in the humiliation and suffering of His humanity He was even below the angels; but that through suffering and death He attained to a glory and honor far superior to that of angels and became the supreme Head and Lord of the Messianic Kingdom, with all creatures beneath His feet.

6. **But one somewhere,** etc., i.e., the Psalmist in Psalm viii. 5-7, which was well known to the Jews, and which St. Paul had already made use of in a Messianic sense in 1 Cor. xv. 26-28 and in Eph. i, 22.

Son of man means the same as "man," to which it is parallel.

That thou visitest him, with so many graces and blessings.

7. *Thou hast made him a little lower than the angels: thou hast crowned him with glory and honor, and hast set him over the works of thy hands:*
8. *Thou hast subjected all things under his feet.* For in that he hath subjected all things to him, he left nothing not subject to him. But now we see not as yet all things subject to him.

9. But we see Jesus, who was made a little lower than the angels, because of the suffering of death, crowned with glory and honour, that, through the grace of God, he might taste death for all.

7-8. In the state of innocence man held in control all material things, all of which were subject to him.

A little, i.e., in degree; but in the application to Christ the meaning is for a "little while," i.e., while in His suffering state our Lord was "a little lower than the angels."

Angels is Elohim in the Hebrew, meaning *God*; but that the signification here is *angels* we are assured by the LXX and the Targum.

Thou hast crowned him with glory and honor. In their application these words refer to our Lord's resurrection and ascension, upon which have followed the preaching of the Gospel and the glorification of the Saviour throughout the world by all peoples.

And hast set him over the works, etc. This clause is not in some of the best MSS., and so is probably a gloss here introduced from Psalm viii.

But now we see not as yet, etc. Man in his glorified state will regain the dominion over nature and the material world which he enjoyed in the state of innocence but lost by sin. In a similar way, all things are not yet perfectly subject to the rule of Christ, since sin and infidelity rebel against His authority; but there will come a time when He will exercise His supreme sovereignty, when all the just will freely obey Him forever and the unjust will be forced to submit to Him.

9. In this verse we are told the reason for our Lord's humiliation in His Incarnation, earthly life, passion, sufferings, and death; He thus was made a little lower than the angels, that is, for a short time He was made inferior to the angels, in order that by "the grace of God," i.e., as a gratuitous gift of God, He might merit His own exaltation as man and our salvation (see Luke xxiv. 26; Phil. ii. 8 ff.).

Might taste death is a Semitic figure of speech, meaning *to die.*

10. For it became him, for whom *are* all things, and by whom *are* all things, when he was bringing many children into glory, to perfect through suffering the author of their salvation.

11. For both he that sanctifieth, and they who are sanctified, *are* all of one. For which cause he is not ashamed to call them brethren, saying:

For all, i.e., for all men; our Lord died for all men without exception (see on 1 Tim. ii. 6).

WHY CHRIST SUFFERED, 10-18

10-18. In these remaining verses of Chapter ii the Apostle digresses to explain our Lord's humiliation, why it was that He became incarnate and suffered, thus for a time becoming lower than the angels. It was all for our sake and our salvation. Sorrow, sufferings, and death in our fallen state are necessary conditions of human life; and He who was to be the Saviour of men must share their nature and sad experiences, in order that He might overcome the power of death, the instrument of Satan, that He who was sinless Himself might satisfy for the sins of His brethren and be a rescue for those who are tempted and sorely tried.

10. Here we are told that it was becoming, though not necessary, that God (who is the final as well as the efficient cause of all things), when bringing men to salvation, should will that Christ, the Saviour of men, should share in their common lot of suffering. God could have chosen other means of saving the world, but for His own wise reasons He has made the way of suffering the royal road to glory.

To perfect. The meaning of the Greek is to "lead to a destined goal." This verb occurs nine times in the present letter, but not once in the best reading of the other Pauline Epistles.

The *adduxerat* of the Vulgate is the translation of an aorist participle, but according to the context it would be better rendered by the present tense here. It is a question of leading to salvation in time, rather than in God's eternal decree. See on Eph. ii. 5-7.

11. Having stated the suitableness of the lot of suffering for the Saviour of mankind, the writer goes on now in verses 11-14 to give the first reason for his statement. It is this: Christ has the same nature as men; but men are subject to suffering and death; therefore, it was becoming that Christ should experience suffering and death.

12. *I will declare thy name to my brethren; in the midst of the church will I praise thee.*

13. And again: *I will put my trust in him.* And again: *Behold I and my children, whom God hath given me.*

Both he that sanctifieth, etc., i.e., Christ, the author of our salvation, and those who are saved have the same origin, namely, God; and having consequently the same nature, they belong to the same family and are brethren. Hence it is that the Saviour, though infinitely superior to other men because of the union of the divine and human natures in the one Divine Person of the Word, does not disdain to address men as His brethren, as the Scripture quotations in the two following verses show.

All of one, i.e., from the one God; less probably, from one man, Adam, as some authorities say.

12. This verse is a quotation from the Messianic Psalm xxi. 23. Our Lord Himself quoted from this Psalm while hanging on the cross (Matt. xxvii. 46; John xix. 24). After having described the humiliation and bitterness of His passion in this greatest of the Passion Psalms, the Messiah looked forward to the glorious issue of it all, to His resurrection and triumph, and in praise and thanksgiving to God for His delivery He declares in the present verse that He will proclaim the divine goodness and mercy to His "brethren," i.e., to His disciples, and to all the faithful gathered together for worship. The history of the Christian Church and of the Gospel verify the fulfillment of the Messiah's promise.

13. In two more citations, drawn from Isaias viii. 17-18, the Apostle wishes to show that Christ really partakes of our nature. Isaias was a figure of the Messiah, and so the latter's experience was foreshadowed in that of the former. In the first of these quotations our Lord is represented as showing His need of trusting in God, as Isaias did, thus proving that He had a human nature which was subject to suffering and in need of succor (Matt. xxvii. 43).

In the second citation, which is from Isaias viii. 18, the author draws a parallel between Isaias and his two sons, on the one hand, and the Messiah and His "children," i.e., mankind, whom God had committed to His care, on the other hand; the Messiah bears a relation to men similar to that which Isaias bore to his two sons,

14. Therefore because the children are partakers of flesh and blood, he also himself in like manner hath been partaker of the same, that, through death, he might destroy him who had the empire of death, that is to say, the devil;

15. And might deliver them, who through the fear of death were all their lifetime subject to servitude.

16. For nowhere doth he take hold of the angels, but of the seed of Abraham he taketh hold.

that is, He has their nature, and so must have part in their sufferings and attain His destiny through suffering.

14-15. In this verse the Apostle gives another reason why Jesus should suffer and die like other men, namely, in order to deliver mankind from the bondage of the fear of death.

Because the children (i.e., mankind) **are partakers of flesh and blood,** i.e., have a suffering, mortal nature, the Saviour would also have such a nature and go through the agony of death. These words and those that follow prove the reality of our Lord's human body against the Docetæ, who maintained that the Saviour's body was only a phantasm.

That, through death, he might destroy, etc. It was Satan that led man into sin, and by divine decree the punishment of sin was death (Gen. iii. 19; Wis. ii. 23-24; Rom. v. 12). According to Jewish conceptions, death meant separation from God and interruption of loving intercourse between the soul and its Maker (Num. xvii. 13, xviii. 5; Ps. vi, xxix, etc.); and hence, before Christ came, mankind were in bondage of the fear of death. But by dying our Lord proved that death was the gateway to life and the prelude to a glorious resurrection of the body and a happy eternity (1 Cor. xv. 21 ff.; Apoc. i. 18). Thus, death, Satan's instrument of terror, has been turned into a means of defeat; for by death Christ has fully atoned for man's sin and thrown open wide to all faithful souls the portals of life without end. The verb "might destroy" here is a common one with St. Paul, occurring some twenty-eight times in his other Epistles.

16. In this verse the writer tells us that, since our Lord came to redeem mankind and not angels, He took human and not angelic nature.

For nowhere (οὐ γὰρ δήπου) means "certainly," "surely." The word δήπου is found only here in the Greek Bible.

17. Wherefore it behooved him in all things to be made like unto his brethren, that he might become a merciful and faithful high priest in things pertaining to God, that he might be a propitiation for the sins of the people.

18. For in that, wherein he himself hath suffered and been tempted, he is able to succor them also that are tempted.

Take hold means, literally, "take by the hand," i.e., help, succor; the Saviour came into the world to succor those who had sprung from Abraham, the father of all God's faithful people, of all those who should believe in Him, Jews and Gentiles alike (Rom. iv. 16-17, ix. 6 ff.; Gal. iii. 6 ff., vi. 16).

17. **Wherefore.** The Greek word is common in this Epistle, but it is not found elsewhere in St. Paul. Since Christ came to the world to help men, it was becoming that He should be like them "in all things," except sin (below, iv. 15), that is, He should have the same human nature, be subject to the same trials and sufferings, etc. The expression, "all things," must not be understood to embrace anything incompatible with our Lord's divinity, grace, or mission. Hence not only sin, but also inclination to evil, ignorance, and the like must be excluded from this statement.

That he might become, etc. Here we have still another reason for the humiliation and sufferings of Christ, namely, that He might be able to feel our needs and miseries, and thus be able the more easily to enter into our lives and be our mediator with God. He was to be our "high priest, etc.," i.e., He was to occupy a position in the New Covenant similar to that of the High Priest of the Old Covenant; He was to be, therefore, "merciful" (i.e., full of sympathy and understanding for our needs and miseries) and "faithful" (i.e., trustworthy in the fulfillment of all His duties and functions) "in things pertaining to God" (i.e., in all religious matters that have to do with man's relations to God), the most important of which was to "be a propitiation, etc." (i.e., to offer an atoning sacrifice to God for sin), as the Jewish High Priest's chief function was to offer an atoning sacrifice on the great Day of Atonement "for the sins of the people" (Lev. iv. 15 ff., xxvi. 1 ff.). As the great Jewish sacrifice was a propitiation for the sins of the Jewish people, so the sacrifice which Christ offered was a propitiation for the sins of all mankind; the former was a type of the latter.

18. In the preceding verse the writer touched on the central thought of the whole Epistle, namely, the high-priestly work of

Christ in being a propitiation for our sins. But the motive of the Incarnation was not only to offer an atoning sacrifice for the sins of men, but also in order that the Saviour might Himself enter into our sufferings and trials, so as to be able to succor us who "are tempted," i.e., who are subject to the sorrows and trials of life and death. Temptation as applied to our Lord here does not mean incitement to sin, of which there could be no question, but trial, as in the wilderness and Gethsemane especially, and throughout our Lord's life in general. The thought of this verse is also characteristic of the Epistle.

CHAPTER III

CHRIST IS SUPERIOR TO MOSES, 1-6

1. Wherefore, holy brethren, partakers of the heavenly vocation, consider the apostle and high priest of our confession, Jesus;
2. Who is faithful to him that made him, as was also Moses in all his house.

1-6. Here we have the second great argument in proof of the Apostle's thesis. We must bear in mind that his thesis is the superiority of the New Dispensation to the Old. The argument to prove this in the two preceding Chapters was the superiority of Christ, through whom the New Law was given, to the angels, who were the mediators in the giving of the Old Law (see on i. 4-14). In these opening verses of the present Chapter the argument is that Christ is superior to Moses, the founder of the theocracy, who delivered to the people of Israel the Law received on Sinai.

Since Christ has been proved superior to the angels, it might seem unnecessary to prove that He is superior to Moses; that conclusion ought to follow as an *a fortiori* inference. But it was not so to the Jewish mind, which regarded Moses above the angels; for the Jews thought that through Moses they had received God's final and complete revelation to mankind. It was, therefore, necessary to prove to them that Christ had a greater authority than Moses enjoyed.

1-2. **Wherefore**, i.e., since Christ has our human nature and is our great high priest, full of mercy and compassion for our suffer-

3. For this man was counted worthy of greater glory than Moses, by so much as he that hath built the house hath greater honor than the house.

4. For every house is built by some man; but he that created all things is God.

ings and miseries, the writer invites his readers to fix their eyes on Jesus, who is God's messenger to us and our mediator with God, and who, like Moses, was faithful in fulfilling all His duties. The deduction here is an inference from what has been said in the two previous Chapters.

Holy brethren is a form of address peculiar to this Epistle, but see Rom. i. 7; Eph. i. 1 ff.; Acts ix. 13.

Partakers, etc., i.e., sharers in the faith and grace of Jesus Christ.

Of our confession, i.e., of the faith we profess.

Who is faithful. The readers of this Epistle who were tempted to disloyalty are to keep in view as their model the loyalty of Jesus, "who was faithful to Him that made Him," i.e., who was loyal to God who invested Him with the high offices of "apostle," in preaching God's revelation to the world, and of "high priest," to offer up an atoning sacrifice for mankind.

As was also Moses in all his house, i.e., as Moses was faithful in teaching and governing the people of Israel (Deut. iv. 5; Exod. xl. 16; Num. xii. 7), who were called the house of God, as in verse 6 below the Christian society is called the family of Jesus Christ (cf. 1 Tim. iii. 15; Eph. ii. 21; 1 Peter iv. 17, where the Christian community is spoken of as the house of God). It is to be noted that Christ's superiority as regards God's people is far greater than that of Moses; for Moses was faithful *in* all the house of God as a servant (ver. 5), whereas Christ was faithful *over* the whole house of God as the son in his own house (ver. 6).

3-4. For goes back to "consider" of verse 1.

This man, i.e., Jesus. The Apostle's first argument here is as follows: Moses was only a part of God's house, that is, of the House of Israel in its covenant relation, though he was indeed a principal part as being God's direct representative and administrator in the whole theocratic family; but Jesus Christ was the builder, that is, the creator and establisher of the whole family of God including Moses, and is consequently deserving of so much greater honor than Moses as the architect is far superior to the thing he has made.

5. And Moses indeed was faithful in all his house as a servant, for a testimony of those things which were to be said;

6. But Christ as Son over his house: which house we are, if we hold firm to the end our confidence and the boasting of our hope.

Hath built. The Greek verb means not only to build, but to furnish and establish.

Every house is built by some man, etc. In Chapter i Jesus was described as the creator of the world; here He is spoken of as the builder of the family or community of God. God has made the Church, as He made the universe, through Christ. In this family of God Moses was but the chief administrator of the orders and sovereign will of Jesus Christ.

5-6. The second argument here is this: Moses was only a servant in the family of God; Christ was the Son of God in that family, and as such heir and master of it.

His house in both verses means God's house, which is the Church. There is continuity and identity, along with development, in God's house both under the Old and under the New Covenant; the Jewish Church was the type, the Christian Church is the anti-type of the same divine establishment.

For a testimony of those things, etc. There are two explanations of this passage: (a) it was the duty of Moses as a servant to make known to the people of Israel all of God's messages to him; (b) the Mosaic legislation and the ceremonies instituted by him pointed to Christ and were a preparation for Christ and the Gospel, and through them, therefore, Moses bore testimony to Christ.

Which house we are, etc. These are familiar Pauline words (cf. 2 Cor. vi. 16; Eph. ii. 21-22). The writer here warns his readers who were in danger of relapse that membership in the house and family of God and the enjoyment of its privileges are dependent on our perseverance in unshaken confidence in the profession of our faith and in the firm hope of future rewards to the end of our lives.

Boasting of our hope (a peculiarly Pauline expression), i.e., boasting that arises from strong hope.

In the Vulgate of verse 6 *sua* should be *eius,* referring to God; and *sumus nos* should be reversed.

7. Wherefore, as the Holy Ghost saith: *Today if you shall hear his voice,*

EXHORTATION TO PERSEVERANCE IN FAITH, 7-19

7-19. Again, as in Chapter ii. 1-4, the writer interrupts his argument to make a practical appeal to his readers (which extends from iii. 7 to iv. 13) to continue firm in their faith, lest they incur a fate similar to that which befell the Israelites of old. Through their unbelief the Israelites of the desert were excluded from entrance into the Promised Land and condemned to die there in their wanderings; they never attained their destined repose in the place which God had prepared for them and wanted them to have, had they remained faithful. In like manner, if Christians lose their faith, they will never know the joy and repose of heaven to which they have been called and of which the Promised Land of Palestine was a type and figure.

This practical exhortation, which runs through the rest of the present Chapter and the greater part of the next, is said to be one of the finest specimens of a sermon or homily and "one of the most perfect examples we possess of the method of preaching in the apostolic age. The author takes a text, expounds its meaning, draws out the ideas involved in it, and then makes a practical appeal to his hearers" (Prof. Andrews, in *Abingdon Bible Commentary, h. l.*).

The exhortation is based on the second part of Psalm xciv, verses 8-11, in which the Psalmist appeals to the people of Israel to give heed to the voice of God and show themselves faithful to the commands of God, lest for their sins they fall under the divine displeasure and punishment, as did the Israelites of old in the desert. In verses 7-11 the Apostle gives the text of the Psalm; in verses 12-14 he applies the words of the Psalm to his readers, showing great concern and fear lest any of them should surrender the Christian faith and revert to Judaism; and in verses 15-19 he explains the meaning of the text, and shows how it was lack of faith on the part of the ancient Hebrews in the desert that excluded them from entrance into the Promised Land.

7. Wherefore. All that follows this word, down to verse 12, is a long parenthesis containing the text of the Psalm; and hence this conjunction does not find its dependent verb till verse 12. The

8. *Harden not your hearts, as at the provocation, in the day of temptation in the desert,*

9. *Where your fathers tempted me with tests and saw my works*

10. *Forty years: For which cause I was offended with this generation, and I said: They always err in heart. And they have not known my ways,*

11. *So I have sworn in my wrath: If they shall enter into my rest.*

connection is as follows: Since no one can belong to the house and family of God unless he remains firm in faith and hope, it is necessary, according to the counsel given in Psalm xciv to the people of Israel, that you Christian brethren should take heed lest any of you abandon the faith you have received.

As the Holy Ghost saith is a regular formula to introduce an inspired Scripture, of which the Holy Ghost is the primary author.

Today is emphatic by its position and means the acceptable time of salvation.

8. **Harden not your hearts,** etc., i.e., do not be stubborn and resist the grace of God appealing to your hearts, as you did at Meribah, the place of strife, and as at Massah, the day of trial, in the desert. In the original Hebrew of the Psalm "provocation" and "temptation" are names of places, Meribah and Massah. At the time in question the Israelites were suffering for want of water in the desert, and they murmured against Moses (Meribah) and tempted God by doubting His providence and His goodness (Massah). See Exod. xvii. 1-7 and Num. xx. 1-13, where these facts are narrated.

9. In this verse God begins to speak to the Israelites in the first person, recalling to their minds how their faithless forefathers "tempted," i.e., put Him to trial by doubting His power and goodness to help them, though they had been witnesses of His miracles in their behalf for forty years.

10. **Forty years.** In the Hebrew text these words are joined to the preceding verse, but in the LXX and St. Jerome they are connected with what follows, meaning that for forty years the Lord was "offended with this generation," i.e., with the faithless Jews in the desert. As a matter of fact, all during their wanderings in the wilderness the Israelites had grieved the Lord by their doubts. Their hearts were perverse, and they paid no heed to God's "ways," i.e., to His precepts, transgressing them at will and in all manners.

11. As a result of their lack of faith, God took a solemn oath

12. Take heed, brethren, lest perhaps there be in any of you an evil heart of unbelief, to depart from the living God.

13. But exhort one another every day, whilst it is called *today,* that none of you be hardened through the deceitfulness of sin.

14. For we are made partakers of Christ; yet so, if we hold the beginning of our substance firm unto the end.

that the Israelites of the desert should all die in their wanderings with the exception of Josue and Caleb, as narrated in Num. xiv. 27 ff., xxxii. 10 ff.; Deut. i. 34.

If they shall enter is a Hebrew idiom meaning, "they shall not enter."

My rest, i.e., the place of repose promised and prepared for them, which in the literal sense was the land of Canaan that the Hebrews were to occupy and enjoy after the fatigue and wanderings of the desert; but in the spiritual sense here applied, "my rest" means celestial beatitude, the eternal Sabbath of heaven, as explained below, in iv. 1-4.

12. The writer now applies the foregoing Psalm verses to his readers (ver. 12-14), warning them in this verse of the danger of apostasy, which, like all personal moral evil, begins in the heart.

13. The Apostle exhorts his readers to give mutual encouragement to one another by word and example constantly throughout their lives, while they have the opportunity: "Whilst you have the light, believe in the light, etc." (John xii. 36; cf. Luke xix. 44).

The deceitfulness of sin. Sin is always a delusion, promising pleasure and satisfaction but leading to sorrow and pain; luring to happiness but terminating in grief. The sin directly in question here is that of unbelief and apostasy, against which the writer is warning.

14. By the faith and grace of Christ to which we have been admitted through Baptism we have become incorporated into Christ, thus partaking of His life and blessings now, with the hope and promise of a fuller share in His divine life hereafter in the world to come; but this is only on condition that we retain unshaken to the end of our lives the foundation of all these present and future graces and benefits, namely, our Christian faith.

If we hold the beginning, etc., i.e., if we hold fast to the faith of which we made profession at the time of our conversion.

Substance is a literal translation of the Greek word here used,

15. While it is said, *Today if you shall hear his voice, harden not your hearts, as at the provocation.*

16. For some who had heard did provoke; but not all that came out of Egypt by Moses.

17. And with whom was he offended forty years? Was it not with them that sinned, whose carcasses were overthrown in the desert?

18. And to whom did he swear, that they should not enter into his rest, but to them that were incredulous?

19. And we see that they could not enter in, because of unbelief.

at least in its later meaning; but according to the sense of the present passage it would probably be rendered better by "confidence."

15-16. In verses 15-19 we have an explanation of the Psalm passage quoted above in verses 7-11. The author tells us who those people were with whom God was angry; they were the people of Israel whom Moses had led out of Egyptian bondage, but whose bones were left bleaching in the wilderness on account of their sins of unbelief.

While it is said. Better, "when it is said." We shall understand these two verses much better if we take them as going together, putting a comma at the end of verse 15, and, with most modern commentators, make verse 16 consist of two interrogations as follows: "Who were they who heard (the voice of God), and provoked (him)? Were they not all those who were led out of Egypt by Moses?" Of the 600,000 Israelites that were led out of Egypt, only Josue and Caleb remained faithful and were permitted to enter the Promised Land (Num. xiv. 38; Josue xiv. 8-9).

17. Those Israelites who sinned by unbelief in the desert perished there in the wilderness, and their corpses were left to rot in the sun. See Num. xiv. 29, with which compare 1 Cor. x. 5, 8.

18. **Incredulous,** better, "disobedient." The Israelites were not only unbelieving, but disobedient; and for these sins they were excluded from the land which God had promised them (Exod. xvi, xvii; Num. xiv, xxi).

19. **We see,** etc., i.e., we know from history. They tried to enter the Promised Land, but the favor of God was not with them and all the adults failed and perished in the desert, except Josue and Caleb (Num. xiv. 28-5).

CHAPTER IV

GOD'S REST STILL AWAITS THOSE WHO WOULD ENTER INTO IT, 1-13

1-13. The writer warns his readers not to miss the opportunity of entering into God's rest; for the promise still holds good, and we who have heard the Gospel message have the chance which the ancient Israelites lost through lack of faith. By embracing the faith we have taken the first step toward making the promised rest our own. God's promise of rest for His people is enduring, and it has been renewed in different ages. God Himself entered upon it at the completion of the work of creation, but He wants to share it with humanity. It was offered to the Israelites of old, but they missed it through disobedience and unbelief. Again it was repeated in the time of David, but without avail. And the very fact that the promise was repeated in the Davidic period, long after the occupation of Palestine by Josue, shows that the rest in question meant more than the possession of the land of Canaan; it is nothing less than a sharing in God's sabbath-rest, which began at the close of creation (ver. 1-10).

The author then seriously admonishes his readers to see that they do not lose their opportunity as did their forefathers. And he warns them that the word of God (that is, the revelation God has given to mankind) is an energizing, penetrating message; it is like a two-edged sword, having one edge of promise and hope, the other of judgment and retribution; it covers man's exterior actions and conduct, and also judges the very thoughts and intentions of his heart and mind. Nothing, he says, is hidden to God; our very souls are naked before the eyes of Him to whom we must give an accounting (ver. 11-13).

The inference from these final words is that, to be condemned, it is not necessary that we be guilty of open disloyalty, unbelief or apostasy, since mere internal acts of this kind are enough to bring us under God's judgment of condemnation.

1. Let us fear therefore lest the promise being left of entering unto his rest any of you should be thought to be wanting.

2. For unto us also it hath been declared, in like manner as unto them. But the word of hearing did not profit them, not being mixed with faith in those things they heard.

3. For we who have believed, are entering into rest; as he said: *So I have sworn in my wrath: If they shall enter into my rest;* and this indeed though the works from the foundation of the world were finished.

1. The readers are warned not to miss their opportunity of entering into God's promised rest, for the promise still holds good.

The promise being left, i.e., being still unrealized.

2. Here the writer tells his readers that to them, as well as to the ancient Israelites, the glad tidings of a future rest have been preached, and that the latter missed their chance because they received the message without faith; they did not believe the things they heard. Faith in the hearer is as necessary as in the preacher, if supernatural results are to be obtained.

Not being mixed with faith, etc. The best reading here has: "Since it was not united with faith in those who heard," i.e., since those who heard the promise of rest did not have faith in it.

3. Here the Apostle tells us that "we who have believed," i.e., we who have accepted the Gospel, have already fulfilled the condition of entering into God's rest, which is eternal beatitude; for the Psalmist informs us in Psalm xciv that God took an oath to exclude from His rest the Israelites of the desert because of their disbelief, not because the promise of the rest was not still open to those who would fulfill its conditions, since indeed it had been open from the beginning, from the day on which God finished the work of creation.

So I have sworn, etc., a quotation of Psalm xciv. 11, where the Psalmist says that God took a solemn oath to exclude from His rest the ancient Israelites because of their lack of faith (see on iii. 11). The Psalmist's exhortation to his contemporaries not to harden their hearts and thus incur exclusion from God's rest is a proof that the rest in question was something beyond the land of Canaan, which they already possessed; it was a sharing in that rest which God had entered upon at the completion of the work of creation, namely, celestial beatitude.

The *ingrediemur* of the Vulgate should be present tense, as in the Greek.

4. For somewhere he spoke of the seventh day thus: *And God rested the seventh day from all his works.*

5. And in this *place* again: *If they shall enter into my rest.*

6. Seeing then it remaineth that some are to enter into it, and they, to whom it was first preached, did not enter because of unbelief,

7. Again he fixes a day, saying in David, *Today,* after so long a time, as it is above said: *Today if you shall hear his voice, harden not your hearts.*

8. For if Josue had given them rest, he would never have afterwards spoken of another day.

9. There remaineth therefore a sabbath-rest for the people of God.

10. For he that is entered into his rest, the same also hath rested from his works, as God did from his.

4-5. The last words of the preceding verse are now explained by citing two texts of Scripture, the first from Gen. ii. 2 (where it is said that the rest of God began at the completion of the work of creation) and the second from Psalm xciv. 11 (where God said that the disbelieving Israelites should not have part in His rest).

For somewhere, i.e., in Gen. ii. 2. See on ii. 2 above.

God rested, i.e., He ceased to create.

And in this place again, i.e., in Psalm xciv. 11.

If they shall enter, etc., i.e., they shall not enter, as in verse 3 above and in iii. 11.

6-10. In these verses the writer tells his readers that God intended His rest for some, at least, and that those who were first invited to share it came short of it through unbelief. Hence it was, he says, that centuries later, in the time of David, the invitation was again issued; and this later call, so long after the entrance into Canaan under Josue, showed that the rest intended was not the mere possession of the country of Palestine, but a sharing in God's own eternal rest, on which He entered at the close of the work of creation.

Unbelief. Better, "disobedience."

Saying in David, i.e., in the Psalm attributed to David, namely, in Psalm xciv.

For if Josue had given them rest, etc., i.e., if the promised rest had been limited to the land of Canaan, God would not have issued another invitation, as He did through the Psalmist.

A sabbath-rest for the people of God, i.e., for Christians. The word "sabbath" means rest from labor; Christians have the opportunity through faith of participating in God's own eternal and

11. Let us therefore strive earnestly to enter into that rest, lest any man fall into the same example of unbelief.

12. For the word of God is living and effectual, and more piercing than any two-edged sword, and reaching unto the division of the soul and the spirit, of the joints also and the marrow, and is a discerner of the thoughts and intents of the heart.

13. Neither is there any creature invisible in his sight; but all things are naked and open to his eyes, to whom our speech is.

blessed rest. From verse 10 it is clear that the eternal rest of God is not secured merely by embracing the faith, but presupposes and follows upon labor in faith; as God rested only after labor, so it must be with us.

11. In verses 11-13 the Apostle concludes the exhortation begun in iii. 7 above. Since so great a reward is waiting for us in the hereafter, we should exert every effort to attain it, remembering the terrible fate that befell the ancient Israelites for their disbelief.

12. Here and in the following verse the writer gives the reason why we should strive with all our might to enter into the rest to which God has invited us. For God has not spoken in vain; His "word" (i.e., the manifestation of His will in revelation) is not dead and inert, but "living," like God Himself, and "effectual" (i.e., producing its effect in reward or punishment) and "more piercing, etc." (i.e., penetrating more deeply into our whole being), than any two-edged sword can penetrate the human body, thus searching the inmost thoughts of the mind and emotions of the heart.

Soul and spirit are but two aspects of the same principle, the former being the source of physical and sensible life and the latter the source and spring of the higher, intellectual life.

13. The thought passes from God's word of revelation to God Himself. As God's word penetrates the soul through and through, so does His gaze; He and His word are alike in searching the whole being of every creature.

Open. More literally, "laid bare." The metaphor is taken from the sacrificial altar, and means to bend back the neck of the sacrificial victim so as to expose the throat fully, in order that the priest or offerer might cut the throat.

To whom our speech is. These words are best explained by the Greek Fathers, St. Thomas, and others, who take them to mean: "to whom we must render an accounting" in the judgment of all our thoughts and actions.

14. Having therefore a great high priest that hath passed through the heavens, Jesus the Son of God, let us hold fast our confession.

Verses 12-13 here should be compared with Isaias xlix. 2, lv. 10-11. Wis. vii. 22-23, xviii. 15-16, Prov. v. 4, Eph. vi. 17, Apoc. ii. 16, xix. 15, with which they have many points in common.

CONFIDENCE IN CHRIST, THE HIGH PRIEST OF THE NEW DISPENSATION, 14-16

14-16. In these verses the Apostle introduces his third principal argument to prove the superiority of the New Dispensation to the Old, namely, the High-priesthood of Christ, which he had already mentioned in ii. 17 and iii. 1, but which will now occupy the rest of the dogmatic part of the Epistle (iv. 14—x. 18). He has proved so far that Christ, the Mediator of the New Dispensation, is superior to the angels (i. 4—ii. 18) and to Moses (iii. 1—iv. 13), who were the intermediaries in the giving of the Old Law. Now he will show that the priesthood of Christ is far more excellent than the priesthood of the Old Law (iv. 14—x. 18).

In the remaining verses of the present Chapter the Apostle says that, since we now have a High Priest who has passed into the very presence of the Father and who has sympathy for us, having experienced all our sorrows save sin, we must approach the throne of grace with all confidence, so as to receive mercy and the grace we need.

14. **Having therefore,** etc., i.e., in view of what has been said above (ii. 17, iii. 1), it is clear that we have a High Priest, and indeed a great High Priest, who is far superior to the angels and Moses of the Old Law. And in contrast with the High Priest of the Old Dispensation, who was accustomed once a year on the Day of Atonement to pass behind the veil of the Temple into the Holy of Holies, into the presence of the Ark which was a symbol of the divine presence, this High Priest of the New Dispensation, who is Jesus the Son of God, "hath passed through the heavens," i.e., behind the curtain which separates this world from the unveiled presence of God, and into the very presence of the Father Himself. Let us, therefore, hold fast to the faith we profess. The readers of the Epistle were in danger of losing their faith.

15. For we have not a high priest, who can not have compassion on our infirmities, but one tempted in all things like as we are, without sin.

16. Let us go therefore with confidence to the throne of grace, that we may obtain mercy and find grace in seasonable aid.

15. And not only has our High Priest entered into the very presence of the Godhead, thereby establishing for us direct communication with the Father, but He also retains close relationship with us and feels for us, because He has lived our life, experienced our sorrows and labors, and has allowed Himself to be tried in all things like ourselves, apart from sin.

Unlike ourselves, who suffer from the effects of original sin, our Lord's temptations were all from without and not at all from within, because there was with Him always perfect harmony between His body and His soul, between His flesh and His spirit. Since our Lord was tempted, He knows how to sympathize with us in our temptations; and since He was sinless, He is able powerfully to plead for us.

16. As our High Priest is seated in the presence of the Father, enthroned above the heavens, and yet is able to sympathize with us and knows all our needs, we can go with confidence to His throne of grace, seeking mercy for our infirmities and the help we need at all times.

Throne of grace is likely an allusion to the mercy-seat above the Ark, between the wings of the cherubim (Exod. xxv. 21), where God manifested Himself in a special manner.

CHAPTER V

JESUS POSSESSED THE QUALIFICATIONS OF A HIGH PRIEST, 1-10

1-10. Every High Priest must, first of all, have the same nature as those for whom he is to act as priest; secondly, he must be able to understand and have sympathy with human frailty; and thirdly, he must have received a divine call (ver. 1-4). Now all these qualifications were found in Jesus Christ: He was made a priest by the Eternal Father at the time of the Incarnation, when He became the divine mediator between God and man, and in the days of His flesh He showed His love and sympathy for mankind and was perfected as man by suffering, thus, through His sacrifice of

1. For every high priest taken from among men, is appointed for men in the things that appertain to God, that he may offer up gifts and sacrifices for sins,

2. Who can have compassion on them that are ignorant and that err, because he himself also is compassed with infirmity.

3. And therefore he ought, as for the people, so also for himself, to offer for sins.

4. Neither doth any man take the honor to himself, but he that is called by God, as Aaron was.

5. So Christ also did not glorify himself, that he might be made a high priest, but he that said unto him: *Thou art my Son, this day I have begotten thee.*

obedience, becoming the source of eternal salvation for all who follow Him (ver. 5-10).

1. Every High Priest must be chosen by God "from among men," i.e., he must have the same nature as men, and be appointed by God on behalf of men "in the things that appertain to God," i.e., in all that has to do with divine worship, "that he may offer, etc." These last words indicate the principal function of the High Priest.

Gifts and **sacrifices,** when used together as here, mean respectively offerings of inanimate objects (such as grain and the fruits of the earth) and animal sacrifices. Taken together, they embrace the whole range of Jewish sacrifices, but the second term here is restricted to sin offerings.

2. **Have compassion.** Literally, "feel for with moderation," "be gentle with."

Ignorant and that err, i.e., those who do not well understand their duty and who are seduced by passion.

With infirmity, moral as well as physical, as is evident from the following verse. There is question of the Jewish High Priest.

3. Not only the Jewish High Priest but also the other priests of the Old Dispensation were under the necessity of offering sacrifices for their own sins, as well as for those of the people (Lev. iv. 3-12, xvi. 6-11). Our Lord, being sinless, is the perfect High Priest to plead for His people.

4. No man should take upon himself the dignity of the priesthood, thus becoming the representative of men with God, unless he has received a divine call, such as was given to Aaron and his sons (Exod. xxviii. 1 ff., xxix. 4 ff.; Num. iii. 10, xvii. 6, 8, etc.).

5. In verses 5-10 the Apostle applies to our Lord the qualifications of a true High Priest, beginning with the last mentioned, and

6. As he saith also in another place: *Thou art a priest for ever, according to the order of Melchisedech.*

7. Who in the days of his flesh, with a strong cry and tears, offering up prayers and supplications to him that was able to save him from death, was heard for his reverence.

showing in this and the following verses how our Lord was called to the priesthood by God. The writer insists on the proof of our Lord's call because, according to His human nature, He was descended through King David from the tribe of Juda, and not like the Jewish High Priests from the tribe of Levi.

So Christ also, etc. Even the Son of God, when He became a priest to mediate between God and mankind, did not take that high honor to Himself, but was called to it by His Father, as is proved in the first place from the Messianic Psalm ii. 7. The words of this Psalm here quoted are understood as addressed to our Lord by the Eternal Father at the moment when He became incarnate; for it was then that He became a Mediator between God and man, and so was called to the priesthood. While on earth, our Lord performed priestly functions, offering Himself at the Last Supper and on Calvary; but from verses 9 and 10 here we gather that the official seal, as it were, was not put on His priesthood until after the Resurrection and Ascension.

This day I have begotten thee. Though our Lord was the eternal Son of the eternal Father, He was begotten as man at the moment of the Incarnation.

6. The consecration of our Lord as priest at the moment when He became incarnate is expressly stated in the Messianic Psalm cix. 4, the full significance of which passage is developed in vii. 1 ff. below. Psalm cix is Messianic in its literal sense. In it the Messiah is described as a king, as an eternal priest, and as a powerful conqueror who will subject all things to Himself.

According to the order, etc. The meaning can be: (a) "according to the likeness or type of Melchisedech," as in vii. 11 below; or (b) "according to the manner or style or fashion of Melchisedech," as in vii. 15, 17 below. See on vii. 1 ff.

7. The reference in this verse is to the whole sacrifice of Christ, which began with the agony in the garden and terminated with His sufferings and death on the cross. Compare this and the following verse with Phil. ii. 5 ff.

8. And whereas indeed he was Son, he learned obedience by the things which he suffered:

9. And being consummated, he became, to all that obey him, the cause of eternal salvation,

Who refers to our Lord; and the phrase, "in the days of his flesh," means His human, mortal life, when He shared our common experience of grief, suffering, and death.

Offering up prayers, etc. Perhaps there is no great distinction to be made between "prayers" and "supplications" here, though the former term may be more definite and the latter more general in character. "Supplications" also carries with it here the thought of greater fervor and intensity.

Offering up, as a priest; the word is the same as that used in verse 1 for "offering gifts and sacrifices."

To him that was able, etc., i.e., to God the Father.

From death. Better, "out of death." Our Lord was not saved from dying, which He did not pray for, but from the effects of death, from the corruption and dominion of death; and this latter was the object of His prayer. Others say, however, that the object of our Lord's petition was perfect resignation and submission to the divine will. In either case He "was heard"; for He calmly resigned Himself to the divine will and plan, meeting death without fear, and on the third day He arose to a glorious and immortal life, thus triumphing over death and its powers.

For his reverence. Better, "because of his reverential fear," i.e., because of the fear, combined with reverence, with which He submitted to the divine will.

8. Though our Lord was the Son of God and the Creator of the world, He submitted Himself as man entirely to the Father's will in all things, and learned obedience in an experimental way by the trials and tests of suffering which He endured. It was only experimentally that our Lord could be said to learn anything, for in Him were all the treasures of wisdom and knowledge from the very beginning of His incarnation (see on Col. iii. 3); and hence it was only as His obedience was put to test and trial by actual suffering that He is here described as learning "obedience by the things which he suffered."

9. Our Lord's sacrifice of obedience as man had a twofold effect: for Himself it brought to completion and perfection His experimen-

10. Called by God a high priest according to the order of Melchisedech.

11. Of whom we have much to say, and hard to be intelligibly uttered, because you are become weak to hear.

tal training as a High Priest, which terminated in His resurrection and glorification (Phil. ii. 8 ff.) ; and for man it became the cause and principle of eternal salvation for all those who obey Him, by following His law and practising His precepts.

Being consummated. Better, "being made perfect," as a High Priest; the allusion is to our Lord's glorification after the resurrection.

10. Since our Lord has all the characteristics of a High Priest, He is rightly addressed by the eternal Father as a "high priest according to the order of Melchisedech." These last words serve as a transition to the proof in Chapter vii of the superiority of the priesthood of Christ to the priesthood of the Old Law; but before entering on that proof the writer stops to discuss the sublimity and difficulty of the subject, the slowness and imbecility of his readers, the dangers in which they live, the duty of persevering in the faith, etc. (v. 11—vi. 20).

Called is better rendered "proclaimed," or "designated," or "addressed." The verb occurs only here in the New Testament.

THE DIFFICULTY OF EXPLAINING THE HIGH PRIESTHOOD OF CHRIST, 11-14

11-14. The author says that the High Priesthood of Christ is going to be hard for him to expound, because of its abstruse nature and because of the weakness and slowness of his readers. They have had the faith long enough to be teachers of it themselves, but the actual facts of their condition are that they need someone to teach them the elements of their religion; spiritually they are mere children.

11. **Of whom.** Better, "on which point," referring to the High Priesthood of Christ, of which that of Melchisedech was a type. The subject will be difficult to expound because of its loftiness and because the readers have grown slow and dull of understanding in spiritual matters; they have neglected their faith, and are suffering the consequences.

12. For whereas for the time you ought to be masters, you have need to be taught again what are the first elements of the words of God, and you are become such as have need of milk, and not of strong meat.

13. For every one that is a partaker of milk, is unskillful in the word of justice, for he is a little child.

14. But strong meat is for the perfect, for them who by custom have their senses exercised to the discerning of good and evil.

12. **You have need to be taught,** etc. Perhaps it is better to read, "you have need that someone teach you, etc." The sense is practically the same in either reading.

The first elements of the words of God, i.e., the rudiments of the Christian revelation.

13. Neophytes in the school of God are not able to understand such high doctrines as the High Priesthood of Christ.

The word of justice is thought, more probably from the context, to mean the correct use of ordinary speech; though it may mean the preaching of justice, which is the solid Christian doctrine of the perfect (ver. 14), embracing the whole field of Christian teaching.

14. Solid Christian doctrine is for those who are mature in faith, for those who by long practice and habits have disciplined their minds and hearts so as to be able to distinguish between the true and the false, between moral good and moral evil.

CHAPTER VI

THE ELEMENTS OF THE CHRISTIAN FAITH, 1-3

1-3. The writer has just told his readers that, whereas they should be full-grown men in faith, they are but infants. Now, while exhorting them to advance beyond the rudiments, he repeats the elementary principles of Christian instruction which formed the basis of their first schooling in the doctrines of faith and practice. These principles were: (a) repentance for sins and faith in God; (b) teaching about different kinds of baptism and the laying on of hands; (c) the doctrine of the resurrection and the eternal judgment. These principles represented the minimum of instruction given to all converts and required of a Christian, but the writer

1. Wherefore, leaving the word of the beginning of Christ, let us press on to things more perfect, not laying again the foundation of repentance from dead works, and of faith towards God,

2. Of the doctrine of baptisms and the imposition of hands, and of the resurrection of the dead and of eternal judgment.

3. And this will we do, if God permit.

would have his readers press on to a complete development of them.

1-2. **The word of the beginning of Christ** is a literal translation of the Greek, but the phrase means the elementary teaching concerning Christ.

Not laying again the foundation, i.e., not repeating the elementary instruction which was given to catechumens.

Dead works, i.e., sinful acts and deeds.

Faith towards God, i.e., in the unity and trinity of God, the Creator and Redeemer of mankind.

Baptisms. The plural here may refer to the difference between the Baptism of Christ, on the one hand, and that of John and the various Jewish washings, on the other hand; or to the triple immersion which was a characteristic feature of the rite in the beginning.

Imposition of hands, i.e., Confirmation, which in early times followed immediately after Baptism.

Resurrection and eternal judgment, pertaining to the end and final goal of life, were naturally included in the instruction given to catechumens.

3. **And this will we do,** i.e., "press on to things more perfect," to a fuller understanding of the teachings of Christ (ver. 1).

THE PERIL OF APOSTASY, 4-8

4-8. In these verses the Apostle stresses the hopeless condition of those who, having embraced the Christian faith and tasted its supernatural fruits, fall away from it, thus crucifying anew the Son of God and making a mockery of Him (ver. 4-6). He concludes his warning by an illustration drawn from nature: those who embrace the faith and keep it are like a fertile field which absorbs the rain and produces fruit, and receives in turn a blessing; while they who yield no fruit of faith and grace are like a barren land, useless in God's sight, and deserving only His curse (ver. 7-8).

4. For it is impossible for those who were once illuminated, have tasted also the heavenly gift, and were made partakers of the Holy Ghost,

5. And have tasted the good word of God, and the powers of the world to come,

6. And have fallen away, to be renewed again to penace, crucifying again to themselves the Son of God, and making him a mockery.

4-6. The Apostle is describing here the blessings of the call to Christianity; and he says that those who have once experienced them and have given them up to the extent of rejecting the primary truths and principles of Christian teaching, are beyond the hope of salvation, simply because they have willfully thrown over the essential means of saving their souls.

For it is impossible, etc. The completion of this sentence is in verse 6, "to be renewed again, etc." The majority of the older Fathers and commentators understood the Apostle to be speaking here of the impossibility of receiving a second time the Sacrament of Baptism, once the Christian faith with all its implications had been abandoned. But St. Jerome and nearly all modern expositors believe there is question in this passage of the moral impossibility of recalling to repentance those who have willfully given up the faith; it is not because they *cannot* be reclaimed, but because they *will not*—they do not want to be recalled from their second sleep of death.

Illuminated, by the reception of Baptism, which translated them from the realm of darkness to the region of light.

The heavenly gift, i.e., the graces and benefits of redemption.

Partakers of the Holy Ghost, i.e., sharers in the gifts and charisms of the Holy Spirit, which were imparted in Confirmation.

And have tasted the good word of God, i.e., have experienced the sweetness of the graces of the Gospel.

The powers of the world to come, i.e., the powers of healing, casting out evil spirits, and working miracles in general, which were possessed by the early Christians.

And have fallen away, i.e., committed the sin of apostasy, totally and finally rejecting the Christian religion with all its spiritual graces and blessings.

To be renewed again, etc. This translation, which follows the Vulgate, is entirely wrong and misleading; the verb is active in the Greek, and so gives the meaning that the impossibility in question

7. For the earth that drinketh in the rain which cometh often upon it, and bringeth forth herbs meet for them by whom it is tilled, receiveth blessing from God.

8. But that which bringeth forth thorns and briers, is reprobate, and very near unto a curse, whose end is to be burnt.

9. But, beloved, we hope of you the better things and nearer to salvation, though we speak thus.

is on the part of the preacher, and not on that of the believer. The meaning is that it is morally impossible for a preacher to awaken again to repentance those who have willfully rejected the Gospel after having once fully accepted it and experienced its wondrous gifts and blessings. Such conscious perverts, as far as in them lies, repeat the crucifixion of Christ and expose again to the scorn and mockery of the unbelieving world the Christ who died for us all. Their sin is like that against the Holy Ghost (Matt. xii. 31 ff.) ; it is an open offence against the known truth and manifest light.

To themselves, i.e., to their own destruction.

The connection between these verses and those that immediately precede is this: Let us pass over the elementary teachings about Christ, which are superfluous for the believing and useless for those who have apostasized. It is impossible by an elementary instruction to call the latter back to faith, for they have received that instruction and have willfully turned their backs upon it.

7-8. In these verses the Apostle means to say that those who make use of the gifts of grace which they receive, receive further graces and blessings from God; while they who abuse the gifts of God, become useless and are accursed of the Giver of all good things. Cf. Matt. vii. 17-19.

WORDS OF ENCOURAGEMENT AND HOPE, 9-12

9-12. After the terrifying doctrines of the preceding paragraph concerning those who lapse and give up the faith, the writer now hastens to encourage his readers, assuring them that he does not expect such things of them. God will never forget their love and the charity they have shown to the saints. May they manifest the same eagerness in realizing to the full the meaning of Christian hope, and follow the example of those who through faith and patience have inherited the promises of God!

9. The harsh words just uttered about the lapsed do not apply to the readers of this Epistle, except as a warning of what might

10. For God is not unjust, that he should forget your work, and the love which you have shewn in his name, you who have ministered, and do minister to the saints.

11. And we desire that every one of you shew forth the same carefulness to the accomplishing of hope unto the end,

12. That you become not slothful, but followers of them who through faith and patience inherit the promises.

happen. Therefore, the writer addresses them as "beloved," and can hope from them works fruitful unto salvation.

The *dilectissimi* of the Vulgate should be *dilecti,* as in the Greek.

10. The Apostle's hope for his readers is grounded on their works of charity in behalf of their fellow-Christians, which charity had for its motive the love of God, for the works were performed "in his name." The meaning of the verse is that, in view of the good works of the faithful performed out of love for God, the Lord in justice will give them the grace and help necessary to persevere in the faith.

This verse proves, therefore, that good works done in a state of grace can merit *de condigno* an increase of grace in this life and eternal glory in the life to come.

11-12. While the readers of this Epistle are zealous and active in works of charity, there is reason to exhort them to show equal zeal and confidence as regards hope. They must keep vividly before them at all times the glorious prospects of their future rewards, and not allow tribulations and sufferings to cause them to relax in doing good. Thus they will become imitators of the saints who have gone before them, whose steadfast faith enabled them to triumph over every obstacle and so obtain the rewards which God had promised them. Examples of these heroes will be found in xi. 1 ff. and xii. 1 ff., below.

The *hereditabunt* of the Vulgate should be in the present tense.

THE CERTAINTY OF OUR PROMISED INHERITANCE, 13-20

13-20. Having just spoken of the promises of God, the author now goes on to show the inviolability of God's word of promise. When God promised to bless Abraham and his seed, he says, He confirmed His promise with an oath, so as to make it doubly sure and convincing. When men wish to strengthen a promise by an oath, they call on one greater than they, namely, God, to stand as guarantee of their contract; but since there is no one greater than

13. For God making promise to Abraham, because he had no one greater by whom he might swear, swore by himself,

14. Saying: *Unless blessing I shall bless thee, and multiplying I shall multiply thee.*

15. And so patiently enduring he obtained the promise.

God, the divine promise made to Abraham had to be assured by an oath in which God swore by Himself. Thus, by two unchangeable things, namely, God's promise and the oath by which He made it doubly secure, we Christians are assured of the fulfillment of our hope of future blessedness; for our hope reaches behind the veil that separates this world from the world to come, and has its anchor in eternity, where God who has made the promise dwells, and where Jesus, our Forerunner, has entered to offer to the Father the merits of His sacrifice for us, having become a High Priest forever according to the order of Melchisedech.

13-15. By introducing the case of Abraham the writer wishes to show that the blessings promised Christians are surely attainable through a patient and faithful fulfillment of the obligations which faith imposes upon us here. The example of Abraham proves this, for to him God made the promise with an oath to bless him and his posterity; and this promise in its literal sense was fulfilled at least in part during the earthly life of the patriarch, and in its spiritual sense it has been completely accomplished in the person of Christ and the blessings that the Saviour has brought to the world.

God making promise to Abraham. See Gen. xii. 2-3, xiii. 14-17, xv. 5 ff., xvii. 5 ff., xxii. 16-17.

Unless blessing, etc. This is the Hebrew manner of introducing an affirmative oath, and the repetition of the words gives a superlative meaning; thus, the sense of the passage is: "I will surely bless thee, I will surely multiply thee."

And so patiently enduring, etc. Many years intervened between the promise made to Abraham and the birth of Isaac, the child of promise (Gen. xii. 4, xxii. 5), and yet the faith and hope of the patriarch remained unshaken; but in a spiritual sense the promise began to be realized without delay, for Abraham was justified and saved through the merits of Christ to come (xi. 13, 39, below), and he thus became the father of all that believe (Gal. ii. 16; John viii. 56).

16. For men swear by one greater than themselves, and an oath for confirmation is the end of all their controversy.

17. Wherein God, meaning more abundantly to shew to the heirs of the promise the immutability of his counsel, interposed an oath,

18. That by two immutable things, in which it is impossible for God to lie, we may have the strongest comfort, who have fled for refuge to hold fast the hope set before us,

19. Which we have as an anchor of the soul, sure and firm, and which entereth in even behind the veil;

16-18. In these verses the writer shows that the promise made to Abraham appertains to Christians, for in them it finds its complete fulfillment. Among men, he says, it is customary when making a promise of something serious to take an oath by calling on God to bear witness that they intend to carry out what they have promised, thus making God a party to their contract. An oath thus puts an end to all further controversy, and places a seal on that which is promised. Hence, God, in order to impress on men His determination to bless all the real descendants of Abraham, confirmed and strengthened His promise by an oath, swearing by Himself since there was no one greater by whom to swear. This promise has been fulfilled, and the blessing has been conferred through Christ, the Messiah, through whom faith and grace are given in this life and glory in the life to come.

The heirs of the promise, i.e., faithful Jews, and especially Christians, who by faith are the true descendants of Abraham (Gal. iii. 29).

Two immutable things, i.e., the promise and the oath. God's oath made His promise more secure and certain only in the eyes of men; but He chose this solemn manner of strengthening His promise in the eyes of men, in order that we Christians "may have the strongest comfort" in taking refuge in the hope that God will fulfill His promise of conferring on us eternal rewards (Rom. viii. 24; Col. i. 5). We take refuge in hope of the future life from the sin, sorrow, and trials of the present life.

19. Which, i.e., hope. Our hope is "sure and firm," because it is anchored in heaven, where God is in His heavenly shrine.

Behind the veil, i.e., behind the veil which separates God's presence from this world; the allusion is to the veil which hung before the Holy of Holies in the Temple, into which the High Priest entered once a year, on the Day of Atonement.

20. Where the forerunner Jesus is entered for us, made a high priest for
ever according to the order of Melchisedech.

20. Not only is our hope anchored in the divine presence, in the
heavenly sanctuary, but Jesus our Forerunner has entered there to
prepare a place for us (John xiv. 2-3) and to be our advocate with
the Father (ix. 24, below).

Made a high priest, etc. By these words the writer skillfully
makes a return to the subject of the High Priesthood of Christ,
which was first introduced in iv. 14-16 and continued in v. 1-10,
but interrupted by the long digression of v. 11—vi. 20. This theme
will now be treated in the four following Chapters, up to the end
of the dogmatic part of the Epistle (x. 18).

CHAPTER VII

THE SUPERIORITY OF THE PRIESTHOOD OF CHRIST, 1-28

1-28. The author now returns to the third great argument in
proof of his thesis, that the New Dispensation is superior to the
Old. This argument is based on the superiority of the Priesthood
of Christ to that of the Old Law. The Apostle had already introduced it in iv. 14-16, and had continued it in v. 1-10, but then felt
it necessary to interrupt his main line of thought in order to give
warning of perils to be guarded against and to offer words of
encouragement to his readers. Now, however, he will take up this
argument and show the force it contains for his purpose. First,
referring to the narrative of Gen. xiv. 18-20, he places before us
a picture of Melchisedech, emphasizing those features in the
patriarch which showed the superiority of his type of priesthood
to that of the Levitical order (ver. 1-3). Next he shows the superiority of Melchisedech to Abraham (ver. 4-10). In the third
place, he discusses the inferiority of the Levitical priesthood, which
was superseded by the perfect priesthood of Christ (ver. 11-25).
Finally, summing up his arguments, he shows that Christ is the
ideal High Priest (ver. 26-28).

1. For this Melchisedech *was* king of Salem, priest of the most high God, who met Abraham returning from the slaughter of the kings, and blessed him:

2. To whom also Abraham divided the tithes of all: who first indeed by interpretation, is king of justice, and then also king of Salem, that is, king of peace:

3. Without father, without mother, without genealogy, having neither beginning of days nor end of life, but likened unto the son of God, continueth a priest for ever.

1-2. In these two verses the writer points out the positive outstanding characteristics of Melchisedech: he is a king and a priest, and he receives tithes. His name means "king of justice"; and Salem, his city, means "peace." Therefore, the heavenly attributes of justice (righteousness) and peace are associated with his person, and these are the qualities so often combined in prophetic pictures of the Messiah (Isa. ix. 7, xi.; Psalms lxxi. 1-3, 7, lxxxiv. 10; Zach. ix. 9 ff.; Mal. iv. 2).

It is disputed whether "Salem" stands for Jerusalem or for a town near Sichem in the vicinity of Gerizim. The question is of no importance for the author's argument, whose only point is that the word means "peace."

Most high God means the true God.

Who met Abraham, etc. After Abraham had defeated the hostile kings from the north who had made war on Sodom and carried away plunder and captives from the cities of the plain, and was returning from the neighborhood of Damascus, whither he had pursued the enemy, he passed through the little domain of Melchisedech; and here it was that Bera, King of Sodom, met Abraham and thanked him for his help, and that Melchisedech brought forth bread and wine and blessed Abraham and thanked God for the victory over the invaders (see Gen. xiv. 1-20).

Divided the tithes, etc. In acknowledgment of the blessing he had received, Abraham gave tithes to Melchisedech of all the spoils he had recovered from the defeated foes.

3. The silence of Scripture about the origin and destiny of Melchisedech makes him an appropriate figure of the Son of God, who as God had no mother and as man no father, whose generation no man knows, and whose eternal life is without beginning or end. In the mention of "genealogy" we likely have an allusion to the

4. Now consider how great this man is, to whom even Abraham the patriarch gave tithes out of the principal things.

5. And indeed they that are of the sons of Levi, who receive the priesthood, have a commandment to take tithes of the people according to the law, that is to say, of their brethren, though they themselves also came out of the loins of Abraham.

6. But he, whose pedigree is not numbered among them, received tithes of Abraham, and blessed him that had the promises.

Levitical priesthood, which with scrupulous care had always to trace its descent back to Aaron.

But likened unto the Son of God, i.e., the silence of Scripture about Melchisedech's father, mother, birth and death, when mystically interpreted, gives him an eternal character and makes him eminently typical of the Son of God; and as he was a priest, and Scripture makes no mention of his death, it is understood that he continues a priest forever. The Apostle is here alluding to the directly and universally accepted Messianic Psalm cix, which in verse 4 speaks of the Messiah as a priest forever according to the order of Melchisedech.

4-6. In verses 4-10 the Apostle shows the superiority of Melchisedech to Abraham. So extraordinary was his dignity that "even Abraham the partiarch," i.e., the father of the chosen people of God, paid him tithes "out of the principal things" (literally, "of the top of the heap," i.e., of the best of the spoils which he had taken in war). This act on the part of the founder and father of the Jewish race showed that he recognized in Melchisedech his superior. Unlike the priests of the Levitical order, who had a right under the Law of Moses to exact tithes from their own people, though they themselves were also children of Abraham, this patriarchal priest, who lived before the Law, could require tithes from Abraham, and his right was not questioned. It was the Law of Moses that gave the Levites the right to tithes, whereas Melchisedech had a right independent of and anterior to that Law. Moreover, Melchisedech tithed Abraham himself, whereas the Levites tithed only the children of Abraham. Another sign of the personal dignity of Melchisedech was the blessing that he imparted to the patriarch to whom had been given the divine promises of blessings for all mankind (Gen. xii. 2-3, xiii. 14 ff., xvii. 1 ff., xxii. 15 ff.).

The sons of Levi who receive the priesthood. Not all the

7. And without all contradiction, that which is less is blessed by the better.

8. And here indeed men that die, receive tithes; but there he of whom it is witnessed that he liveth.

9. And, so to speak, even Levi who received tithes, paid tithes in Abraham;

10. For he was yet in the loins of his father, when Melchisedech met him.

11. If then perfection was by the Levitical priesthood (for under it the people received the law), what further need was there that another priest should rise according to the order of Melchisedech, and not be called according to the order of Aaron?

12. For when the priesthood is changed it is necessary that a change also be made of the law.

descendants of Levi were priests, but only those who were of the family of Aaron; all the rest were called Levites, and their duties were concerned with the material ministries of the Temple.

Whose pedigree is not numbered, etc., i.e., who in no way belonged to the tribe of Levi.

7. A benediction, as such and at the time it is given, is always the sign of superiority in the one who imparts it to the one who receives it. Therefore, Melchisedech in blessing Abraham showed his superiority to the patriarch and to the Levites who descended from him.

8. Another sign of the superiority of the priesthood of Melchisedech is in this, that, whereas the Levitical priests die one after another, he lives forever, at least in so far as the testimony of Scripture is concerned: Scripture tells us that they die, but makes no mention of his death; it speaks of their successors, but says nothing about his.

9-10. Even Levi and the Levites, who received tithes from their own brethren, paid tithes to Melchisedech in the person of Abraham their father, and they and their priesthood, therefore, are inferior to him and his priesthood.

The phrase "so to speak" is found only here in the New Testament, but it is classical and Philo frequently employs it.

11-12. In verses 11-19 the Apostle points out the failure and ineffectualness of the Levitical priesthood and of the Old Law which had grown up around it, and in verses 20-25 he shows the perfection and effectiveness of the priesthood and the new code introduced by Jesus.

If then perfection was by the Levitical priesthood, etc. The ancient code had grown up around the Levitical priesthood, which

13. For he, of whom these things are spoken, is of another tribe, of which no one attended on the altar;

14. For it is evident that our Lord hath sprung out of Juda, in which tribe Moses spoke nothing concerning priests.

15. And this is yet far more evident if according to the similitude of Melchisedech there ariseth another priest,

16. Who is made not according to the law of a carnal commandment, but according to the power of an indissoluble life.

was its centre and core; it depended on the priesthood for its efficacy and success; if the priesthood failed, the whole system became void and useless. But the Levitical priesthood did fail, it did not secure moral perfection for men; and this is why the Psalmist in Psalm xciv. 4 proclaims the advent of a new system in the Messiah which would be independent of the line of Aaron and according to the order of Melchisedech. Since, therefore, the Law centred about the priesthood and depended on it, it follows that, when the priesthood failed, the whole legal system also failed and became obsolete and useless.

13-14. **For he, of whom,** etc., i.e., the Messiah, who is the subject of Psalm xciv. As a matter of fact, the Levitical priesthood has failed, and with it the entire old system has gone, in so far as it depended on the priesthood. Nor is there to be any reformation of the discarded code; for He whom the Psalmist announced as the author of a new priesthood and a new law was of the tribe of Juda, and had nothing to do with the ancient tribe of Levi which provided the ministers of the old altar. Since, then, our Lord is a priest, and not of the tribe of Levi but of the tribe of Juda, it follows that the Law has been superseded, because a new priesthood has arisen.

Our Lord. See on 1 Tim. i. 14; 2 Tim. i. 8.

15-16. **And this is yet far more evident,** i.e., that the ancient Levitical system had to go, and that it had to be superseded by a new priesthood, is evident not only from its imperfection and from the fact that a new priest was to arise outside the line of Levi (ver. 11-14); but also, and even more so, is this evident when we see arise another priest who is constituted in a wholly different manner, in no wise depending on the Law, but being made according to the type and fashion of Melchisedech; not deriving His priesthood from carnal and external descent, but from "the power

17. For he testifieth: *Thou art a priest for ever, according to the order of Melchisedech.*

18. There is indeed a setting aside of the former commandment, because of the weakness and unprofitableness thereof,

19. (For the law brought nothing to perfection) but a bringing in of a better hope, by which we draw nigh to God.

20. And inasmuch as it is not without an oath (for the others indeed were made priests without an oath;

21. But this with an oath, by him that said unto him: *The Lord hath sworn, and he will not repent, Thou art a priest for ever*) ;

22. By so much is Jesus made a surety of a better testament.

of an indissoluble life." The Greek expression for "far more evident" here is not found elsewhere in the New Testament.

Not according to the law, i.e., not according to the Mosaic legislation, which required that the priests should come from the family of Aaron in regular succession. This prescription of the Law of Moses was called "a carnal commandment," because it referred to mortal men who transmitted the priesthood from father to son according to carnal descent, or because it was merely external and subject to earthly limitations and human relationships. The priesthood of Christ, on the contrary, is not dependent on something external and changeable, but is derived from a power which is internal and depends on a life which is eternal, and therefore unchangeable. The Greek for "indissoluble" occurs only here in the New Testament.

17. The Psalmist (Ps. cix. 4) had foretold that the Messiah should be a priest forever according to the order of Melchisedech, and our Lord by His risen and immortal life has fulfilled this prophecy; He conquered death in His resurrection, and now He liveth evermore.

18-19. Now we have given the reason why the Levitical code and the ancient legislation came to an end: they were impotent to produce moral perfection, they could not effect man's justification from sin and lead him to eternal salvation; and in this sense they were weak and unprofitable. But the Law was not altogether useless, for it was a shadow of things to come and a prelude to a higher hope by which we draw near to God. It is the New Law and the priesthood of Christ that lead to perfection and to eternal life.

20-22. The superiority of the priesthood of Christ to the Levitical system is further proved from the fact that it was instituted with

23. And the others indeed were made many priests, because by reason of death they were not suffered to continue;

24. But this, for that he continueth for ever, hath an everlasting priesthood.

25. Whereby he is able also to save for ever them that come to God by him, always living to make intercession for us.

a solemn oath on the part of God, whereas the priests of the Old Law were constituted such without an oath. An oath is used only in matters of greater importance, and it gives firmness and stability to the thing sworn to. Speaking through the Psalmist (Ps. cix. 4), God took an everlasting oath that Christ was to be a priest forever. In proportion, therefore, as the priesthood of Christ rests on the solemn oath of God, in the same proportion is our Lord made the surety of a more excellent covenant than that which existed under the Old Dispensation.

For the others, i.e., the Aaronic priests.

But this with an oath, etc., i.e., Christ our Lord was made a priest by God the Father who, in the words of Psalm cix. 4, said to Him with a solemn oath which He will never revoke: "Thou art a priest for ever."

By so much is Jesus, etc. Since the priesthood of Jesus has been set up with an oath, it follows that the whole New Testament which centres about that priesthood has also been established with an oath, and our Lord is our assurance that the promises contained in the New Law will be fulfilled; it is He who has satisfied for our sins and merited for us the graces by which we can keep His commandments and save our souls.

Here in verse 22 we have for the first time the introduction of the idea of a New Covenant or Testament, which is developed in Chapter viii.

23-25. The author now gives other reasons to show how the new priesthood is superior to the old. In the old system the priests were many in number and were always succeeding one another, because death was constantly thinning their ranks; there was no permanency about them, and their office was consequently transitory. But in the new system we have one supreme Mediator who abides forever, and whose priesthood does not change. Thus, it follows from this perpetual and unchanging priesthood of the New Law that Jesus Christ, our great High Priest, is able "to save for ever" (i.e., at

26. For it was fitting that we should have such a high priest, holy, innocent, undefiled, separated from sinners, and made higher than the heavens;

27. Who needeth not daily as the *other* priests to offer sacrifices first for his own sins, and then for the people's; for this he did once, in offering himself.

28. For the law maketh men priests, who have infirmity; but the word of the oath, which followed the law, setteth up the Son who is perfected for evermore.

all times) those who draw near to God through Him; He is always living "to make intercession for us" (i.e., to exercise His priesthood in our behalf).

The words translated "for ever" (ver. 25) may also be rendered "to the uttermost," i.e., completely, in the fullest degree.

The human priests of the New Law are but vicars of Jesus Christ, ministers employed by Him to discharge in His name certain visible and external functions here on earth; and the sacrifice which they offer is identical with His sacrifice.

26-28. The author now returns to the thought of Jesus Christ as High Priest, having established the superiority of His priesthood to that of the Levitical system. Christ is indeed the ideal High Priest, because He possesses perfect intrinsic holiness and is entirely apart from sin and sinners; He surpasses in sanctity all creatures and is seated above the heavens at the right hand of the Father Almighty. Unlike the Levitical priests who were under the necessity of offering sacrifices continually, first for their own sins and then for the sins of the people, Christ had no sins of His own to expiate, and for the sins of the people He offered Himself once and for all.

The reason why the Jewish priests had to offer sacrifices for their sins was that the Law of Moses chose as its priests men who were subject to moral infirmity, men who were sinners; but the High Priest of the New Law, whom the Eternal Father constituted such with an irrevocable oath, as declared by the Psalmist centuries after the Law was given (Ps. cix. 4), is the Son of God Himself, and therefore sinless and perfect from eternity.

The word "daily" in verse 27 causes a difficulty, since the Jewish High Priest did not offer sacrifice every day, but only once a year on the Day of Atonement, when he offered sacrifice first for himself and then for the people. But the author is here speaking of the Levitical system in general and of all the Jewish priests and sacrifices. Many of these sacrifices were offered daily, and all of them were directly or indirectly ordained to the expiation of sins of the priests and of the people (Exod. xxix. 38 ff.; Lev. vi. 14; Num. xxviii. 3 ff.). According to Philo, the High Priest himself offered sacrifice daily. Whether he did or not, he could be said to have part in the daily sacrifices of the inferior priests, since they performed their functions subject to his authority and jurisdiction. At any rate, our author is thinking of the need of repetition of the ancient sacrifices as contrasted with the one, all-sufficient, and eternal sacrifice of Christ, which was offered once in a bloody manner on the cross and is perpetuated to the end of the world in an unbloody manner on our altars through the holy sacrifice of the Mass.

CHAPTER VIII

CHRIST A HIGH PRIEST IN THE HEAVENLY SANCTUARY, 1-5

1. Now of the things which we have spoken, this is the chief point: We have such an high priest, who is set on the right hand of the throne of majesty in the heavens,
2. A minister of the holies, and of the true tabernacle, which the Lord hath pitched, not man.

1-5. The author continues his proof of the superiority of the New Dispensation to the Old from the superiority of its priesthood. In iv. 14—vii. 28 he has been showing the superiority of the priesthood of Christ to the Levitical priesthood, arguing from the greater dignity of the Person who is the High Priest of the Christian Dispensation, as compared with the priests of the Old Law; Christ is the ideal High Priest. In the present Chapter he will show how far the ministry of Christ surpasses that of the Levitical system, (a) because it is exercised in the heavenly Sanctuary (ver. 1-5), and (b) because it is a part of a new and better Covenant (ver. 6-13).

1-2. Now of the things which we have spoken, i.e., the chief feature about the priesthood of which we are speaking is this, that we Christians have a High Priest who is enthroned in heaven and

3. For every high priest is appointed to offer gifts and sacrifices; wherefore it is necessary that this one also should have some thing to offer.

who exercises His ministry in the heavenly Sanctuary, which the
Lord, and not man, has built.

Chief point. The Greek expression may also be rendered "sum,"
i.e., compendium; but the writer is not recapitulating his previous
arguments. He is introducing a new idea: Christ is not only the
ideal High Priest, but He exercises His office in the ideal Sanctuary in heaven, where He is enthroned at the right hand of God
the Father.

Minister. The Greek denotes an officiating priest.

Holies is a literal translation of the Greek, but, since the word
is here parallel to "tabernacle," it clearly means "sanctuary," as
also in ix. 8, x. 19, xiii. 11.

The true tabernacle, as distinguished from the earthly tabernacle, which was its shadow or figure.

3. Every High Priest is appointed to offer gifts and sacrifices,
and therefore Christ, the ideal High Priest, who resides in heaven
and exercises His ministry in the heavenly Sanctuary, must have
something to offer there. The gifts and sacrifices that He offers
and presents are His prayers in our behalf (vii. 25), the blood He
shed for us on the cross, and Himself (ix. 14; Eph. v. 2).

This great theme of the priestly functions that are performed in
the heavenly Sanctuary is developed in Chapter ix. 11-28, x. 5-7,
11, 12, 14. But here it may be well to note the following opinions
regarding the sacrifice of Christ: (a) the Socinians held that Christ
offered no sacrifice on earth, but became a High Priest only after
His Ascension into heaven and offers His sacrifice there, which
opinion is contrary to the teaching of St. Paul on the sacrificial
death of Christ; (b) Thalhofer (Cath.) taught that Christ offers in
heaven a true and proper sacrifice, which consists exclusively in
the internal offering of His will, but this is contrary to the accepted
notion of sacrifice, which must be an external act; (c) Condren
(Cath.) says that Christ completes in heaven the sacrifice of the
cross by communion with the Father, but this would make the
sacrifice of Calvary incomplete; (d) the common Catholic teaching
is that in heaven Christ neither offers a new sacrifice, nor completes His earthly sacrifice, but applies there the merits of the

4. If then he were on earth, he would not be a priest: seeing that there are *others* to offer gifts according to the law:

5. Who serve unto the copy and shadow of heavenly things. As it was answered to Moses, when he was to finish the tabernacle: See (saith he) that thou make all things according to the pattern which was shewn thee on the mount.

sacrifice He offered here on the cross. Moreover, through His ministers on earth Christ continues in the Mass the sacrifice once offered on the cross.

4. Since our Lord in His human nature was descended from the tribe of Juda, and not from the tribe of Levi, He could not be a priest and exercise priestly functions on earth according to the Levitical system prescribed by Moses. The ministry of the earthly sanctuary is taken care of by those who are priests in the Levitical sense, and who offer gifts according to the Law of Moses. This verse implies that the Jewish priests were still performing their functions in the Temple when this letter was written.

The *essent* and *offerrent* of the Vulgate should be in the present tense, as in the Greek.

5. The Levitical priests exercise their ministry and offer their sacrifices in an earthly sanctuary which is but a copy and shadow of the true heavenly Sanctuary where Christ is officiating. The author appeals to Exod. xxv. 40 to prove that the earthly tabernacle was but a copy and shadow of the heavenly one, for Moses had it built according to the pattern which God gave him on Mount Sinai. The Levitical priesthood, sanctuary and sacrifices were only shadows of Christ's priesthood, the heavenly Sanctuary and oblation; hence the vast superiority of the latter to the former.

CHRIST THE MEDIATOR OF A NEW AND BETTER COVENANT, 6-13

6-13. The superiority of the priesthood of Christ to that of the Old Dispensation is again manifest in the greater excellence of the Covenant of which He is the minister and mediator. The New Covenant is superior to the Old because it is based on superior divine promises. That the Old Testament was faulty, God Himself bore witness when through Jeremias He pronounced judgment upon it and promised the new and better one which has been fulfilled in the new relationship established between God and man by

6. But now he hath obtained a better ministry, by how much also he is a mediator of a better testament, which is established on better promises.

7. For if that former had been faultless, there should not indeed a place have been sought for a second.

8. For finding fault with them, he saith: *Behold, the days shall come, saith the Lord, and I will perfect unto the house of Israel, and unto the house of Juda, a new testament;*

Jesus Christ. The Old Law was external, written on tables of stone; the New Law is inscribed on the heart. The Old Law was given to the nation as a whole; the New Law speaks to the individual, instructing every man in the knowledge of God and leading to the forgiveness of men's sins. Thus, by speaking of a "new" Covenant God implied the transient character and the ultimate disappearance of the old order, which was to be superseded by a new and better one.

6. **But now,** etc., i.e., as things are actually, the priesthood of Christ is as far superior to that of the Levitical system as the new relationship which He has established between God and man is superior to the one that existed under the Old Law.

A Mediator. Christ is to the New Law what Moses was to the Old, and more; for, like Aaron, He is also a High Priest. Through the revelation He gave to the world, and through His sufferings, oblation on Calvary, and His death, He is both the Mediator and the High Priest of the New Dispensation.

Better promises. The Levitical system was based on material promises of the Land of Canaan (Deut. xxviii. 1 ff.), whereas the New Covenant rests on spiritual promises, such as grace, the remission of sins, life everlasting, and the like, as described in the quotation that follows from Jeremias.

7. The Old Law did not lead men to perfection and salvation; it was defective, as God's words to Jeremias clearly prove. Hence it had to be superseded by a new and better one.

8. In verses 8-12 the author now proves by a quotation from Jeremias (Jer. xxxi. 31-34) that on God's own testimony the Old Covenant established through Moses on Mount Sinai was unsatisfactory, and that it was to be superseded by a new and perfect one. The quotation from the prophet, being according to the LXX, differs slightly from the Hebrew.

Finding fault, etc., i.e., God reproaches the people of Israel for

9. *Not according to the testament which I made to their fathers, on the day when I took them by the hand to lead them out of the land of Egypt, because they continued not in my testament, and I regarded them not, saith the Lord.*

10. *For this is the testament which I will make to the house of Israel after those days, saith the Lord: I will give my laws into their mind, and in their heart will I write them, and I will be their God, and they shall be my people;*

11. *And they shall not teach every man his neighbor and every man his brother, saying, Know the Lord; for all shall know me from the least to the greatest of them,*

12. *Because I will be merciful to their iniquities, and their sins I will remember no more.*

their failure to fulfill their part of the Old Covenant, and promises to establish a new alliance with the nation.

The days shall come refers to the Messianic era.

9. The New Covenant will differ in character from that established on Mount Sinai after the release of the Israelites from the bondage of Egypt, for the latter was set aside because of the failure of the people to fulfill their part of the agreement.

10. The author begins now to describe the positive character of the New Covenant which God promised to establish in Messianic times: it will be internal, written on the hearts of the people, and the relation which it will effect between God and His people will be far more intimate than before; God will enrich them with His benefits and lead them to salvation, while they will render Him a service worthy of Him.

11. Under the New Covenant the knowledge of God will become universal, not confined to any one people or class, as was the case under the Old Law. This does not mean that there will be no need of a teaching authority in the Church, for otherwise the teaching of this very letter would be superfluous, and St. Paul could not have so often insisted elsewhere on the necessity of teaching and of sound doctrine (cf. Eph. iv. 11 ff.; Gal. i. 18 ff.; 1 Tim. iii. 15, iv. 11, 13, 16; 2 Tim. ii. 2, iv. 2, 5; Titus i. 5, 9, ii. 1, etc.). The meaning, therefore, here is that under the New Covenant there will be a much greater outpouring of grace on the teacher and the hearer, that the law will be far simpler to understand, that it will not be confined to the Jews but will be extended to all peoples, etc.

Neighbor is "fellow-citizen" in the Greek.

12. In consequence of this new relationship between God and His people, and of the grace which the New Law will confer, God

13. Now in saying a new, he hath made the former old. And that which decayeth and groweth old is near its end.

will remit the sins and blot out the transgressions of His people. The Old Law had no power to forgive sins, because it did not confer grace; and hence it could not remove the principal obstacle to union between God and His people.

13. When God through Jeremias spoke of the future Covenant as "new," He indicated that the Old Law was already in decay and near its end. Hence the Old Testament itself contains a prophecy of its supersession by a new and better alliance.

CHAPTER IX

THE SUPERIOR EXCELLENCE OF CHRIST'S SACRIFICE, 1-28

1. The former indeed had also justifications of *divine* service, and an earthly sanctuary.

1-28. In the preceding Chapter the author has shown us how Christ was the ideal High Priest, exercising His functions in the heavenly Sanctuary, and the Mediator of a new and better Covenant. Here in the present Chapter he will show how our Lord offered the ideal sacrifice, excelling by far the sacrifices of the Levitical order. To prove this, he first contrasts the ancient Tabernacle, its furnishings, and defective worship with the greater and more perfect Sanctuary into which Christ has entered, and the perfect and everlasting sacrifice which Christ has offered to God (ver. 1-14). Then he explains the necessity and value of the one and all-sufficient sacrifice which Christ has offered for sin (ver. 15-28).

1. In verses 1-5 we have a description of the Mosaic Tabernacle and its furnishings, to which and its services the author always refers rather than to the Temple of his own time. His aim here is to give us an idea of the splendor which attended and surrounded the ancient Jewish worship.

The former. No substantive is expressed, but "covenant" is to be understood, as is evident from the preceding chapter.

Justifications, i.e., ordinances, or arrangements for divine wor-

2. For there was a tabernacle made, the first, wherein were the candle-stick, and the table, and the setting forth of loaves, which is called the holy.

3. And behind the second veil, the tabernacle, which is called the holy of holies,

ship ordained by God. The ancient Sanctuary is called "earthly" or "of this world," as contrasted with the heavenly Sanctuary where Christ officiates.

2. **A tabernacle.** The reference is to the Mosaic Tabernacle, which consisted of a vestibule and two main parts, called the Holy Place and the Most Holy Place or Holy of Holies. Both of these main parts were called tabernacles or tents. The vestibule was sepa-rated from the Holy Place by a curtain or veil, and a second curtain or veil hung between the Holy Place and the Holy of Holies. The author will now describe the furnishings of these two main parts of the ancient Tabernacle of the wilderness; he is not concerned with the Temple of his own day, in which there was no ark, or mercy-seat, or Shechinah, and probably no seven-branched candle-stick. These furnishings had disappeared with the exile.

The first, i.e., the outer tent, the Holy Place, into which the vestibule opened and which contained "the candlestick" or lamp-stand with seven lamps (Exod. xxv. 31-40), "the table" for the loaves of shewbread (Exod. xxv. 23-30), and "the setting forth of loaves," or the shewbread of twelve cakes set out in two rows on the sacred table (Exod. xxv. 30; Lev. xxiv. 5-9).

Which is called the holy, i.e., this first tent is called the Holy Place. It is remarkable that our author makes no mention of the altar of incense among the furniture of the Holy Place or outer tent, probably because he is confining his description to what is found in Exod. xxv and xxvi, or because he possessed more defi-nite information regarding its introduction and position than we have, as given later in Exod. xxx; for from 3 Kings vi. 22 and Exod. xl. 5 it would seem that the altar of incense was in the Most Holy Place. See below, on verses 4-5.

3. A first veil hung between the Holy Place and the vestibule and outer court, and a second one between the Holy Place and the Most Holy Place or innermost Sanctuary. By the first veil the laity and the Levites were excluded from the Holy Place; and by the second all were excluded from the Most Holy Place, except the High Priest on the Day of Atonement.

4. Having a golden censer, and the ark of the covenant covered about on every part with gold, in which was a golden pot that had manna, and the rod of Aaron, that had blossomed, and the tables of the covenant;

5. And over it were the cherubim of glory overshadowing the mercy-seat, of which it is not needful to speak now particularly.

4-5. We now have a description of the furniture of the Most Holy Place.

Having a golden censer. Since there is no mention in the Old Testament of a "golden censer," many scholars think the Greek word here so translated should be rendered "altar of incense." But to this it is objected that the altar of incense belonged to the Holy Place (Exod. xxxvii. 25-29). The best explanation is that the altar was so intimately connected with the Most Holy Place that it could be said to belong to it; for, because of its atoning power, Exod. xxx. 10 speaks of it as the Holy of Holies, and Exod. xxx. 6 and xl. 5 say it was placed before the mercy-seat. At any rate, it was separated from the Most Holy Place only by the second veil, and this was drawn on the Day of Atonement; and thus on that day the altar of incense became intimately associated with the High Priest's services in the Most Holy Place.

The ark of the covenant (Exod. xxv. 10-12) was a box made of acacia wood and covered with gold inside and outside.

A golden pot that had manna (Exod. xvi. 32-35), which was a memorial of the gift of manna in the wilderness.

The rod of Aaron, etc. (Num. xvii. 1-10), which symbolized that the priesthood belonged to the tribe of Levi.

Tables of the covenant (Deut. x. 2-8) were the tables of stone on which the commandments were written.

The cherubim of glory (Exod. xxv. 18-22; Lev. xvi. 2), i.e., the two cherubim of gold with outstretched wings between which rested the Shechinah, or luminous cloud of divine glory, which was the symbol of God's presence, or the medium by which His presence was manifested.

The mercy-seat or kapporeth (Exod. xxv. 17-22) was a square slab made of wood that served as a lid for the ark. It was sprinkled with sacrificial blood on the Day of Atonement, and thus got its name of "mercy-seat," or literally, "means of propitiation," because it signified God's compassion and readiness to forgive sin.

The author has said enough to give us an idea of the furniture

6. Now these things being thus ordered, into the first tabernacle the priests indeed always entered, accomplishing the offices of sacrifices;
7. But into the second, the high priest alone, once a year, not without blood, which he offereth for his own and the people's ignorance,
8. The Holy Ghost signifying this, that the way into the holies was not yet made manifest whilst the former tabernacle was yet standing.

and rich meaning of the ritual of the Tabernacle, but he says it is not possible to discuss all the symbolism and its significance which the contents of the ancient Sanctuary shadowed forth.

6-7. Having given us the furniture of the Tabernacle and a general idea of its symbolism, the author now in verses 6-10 describes the Levitical worship. The Levites did not enter the Holy Place, but the priests officiated there at least twice every day, entering every morning and every evening to offer incense, to prepare and light the candles, etc. (Exod. xxx. 7 ff.), and on Saturdays to renew the shewbread (Lev. xxiv. 8). But the Holy of Holies was entered only by the High Priest once a year, on the Day of Atonement. On this day, however, the High Priest went into the Most Holy Place several times. The ceremonial was as follows: in the court he first killed the bullock which was the sin-offering for himself and the priesthood, and then taking some of its blood he entered the Most Holy Place and sprinkled it on the mercy-seat, thus cleansing, consecrating, and making atonement for himself and the priesthood. Returning to the court he killed the goat, which was the sin-offering for the people, and sprinkled its blood in the same place. The altar of incense in the Holy Place and the altar of burnt offerings in the outer court were also cleansed by the blood of both victims (cf. Lev. xvi. 12-16; Num. xv. 22 ff.).

People's ignorance, i.e., sins committed through ignorance.

8. The author now explains the meaning of the regulations relative to entrance into the Holy of Holies. He says that the Holy Ghost, the author of the Law and of Scripture, meant to show by the arrangement which permitted only the High Priest to enter the Holy of Holies once a year that under the worship connected with the Tabernacle there was no free access to the presence of God. Only the High Priest had this privilege, and that only once a year, as long as the ancient Sanctuary existed. Thus, from the Holy of Holies all were excluded but the High Priest, and from the Holy Place all but the priests.

9. Which is a parable of the time present, according to which gifts and sacrifices are offered, which can not, as to the conscience, make him perfect that serveth, only in meats and in drinks,

10. And divers washings, and justices of the flesh laid on them until the time of reformation.

11. But Christ being come, a high priest of the good things to come, by a greater and more perfect tabernacle not made with hand, that is, not of this creation:

12. Neither by the blood of goats, and of calves, but by his own blood, entered once into the holies, having obtained eternal redemption.

The term "tabernacle" here comprises both tents, the Holy of Holies and the Holy Place.

9-10. **Which,** i.e., which Tabernacle. The Greek clearly shows that this is the meaning, and hence the Vulgate *quæ* should be *quod*. The meaning of the verse is that the Tabernacle with its exclusive arrangements was "a parable" (i.e., a sign or symbol) "of the present time" (i.e., of conditions as they were under the Old Law), before the full inauguration of the Gospel Dispensation; which parable showed that under the Old Covenant man's access to and fellowship with God was very much restricted, and that the gifts and sacrifices offered by the priests and the ceremonies performed were only external ordinances having but external effects, utterly unable to perfect man in his inner life and soul, and that they therefore had only a temporary value, being imposed "until the time of reformation," i.e., until the establishment of the New Covenant and the inauguration of the Messianic era, which took place in its fullness on the first Christian Pentecost. The complete and final annulment of the Old Covenant was effected with the fall of Jerusalem and the destruction of its Temple and worship in the year 70 A.D.

11-12. In verses 11-14 the author describes the greater efficacy of the sacrifice of Christ, showing that our Lord offered the ideal sacrifice.

But Christ, being come, i.e., Christ having arrived on the scene.

Of the good things to come, i.e., of the blessings they would enjoy who would belong to His Church. Another equally good reading has: "Of the good things that have come," i.e., that are already enjoyed by those who have embraced Christianity. The author now gives two reasons to show how the work of Christ surpassed that of the Jewish High Priest: (a) He entered into the

13. For if the blood of goats and of oxen, and the ashes of a heifer being sprinkled, sanctify such as are defiled, to the cleansing of the flesh,

14. How much more shall the blood of Christ, who by his eternal Spirit offered himself unspotted unto God, cleanse our conscience from dead works, to serve the living God?

ideal Sanctuary in heaven; (b) He offered a perfect sacrifice—His own blood which, being of infinite value, needed not to be repeated, but has wrought an eternal redemption. The Jewish High Priest entered only an earthly Sanctuary which belonged to the world of created things, and the sacrifices which he offered consisted of the blood of animals and had to be repeated continually because imperfect.

In verse 11 of the Vulgate *assistens* should be *apparens* and the *aut* in verse 12 should be *et*, to agree with the Greek.

It is to be noted that many of the Fathers understood "tabernacle" of verse 11 to refer to our Lord's body or the sacred humanity, as in x. 20 below; but such an interpretation seems to be out of line with the author's argument here, where he is contrasting Christ's entrance with His body into heaven with the entrance of the Jewish High Priest into the Holy of Holies on the Day of Atonement.

13-14. The author does not deny all value to the ancient sacrifices; but here, by an argument from less to greater, he shows how the blood of Christ has wrought an eternal redemption. Referring to the sacrifices of the Day of Atonement, when a bullock and a goat were slain and their blood used for cleansing and purifying (Lev. xvi. 16, 21), and to the sacrifice of the Red Cow (Num. xix. 18), whose ashes mixed with water served to cleanse from legal defilement, he says, if these external rites of the Old Law were able to confer a purification, even though it was merely of the flesh and external, how much more will the blood of Christ, who by His eternal Spirit offered Himself unblemished to God, purify our conscience from the works of sin and enable us to offer a worthy service to the living God. The author is arguing that the greater the victim, the greater the fruit of its sacrifice. Now, in the sacrifice of Christ we have (a) the life-blood of a Person, not of an animal; (b) that Person is Christ, the anointed of God; (c) Christ's sacrifice is a self-oblation, and not something external to Him, for He was the victim and priest on the cross and now in the heavenly

15. And therefore he is the mediator of a new covenant, that since death has taken place for the redemption of those transgressions which were under the former covenant they that are called may receive the promise of eternal inheritance.

Sanctuary; (d) He is a victim without blemish, not only in body like the ancient victims, but also in spirit; (e) He offered Himself through His eternal Spirit, or that indwelling power of divinity which enabled Him to rise from the dead and gave Him an "indissoluble life" (vii. 16).

Some authorities understand "eternal Spirit" here to mean the Holy Ghost, but this is improbable since there is no definite article in the Greek.

15. In verses 15-22 the author wishes to show his readers, who might otherwise be scandalized at the death of Jesus, how that death was necessary for the redemption of mankind. He bases his argument on the double meaning of the Greek word διαθήκη, which may signify either a covenant or a will and testament. In verses 15-17 he uses the word in both senses, as a covenant and as a will or testament, after first recalling the idea of Chapter viii. 6-13, where it was shown that Christ is the Mediator of a new and better Covenant; and then in verses 18-22 the same word is employed in the more precise and Hebrew sense of covenant.

In verses 15-17, therefore, the writer shows how the death of Christ was necessary in order that the will and testament which He made might have its effect. A will or testament becomes effective and binding only on the death of the testator, and since the New Testament is Christ's will, as well as His Covenant, it could not have its effect and force without His death.

And therefore, i.e., because the sacrifice which Christ has offered is of so great value, or because He has redeemed us with His blood and has purified our conscience and reconciled us to God (ver. 14), He has become "the mediator of a new covenant," as was explained in viii. 6-13, in order that what took place under the Old Covenant with regard to men's sins might occur with greater efficacy under the New Covenant: under the Old Covenant the death of victims was necessary in order that by their blood men might be purified from their transgressions, and that the High Priest might be able to enter the Holy of Holies; so in like manner under the New Covenant the death of a more perfect victim, namely, Christ Him-

16. For where there is a testament, the death of the testator must of necessity come in.

17. For a testament is of force after men are dead: otherwise it is as yet
of no strength whilst the testator liveth.

18. Whereupon neither was the first indeed dedicated without blood;

19. For when every commandment of the law had been read by Moses to
all the people, he took the blood of calves and goats, with water and scarlet
wool and hyssop, and sprinkled both the book itself and all the people,

self, was necessary in order to give to those ancient sacrifices all
the efficacy they possessed and to secure to all who are called to
the true faith the means of attaining to eternal beatitude and of
entering their heavenly abode. This seems to be the meaning of
a very obscure verse on which long treatises have been written.

If we do not connect "and therefore" at the beginning of the
verse with what immediately precedes in verse 14, we cannot do
better than translate with the Westminster Version as follows:
"For this, then, is he the Mediator of a new testament, that whereas
a death hath taken place, etc."

16-17. Having just spoken of the necessity of a death and of an
inheritance, the writer now goes on to show in these two verses
that the death of Christ was necessary from the fact that the new
alliance which He established was His will and testament. He is
here using the word διαθήκη in its Greek and Roman sense of will
or testament; and he says that, since no will takes effect until after
the death of the testator, the death of Christ was necessary that
we Christians might get possession of our inheritance of eternal
life. The death of Jesus, therefore, was not a sign of weakness,
but was rather an essential condition of the establishment of the
Messianic kingdom and of the inheritance of those Messianic blessings of which Jesus was the primary heir and the sole dispenser.

18. The writer now returns to the Hebrew meaning of the word
διαθήκη, and says that even the "first" (i.e., the Sinaitic Covenant)
was not "dedicated" (i.e., inaugurated) without the bloody sacrifice
of victims, referring to the account given in Exod. xxiv. 1 ff. The
inference is that the death of Jesus was necessary also for the
establishment of the New Covenant, as the death of animals was
necessary for the inauguration of the Old Covenant.

19. **For when every commandment,** etc. The reference is to
Exod. xxiv, where we are told that, after Moses had read to the

20. Saying: *This is the blood of the testament which God hath enjoined unto you.*

21. The tabernacle also and all the vessels of the ministry, in like manner, he sprinkled with blood.

22. And almost all the things, according to the law, are cleansed with blood, and without shedding of blood there is no remission.

people all the commands of God as contained in the Law and had received the people's promise to obey them, he erected an altar and sacrificed certain victims, sprinkling the blood partly on the altar and partly on the people, thus establishing the covenant relationship between God and His people. The writer here makes several additions to the narrative of Exod. xxiv, which he probably had derived from traditional sources of information. The added details are: (a) the mention of goats; (b) of water, scarlet wool, and hyssop; (c) the sprinkling of the Book of the Covenant.

20. **This is the blood,** etc, i.e., this is the blood with which God confirms and seals the covenant which He has made in favor of His people. Our Lord used these same words in the institution of the Holy Eucharist (Matt. xxvi. 28; Mark xiv. 24), thus showing that the Old Covenant was a figure of the New, and that the blood of victims was a type of the blood which He Himself shed for the remission of the sins of all mankind and which He has left us in the Holy Eucharist.

21. As the Tabernacle was not yet erected when the Sinaitic Covenant was established, this verse must refer to an event of a later date. Perhaps the reference is to what took place at the dedication of the Tabernacle (Exod. xl. 9 ff.; Lev. viii. 30 ff.), as some of the ceremonies here recorded are not directly mentioned elsewhere in Sacred Scripture. Of course, we know that the cleansing of the Tabernacle and its vessels by the sprinkling of blood was the chief feature of the Day of Atonement (Lev. xvi. 16, 19), and the sacrifices of that feast were but the yearly renewal of those that were offered at the inauguration of the Covenant.

22. **Almost all,** etc. Exceptions are recorded in Exod. xix. 10, 14; Lev. v. 11 ff., xvi. 26 ff.; Num. xxxi. 22 ff. Blood was the recognized means by which the Tabernacle and its vessels were consecrated and purified. It was also the blood of the sacrifices at the inauguration of the Covenant that established fellowship between God and His people, and the yearly renewal on the Day of

23. It is necessary therefore that the patterns of heavenly things should be cleansed with these; but the heavenly things themselves with better sacrifices than these.

Atonement of those inaugural sacrifices with cleansing and sanctifying blood renewed and restored this covenant relationship when it had become marred or destroyed by sin. Thus, sacrificial blood was the divinely established means by which fellowship between God and His people was maintained, and, as the sacrifice of Jesus was the antitype and fulfillment both of the inaugurating sacrifice and its yearly renewal on the Day of the Atonement, it is by His blood, poured out on the cross and offered daily in the Holy Sacrifice of the Mass, that fellowship between God and His people is now established and maintained, and restored when lost by sin.

There is no remission, i.e., no forgiveness of sins. The remission of sins here in question was only external and legal, by which one escaped the threats and punishments of the Law. The true and internal remission of sins has always been only through the merits of Christ—under the Old Covenant through the merits of Christ prefigured and foreseen, and under the New Covenant through the same merits actually realized in the sacrifice and death of Jesus.

23. In verses 23-28 the author draws a parallel between the acts of the Jewish High Priest on the Day of Atonement and their fulfillment by our Lord in the heavenly Sanctuary, showing at the same time the relation between the ideal sacrifice and the ideal Sanctuary.

It being necessary, etc. The writer is deducing a conclusion, and he wishes to say that, since by divine ordination it was necessary that "the patterns of heavenly things, etc." (i.e., the earthly Tabernacle and its vessels), should be cleansed and purified by the blood of sacrificial victims, so "the heavenly things, etc." (i.e., the ideal Sanctuary in heaven), require dedication by the blood of a far more excellent victim, namely, Christ Himself. The heavenly Sanctuary cannot be said to need purification in itself, but only by reason of its contact with sinful worshippers. Of course, it is also true that the Priest and Victim who entered it, and who abides there forever, is He before whom "the very heavens are not clean."

With better sacrifices. The plural is used generically, to express a class with which the many sacrifices of the Old Law are contrasted.

24. For Christ is not entered into the holies made with hands, the patterns of the true, but into heaven itself, that he may appear now in the presence of God for us.

25. Nor yet that he should offer himself often, as the high priest entereth into the holies, every year with the blood of others;

26. For then he must needs have suffered often from the beginning of the world: but now once at the end of the ages, he hath appeared for the destruction of sin by the sacrifice of himself.

24. Unlike the Jewish High Priest, Christ has not entered an earthly Sanctuary, which was a mere type of the true one in heaven, but He has passed into heaven itself; nor again, like the ancient High Priest on the Day of Atonement, has He come into the presence of a mere symbol of the divine presence, but into the very presence of God Himself, meeting the Father face to face.

That he may appear now, etc. The Jewish High Priest entered the Holy of Holies for a few moments once a year, but Christ's appearance in heaven is a continued manifestation in our behalf, so that, as He and the Father now stand face to face, we also by His merits may realize the divine fellowship, here through grace and hereafter in glory.

The *Jesus* of the Vulgate should be *Christus,* as in the Greek.

25. The Jewish High Priest entered the earthly Sanctuary once every year to offer the blood of a bullock and of a goat, the repetition being due to the imperfection of the sacrifice he offered; but Jesus, Priest and Victim of the perfect sacrifice of the New Covenant, has entered into the Sanctuary of heaven once for all to present for us the merits of His sacrifice.

The Feast of the Atonement was the greatest of the Jewish Calendar, and its ceremonies were the most elaborate of the Jewish ritual; and therefore our author, by stressing the superiority of the sacrifice, sanctuary, and ritual of the New Covenant, gave a powerful argument in favor of the Gospel as compared with the Old Law, and thus greatly strengthened in the new faith those who had been tempted to waver and fall back into Judaism.

26. The reason why Christ needed to suffer and die only once is found in the entire completeness and sufficiency of His sacrifice. Had His sacrifice been incomplete, He would have had to suffer and die often from the beginning of the world up to now, for sin has been rampant in the world all along and only the blood of Christ has the power to remit it.

27. And as it is appointed unto men once to die, and after this the judgment,

28. So also Christ was offered once to exhaust the sins of many; the second time he shall appear without sin to them that expect him unto salvation.

But now once for all Christ has appeared "at the end of the ages," i.e., in the Messianic era, which began with the birth of Jesus and will last till the end of time, and His coming has been for the abolition and "destruction of sin" by means of His sacrifice and death on the cross. A further sacrifice, therefore, is not necessary.

The "appearing" of verse 24 was before God the Father in the heavenly Sanctuary, but in the present verse it refers to our Lord's manifestation before men at the Incarnation; a different Greek word is used in this verse.

From verses 25 and 26 it is clear that the sacrifice of Jesus is superior to all the ancient sacrifices, because it has the power of remitting sins, internally and really, and it is complete and final, thus making another sacrifice unnecessary.

27-28. These verses imply a double comparison: first, between the death of men and their reappearance in judgment, and the death of Jesus and His reappearance in glory at the end of the world; and secondly, between the coming forth of the High Priest from the Holy of Holies on the Day of Atonement and the final coming of Jesus to call the just to their rewards.

The judgment. This may mean the particular judgment at death, but the parallel with our Lord's final appearance is better sustained by understanding the general judgment at the end of the world.

The sins of many. Christ died for all mankind, though all do not choose to make use of the graces and merits thus put at their disposal.

Without sin. Our Lord's second appearance will have no connection with sin; it will be a coming in glory to those faithful souls who will be prepared and waiting for Him.

CHAPTER X

THE SUPERIORITY OF CHRIST'S SACRIFICE, 1-18

1. For the law having a shadow of the good things to come, not the very image of the things; by the selfsame sacrifices which they offer continually every year, can never make the comers thereunto perfect;
2. For then they would have ceased to be offered, because the worshippers once cleansed should have no conscience of sin any longer:

1-18. The Apostle continues here the subject discussed in the preceding Chapter, adding new thoughts and illustrations to the arguments already given. First he contrasts the one sacrifice of Christ with the many Levitical sacrifices (ver. 1-10), and then speaks of the perfection of the New Covenant established by Christ, citing again, as in viii. 8-12, the famous passage of Jeremias xxxi. 31-34 to prove that in the New Dispensation there is union with God and complete reconciliation between man and his Creator (ver. 11-18).

1. Since the Law was only the shadow "of the good things to come" (i.e., of the Messianic blessings revealed in the Gospel), and "not the very image" (i.e., not the realization of those benefits), it was impossible that the ancient sacrifices, in which the Law centred and which were offered annually on the Day of Atonement, should ever make "perfect" (i.e., cleanse interiorly and sanctify) those who came to worship God through them.

Image is here contrasted with "shadow"; the former is an exact reproduction of a thing, whereas the latter is only a general outline.

2. In verses 2-4 the Apostle gives arguments to show the inefficiency of the Jewish sacrifices to make perfect those who worshipped through them. They never took away the sense of sin from the hearts of the worshippers, and hence they had to be continually repeated, whether the people were guilty of new sins each year or not. On the contrary, the sacrifice of Christ has satisfied for the remission of all sins for all time. St. Chrysostom remarks

3. But in them there is made commemoration of sins every year:

4. For it is impossible that with the blood of oxen and goats sin should be taken away.

5. Wherefore when he cometh into the world, he saith: *Sacrifice and oblation thou wouldest not: but a body thou hast fitted to me:*

6. *Holocausts for sin did not please thee.*

at this place that, while we offer to God every day the Sacrifice of the Mass, it is not a new sacrifice; for we always offer the selfsame sacrifice which Christ offered, the Victim and the great High Priest being always the same, namely, Christ Himself, and the human priests being but Christ's vicars and ministers in the visible and material realm. Cf. also Theophylact and St. Thomas, *h. l.*

3. All that the Levitical sacrifices could do was to keep alive a sense of sin, and this their repetition each year effected. St. Chrysostom says: "They served as an accusation of weakness, not a display of strength." Of course, they were also a perpetual symbol of the real sacrifice of Christ, to which they pointed and directed those who were longing for redemption and forgiveness. Thus, instead of removing sins these ancient sacrifices only intensified the consciousness of guilt. This is familiar Pauline doctrine, found in Rom. iii. 20, v. 20; Gal. iii. 19, etc.

4. The invalidity of the Old Law sacrifices to remit sins is evident from their very nature, for there is no proportion between them and the result sought. It is impossible that the blood of irrational animals of itself should be able to cleanse the guilty conscience of an intelligent and free creature. The sins that were actually forgiven under the Old Law were remitted through the power of the blood of Christ which those ancient rites prefigured. It was only as symbols of Christ's sacrifice, therefore, that the Levitical sacrifices had any real validity.

5-6. In the preceding verses the author has been repeating in other words arguments already given to show the failure of the Jewish sacrifices. Now he introduces a new and more powerful argument based on Psalm xxxix. 7-9 according to the LXX. From that text he proves that centuries before the coming of Christ it was announced that God was not pleased with the ancient sacrifices, and that they would be superseded by the perfect sacrifice of the will of Christ. The Psalm is certainly Messianic, and the verses here quoted represent the Messiah as saying at the moment of His

7. Then said I: Behold I come (in the head of the book it is written of me), that I should do thy will, O God.

incarnation that all the ancient sacrifices were unpleasing to God, because inadequate for human needs, and that consequently a body had been especially prepared for Him by God the Father which should be the organ and instrument of a sacrifice of perfect obedience and absolute submission of His will to the divine will. Such a sacrifice would be worthy of God, since it was the sacrifice of the Son of God, and sufficient atonement for man's sins.

Wherefore, i.e., because of the imperfections of the Jewish sacrifices.

When he cometh into the world, i.e., when the Messiah became incarnate.

Sacrifice and oblation, i.e., bloody and unbloody offerings.

Thou wouldst not, i.e., Thou didst not desire, because of their inefficacy.

A body thou hast fitted for me. So the LXX; the Hebrew has: "Ears thou hast digged (i.e., opened) for me," so that the will of the Father might be readily perceived and obeyed. According to the LXX rendering, the body has been prepared to act, to carry out the behests of the divine will. Hence, the underlying meaning is the same in both translations.

Holocausts were bloody offerings, all of which were entirely consumed by fire on the altar.

Sin-offerings. Our Vulgate has missed this correct rendering of the Hebrew and the Greek. Thus, the terms here employed cover the whole range of Jewish sacrifices, with none of which was the divine will pleased; God wanted a complete obedience and an entire spiritual consecration.

7. Then said I, etc. Having understood the divine will, the Messiah replies that He is ready to do it, that is, He is prepared to sacrifice Himself, to consecrate His life to complete obedience in accordance with prophecy, for the whole Old Testament speaks of His advent.

The head of the book. Rather, "the roll of the book," i.e., the entire Old Testament regarded as a book of prophecy about the Messiah. The Old Testament was written on strips of parchment or vellum, which were then wound about a roller, and the whole

8. In saying above: *Sacrifices, and oblations, and holocausts and sin-offerings thou wouldest not, neither are they pleasing to thee,* which are offered according to the law.

9. *Then said I: Behold, I come to do thy will, O God.* He taketh away the first that he may establish that which followeth.

10. In the which will we are sanctified by the oblation of the body of Jesus Christ once.

11. And every priest indeed standeth daily ministering, and often offering the same sacrifices, which can never take away sins.

12. But this man offering one sacrifice for sins for ever sitteth on the right hand of God,

13. From henceforth waiting until his enemies be made his footstool.

14. For by one oblation he hath perfected for ever them that are sanctified.

book was called a roll. This phrase here, "the head of the book, etc.," is to be read as a parenthesis.

8-10. The Apostle makes application of the words just quoted from the Psalmist, saying that according to those words of prophecy the ancient sacrifices which were offered as prescribed by the Law have been superseded by the new and perfect sacrifice which Christ has offered to the Father, and that we, by virtue of that perfect sacrifice of Christ, have been "sanctified," i.e., dedicated to God. What Christ did and endured for us in the days of His flesh has merited for us this sanctification and dedication.

The argument developed here in verses 5-10 must have powerfully influenced the readers of the Epistle who were wavering in their Christian faith; for it showed that by the mouth of the Psalmist the Old Testament itself condemned the Jewish sacrificial system, foretold its abrogation, and prophesied the perfect sacrifice of Christ and the establishment of the new type of religion introduced by Him. With such evidence drawn from the Old Law itself, how could any Jewish Christian think of forsaking Christianity and lapsing into Judiasm?

11-14. In these verses the writer institutes a comparison between Jesus and the ordinary Jewish priests, in order to show how far the sacrifice of the former surpasses the offerings of the latter. Every day those ancient priests stood at the altar of holocausts, offering the same sacrifices (Exod. xxix. 38 ff.), but to no avail, so far as the real forgiveness of men's sins was concerned; but Christ offered one sacrifice for the sins of all the world, and then, as proof of the finality and completeness of His work, took His

15. And the Holy Ghost also doth testify *this* to us. For after having said:

16. *And this is the testament which I will make unto them after those days, saith the Lord: I will give my laws in their hearts, and on their minds will I write them;*

17. *And their sins and iniquities I will remember no more.*

18. Now where there *is* a remission of these, there is no more an oblation for sin.

seat in triumph at the right hand of the Father in heaven, there continuing His priestly activity in the ideal Sanctuary and exercising His sovereign rule until the final victory, when all enemies shall be made subject to Him, as has been foretold in the Messianic Psalm cix., verse 1 (ver. 11-13), and as St. Paul has written elsewhere (1 Cor. xv. 25). And the reason why Jesus now reposes in heaven, not needing to renew His sacrifice on earth, is that by the one oblation of Himself on the cross He has provided the means and merits of justification and sanctification for all mankind down to the end of the world; all that now remains for men to do is by faith and charity to apply these amassed merits and graces to their own souls. Of course, we cannot make use of Christ's merits and graces without the special help of God, but that help is never wanting to anyone who is willing to co-operate with it.

15-18. The author now clinches his argument by a reference to Jeremias' prophecy regarding the New Covenant, which was previously cited in viii. 8-12.

And the Holy Ghost also doth testify, etc., i.e., the Holy Spirit of God, speaking through the prophet Jeremias, bears witness that the remission of sins which the Levitical sacrifices were unable to effect has been obtained under the New Covenant by the one sacrifice of Jesus Christ. The main point in citing the prophet's words this time is not to show the establishment of a New Covenant, but to emphasize the fact that by the sacrifice of Christ, which is the heart of the New Covenant, sins have been remitted and the power of sin has been destroyed. Therefore, to seek now further means or other sacrifices for remitting sins is an injury to the sacrifice of Christ, as implying its insufficiency and incompleteness. Hence, all the Jewish sacrifices are out of date and useless, and it would be seriously wrong to return to them; they and their priesthood have been superseded for all time to come by the vastly more perfect priesthood and sacrifice of Jesus Christ.

EXHORTATION TO PERSEVERANCE IN FAITH, 19-39

19. Having therefore, brethren, full freedom to enter into the holies by the blood of Jesus,

20. A new and living way which he hath dedicated for us through the veil, that is to say, his flesh,

21. And a high priest over the house of God,

19-39. Here we have the beginning of the Moral Part of the Epistle (x. 19—xiii. 17), on which see *Introduction*, No. V, C. The author first makes a moral and spiritual appeal, telling his readers that their faith should give them great confidence, (a) because now through Christ we all have free entrance into the immediate, presence of God, and (b) because we have in Christ a High Priest who presides over the house of God and to whom we can come without faltering, provided our approach is with a sincere heart, with full assurance of faith, with a purified conscience, and with bodies washed by the regenerating waters of Baptism (ver. 19-25). He then warns them, as before in vi. 4-8, of the perils of apostasy, holding that only a terrible fate can await those who have willfully trampled under foot the Son of God, profaned the blood of the Covenant, and insulted the Holy Spirit of God (ver. 26-31). Finally, he bids them take courage and hope in recalling the early days of their faith, when they and others had so much to suffer and bore their persecutions and privations bravely. In view of the confidence and steadfastness then manifested, they must not waver or shrink back now; they must not lose the reward of their earlier sacrifices; they must press on to the crown of eternal life, for the struggle will not be long for any of them (ver. 32-39).

19-21. Under the Old Dispensation only the High Priest had the right to enter the Holy of Holies of the Tabernacle; but now, says the Apostle, we all are perfectly free, by virtue of the blood of Jesus and our union with Him, to enter the heavenly Sanctuary, into the very presence of God in heaven. Jesus has led the way to that Sanctuary, passing thither "through the veil" of His body, through His suffering humanity, and thus opening it to everyone. The way He traversed is called "new," because until He passed through it we knew it not, it was closed to us; it is also said to be a "living way," because it leads to a life of grace and glory, and because He who first entered by it is the way, the truth, and the

22. Let us draw near with a true heart in fullness of faith, having our hearts sprinkled from an evil conscience, and our bodies washed with clean water.

23. Let us hold fast the confession of our hope without wavering, for he is faithful that hath promised.

24. And let us consider one another, to provoke unto charity and to good works;

25. Not forsaking our assembly, as some are accustomed to do; but comforting *one another,* and so much the more as you see the day approaching.

life (John xiv. 6; cf. Eph. ii. 18, iii. 12). And not only have we this free access to the throne of God and this opened way, but Jesus is our great High Priest who is now actually exercising His priestly functions for us in the heavenly Sanctuary, and has authority over the whole "house of God," i.e., the Church Militant and Triumphant. See Eph. i. 22; 1 Tim. iii. 15.

In the Vulgate of verse 19 *Christi* should be *Jesus.*

22-23. With the three sources of confidence and assurance just mentioned in the preceding verses the Apostle bids us draw near to God and the throne of grace, but with sincerity of heart, fullness of faith, a purified conscience, and a body over which have flowed the cleansing waters of Baptism; and he further exhorts his readers who were tempted to waver in their faith to "hold fast" to the profession which they made at the time they were baptised and received into the Church.

Hearts sprinkled. The reference is to the physical purification by blood according to the Law, spoken of above in ix. 19-22. Our hearts are purified by the blood of Christ, as St. John says (1 John i. 7). The water of Baptism is called "clean water" because of its cleansing effects on the soul; while washing the body physically, it cleanses the soul spiritually.

For he is faithful, etc., i.e., God who has promised the rewards of the future life will keep His promise, if we do our part.

24-25. Our faith and hope must issue in works of charity and mutual helpfulness; we must emulate one another in the exercise of charity and the performance of good works. None should withdraw from the Christian assembly, from the coming-together of the faithful to celebrate the divine mysteries and receive instruction, where mutual comfort and exhortation were given. The chief purpose of the Christian assembly was to celebrate the Holy Eucharist, as we are told in 1 Cor. xi. 20. This fidelity to Christian fellowship

26. For if we sin willfully after having the knowledge of the truth, there is now left no sacrifice for sins,

27. But a certain dreadful expectation of judgment, and the rage of a fire which shall consume the adversaries.

28. A man making void the law of Moses dieth without any mercy under two or three witnesses:

29. How much more do you think he deserveth worse punishment who hath trodden under foot the Son of God, and hath esteemed the blood of the testament unclean by which he was sanctified, and hath offered an affront to the Spirit of grace?

and service was all the more necessary in view of the fact that the day of death and judgment was not far off for any one of the faithful.

As some are accustomed to do. It seems that some of the faithful had withdrawn from the Christian gatherings, perhaps out of human respect or for fear of persecution.

26-27. To render his readers ever more firm and steadfast in their faith, the Apostle now (ver. 26-31), as before in vi. 4-8, sets before them the terrible consequences of apostasy.

If we sin willfully, i.e., by deliberately rejecting the faith, after having had a "knowledge of the truth" (better, "perfect knowledge of the truth," i.e., of the teachings of the faith of Christ), there can be no hope of salvation, as long as we remain in that condition of mind and soul, because the sacrifice for sin which Christ has given is God's final offer to man, the sole means of obtaining forgiveness. On the contrary, there awaits the wretched victims of this state of soul "a certain" (i.e., some sort of) "dreadful expectation of judgment" from God and a punishment which is described as a consuming fire (cf. xii. 29 below; also Isa. xxvi. 11).

28-29. The writer here confirms what he has just said by an argument from less to greater drawn from Deut. xvii. 2 ff., where there is question of idolatry, and so of apostasy from the true faith. He says if, under the Law of Moses, one who on the testimony of two or three witnesses was guilty of such a sin had to suffer death, how much more does he deserve a worse punishment who has apostasized from the faith of Christ under the Gospel Dispensation. For such a one has despised the Son of God, has set at naught the blood of Christ by which the New Covenant has been sealed and ratified and he himself sanctified, and has insulted the Holy Ghost, the author and dispenser of the grace which Christ's blood

30. For we know him that hath said: *Vengeance belongeth to me, and I will repay.* And again: *The Lord shall judge his people.*

31. It is a fearful thing to fall into the hands of the living God.

32. But call to mind the former days wherein, being illuminated, you endured a great fight of afflictions.

33. And on the one hand indeed, by reproaches and tribulations, were made a gazingstock; and on the other, became companions of them that met a similar fate.

34. For you both had compassion on them that were in bonds, and took with joy the being stripped of your own goods, knowing that you have a better and a lasting substance.

has merited for us. The sin here described is like the sin against the Holy Ghost, spoken of in Matt. xii. 31 ff., and Mark iii. 22 ff.

30. The certainty of God's punishment of the sin of apostasy is made clear by an appeal to God's own words in Deut. xxxii. 35-36. The first quotation, "vengeance belongeth to me, etc.," is not strictly according to either the Hebrew or the LXX, but is found in the same form in Rom. xii. 19, where, however, the application is different. This is the only Old Testament quotation in the Epistle which is not according to the LXX.

31. **Hands of the living God,** i.e., a God of power and activity. The reference is to Deut. v. 26.

32. After his severe words about the fate of those who apostasize, the Apostle now (ver. 32-39) gives his readers some words of encouragement and hope, as he did before in vi. 9, following a passage of similar severity. They will be heartened in their present trials by recalling the persecutions and sufferings they endured soon after their Baptism and reception to the faith. If they could stand so much then, they ought to be able to stand more now when their faith should be stronger.

33-34. In those early days of their Christian profession the faithful had much to suffer individually in mind and body, and also shared in the sorrows and trials of their brethren who had met a similar fate and had been cast into prison; and they took with joy the plunder of their own possessions, knowing that there awaited them hereafter riches that would endure, "treasures in heaven, where neither the rust nor moth doth consume, and where thieves do not break through, nor steal" (Matt. vi. 20).

The reading of the last clause is not certain. According to the Sinaitic MS. we should read: "Knowing that you have your own

35. Do not therefore lose your confidence, which hath a great reward.

36. For patience is necessary for you, that, doing the will of God, you may receive the promise.

37. For yet a little and a very little while, and he that is to come, will come, and will not delay.

38. But my just one shall live by faith; but if he withdraw himself, he shall not please my soul.

selves as a better and abiding possession," i.e., the retention of their own souls and consciences will console them in the loss of temporal goods.

35-36. Having therefore suffered so much already, the Christians must not fall away now and thus lose the merits of their former faith and good works. They have need of patience, and, doing the will of God, they should offer to Him the true sacrifice of obedience, as Christ their Master did (x. 7), and receive in due time the eternal inheritance promised them (ix. 15).

37-38. The readers will find further consolation and hope in the reflection that their struggle will not be a long one, nor their rewards long delayed. This is proved by a free citation of the LXX of Habacuc ii. 3-4, introduced by the phrase, "for yet a little and a very little while," from Isaias xxvi. 20.

He that is to come, or more literally, "the coming one," was a Messianic phrase, and so meant here the coming of Christ as judge, whether at the hour of death for the individual or at the end of the world for the race. Soon at longest the Lord will come, to render to each one according to his works. It is probable, however, that the reference here is to the destruction of the city of Jerusalem, which had been predicted by our Lord (Matt. xxiv. 34).

My just one, etc., i.e., he who has been justified by sanctifying grace and has remained faithful shall be sustained by his faith in the struggles of this life and shall attain to life eternal in the world to come. This same quotation St. Paul makes use of in Rom. i. 17 as the basis of his doctrine of justification by faith. Faith here means steadfast confidence.

But if he withdraw himself, etc., i.e., if he abandons his faith and falls into apostasy, he shuts himself out from the divine favor and incurs the punishment his sin deserves.

The Hebrew of this passage of Habacuc differs considerably from the LXX. In their literal meaning the prophet's words had reference to the liberation of the Chosen People from Babylonian

39. But we are not the children of withdrawing unto perdition, but of faith to the saving of the soul.

captivity, but spiritually they referred to the Messiah, who would deliver from sin those who would believe in Him and would give them life eternal.

Vivit in the Vulgate should be future, as in the Greek.

39. The writer reassures his readers that they have not fallen away from the faith; they are children of faith and will save their souls. The introduction of the word "faith" here prepares the author for the next great subject of his Epistle.

CHAPTER XI

FAITH DESCRIBED AND ILLUSTRATED, 1-38

1. Now faith is the substance of things to be hoped for, the evidence of things that appear not.

1-38. The close of the preceding Chapter has shown that faith is essential to salvation, and hence the author will now describe so important a virtue and illustrate its value and power by citing some of the religious heroes of the past. These examples of what faith has done for so many of those ancient saints whom Jewish history most revered will be especially consoling to the readers of this Epistle, for it will show them that their own Christian faith is not something new and distinct from the religious assurance and conviction which sustained their ancestors, but rather a continuation of the same sustaining virtue, only on a much more elevated plain.

1. We have not here a strict definition of the virtue of faith, but rather a description of some of the practical results which faith produces in those who possess it.

The word *hypostasis,* here translated "substance," may be taken subjectively, for *assurance* or *firm confidence*; or objectively, for *basis* or *foundation*. The Greeks understood it in this latter sense, as that which gives substance and reality to the things hoped for. This sense would be presupposed to the former meaning any way; it is the firm foundation which produces the firm confidence and assurance, though assurance or firm confidence seems to be the more direct meaning of the term here.

2. For by this the ancients obtained a testimony.

3. By faith we understand that the world was framed by the word of God; that from invisible things visible things might be made.

4. By faith Abel offered to God a better sacrifice than Cain, by which he obtained a testimony that he was just, God giving testimony to his gifts; and by it he being dead yet speaketh.

5. By faith Henoch was translated, that he should not see death; and he was not found, because God had translated him: for before his translation he had testimony that he pleased God.

The word translated "evidence" may also be taken objectively as *proof,* or subjectively as *conviction,* or the result of proof or demonstration. Perhaps the subjective meaning is the one intended here. Thus, by faith we are *assured* of the future things for which we hope, and *convinced* of the reality and certainty of the things we do not see.

2. Because of their faith God bore witness to the ancient saints of Israel, causing them to be praised in Sacred Scripture as holy and acceptable to Him.

3. The Apostle will now give some examples of faith, beginning with the work of creation. We know through faith, he says, that the world was created by God's fiat, for so it was revealed to the ancient patriarchs and has been handed down to us in the Sacred Scriptures (Gen. i. 3, 6, 9, ff.).

The world. Literally, "the ages," as in i. 2.

That from invisible things, etc. The visible universe was created by God out of nothing, that is, from no pre-existing matter; all things visible have come from God, formed according to His invisible idea. Therefore, all materialistic explanations of the origin of the world are wrong.

4. It was faith that directed Abel to offer God a more worthy sacrifice than his brother Cain (Gen. iv. 2 ff.), for by faith he was able to recognize more clearly the supreme excellence and the sovereign rights of God. Because of this faith God bore testimony to Abel that he was just, and that his gifts were acceptable to Him (Gen. iv. 4).

And by it, etc. The reference may be to the voice of Abel's blood crying to heaven for vengeance (Gen. iv. 10), or to the fact that Abel, though dead, still speaks by his blood and example (Matt. xxiii. 35).

5. Henoch. See Gen. v. 21-24.

6. But without faith it is impossible to please him. For he that cometh to God, must believe that he is, and is a rewarder to them that seek him.

7. By faith Noe, having received an answer concerning those things which as yet were not seen, moved with fear, framed the ark for the saving of his house, by the which he condemned the world; and was instituted heir of the justice which is by faith.

8. By faith he that is called Abraham, obeyed to go out into a place which he was to receive for an inheritance; and he went out, not knowing whither he went.

Pleased God. The Hebrew has: "Walked with God." It was Henoch's faith that made him pleasing to God, and that enabled him to commune with God, as the following verse shows.

6. The fact that we cannot please God without faith is a proof that Henoch had faith. The minimum required for salvation is to *believe* that God exists and that He rewards His servants. A mere scientific acceptance of God's existence, which we can get by the due exercise of reason, is not sufficient for merit, since it is not free; whereas acceptance on faith is always free.

Deo of the Vulgate is not expressed in the Greek.

7. Noe believed God's revelation about a flood to come, and prepared an ark against it, thus manifesting his faith in God and at the same time condemning the unbelieving world around him (Matt. xxiv. 37 ff.). His faith saved him and made him "heir," i.e., possessor, of the justification which is through faith.

8. As Abraham was the supreme example of faith among the Jews, the writer now dwells at length on his faith. The great patriarch's faith is illustrated: (a) by his obedience to the call of God to go forth from his own country in search of the Promised Land and his wanderings in that strange land (ver. 8-10); (b) by the confidence with which he and his wife Sara received God's promise of offspring (ver. 11-12); (c) by his willingness to sacrifice Isaac (ver. 17-19).

The call of God came to Abraham in Ur of the Chaldees, and in obedience to it he left home and kindred, wandering and enduring privations and hardships in search of the land of Canaan which God had promised to give to him and his descendants (Gen. xii. 1 ff.).

That is called Abraham. Here the author alludes to the fact that God, as a mark of special favor, changed the patriarch's original name Abram to Abraham (Gen. xvii. 5).

9. By faith he abode in the land as a stranger, dwelling in cottages, with Isaac and Jacob, the co-heirs of the same promise.

10. For he looked for a city that hath foundations; whose builder and maker is God.

11. By faith also Sara herself, being barren, received strength to conceive seed, even past the time of age; because she believed that he was faithful who had promised.

12. For which cause there sprung even from one (and him as good as dead) issue like the stars of heaven in multitude. and like the sand which is by the seashore innumerable.

13. All these died according to faith, not having received the promises, but beholding them afar off, and saluting them and confessing that they are pilgrims and strangers on the earth.

14. For they that say these things do signify that they seek a country.

15. And truly if they had been mindful of that from whence they came out, they had doubtless time to return.

16. But now they desire a better, that is to say, a heavenly country. Therefore God is not ashamed to be called their God; for he hath prepared for them a city.

9. Faith not only made Abraham obedient to the call of God, but also gave him patience to wait for the fulfillment of God's promises, dwelling as a sojourner in a foreign country. His son, Isaac, and his grandson, Jacob, persevered in the same faith, never doubting the promise of God. Cf. Gen. xii. 8, xiii. 3, xvii. 1 ff.

10. Abraham was sustained in his faith by the conviction that there was an abiding city awaiting him hereafter in heaven, a city whose architect and master-builder is God. The land of Canaan which God had promised him was but a figure of an eternal inheritance which God would bestow upon him above.

A city that hath foundations means the heavenly Jerusalem (xii. 22; Gal. iv. 26; Apoc. xxi. 2).

11-12. Though Sara was already ninety years of age when she received the promise of a son, she believed, even if somewhat less promptly than Abraham, and as a result she was given the power to conceive (Gen. xvii. 17). Likewise, though far beyond the age of begetting children, Abraham, as a reward of his faith, became the father of a posterity as numerous as the stars of heaven and the sands on the sea-shore (Gen. xxi. 17; cf. Rom. iv. 19).

13-16. In these verses the author interrupts his argument to reflect on the great faith of the patriarchs, Abraham, Isaac and Jacob. The vision which faith had disclosed to them was too glorious to find its realization during their lifetime, or on earth.

17. By faith Abraham, when he was tried, offered Isaac, and he that had received the promises offered up his only-begotten son,

18. To whom it was said: *In Isaac shall thy seed be called:*

19. Accounting that God is able to raise up even from the dead. Whereupon also he received him for a parable.

20. By faith also of things to come, Isaac blessed Jacob and Esau.

21. By faith Jacob dying, blessed each of the sons of Joseph, and adored the top of his rod.

The fulfillment of the divine promises they saw dimly in the far future; but they were not disappointed, for they sought a city not made with hands, eternal in the heavens. Therefore, God recognized their faith and bestowed on them a celestial home. If the "country" they sought had been the earthly one whence they had come, they could have returned to it; but the object of their quest was "a heavenly country."

17-19. The faith of Abraham was sorely tried when God demanded of him the sacrifice of his son Isaac, but the aged patriarch did not waver (Gen. xxii. 1-18). Isaac was indeed the son of promise, who had been born of a freewoman, and on whom the future depended; but at God's command Abraham made ready to immolate him, feeling sure that He who had given this son in the first instance by a miracle, could restore him if necessary by a second miracle.

Isaac is called "the only-begotten son," because to him alone were the promises made, Ishmael being excluded from them.

Whereupon also he received him for a parable, i.e., as a reward of his faith Abraham received his son safely back from the jaws of death, and this delivery made Isaac a "parable," i.e., a figure or type of the sacrifice and resurrection of Christ.

20-21. Isaac and Jacob respectively pronounced blessings on their descendants, assuring them that God's promises to Abraham would be fulfilled for them and their children.

Each of the sons of Joseph, i.e., Ephraim and Manasses (Gen. xlviii. 1-20).

Adored over the top of his staff, i.e., he bowed in reverence to God, leaning on his staff (Gen. xlvii. 29-31). The Hebrew of this phrase reads: "He did homage toward the head of his bed," i.e., Jacob worshipped God, bowing in reverence toward the head of his bed.

22. By faith Joseph, when he was dying, made mention of the going out of the children of Israel; and gave commandment concerning his bones.

23. By faith Moses, when he was born, was hid three months by his parents; because they saw he was a comely babe, and they feared not the king's edict.

24. By faith, Moses, when he was grown up, denied himself to be the son of Pharao's daughter,

25. Rather choosing to be afflicted with the people of God, than to have the pleasure of sin for a time,

26. Esteeming the reproach of Christ greater riches than the treasures of the Egyptians. For he looked unto the reward.

27. By faith he left Egypt, not fearing the fierceness of the king; for he endured as seeing him that is invisible.

22. By faith Joseph was convinced that the Israelites would be delivered from the bondage of Egypt, and that his own bones would be laid to rest in the Promised Land (Gen. i. 24-25).

23-26. See Exod. ii. 2, 11. It was an act of faith on the part of the parents of Moses to hide their son away in defiance of the royal decree. It was likewise an act of faith on Moses' part that moved him to decline the royal position and prerogatives and identify himself with his own outcast people.

Esteeming the reproach of Christ, etc. Here we have the motive which actuated Moses in bearing his sufferings. As a figure and type of the Christ, he had much to suffer, both from his own people and from strangers. But faith in the Messiah to come was his guiding principle, and he associated his sufferings with the future outrages and persecutions borne by our Saviour for the salvation of the world (Rom. xv. 3). He looked beyond his present distress to the reward that awaited him in the hereafter. What a powerful example Moses afforded to the readers of this Epistle, who were tempted to waver under persecution!

27. **He left Egypt, not fearing,** etc. Many scholars find here an allusion to the final Exodus from Egypt; but the following verse requires us to find in these words an event prior to the Passover which preceded the Exodus. Therefore, the majority of expositors say the reference here must be to the flight of Moses to Madian, as narrated in Exod. ii. 14 ff. But there it is said that he fled from the face of Pharaoh, whereas here we are told that he did not fear the fierceness of the king. The best explanation seems to be that, while at the moment in question Moses felt the extrem-

28. By faith he celebrated the pasch and the shedding of the blood, that he who destroyed the first-born might not touch them.

29. By faith they passed through the Red Sea, as by dry land; which the Egyptians attempting were swallowed up.

30. By faith the walls of Jericho fell down, by the going round them seven days.

31. By faith Rahab the harlot perished not with the unbelievers, receiving the spies with peace.

32. And what shall I yet say? For the time would fail me to tell of Gedeon, Barac, Samson, Jephte, David, Samuel, and the prophets,

33. Who by faith conquered kingdoms, wrought justice, obtained promises, stopped the mouths of lions,

ity of the situation and did retire for a time from the presence of the king, still he was so confident of divine help and final success that he was not turned aside from his purpose and clung to his own people, instead of throwing in his lot with the Egyptians.

28. Moses' next act of faith is seen in his obedience to the commands of God regarding the keeping of the Passover and the sprinkling of the blood on the lintels and door posts that the destroyer "of the first-born might not touch them" (Exod. xii. 12-48).

29-31. The march through the Red Sea (Exod. xiv. 13 ff.) and around the walls of Jericho (Jos. vi. 1 ff.) were powerful acts of faith on the part of the whole people; and the faith of Rahab saved herself and her family from the common fate that befell the faithless inhabitants of Jericho. This woman was a stranger and a sinner, and yet she received the spies sent to Jericho by Josue because she believed in the God of Israel who has done so much for His people (Jos. ii. 1 ff.).

32. In verses 32-38 the writer gives a brief statement of some of the illustrations of faith found in great leaders of Israel from the conquest of the Promised Land under Josue down to the time of the Machabees. The names enumerated do not follow a chronological order; on the contrary, the name which appears second in each pair in this verse preceded the other in time. He speaks first of the exploits of four great judges, and then of the achievements of David, Samuel and the Prophets.

33. Many of the phrases in this and the following five verses are quite general and applied to a number of the heroes mentioned; others are more specific and refer to some definite event in the history of Israel.

34. Quenched the violence of fire, escaped the edge of the sword, recovered strength from weakness, became valiant in battle, put to flight the armies of foreigners.

35. Women received their dead raised to life again. But others were racked, not accepting deliverance, that they might find a better resurrection.

36. And others had trial of mockeries and stripes, moreover also of bonds and prisons.

37. They were stoned, they were cut asunder, they were tempted, they were put to death by the sword, they wandered about in sheepskins, in goatskins, being in want, distressed, afflicted,

38. Of whom the world was not worthy; wandering in deserts, in mountains, and in dens, and in caves of the earth.

39. And all these being approved by the testimony of faith, received not the promise,

40. God providing some better thing for us, that they should not be perfected without us.

Obtained promises, i.e., particular promises which were subordinated to the one great promise (ver. 39).

Stopped the mouths of lions. See Dan. vi. 22.

34. **Quenched the violence of fire.** See Dan. iii. 17; 1 Mach. ii. 59.

35. **Women received their dead,** etc., like the widow of Sarepta (3 Kings xvii. 23) and the Sunamite (4 Kings iv. 36).

Others were racked, etc., referring to the martyrdom of Eleazar and the seven brothers (2 Mach. vi-vii).

A better resurrection, in life eternal.

36. This verse refers especially to the tortures of the seven brothers and their mother (2 Mach. vii. 1 ff.). Most of the sufferings mentioned in this and the two following verses were experienced by the faithful during the persecution of Antiochus Epiphanes.

37. Zachary, son of Joiada, was "stoned" (2 Paral. xxiv. 20 ff.). According to Jewish tradition Isaias was sawn asunder (*The Ascension of Isaias,* v, 1-14).

38. Those faithful servants of God were treated as outcasts by a world that was not worthy of them.

GENERAL CONCLUSION, 39-40

39-40. All those heroes of the past gained a reputation for faith and to a certain extent realized the divine promises, but the promised Messiah they did not live to see. Without any fault of theirs,

the supreme reward of faith was denied to them, being reserved
for us of a later date; but with us they have entered into the full
inheritance of faith, being admitted to the glory of heaven through
the Messianic blessings brought to the world by Christ.

That they should not be perfected without us. The faith of
the heroes of the past has been perfected through the revelation
vouchsafed to us.

CHAPTER XII

EXHORTATION TO CONSTANCY, 1-13

1. And therefore, we also having so great a cloud of witnesses over our
head, laying aside every weight and sin which surrounds us, let us run by
patience to the fight proposed to us;

2. Looking on Jesus, the author and finisher of faith, who having joy set
before him, endured the cross, despising the shame, and now sitteth on the
right hand of the throne of God.

1-13. The Apostle now applies to his readers what has just been
said in the preceding Chapter. He exhorts them to remain steadfast in their faith, thus imitating those illustrious examples of the
past, and especially Christ Himself (ver. 1-3). Our sufferings are
a sign of God's fatherly care for us as His sons; He knows that
discipline is good and necessary for us, and He wants to lead us
to perfection (ver. 4-13).

1-2. The writer describes the Christian life as a race, like the
contests often witnessed in the Greek amphitheater. The metaphor
is a familiar one with St. Paul (1 Cor. ix. 24-25; Phil. iii. 12-14;
2 Tim. iv. 7-8). The racers in the games were surrounded by
spectators. They put off all superfluous clothing and reduced their
flesh by training, so as to be able to exert their maximum strength
and gain the greatest speed, and they kept their eyes steadily fixed
on the goal.

In a similar manner the runners for the prize of eternal life must
act. They are in the arena of life, and the heroes enumerated in
the previous Chapter are watching their struggle. They must put
away all the entanglements of sin and run with patient steadfastness
the way before them, looking to Jesus as their goal, who is the
author and perfecter of their faith, and who, for the joy that would

3. For think diligently upon him that endured such opposition from sinners against himself; that you be not wearied, fainting in your minds.

4. You have not yet resisted unto blood, striving against sin;

5. And you have forgotten the consolation, which speaketh to you, as unto children, saying: *My son, neglect not the discipline of the Lord; neither be thou wearied whilst thou art rebuked by him,*

6. *For whom the Lord loveth he chastiseth; and he scourgeth every son whom he receiveth.*

be afforded by our redemption and His own glorification as man, gladly endured the sufferings and shame of His passion, and now sits in triumph at the right hand of the Father in heaven.

Which surrounds us, like an encircling robe. The Greek word for "surrounds" means, more literally, "easily besets." It is found only here and is of uncertain meaning, but it surely refers to the internal and external encumbrances of sin, to the hampering effect of sin on the soul.

Now sitteth on the right hand, etc. This is the glorious reward which our Lord's sufferings merited for His humanity. Note the difference in time of the verbs which express our Lord's sufferings and His glorification, "endured," "sitteth." The former expresses something that was passing and that came to an end, while the latter (in the perfect tense in the Greek) signifies that Christ has taken His seat for all future time at the right hand of the Father.

3-4. Meditation on the passion and sufferings of Christ would give greatest encouragement to the readers of the Epistle who were tempted to falter in their Christian loyalty and devotion under the pressure of persecution by their enemies. The writer has already shown in ii. 10 and v. 8-9 that Christ Himself was made perfect and learned obedience by the things which He suffered. He, therefore, now exhorts his readers to follow the example of their Master. Surely their sufferings have not yet equalled His.

The *enim* of the Vulgate in verse 4 is not expressed in the Greek.

5-6. The writer now bids his readers remember what God has said in the words of Prov. iii. 11-12, where suffering is described as the chastening of the Lord; the Lord admits no one to His love whom He does not chastise and subject to discipline. Of course, it does not follow from this that all who suffer are beloved of the Lord, because sin brings its own punishment here and now, and the sinner is often scourged by the results of his sins without being

7. Persevere under discipline. God dealeth with you as with *his* sons; for what son *is there* whom the father doth not correct?

8. But if you be without chastisement, whereof all are made partakers, then are you bastards, and not sons.

9. Moreover, we have had fathers of our flesh for instructors, and we reverenced them: shall we not much more obey the Father of spirits and live?

10. And they indeed for a few days, according to their own pleasure, instructed us; but he, for our profit, that we might receive his sanctification.

11. Now all chastisement for the present indeed seemeth not to bring with it joy but sorrow; but afterwards it will yield, to them that are exercised by it, the most peaceable fruit of justice.

12. Wherefore lift up the hands which hang down and the feeble knees,

13. And make straight steps with your feet, that no one halting may go out of the way; but rather be healed.

moved to better ways. But the way of the cross and of suffering is the only road to heaven.

7-8. Persevere under discipline. The Greek means: "It is for the sake of discipline that you have to suffer." God is treating the Christians as sons, and suffering is necessary for the upbuilding and perfecting of character. Hence, if they had not to endure these hardships, it would be a sign that they were not in God's favor as sons.

9-10. Here the Apostle tells us that we all have had our earthly fathers who chastised and instructed us in our youth, and yet we revered them. How much more then should we reverently accept the discipline of the Father and Creator of our spirits and spiritual life who is training us for eternity! Those human parents were preparing us for this present brief life and according to their own conceptions and standards, which were sometimes erroneous; but God's discipline is always perfect, and the end He has in view is our sanctification, to make us partakers of His own holiness here through grace and hereafter in glory.

11. All discipline seems hard and irksome at the time, but when it comes from God its final issue is always peace and holiness; everything good has to be purchased at a price proportionate to its value. As athletes are hardened and strengthened by physical exercise, so Christians by moral discipline are developed, strengthened and perfected in their character and made ready for the life to come.

12-13. There is a reference in ver. 12 to Isaias xxv. 3, and in

14. Follow peace with all men, and holiness; without which no man shall see God:

15. Looking diligently, lest any man be wanting in the grace of God; lest any root of bitterness springing up do hinder, and by it many be defiled.

16. Lest there be any fornicator, or profane person, as Esau; who for one mess sold his first birthright.

ver. 13 to Prov. iv. 26. In view of what has just been said, the writer tells his readers to take courage in their sufferings and tribulations. They must not let their hands hang listlessly down nor their feet grow weak. They must have regard for the fainting souls of their brethren and try to smooth the path for them, so that legs which are already lame may not be put out of joint by the roughness of the road they have to walk, but may rather be healed. Such is the meaning of the Greek of verse 13, which our version and the Vulgate do not clearly bring out.

EXHORTATION TO VARIOUS VIRTUES, 14-29

14-29. The writer now appeals to his readers to keep before their minds two supreme requirements of the Christian life, namely, peace and holiness, which must be cultivated both for personal and community reasons (ver. 14-17). The warning words here addressed are then made more emphatic by a consideration of the severity and awfulness of the Old Covenant as contrasted with the mercy and sublimity of the New, which shows the vast superiority of the latter (ver. 18-24). The inference to be drawn from this comparison is that the duties and responsibilities imposed by the Gospel are far greater than those involved in the Law. Therefore, if God severely punished the violation of the commands given at Sinai, how much greater will be the penalty they must pay who are deaf to the voice that speaks through the New Dispensation (ver. 25-29)!

14. Follow peace with all men. The same thought is in Rom. xii. 18. The faithful are to try to have peace and harmony among themselves, and, as far as Christian principles will permit, with outsiders as well.

15-16. Christians must not only be solicitous about their own personal sanctification, but also about that of their fellow-Christians. No one must be allowed to fall away from the grace of God, thus becoming a source of scandal and contamination for others.

17. For know ye that afterwards, when he desired to inherit the benediction, he was rejected; for he found no place of repentance, although
with tears he had sought it.

18. For you are not come to a mountain that might be touched, and a
burning fire, and a whirlwind, and darkness, and storm.

19. And the sound of a trumpet, and the voice of words, which they that
heard excused themselves, that the word might not be spoken to them;

20. For they did not endure that which was said: *And if so much as a
beast shall touch the mount it shall be stoned.*

21. And so terrible was that which was seen, Moses said: *I am frighted
and tremble.*

Root of bitterness, etc., is a reference to Deut. xxix. 18; it
means here a cause of infection for others. Nor must anyone be
allowed to fall into apostasy, thus becoming guilty of spiritual
adultery by violating his covenant relationship with God, as did
Esau (Gen. xxv. 30 ff.).

Profane person, i.e., one who is earthly and material in his
desires and aims, caring nothing for spiritual things.

17. **He found no place of repentance.** It was not the forgiveness of his sin that Esau sought in vain with tears, but the recovery
of the forfeited blessing (Gen. xxvii. 34, 38). He wanted to undo
the natural consequences of his act, which even a true repentance
could not remove. Had Esau ever sincerely repented of his sin,
its guilt would have been remitted, though the lost blessing could
not be regained.

18-21. In verses 18-24 the writer enters upon a comparison of
the natures of the Old and New Covenants, showing that, whereas
the Old was one of dread warnings and threats, the New invites
to a glad and glorious fellowship. And because of this very difference, he says, those who become unfaithful to the latter are far
more guilty than those who disobeyed the former. The characteristic of the Old Law was fear, that of the New Law is love. How
terrible, therefore, will be the fate of those who turn their backs
on the law of love! And how much greater sanctity, consequently,
is required of us Christians than was expected of the Israelites
of old!

In these verses we have a description of the physical phenomena
which accompanied the giving of the Law on Sinai (Exod. xix. 1
ff., xx. 1 ff.; Deut. iv. 11 ff.), and the consequent fear that filled
the attending multitude, and even Moses to whom the revelation

22. But you are come to mount Sion and to the city of the living God, the heavenly Jerusalem, and to the company of many thousands of angels.

23. And to the church of the first born, who are written in the heavens, and to God the Judge of all, and to the spirits of the just made perfect,

24. And to Jesus the mediator of the new Testament, and to the sprinkling of blood which speaketh better than that of Abel.

was made. So awful was the voice there heard that they prayed not to hear it again; and so holy was the mountain that, if even a dumb animal trespassed upon it, it was immediately stoned to death (Exod. xxix. 12 ff.). In some MSS. of verse 18 there is no word corresponding to "mountain," but it seems to be implied and required by the context. The words attributed to Moses in verse 21 are not found in the Old Testament, but perhaps the writer is drawing on tradition. Words somewhat similar, uttered on another occasion, are found in Deut. ix. 19.

The awful and unapproachable mountain described in these verses is a symbol of a dreadful and forbidding God, whom the ancient Israelites might well fear. But in the following verses the writer will give us the very different picture of the New Covenant and of the God revealed therein.

22-24. In these verses the author tells us something of the beauty and transcendent character of the New Dispensation, of which Mount Sion was the symbol even under the Old Dispensation. Through their faith Christians have not been led to a mountain of warning and terror like Sinai, but to the Church Militant and Triumphant, of which Sion and Jerusalem were the material symbols. And the vision which meets their eyes is one, not of dread and foreboding, but of peace and festive joy, of a vast assembly composed of thousands of angels, of the faithful on earth, and of the blessed spirits of the Old and New Dispensations who have entered into their eternal rewards in heaven; and in the midst of all this innumerable gathering stands God Himself, the Judge of all mankind, and Jesus Christ, the Mediator of the New Covenant, who has offered the perfect sacrifice of His own blood, by which the New Covenant is ratified and the sins of men washed away.

First born most probably refers to regenerated men on earth, who are called the "first born" of God by comparison with the rest of men who remain in darkness and infidelity. With less probability of correctness some authorities understand the phrase to be in apposition to "thousands of angels."

25. See that you refuse him not that speaketh. For if they escaped not who refused him that spoke upon earth, much more *shall not* we, that turn away from him that speaketh to us from heaven.

26. Whose voice then moved the earth; but now he promiseth, saying: *Yet once more, and I will move not only the earth, but heaven also.*

27. And in that he saith, *Yet once more,* he signifieth the translation of the moveable things as made, that those things may remain which are immoveable.

28. Therefore receiving an immoveable kingdom, let us be thankful. and thus serve, pleasing God, with fear and reverence.

29. For our God is a consuming fire.

And to the sprinkling of blood, etc.   The allusion is to Gen. iv. 10, where it is said that the blood of Abel cried to heaven for vengeance; but the blood of Jesus speaks of a far better sacrifice, which calls for mercy and pardon.   The allusion, however, may be, not to Abel's blood crying from the ground to heaven, but to his "better sacrifice" (xi. 4), compared with which the sacrifice of Jesus is better still.

25. In verses 25-29 we have an appeal based on the pictures just drawn of the Old and New Covenants (ver. 21-24), which shows the greater obligations that rest on the faithful of the New Law. Christians must see that they do not repeat the error of the Jews who refused to listen to the voice of God speaking to them from Sinai; if they were punished, how much more shall we have to suffer if we fail to heed the divine voice that speaks to us from heaven!

26-27. At Sinai God's voice shook the earth (Exod. xix. 18), and the prophet Aggeus (ii. 6, 7, 21) tells us that once more, at the end of time, the same divine voice will shake the whole world. This prophecy has yet to be fulfilled, as the words, "yet once more," clearly indicate.   In this final shock all created, material things will perish, but spiritual realities will survive unshaken and unharmed. The latter will remain because they are imperishable.   All material and sensible things are but the shadows, the perishing copies of their heavenly archetypes.   "The earthquake which dissolves and annihilates things sensible is powerless against the Things Invisible. The rushing waters of the cataract only shake the shadow of the pine" (Farrar, *h. l.*).

28-29. Since, therefore, we Christians belong to the unshakable kingdom which Christ has established, and which is destined to endure forever, "let us be thankful" for the grace of faith which we have, and hold to it firmly, thus offering to God a service worthy of Him, with fear and awe; for "our God is a consuming fire," both under the Old Dispensation (Deut. iv. 24) and in the New (2 Thess. i. 8), i.e., He will destroy all His enemies and the vio-lators of His Law, especially all apostates from the faith.

CHAPTER XIII

CONCLUDING EXHORTATIONS, 1-17

1. Let the charity of the brotherhood abide in you.
2. And hospitality do not forget; for by this some, being not aware of it, have entertained angels.
3. Remember them that are in bonds as if you were bound with them; and them that are ill-treated, as being yourselves also in the body.

1-17. In these closing verses the Apostle first exhorts his readers to the practice of various virtues, reminding them especially of brotherly love, hospitality, kindness to prisoners and the suffering, purity of life, and contentment (ver. 1-6). He then calls to their minds the example of their religious leaders, the need of steadfast-ness in spirituality, the difference between the Jewish sacrifice of the Atonement and the sacrifice of Christ, and finally repeats the injunction of obedience to superiors (ver. 7-17).

1. Everywhere in the New Testament the phrase "brotherly love," or "charity of the brotherhood," means love of one's fellow-Chris-tian. The term "brother" is one of the earliest designations for a member of the Christian community (1 John iv. 20; Rom. xii. 13, 20; 1 Cor. v. 12; 1 Thess. iv. 9, etc.). The words "in you" are not expressed in the Greek but are implied.

2. Hospitality was cultivated by both Jews and pagans. It was a virtue especially recommended in early Christian times in imita-tion of the charity of Christ and because of persecution, by which Christians were often despoiled of their goods. The exceeding diffi-culties of travel also made the exercise of this virtue most helpful and necessary.

Have entertained angels. The writer is referring to the cases of Abraham, Lot, and Tobias (Gen. xviii. 2, xix. 3; Judg. xiii. 2 ff.).

3. In this verse the writer reminds his readers that it is the duty of charity to suffer with those who suffer, and that, since they have the same frail nature as their brethren and so are exposed to the

4. Let marriage be honorable in all, and the bed undefiled. For fornicators and adulterers God will judge.

5. Let your manners be without covetousness, contented with such things as you have; for he hath said: *I will not leave thee, neither will I forsake thee.*

6. So that we may confidently say: *The Lord is my helper: I will not fear what man shall do to me.*

7. Remember your prelates who have spoken the word of God to you; whose faith follow, considering the outcome of their manner of life.

8. Jesus Christ, yesterday and today and the same for ever.

9. Be not led away with various and strange doctrines. For it is best that the heart be established with grace, not with meats; which have not profited those that walk in them.

same dangers, they may soon find themselves in the same condition. These considerations ought to appeal to their charity and compassion.

The Greek rendered *laborantium* by the Vulgate really means "to suffer adversity."

4. An exhortation to respect marriage in all its aspects, and to observe conjugal chastity.

In all may mean "in all respects," or "by all" who have contracted matrimony, or "among all," that is, by everybody. The phrase does not mean that all should marry, for St. Paul has not forgotten what he wrote about the superiority of the state of virginity in I Cor. vii.

5-6. Christians must also be free from avarice and from too much attachment to things of this world, for God has assured us that He will never abandon the faithful soul in its need. The references here are to Deut. xxxi. 6; Josue i. 5; Psalm cxvii. 6. Cf. also Matt. vi. 31, 34.

7. In verses 7-17 the Apostle has especially in mind the danger in which his readers stood of giving up their Christian faith and going back to Judaism. He therefore begins by calling to their minds for imitation those Christian leaders—the bishops, priests, and deacons—who first preached the Gospel to them, who continued firm in the faith to the end of their lives, and some of whom, like St. James and St. Stephen, were martyred for their faith. The glorious life and death of these early leaders ought to be an example for the readers of this Epistle, who under stress of persecution were tempted to waver in their faith.

8-9. Although the human leaders and preachers of the Christian

10. We have an altar, whereof they have no power to eat who serve the tabernacle.

11. For the bodies of those beasts, whose blood is brought into the holies by the high priest for sin, are burned without the camp.

faith come and go, Jesus Christ, who is the object of that faith, remains forever unchanged. Such as He was proved to be in the past, He is now and will continue to be for all eternity. And His doctrine is like Himself, unchangeable and everlasting. The faithful, therefore, must not permit themselves to be led astray by new and strange doctrines which are not in conformity with the Gospel that has been preached to them; nor must they be trying to add to Christianity the outward forms of Judaism about various kinds of food, which were of no use to the Jews themselves who practised them under the Law. Far more important for salvation than these external ordinances is inner grace from God, which makes the heart strong and firm in sanctity. In speaking of "meats" here the writer has in mind the Jewish sacrificial banquets, as is evident from the following verse.

10-11. In verses 10-14 the author shows the difference between Christianity and Judaism, from which it follows that Christians should take no part in Jewish worship. We Christians, he says, have an altar and a sacrifice of which we partake, but of which "they," i.e., the Jewish priests and faithful, have no right to eat. Even among their own Jewish sacrifices there were some, like the great sin-offering on the Day of Atonement, the flesh of which the priests and Levites were not allowed to eat, since it all had to be burned outside the camp while the Jews were in the desert, and outside of Jerusalem after the temple was built (Lev. vi. 30, iv. 3-21). Now, the sacrifice of Jesus was the fulfillment of the sacrifice of the Day of Atonement, and so He was immolated outside the city; and therefore also, because of the typical relationship between the sacrifice of Jesus and that of the Day of Atonement, the Jews were excluded from partaking of the fruits of the Christian altar. Such seems to be the Apostle's argument in these difficult verses.

The word "altar" in verse 10 is understood by some to mean the altar of the cross, but by others the Eucharistic altar. In this latter opinion there would be a real eating of the body of Christ in the Eucharist, whereas in the former view there would be a sharing in

12. Wherefore Jesus also, that he might sanctify the people by his own blood, suffered without the gate.

13. Let us go forth therefore to him without the camp, bearing his reproach.

14. For we have not here a lasting city, but we seek one that is to come.

15. Through him therefore let us offer the sacrifice of praise always to God, that is to say, the fruit of lips confessing to his name.

16. And do not forget to do good, and to impart; for by such sacrifices God's favor is obtained.

the fruits of His passion. Some expositors think the "altar" here must be the altar in the heavenly Sanctuary, and not the cross, since the altar was not the place where the victim was slain, but where its blood was solemnly offered to God. It is to be noted that the Council of Trent did not use verse 10 here as a proof of the sacrificial character of the Eucharist.

The reference in verse 11 is to the sin-offering on the Day of Atonement, the blood of which was brought by the High Priest into the Holy of Holies and sprinkled on the mercy-seat, while the flesh was entirely burned in the fire. In the minor sacrifices for sin the priests and Levites partook of the flesh of the victims (Lev. vi. 25-29).

12. The purpose of the sacrifice which Jesus offered on the altar of the cross, "without the gate" (i.e., outside the city of Jerusalem; cf. Matt. xxvii. 32; John xix. 20), was the expiation of the sins of the world and the sanctification of all mankind.

13-16. In these verses the author makes a final appeal to his readers to go forth from the Jewish camp and city, that is, to renounce forever Judaism and the Jewish community, and through faith to unite themselves to Christ, showing themselves willing to share in His shame and sufferings that they may have part in His glory. He reminds them that they must not shrink from suffering and the loss of temporal goods, for there is nothing permanent here, and we seek an eternal city in the world to come, of which we are already citizens through the faith we profess. Instead of animal sacrifices, we should continually offer to God through Christ the sacrifice of praise which proceeds from lips that make public confession of Christ. This is a far more pleasing sacrifice than that of a lamb or a bullock, because it is the offering of the heart. Moreover, we must not forget the sacrifice of charity and beneficence, which is always pleasing to God.

The fruit of lips, etc. This is an Old Testament phrase accord-

17. Obey your prelates, and be subject to them. For they watch as having to render an account of your souls; that they may do this with joy and not with grief. For this is not expedient for you.

18. Pray for us. For we trust we have a good conscience, being willing to behave ourselves well in all things.

ing to the LXX (Isa. lvii. 19; Osee xiv. 2). The sacrifice of the lips and the heart is a continual one, and so unlike the Jewish sacrifices which took place only occasionally, on certain days or at certain hours of the day.

To impart, i.e., to share our possessions with others, to give alms.

17. In verse 7 the Apostle spoke of the religious leaders in the Church who had completed their work and entered into rest. Now he asks obedience and respect for those who were actually presiding over the Christian community when this letter was written. These spiritual superiors have a heavy duty to perform, for they are charged with the spiritual welfare of their subjects and will have to give an account of their stewardship to God. If the faithful make this burden heavier by disobedience and disloyalty, they themselves will be the losers.

CONCLUSION, 18-25

18-25. Here the Apostle first asks the prayers of his readers. His conscience bears him witness that he has done his best for them. One result of their prayers will be that he may be able to see them sooner (ver. 18-19). Then he utters a prayer for them, which takes the form of a magnificent doxology and embodies the main themes of the Epistle (ver. 20-21). Some final messages terminate the letter (ver. 22-25).

18. This verse affords the first personal note in the Epistle. The writer requests the prayers of his readers, which is a frequent practice with St. Paul (Rom. xv. 30; Eph. vi. 19; Col. iv. 3; 1 Thess. v. 25; 2 Thess. iii. 1).

For we trust, etc. The readers may not have agreed with the writer in all respects, but his own conscience is clear; and he feels he has always lived for the highest ends. This appeal to his conscience is also characteristic of St. Paul (Acts xxi. 20, xxiii. 1, xxiv. 16; 1 Cor. iv. 4; 2 Cor. i. 12, etc.).

19. And I beseech you the more to do this, that I may be restored to you the sooner.

20. And may the God of peace, who brought again from the dead the great pastor of the sheep, our Lord Jesus Christ, in the blood of the everlasting testament,

21. Fit you in all goodness that you may do his will; doing in you that which is well pleasing in his sight, through Jesus Christ, to whom be glory for ever and ever. Amen.

19. The first person plural is here dropped for the first person singular.

That I may be restored. The same thought is expressed in Phlm. 22. The word "restored" shows the writer was with his readers at a previous date.

20. In this and the following verse the Apostle prays for his readers, and his prayer takes the form of a greater doxology. Those Jewish Christians were torn by temptations from within and persecutions from without, and so the writer asks "the God of peace" to comfort and fortify them that they may remain firm in the faith.

Who brought again from the dead. Though the Ascension and Glorification of Christ are frequently referred to in the Epistle, this is the only direct allusion to the Resurrection. Jesus was raised from the dead by the Eternal Father as a reward for the blood which He shed in establishing the New Covenant. His bloody death on the cross thus merited for Him, as well as for us, a glorious resurrection.

The great pastor of the sheep. Our Lord describes Himself as the Good Shepherd in John x. 11-17.

In the blood, etc., i.e., in virtue of the blood, etc. The resurrection followed the outpouring of the blood on the cross as a reward and recompense (St. Thomas, *h. l.*). The most recent non-Catholic scholars, however, understand this last phrase as indicating the end and purpose of the Resurrection. Jesus, they say, was raised from the dead that He might offer His blood (i.e., the risen life) in the heavenly Sanctuary. Thus, these authorities make the establishment of the New Covenant and the actual work of atonement follow the Resurrection, and they maintain that this teaching is characteristic of the Epistle.

21. Now comes the actual prayer for the readers.

22. And I beseech you, brethren, that you suffer *this* word of consolation. For I have written to you in a few words.

23. Know ye that our brother Timothy is set at liberty; with whom (if he come shortly) I will see you.

24. Salute all your prelates, and all the saints. The brethren from Italy salute you.

25. Grace be with you all. Amen.

Doing in you, etc., i.e., accomplishing in you by means of His grace that which is pleasing to Him. God must give both the good will and the movement of the will (see on Phil. ii. 13).

To whom be glory, etc., may refer to God the Father, as in most doxologies of the New Testament, or to Christ, as the construction here would seem to indicate.

22. The writer asks his readers to accept in the right spirit the strong appeal he has made to them to persevere firm in the faith. He might have said much more to them on the grand subjects treated.

23. Timothy seems to be well known to the readers of the Epistle; and the words, "is set at liberty," would appear to suggest that he has been in prison, but is now set free; or they may mean simply that he is now freed from the task which was committed to him. If imprisonment is here referred to, nothing further is known of it.

24. The writer sends his salutations to all the faithful and their pastors.

The brethren from Italy means Christians living in Italy, if the letter was written from Rome or some place in Italy to readers elsewhere; but if the letter was addressed to Italy, the phrase would seem to refer to Italians who were living outside of Italy and who were sending greetings to their fellow-countrymen at home. See *Introduction* to this Epistle, Nos. II and III.

25. **Grace be with you all.** This blessing is identical with that of Titus iii. 15.

INDEX

A

Aaron, family of, II, 399.

Abba, Father, I, 128, 630.

Abel, Abel's blood crying to heaven for vengeance, II, 432.

Abraham, was justified by faith, I, 68, 614; justified by faith before he was circumcised, I, 72; time of justification, I, 73; spiritual father of the Jews, I, 74; model of all the Gentiles, I, 74; promise of Land of Canaan made to Abraham, I, 75; promise and inheritance did not depend on the observance of the Law, I, 75; faith reputed to Abraham unto justice, I, 77; spiritual father of Gentiles as well as Jews, I, 77; positive divine precepts given to Abraham, I, 109; promise made to Abraham, I, 145; spiritual children of, I, 147; differences between Abraham's two sons, I, 637; God's promise to Abraham appertains to Christians, II, 394; gave tithes to Melchisedech, II, 397; superiority of Melchisedech to, II, 398; God's call to Abraham, II, 433; supreme example of faith, II, 433; faith sorely tried, II, 435.

Abstinence, I, 218.

Achaia, a Roman province, I, 463; one of two provinces into which the Romans divided Greece, II, 205.

Achaicus, Corinthian Christian, I, 443.

Adam, sin and death came by Adam, I, 86; physical and moral head of human race, I, 87; all men have sinned in Adam, I, 87; pernicious effects of Adam's sin, I, 87; a figure or type of Christ, I, 89; points of difference between Adam, the type, and Christ, the antitype, I, 90; positive divine precepts given to Adam, I, 109; the first and last Adam, I, 431; Adam's precedence over Eve, II, 274.

Adeney, admits authenticity of Colossians, II, 150; supports authenticity of Pastoral Epistles, II, 248.

Adoption of sons, I, 128, 627.

Adversaries of Paul, see **Judaizers.**

Agape, abuses at Corinth condemned by Paul, I, 371; extension of this custom in the early Church, I, 374.

Agar, the type of the first Covenant, I, 637.

Ahern, on authenticity of Pastoral Epistles, II, 252.

Air, popularly regarded by Jews as the abode of evil spirits, II, 41.

Alexander, Christian heretic, II, 269, 318.

Alexander of Alexandria, declares Paul was author of Hebrews, II, 338.

Alford, Dean, supports authenticity of Pastoral Epistles, II, 247.

Almsgiving, fruits of, I, 528.

Alpheus, I, 593.

Altar, Christian, Jews excluded from, II, 448.

Altar of Incense, Jewish, II, 411.

Amen, use as the response to prayers, I, 405, 472.

Ampliatus, Christian convert, I, 236.

Anathema, I, 144, 385, 445, 587.

Andronicus, Christian convert, I, 235.

Angels, four choirs of celestial beings, II, 38; nine orders and three hierarchies, II, 38; good

453

God the ultimate end of all the labors and sufferings of the Apostles, I, 496; jealousy of, I, 538; eternal decree of salvation, II, 29; mystery of God's will, II, 31; the divine dispensation, II, 31; God's inheritance, II, 32; God's glory, II, 33; God's glory the end of all His gifts, II, 35; God's power, II, 40; manifold wisdom, II, 52; eternal purpose, II, 54, 57; fatherhood of God, II, 59; the riches of His glory, II, 60; God's glory last end of all virtue and good works, II, 109; God's vengeance, II, 230; God's love is gratuitous, II, 240; absolute gratuitousness of the works of God's love, II, 337; "temptation" by Israelites, II, 375; God's "Word" is His will, II, 382; God's promise to Abraham, I, 75; II, 394; God's oath to Abraham, II, 395.

God, Mocking of, to profess Christianity and obey the flesh, I, 655.

Godet, favors authenticity of Ephesians, II, 13; admits authenticity of Colossians, II, 150; supports authenticity of Pastoral Epistles, II, 248.

Goodness, II, 81.

Gospel, difference between true and false, II, 129. See also Covenant.

Governments in the Church, I, 393.

Grace, is the formal cause of justification, I, 63; grace did more abound, I, 94; grace came not from the Law but living faith in Christ, I, 106; we can never be absolutely certain that we are in a state of grace, I, 129; grace sufficient for salvation, I, 156; the work of the preacher is vain and useless without grace of God, I, 288; diversities of graces, I, 386; excellence of the grace of God, I, 530; state of grace, I, 561; grace the supernatural principle of the spiritual life, I, 655; the riches of His grace, II, 30; grace transforms us into the likeness of Christ, II, 43; necessity of grace, II, 108; grace of the Apostolate, II, 108; sanctifying grace, the temporal cause of salvation, II, 302; graces of Christianity are to be shown to outsiders, II, 336; inner grace, far more important for salvation than ordinances, II, 448. See also *Gratiae gratis datae*.

Grace . . . peace, form of wellwishing, I, 29, 585; II, 24.

Grace of healing, as gift of the Holy Spirit, I, 387.

Gratiae gratis datae, definition, I, 198, 383; as opposed to *gratia sanctificans* or *gratum faciens*, I, 384.

Gratitude to God, II, 84; gratitude for the gift of faith, II, 445.

Grecian Games, I, 350.

H

Haggadoth, Jewish Apocryphal book, II, 252.

Harden one's heart, II, 380.

Harnack, on the destination of Romans, I, 15; favors authenticity of Ephesians, II, 13; accepts authenticity of Colossians, II, 150; accepts authenticity of 2 Thess. on purely internal grounds, II, 198; thinks 1 Thess. was addressed more directly to Gentile and 2 Thess. to Jewish group in Thessalonian Church, II, 198; maintains no proof can be given that Paul was not released from his first Roman captivity, II, 249; takes middle position on question of authenticity of Pastoral Epistles, II, 249.

Harrison, takes middle position on question of authenticity of Pastoral Epistles, II, 249.

Harvest, depends chiefly upon the kind of seed sown and soil, I, 655.

Hatch, contests genuineness of Pastoral Epistles, II, 248.

Hatred of God, I, 152.

Haughtiness, I, 40.

Hausrath, takes middle position on question of authenticity of Pastoral Epistles, II, 249.

INDEX

spite of Jewish incredulity God is faithful to His promises, I, 146; rejection foretold in Osee and Isaias, I, 160; culpability of the Jews, I, 162; Jews are responsible for their rejection, I, 162; misunderstood the justice of God, I, 165; refused to believe in the Gospel, I, 171; Jews could not plead obscurity in the preaching of the Gospel, I, 174; rejection of Jews only partial, I, 176; rejection of Jews served for the conversion of the Gentiles, I, 181; final conversion of Israel to Christianity, I, 189; Jews' present incredulity will not hinder the final realization of God's promises, I, 190; Old Testament still a veiled book to the Jews, I, 488; under the Law, Jews were like minors, I, 628; all Jews were baptized in Moses, I, 352; Jewish Paschal supper, I, 378; Jewish converts must not return to the Law, I, 606; according to popular Jewish belief air was the abode of evil spirits, II, 41; principal crimes of the Jews, II, 210; dispersion of the Jews forecast by St. Paul, II, 211; Jews were obliged to teach the Scriptures to their children, II, 316; Jewish sacrifices, II, 385; Jewish washings, II, 390; Jewish priests, II, 403; Jewish sacrificial banquets, II, 448. See also Judaism; Judaizers.

Joseph, sons of, II, 435; faith of Joseph, II, 436.

Josue, I, 354.

Joy, definition, I, 219.

Judaism, adoption by Gentiles would be a return to paganism, I, 647; comparison with Christianity, II, 448.

Judaizers, activities in Rome, I, 239; at Corinth, I, 350; at Corinth, sought to destroy Paul's authority by defaming him, I, 468; Judaizers in Corinth charge Paul with fickleness, I, 469; adulterated the word of God, I, 481; Paul defends himself against Ju-

daizers in Corinth, I, 531; preached "another Christ," I, 539; Judaizers, champions of the Law, I, 542; Judaizers called "false brethren," I, 547; among the Galatians, I, 572; arguments of Judaizers, I, 572; campaign of Judaizers against St. Paul, I, 577; Judaizers destroy Gospel by adding to and subtracting from it, I, 586; the so-called Gospel preached by the Judaizers to the Galatians, I, 587; entered Church by stealth, I, 598; Judaizers of Antioch, I, 606; Judaizers in Galatia, I, 610, 634; Judaizers persecuted St. Paul and the faithful Christians, I, 641; Judaizers insisted on circumcision as essential to salvation, I, 643; claimed that Paul himself was in favor of circumcision, I, 646; motive of Judaizers' actions, I, 656; proof of insincerity, I, 657; scandalous lives of Judaizers, II, 101, 135; some Judaizers maintained that Mosaic observances were the necessary gateway to Christianity, II, 112; dangers of Judaizers to Philippians, II, 129; indignant denunciation of Judaizers by St. Paul, II, 130; false notion of circumcision, II, 130; Judaizers' activities at Colossæ, II, 146; Judaizers taught false asceticism at Colossæ, II, 172; errors had root in Judaism, II, 264; Judaizers of Crete, II, 332.

Judgment, judgment seat of God, I, 216; all must appear in the General Judgment, I, 500; preparation for Judgment, I, 654; Day of Jesus Christ, II, 108; the final judgment, II, 138; Judgment of the wicked, II, 230; death and judgment appointed for all men, II, 420; dreadful expectation of judgment, II, 428. See also Parousia, II, 428.

Judgment, used for chastisement, I, 381.

Judgment, Moral, II, 73.

Julia, Christian convert, I, 238, 240.

Trent to prove that Orders is
a true Sacrament, II, 301.

Ordination, I, 473.

Origen, on the names Saul and
Paul, I, ix; attributes fourteen
Epistles to St. Paul, I, xxx; appreciation of literary style of
Epistles, I, xxxix; says Romans
had a dogmatic purpose, I, 7; on
destination of Ephesians, II, 12;
quotes Colossians, II, 150; testimony on authenticity of Pastoral Epistles, II, 248; opinion on
Hebrews, II, 341.

Osee, foretold rejection of Jews,
I, 160.

Ox, muzzling forbidden by Mosaic Law, I, 344.

P

Pagans, natural knowledge of God
was possible for pagans, I, 35;
lapsed into idolatry through sin,
I, 34; unnatural vices of pagans,
I, 39; degradation of the pagan
world, I, 42.

Pain of loss, II, 231.

Pantænus, opinion on authorship
of Hebrews, II, 342.

Papias, declared St. Peter was
founder of the Roman Church,
I, 2; cites Paul also as co-
founder, I, 3.

Parable, use of term by Paul, II,
413.

Paradise, I, 552.

Parchments, II, 320.

Parents, duties, II, 178. See also
Marriage, Family.

Parousia, no reference to time of
Parousia in 1 Cor. iii, 15, I, 292;
the just who are living at the
second Coming of Christ shall
not die, I, 434; Paul did not believe it imminent, I, 436; St. Paul
had no revelation regarding the
time of the Second Advent, I,
500; supposed difference in
Paul's teaching to Thessalonians,
II, 199; Parousia and those who
have died previously, II, 218; St.
Paul's teaching on its imminence, II, 219 ff.; the Day of the
Lord is uncertain, II, 221, 224,

235; "times and moments" referred to time of the Parousia,
II, 222; Antichrist must appear
before, II, 232; Parousia is not
yet, II, 232; great events that
shall precede, II, 234; the brightness of His coming, II, 237;
Second Coming of Jesus Christ
will occur in His time, II, 297;
the blessed hope of the coming,
II, 335.

Partakers of the Holy Ghost, II,
391.

Pasch, Christ our Pasch is sacrificed, I, 310.

Passions, II, 311.

Passions of sins, I, 108.

Passover, Christ was the Passover,
I, 307.

Pastor of Hermas, probably acquainted with Hebrews, II, 341;
refers to Philippians, II, 102.

Pastoral Epistles, see Epistles,
Pastoral.

Pastors and doctors, use of terms
by Paul, II, 69; pastors in early
Church, II, 69.

Patience, characteristic of worthy
Christian, II, 65; "unto all
patience," II, 157.

Patriarchs, Old Testament Patriarchs received grace to observe
the Law, I, 105.

Patterns of heavenly things, II,
418.

Paul, Saint, birth and education,
I, ix; knowledge of Greek, I,
x, 16; was at all times an Israel-
ite, I, x; learned the handicraft
of dressing tents, I, x; studied
at the school of Gamaliel, I, x;
conversion and early labors, I,
xi; rationalists give natural explanation of the conversion of
St. Paul, I, xiii; retired to
Arabia, I, xiv; attempts to convert Jews of Damascus, I, xv;
labors with Barnabas at Antioch,
I, xv; ordained bishop, I, xv; the
First Missionary Journey, I, xvi;
attends Council of Jerusalem, I,
xvii; Second Missionary Journey, I, xviii; Third Missionary
Journey, I, xix; arrest and cap-

tions to Timothy, II, 258, 259; near to death in writing, 2 Tim., II, 314; last appeal to Timothy, II, 317.

Pauline Privilege, I, 329.

Peace, effect of justice and sanctity, I, 218; the bond of peace, II, 65; Paul admonishes Philippians to cultivate peace, II, 126; peace of God which surpasseth all understanding, II, 139; Christian peace, II, 442; warnings against peace disturbers, I, 239.

Pedagogues, in Apostolic times, I, 302.

Pelagians, I, 150, 299; use Rom. ii. 14, to support their heresy, I, 47; Pelagians denied all need of grace, I, 484; beliefs contrary to 2 Tim. i. 9, II, 302.

Penance, necessary for those who have sinned, I, 559.

Perdition of the damned, II, 136.

Perfection, Christian, I, 279; II, 60; Jesus Christ is the standard of perfection, II, 70; perfection can be won only by great effort, II, 133.

Persecution, I, 646.

Perseverance, I, 655; II, 439; final perseverance, II, 125.

Persis, Christian convert, I, 237.

Perverts, repeat the crucifixion of Christ, II, 392. See also Apostasy.

Peter, recognized as founder of Roman Church by unanimous decision of antiquity, I, 2; came to Rome in 42, I, 3; Paul appeals to Peter's authority, I, 343; Cephas, Aramaic equivalent, I, 601; traditional founder of Church at Antioch, I, 602; regarded by Paul as superior, I, 603; authority and influence in early Church, I, 604, 605; rebuked by Paul, I, 605; probably refers to Ephesians in his first Epistle, II, 12.

Pfleiderer, doubted authenticity of Ephesians, II, 13.

Pharao, why God permitted him to misuse his free will, I, 155.

Pharisaical scandal, I, 340.

Philastrius, Saint, attributes fourteen Epistles to St. Paul, I, xxx; tells why early Western Churches suspected authenticity of Hebrews, II, 342.

Philemon, native and early convert of Colossæ, II, 145, 151; correspondent of St. Paul, II, 184.

Philemon, Epistle to, Introduction, II, 184; date and place of composition, II, 16 f.; occasion and purpose, II, 184; date and place of composition, II, 185; authenticity, II, 185; analysis, II, 187; bibliography, II, 187.

Philetus, errors of, II, 308.

Philip of Bethsaida, Saint, Apostle, resided in Hierapolis, II, 144.

Philippi, City of, II, 97; the Church of Philippi, II, 98; Paul's first converts in Philippi, II, 98; discordant elements among the Philippian Christians, II, 118.

Philippians, Epistle to the, date and place of composition, II, 16 f.; introduction, II, 97; occasion, purpose and character of the Epistle, II, 100; authenticity and integrity, II, 102; analysis of contents, II, 103; body of the letter, II, 103; bibliography, II, 105; Epaphroditus, the bearer of Philippians, II, 117.

Philologus, Christian convert, I, 241.

Philosophy, use in preaching, I, 270; definition of term as used by Paul, II, 168.

Phœbe, deaconness of Cenchræ and bearer of Romans, I, 232.

Pillar and ground of truth, II, 281.

Pillar of cloud, I, 352.

Plummer, supports authenticity of Pastoral Epistles, II, 248.

Plutarch, on unnatural vices of pagans, I, 39.

Polycarp, cites from eight and alludes to four other Epistles, I, xxx; quotes from Romans, I, 10; enumerates vices of the Philippians, I, 254; refers to Ephesians, II, 12.

Potter, and a vessel of clay, I, 157.

Power, definition, I, 422; power of administration comes radically

Q

Quartus, Roman Christian, I, 243.
Quietism, opposed to Rom. ii. 7, I, 45.

R

Rabbins, would not admit that a Gentile who observed the Natural Law could be saved, I, 52.
Race, metaphor for Christian life, I, 350, 644; II, 116, 134.
Rahab, faith of, II, 437.
Ramsay, supports authenticity of Pastoral Epistles, II, 248.
Rationalists, account of Paul's conversion, I, xii.
Reason, Human, can attain knowledge of the existence of a Creator, I, 36.
Rebecca, I, 149.
Reconciliation, with God through Christ, II, 159.
Redeeming the time, II, 83, 180.
Redemption, is the ransom paid by Christ for our delivery from sin, I, 63; Redemption of Christ is the meritorious cause of justification, I, 63; Redemption equals creation in its extension, II, 32; final redemption, II, 34.
Red Sea, march through the, I, 352; II, 437.
Reformation, Time of, meaning of phrase, II, 413.
Reiche, on Paul's purpose in writing Romans, I, 6.
Remarriage, incompatible with ministerial service of Christ, II, 289.
Renan, account of Paul's conversion, I, xiii; doubted authenticity of Ephesians, II, 13.
Reprobation, I, 151, 562; negative reprobation, I, 152; positive reprobation, I, 158.
Responsibilities, personal, I, 654.
Rest, God's, awaits those who would enter into it, II, 379; sabbath-rest for the people of God, II, 385.
Resurrection of Christ, gave the seal of divine approbation to all Christ's other miracles and all His doctrines, I, 80; represented by Baptism of immersion, I, 96; attributed to the power of the Father, I, 97; resurrection of Jesus and of all the dead is attributed to the Father, I, 126; necessity of believing in the Resurrection of Christ, I, 417; Christ's Resurrection includes the resurrection of all men, I, 420; mystical explanation given by heretics of Resurrection, II, 309; directly referred to in Hebrews, xiii, 20, II, 451.
Resurrection of the body, the last fruit of our consummate adoption, I, 133; belief in resurrection from the dead, I, 169; resurrection of the body stumbling-block to many of the pagans, I, 413; some Corinthians denied resurrection of the dead, I, 418; resurrection of the just, I, 412 ff., 418, 420; qualities of the risen body, I, 427, 428; among the risen bodies of the just there will be a vast variety according to their respective merits, I, 430; contrast between our mortal and risen bodies, I, 430; difference between natural and spiritual body, I, 431; intepretation of I Cor. xv. 51, I, 435; the just shall rise clothed with glorified bodies, I, 436; resurrection confirmed by Paul, I, 498; general resurrection of all the just, II, 133; doctrine of resurrection included in instruction given to catechumens, II, 390.
Revelation, speaking in revelation or in knowledge, I, 402; revelation of God is an energizing message, II, 379.
Revelations of Paul, I, 551.
Reviviscence, through penance of merits lost by mortal sin, I, 613.
Reward, each one rewarded in proportion to his labors, I, 289; reward of the saved, I, 291; eternal reward, II, 229.
Rhetoric, use in preaching, I, 270.
Riches in glory, II, 143.
Right hand, the place of honor, II, 38.
Robber Synod, of Ephesus, II, 6.